The Ever-Fixed Mark:
Shakespeare on Love, Women, and Human Nature

By
Thomas P. Brackshaw

Library of Congress Control Number: 2021904665

ISBN: 978-1-7367522-0-3 (Print)
          978-1-7367522-2-7 (ebook)

Send questions or comments to:
markfixed1616@gmail.com

To J. Arthur and Normand, the educators that sparked and encouraged my interest in Shakespeare, but most of all to my dearest wife, Maureen, for her patience and her support during the writing itself. Any wisdom within these chapters came through them to me.

A Shakespearean definition of love

Sonnet 116

Let me not to the marriage of true minds
Admit impediments; love is not love
Which alters when it alteration finds,
Or bends with the remover to remove.
O no, it is an ever-fixed mark
That looks on tempests and is never shaken;
It is the star to every wand'ring bark,
Whose worth's unknown, although his highth be taken.
Love's not time's fool, though rosy lips and cheeks
Within his bending sickle's compass come,
Love alters not with his brief hours and weeks,
But bears it out even to the edge of doom.
If this be error and upon me proved,
I never writ, nor no man ever loved.

The rationale for the book title, the book cover art, and the main argument of the following chapters are all derived from this definition, which promotes love's miraculous constancy as the guiding principle for human nature.

Contents

Why Shakespeare?

It's difficult to avoid becoming disillusioned by the prevalent self-promotion and entitlement that drives the behavior of celebrities, athletes, politicians, business leaders, and some individuals these days. The question is, how are we to act in the midst of all this? Join the crowd? Or try to do what's right? Is it even possible anymore to distinguish between what's good and what isn't? Our secular age has made those questions a matter of epistemology, the branch of philosophy that deals with understanding how we know what we know, and philosophy has argued recently that, if there is such a thing as moral truth, it is subjective and internal rather than objective and normative. Moreover, anthropology and sociology seem to supply supporting evidence: even though western societies don't find murder acceptable, it is argued, cannibals consider ritual murder perfectly normal, proof that morality is relative to culture. And if there really are no moral absolutes, what's right must be defined within a particular situation or experience. The consequences of that assumption, however, are quite profound. Absent any behavioral absolutes, one person's perception of what's true, what's right or wrong, is just as valid as another's, reinforcing the most negative aspects of individualism. Unfortunately, that seemingly tolerant worldview has led our culture into all sorts of discord and mayhem.

This is not at all how Shakespeare thought about moral truth, however. While his 116th sonnet, the source of this book's title and cover art, is often considered a definition of love, which it is, it is also about how and where a constant and reliable definition of right and wrong can be derived. That's a lot to put into a fourteen line poem, but he was able to do so because he spent his theatrical career writing plays on the archetypal conflict between good and evil, an old but persistently fascinating framework for storytelling. For many, a good story doesn't seem possible without a formidable scoundrel. But the widespread appeal of such conflict endures because the battle subtly incorporates an age-old, seemingly unanswerable question about existence: why is there evil in the world? Christianity submits its answer, of course, but, individuals will always struggle to understand that intractable fact.

This is precisely why moral opposites are visible in the *Book of Genesis*, in Milton's *Paradise Lost,* in Conrad's *Heart of Darkness*, in the signature white or black hats of the American western, and in the stark contrast between hero and villain in much contemporary cinema. Unfortunately, however, a quick review of popular books and films indicates that the lack of a functional moral framework in western civilization renders it incapable of seeing much beneath the surface of these ubiquitous struggles between good and evil. To be recognizable these days, bad has to be very bad. Today, characters are either morally ambivalent and therefore pathetic antiheroes or cartoon-like opponents who assert their wills with intimidating firepower.

In contrast to our willing embrace of either a tolerant moral ambivalence or moral oversimplification, preceding eras lived within a framework, provided by religion, that could distinguish between the good and evil that inhabited their lives. Part of what makes Shakespeare's plays so different from modern stories is that he wrote within such a framework. With the possible exception of characters like Richard III from his early histories, he had little interest in the one-dimensional characterizations that occupy so much space in the media of contemporary culture. Being far more interested in the causes, the processes, and the consequences that identify what is actually evil, he pays considerable attention to what makes human nature so vulnerable to the intricate machinery of

2

traits. Over the next fifteen years of his career on the London stage, he would anatomize exactly how the very strengths that are legitimate sources of human satisfaction, like love and innocence, all too easily become our greatest weaknesses. Though Shakespeare's sympathy for such vulnerability is obvious, his plays also show that the world exacts a price for such innate frailties.

For all its obvious merits, Romeo and Juliet does not yet exhibit Shakespeare at his most mature. Each of the subsequent plays will show remarkable advancements in all aspects of theatrical composition. Perhaps the most remarkable of these is his facility for making stage personalities seem so amazingly life-like. For at least the past 150 years, Shakespeare's characterizations have received enthusiastic and, to many minds, justified praise for their complex but balanced view of human nature. The Romantic poet-critic Samuel Coleridge and the Victorian William Hazlitt popularized this view which reached its early twentieth-century apogee with A.C. Bradley's influential Shakespearean Tragedy, at one time required reading in college Shakespeare classes. More recently in his *Shakespeare: The Invention of the Human,* renowned Yale professor, Harold Bloom, places himself squarely within this camp as he examines all 36 plays chronologically. Besides the intriguing title, it is an interesting book for multiple reasons, the first of which, of course, is his appreciation for Shakespeare's characterizations, his uncanny ability to give voice to what seem to be real, living, breathing characters with distinct personalities. This ability to imbue stage personalities with living vitality is what Bloom labels the invention of the human. And the plays are replete with examples. The nurse from *Romeo and Juliet,* for instance, has an unmistakable personality that perfectly captures a talkative woman's well-intentioned recollections of the child she raised from infancy:

Even or odd, of all days in the year,
Come Lammas-eve at night shall she be fourteen.

> Susan and she—God rest all Christian souls!—
> Were of an age. Well, Susan is with God,
> She was too good for me. But as I said,
> On Lammas-eve at night shall she be fourteen,
> That shall she, marry, I remember it well.
> "Tis since the earthquake now aleven years,
> And she was wean'd—I never shall forget it— .
>   (1.3.16-24)

Like many talkative people, the nurse gets easily sidetracked from her main point by memories of tangentially related people and events: a deceased child, a husband's joke. Her thoughts tumble out faster than her words can accommodate, and she has to circle back to the topic at hand with "but as I said. . . ."

An early play, *Romeo and Juliet* already demonstrates the author's remarkable ear for the kind of phrasing and rhythm that differentiates one individual from another. Bloom contends that this aptitude sets Shakespeare apart from any other playwright, ever. What Shakespeare develops, however, is much more than a gift with language. Captivated by two of Shakespeare's characters, Bloom goes on to describe in more detail what makes these stage personalities unique:

> Falstaff and Hamlet palpably are superior to everyone else whom they, and we, encounter in their plays. This superiority is cognitive, linguistic, and imaginative, but most vitally it is a matter of personality. Falstaff and Hamlet are the greatest charismatics: they embody the Blessing, in its prime Yahwistic sense of "more life into a time without boundaries" (to appropriate from myself). Heroic vitalists are not larger than life; they are life's largeness. Shakespeare, who seems never to have made heroic or vitalistic gestures in his daily life, produced Falstaff and Hamlet as art's tribute to nature. More even than all the other Shakespearean prodigies –Rosalind, Shylock, Iago, Lear, Macbeth, Cleopatra—Falstaff and

> Hamlet are the invention of the human, the inauguration of
> personality as we have come to recognize it. (4)

For the first time in English literature, characters have been given a complex inner reality that finds expression in the words they use and the decisions they make. They are distinct, individual, and full of vitality. They speak with distinct voices, use language differently, see the world uniquely, just as living people do. Though lovers of Chaucer's wife of Bath may disagree, Shakespeare's art, Bloom argues, transformed perceptions of what it means to be human. Hence the title of his book.

What's more, this new realism was more than a mere literary accomplishment. According to Bloom, art and life intersected in a new and startling way because of Shakespeare, who not only changed how human experience was depicted through literature but changed prevailing notions of what it meant to be human. Because of Shakespeare's facility with language, his ability to reflect the inner assumptions and attitudes that motivate his characters to act, he created a rudimentary awareness of human psychology long before that existed as a subject of study. This achievement transformed the way people thought of and spoke about others. Unlike any previous dramatist, Shakespeare's ability to re-create particular and distinguishable human vitality served to draw his audience into the lives of his characters, and by doing so, instructed them about the complexities of human personality. According to Bloom, Shakespeare's gift captures not only the interior reality of his characters but also how that manifests itself within what can only be called their approach to life: their propensity for selfish or selfless existence, for joy or sorrow, for freedom or responsibility, for love or its many opposites, for any of the infinite choices available from the banquet of human experience. Keenly observant of people and the language they used, Shakespeare peopled his imaginary worlds with unique personalities that his audiences, then and now, were taught to comprehend. For the first time in the history of English literature, Shakespeare provided his audiences with the opportunity to observe, listen to, comprehend, and empathize with others around them.

But his purpose went beyond recreating lifelike characters. With great subtlety, he incorporates a phrase, an event, a contrasting personality to guide our interpretation of the people and events within his stories. It is nuance, the ability to clarify complexity, that makes Shakespeare's characterization so special. None of the main characters from the mature plays could ever be identified as types. They are never cartoonish symbols for an idea. By way of contrast, rival playwrights like Chris Marlowe and Ben Jonson wrote well-received plays with characters that were unable to escape the limitations of established dramatic types. As characters, they possess little if any depth. They are all heroic power like Marlowe's Tamburlaine, the Scythian shepherd who conquered the known world and taunted those he defeated with the kind of bombastic rhetoric that thrilled his Elizabethan audiences; or like Ben Jonson's greatest comic creation, Volpone, the main character in what one editor described as "a savage and sardonic satire on human greed and rapacity." Though Elizabethan audiences loved both plays, these characters exist as two-dimensional symbols for a concept. Not surprisingly, as a result, both plays have faded into relative obscurity. Bloom clearly recognizes how different Shakespeare's plays are from those of lesser artists, and he deserves credit for that alone.

That unabashed love and admiration for Shakespeare once again align him with traditional critics like Coleridge, Hazlitt, and Bradley. It is a position that sets him at odds with many peers who now occupy positions within his profession. While current academic trends suggest Shakespeare's plays often reflect the flawed social, economic, and political assumptions and attitudes of his era, a notion Bloom finds irrelevant, he goes on to propose an alternative approach to the plays:

The other way of exploring Shakespeare's continued supremacy is rather more empirical: he has been universally judged to be a more adequate representer of the universe of fact than anyone else, before him or since. This judgment has been dominant since at least the mid-eighteenth century; it has been staled by repetition, yet it remains merely true, banal as resentful theorists find it to be. We keep returning to Shakespeare because we need him; no one else gives us so much of the world most of us take to be fact. (16-17)

Bloom's vigorous defense of Shakespeare's continuing relevance is intended to counter the illiberal biases of the New Historicism so prevalent in current academic hallways. This school of critical theory began with legitimate questions about how and why the long-accepted canon of western literature had been established, why it consisted almost entirely of dead white men, and what that implied about western culture. The most obvious consequences of this examination have been twofold: first, it opened up the canon to other English language authors, including women, people of color, and those with non-standard sexual orientations; second, it validated the conviction that authors of the older, accepted canon could and should be judged on their failure to recognize their underlying assumptions about imperialism, race, gender, and sexuality. It is a legitimately debatable point that the first of these consequences may have been worthwhile. But the second is not only anachronistic but discredits authors like Shakespeare for holding viewpoints for which their culture offered no alternatives. While the New Historicism asserts that that is precisely the problem, their judgments have served as an indictment not only of that older, established canon of authors but of an entire history and culture as well. One of Bloom's premises is that such judgments are exceedingly narrow and go so far outside the normal boundaries of what literary criticism should entail that they become irrelevant.

Now it is certainly beyond obvious that Shakespeare's art was a product of an Elizabethan culture that was much different from our own, so it shouldn't be surprising that his plays don't meet many current expectations about race, gender, or politics. How could they? Yet despite this disjuncture, devoted followers go on reading and discussing Shakespeare's plays anyway, and, as Bloom is arguing, they most probably do so because the plays clarify essential truths about human experience. Those "facts" have far more to do with the psychological, emotional, and spiritual verities that undergird human action, even today, than with the ancillary issues currently occupying many apologists on university faculties. While treatises on the political, gender, economic, or social aspects of the plays can enlighten our understanding of the Elizabethan milieu and how it was different from our own, they tend to reveal far more about the critic's political and cultural positions than they do about Shakespeare's art. It may have become banal, as Bloom observes, to say that Shakespeare is one of the great literary artists in English literature, but that does not make it less true. If anything, it obligates teachers of literature to clarify why that is so, a goal that is being ill-served by New Historicism.

The contention between these two vastly different critical attitudes has to do with different assumptions about the purpose of literature. Proponents of New Historicism assume that literature should describe the wide range of human experience, a pluralism that appeals to the egalitarian leanings of liberal western democracies. Readers need to hear voices different from their own, the argument goes, so that empathy for different others is increased, so societies become more tolerant and inclusive. Perhaps this is a worthwhile goal, but Elizabethan authors set pen to paper for an altogether different reason. The late sixteenth and early seventeenth centuries during which Shakespeare worked assumed that literature's purpose was to convey moral instruction, a position that was carefully articulated in Sir Phillip Sydney's

A Defense of Poesy, an influential treatise for the writers of that time. Sidney argued that literature deserved a place in his society because it could both entertain and instruct, that literature's ability to delight, in fact, expedited the instruction. Not surprisingly, the lessons conveyed were largely defined by the religious and moral norms of that culture. For the Elizabethans, literature helped people distinguish between right and wrong, something far different from the goals of tolerance and inclusivity. The logical fallacy of New Historicism, therefore, is very much like observing that a cow cannot run as fast as a horse and then blaming the cow for not being a horse, a bias that renders it irrelevant and undeserving of any serious attention. The premise, which would certainly please aficionados of polo, may be fair enough, but the conclusion would alarm anyone who liked butter or cheese, particularly if they were also considered defective for their preference. Cows deserve to be evaluated for what they are. Shakespeare is no different.

As with any literary period, historical perspectives on Shakespeare may indeed provide interesting context but they are far from sufficient. On this matter, then, Bloom is absolutely right. Shakespeare deserves to be evaluated for what he achieved rather than chastised for failing to meet an anachronistic goal imposed by a period far different from his own. A more objective approach for those who earnestly seek to understand the plays is to confront the basics of the texts themselves. For most readers, this needn't be complicated. Who are these characters and what are they like? What action is being described? Why does the play end as it does? Most readers simply want to understand why these characters say and do what they do, and they want to perceive some linkage between those actions and the consequences that follow. Because these fundamental questions are essentially moral (decisions and actions have consequences), they correlate well with a culture that assumed literature's purpose was to convey moral instruction. The alignment of Elizabethan assumptions

11

about literature with the instinctive search for answers to such fundamental, moral questions, therefore, cannot help but lead to a valid appreciation of Shakespeare's art.

Ironically, however, Bloom's book could have benefited from more historical context, from an acknowledgment of the ways the Elizabethan and modern periods are different. Despite his sound judgments about Shakespeare's characters and the value of his artistic achievements, he strives to make Shakespeare relevant to a modern audience by a conviction that, beginning with *Hamlet*, the plays exhibit a deepening and persistent nihilism. This squares neatly with the existentialism popularized by twentieth-century writers like Camus, who proposed that the only question that matters is what prevents each of us from committing suicide. For Camus, it was a question about the purpose and meaning of life in a universe where God no longer existed, where man was alone and fully responsible for his actions. The nihilism that Bloom sees in the later plays also squares neatly with a culture that believes values are relative, that situations should determine what is right or wrong, that a person's life experience is sufficient validation of whatever decisions he may make, no matter how that affects others. In this prevalent spirit of tolerant acceptance, one person's good is no better or worse than another's. Nihilism follows quite naturally from the dysfunctional morality that these viewpoints justify. But, as previous paragraphs have already suggested, a world emptied of all meaning and purpose is the very negation of those beliefs the Elizabethans hoped literature would clarify and inspire its audience to perpetuate.

At one point, Bloom is careful to distinguish between the author's spiritual state and the dramatic characters whose words supposedly reflect a sense of life's inescapable meaninglessness. But that brief and easily overlooked acknowledgment is eventually overwhelmed by the consistent commentary from that perspective until author and theme converge. As his chapters unfold, it seems inconceivable that an author consistently depicting nihilism in his characters would not succumb to nihilism in his thinking. Bloom's far-ranging chapter on *Hamlet*, the play that supposedly begins this slide into spiritual indifference, contains many passages similar to the following:

> No one is ever going to call Hamlet "the joyous Dane," yet a consciousness so continuously alive at every point cannot be categorized simply as "melancholy." Even at its darkest, Hamlet's grief has something tentative about it. "Hesitant mourning" is almost an oxymoron; still, Hamlet's quintessence is never to be wholly committed to any stance or attitude, any mission, or indeed to anything at all. . . . He has no center. . . . (406)

Bloom is referring to Hamlet's continuous repurposing of identity, beginning as Denmark's prince, then student, then moving to failed avenger of a murdered father, to an actor pretending madness, to director of "The Mousetrap" to catch the conscience of a murderer, to moral reformer of a sinful mother, and finally the jester who mocks a brother's extravagant grief at Ophelia's grave. Forced to play many, sometimes uncomfortable roles, Bloom argues, the prince loses all moral direction and is unable to move forward until Claudius's final act of treachery leaves him no choice. Bloom concludes that Hamlet "can and does repair to that nothing at sea, and he returns disinterested, or nihilistic, or quietistic, whichever you may prefer" (431). Because values such as love and loyalty that might have moved Hamlet to action have disappeared in the whirlwind vortex of finding a workable identity capable of revenge, life has lost any meaning, and what remains is this soul-destroying indifference that renders him a "villain-hero," to use Bloom's phrase, morally empty and finally capable of murder. After Hamlet, Bloom maintains, all of Shakespeare's tragic heroes lose any functional moral or spiritual compass that might have guided their decisions. Emptied of purpose, all suffer through

13

nihilism's dark night of the soul.　If this were true, Shakespeare's dramatic world would be bleak reading indeed.

But in the aggregate, they aren't.　Though Bloom is not alone in this peculiarly modern assessment of Shakespeare's mature dramas, several closely related factors argue strongly against it.　The most significant of these may be the historical context in which Shakespeare wrote.　That context was inescapably Christian, a religion that recognizes both hope and joy in the midst of suffering.　In a small, previously influential but now nearly forgotten book, E.M.W. Tillyard documented just how influential Christian orthodoxy remained in Shakespeare's time.　He observed that many readers today

> . . . still think of the Age of Elizabeth as a secular period between two outbreaks of Protestantism: a period in which religious enthusiasm was sufficiently dormant to allow the new humanism to shape our literature.　They admit that the quiet was precarious and that the Puritans were ever on the alert. . . . They do not tell us that Queen Elizabeth translated Boethius, that Raleigh was a theologian as well as a discoverer, and that sermons were as much a part of an ordinary Elizabethan's life as bear-baiting.　(3)

Tillyard's point is that the Elizabethans were still very much in the thrall of Christian thinking.　Boethius, a sixth-century Roman consul who was jailed and eventually executed, wrote *The Consolation of Philosophy* while in prison.　One of the most influential works of the subsequent medieval period, it taught acceptance of hardship in a spirit of philosophical detachment, an outlook that resonated strongly with Christian thinkers of the time. That Elizabeth, queen of England, would spend time translating Boethius from Latin to English indicates her desire to share those insights with her subjects. Similarly, the explorer Raleigh was motivated, in part, to expand God's kingdom into the New World.　And sermons by that poet and reluctant Anglican minister, John Donne, are minor literary artifacts in themselves.　Alive and well in

14

Elizabethan England, Christianity provided both meaning and purpose. While multiple historical factors were already beginning to erode the hold that Christianity exercised upon that culture, that process would not approach completion until some 400 additional years had passed. In many ways, therefore, it is accurate to say that Elizabethan England was much closer to the very religious, very Christian Middle Ages than it is to our far more secular times.

And because the Elizabethan period was inescapably Christian, that faith's foundational principles were the guiding light of everyday existence. Admittedly, those principles were not always fully understood or fully implemented, but the culture offered no alternative value system. Surprisingly, modern critics and commentators have largely ignored Christianity's influence on the culture from which these plays emerged. Yet evidence for that influence is everywhere in Elizabethan England, rendering it very different from our own secular age, which tries very hard to separate church from state, to isolate religious conviction entirely into the personal sphere where it is prone to wither and die. In Shakespeare's culture, though, Christianity influenced every aspect of daily life, including politics, where the full force of the state could be exercised upon anyone who deviated from proscribed beliefs. Two fellow playwrights with whom Shakespeare had worked suffered grievously for even the appearance of non-conforming religious views. One was Shakespeare's very famous theatrical peer, Christopher Marlowe, who was found to have documents questioning the divinity of Jesus. For that infraction, he was killed in a barroom brawl, very likely by several of the queen's henchmen. The other acquaintance was Marlowe's one-time roommate, Thomas Kyd, another famous playwright who authored *The Spanish Tragedy*, considered a precursor for *Hamlet*. He was tortured and his writing hand crippled simply for having once roomed with Marlowe. In Elizabeth's England, a person's religious convictions could very well be a matter of life or death. And as perhaps the most prominent member of a theater company sponsored by royal authorities, Shakespeare never appears to have expressed opinions deviating from orthodox religious doctrine. Given his prominent position near the royal court, it would have been foolish to do otherwise.

While state suppression of religious dissent cowed authors from contradicting or even explicitly discussing accepted theology, the basic tenets of Christianity were inescapably part of everyone's life. Because of the inherent danger of religious statements as well as the crown's censorship of every theatrical script, Shakespeare, like all the major playwrights, carefully avoided religious issues and focused on human behavior and life's difficult moral choices. In *King Lear*, for example, one of the characters, the elderly Duke of Gloucester, is cruelly blinded by one of the play's many villains and cast out into the stormy night. Suffering grievously, he observes bitterly that men are like flies to the indifferent gods "who kill us for their sport." Out of context, his sentiment would seem to support Bloom's assertion of a prevalent nihilism in Shakespeare's later plays. Gloucester's despair, however, is soon contradicted by the healing love of the very son he rejected. As Alfred Harbage suggests in his reflections on Shakespeare's moral vision:

> If *King Lear* had meant to its audience what it is sometimes said to mean, there would have been panic at the Globe. The people there. . . did not want to hear that life is a tale told by an idiot or that clouds of glory trail in the Boar's Head Inn. They were not prepared for a two-hour operation in which old principles were cut away and new ones grafted in. They were too frugal to sacrifice to the day's entertainment the truths they lived by, and accept in exchange for sheer loneliness and fear. (*As They* 117)

Given the Elizabethan period's deep Christian roots, this seems eminently sane. Rather than Bloom's very contemporary nihilism, the aggregate impression given by Shakespeare's plays seems far more spiritually hopeful. In his dramatic world, there is detectable evidence of a God who redeems. Modern, secularized man may promote the courage to confront a morally vacuous and meaningless universe, but this was not how Elizabethans, including Shakespeare, saw man's place in the world. Harbage makes a far more compelling case because he accounts for the cultural assumption of the period as well as the textual evidence. Shakespeare did not succeed artistically and financially by defying the moral and spiritual norms he shared with his audience. Quite the opposite, in fact. He succeeded by reminding them of the full implications of the truths that supposedly guided their daily lives. He used the stage to show them what they already accepted as right and good.

That Shakespeare repeated the commonly held moral and religious assumptions of his age implies another limitation of Bloom's emphasis on the characters, which, in his book, seem to exist as entities disembodied from their own stories only to become subjects swirling within the critic's fertile consciousness. Dramatic characters exist within the context of their plots, which deserve equal importance. Forged at the intersection of character and action, the morality of behavior is defined by a character's decisions and the consequences that result from those. Once again in *Lear*, perhaps the greatest tragedy ever written, the Duke of Albany, who is married to a particularly wicked daughter of the protagonist, is astonished by her depraved indifference to the suffering she has willfully inflicted upon her father. Though each of Lear's two eldest daughters receives half of his kingdom when he chooses to retire, they deny him even basic shelter when his presence in their homes becomes inconvenient. The understandable anguish Lear experiences from their ingratitude breaks his hold on reality, and the aged king slides into a temporary madness. Looking at his wife, the virtuous Albany struggles to comprehend the ungrateful sisters and his brother-in-law, the Duke of Cornwall, who has supported their decisions. In Albany's view, they have relinquished all semblance of human decency. Note the prevalent animal imagery:

> What have you done?
> Tigers, not daughters, what have you perform'd?
> A father, and a gracious aged man,
> Whose reverence even the head-lugg'd bear would lick,
> Most barbarous, most degenerate, have you madded.
> Could my good brother suffer you to do it?
> A man, a prince, by him so benefited!
> If that the heavens do not their visible spirits
> Send quickly down to tame [these] vild offenses,
> It will come,
> Humanity must perforce prey on itself,
> Like monsters of the deep. (4.2.39-49)

Albany's speech reflects an understanding that the sisters have violated every natural bond of respect, appreciation, and love that should normally exist between children and parents. Such inhumane behavior, in his view, can only lead to chaos. Whatever Lear's faults, he has dealt generously with these two daughters, and because they value their interests more than anyone else's, neither of them has the moral or emotional capacity to repay his generosity. Greed and self-regard drive their cruel indifference to natural bonds, and instead of the limitless love they falsely promised earlier, they sow division, suffering, and death. Albany's words are eerily prophetic: habitually motivated by self-interest, the two sisters end up poisoning each other as they vie for the affection of Gloucester's bastard son, Edmund. Writing from a system of widely shared and deeply felt Christian values, Shakespeare clearly understood that such obsessive self-regard is inevitably blind to more significant emotional, social, historical, and spiritual consequences. It is in this intersection between character and action that Shakespeare's most moving insights are to be found. Unfortunately, Bloom's preoccupation with character renders his book oddly

18

unhelpful for any inquisitive reader seeking clarification of any particular play.

While commentary on the plays is full of disagreements, most everyone agrees that Shakespeare was exceedingly proficient at transforming dull source material into theatrical gold. Because he knew how to stage a good story, each play contained a clearly defined conflict between likable people and a villain which quickly propelled the story forward. And whatever form the resolution took, it inevitably reflected the moral values widely accepted by believing Elizabethans. For them, these plays were both compelling and reassuring because they assume a universe based on a set of unchanging principles and values informing human life and giving it meaning, a meaning that could be preserved or lost by human will. A sense of hopeless nihilism, therefore, was not inevitable but was the final, spiritual consequence of consistently making wrong choices, of never recognizing and repenting of sin. Witnessing the emotional power of a medieval morality play like *Everyman*, whose main character is torn between a good angel and a bad one, is to comprehend just how significant this spiritual battle was for the Elizabethans. Making the right choices, laid out in Scripture's huge historical sweep, was man's purpose in life. As Tillyard notes,

> . . .the other set of ideas that ranked with [the idea of universal order] was the theological scheme of sin and salvation. However widely biblical history was presented in medieval drama and sermons . . ., the part of Christianity that was paramount was not the life of Christ but the orthodox scheme of the revolt of the bad angels, the creation, the temptation and fall of man, the incarnation, the atonement, and regeneration through Christ. (18)

This huge arc of Biblical history formed the basis for late medieval plays, and it was out of that tradition that Elizabethan drama emerged. So it's not that Elizabethans were unfamiliar with nihilism. The nihilism in the *Book of*

Ecclesiastes, for example, would certainly have been recognizable to them, but they would also be aware that it was the result of Solomon's self-indulgent and sinful past. They would see nihilism as a consequence of man's innate desire to follow his own will rather than God's. This was Solomon's sin, and the despair he felt and recorded in *Ecclesiastes* was the consequence of that. But such nihilism was by no means inevitable, an inescapable condition of human existence, as the moderns would have it. That kind of nihilism is a product of a world that has excised the concept of sin and embraced the primacy of self. For the Elizabethans, who were very aware of free will, sin was an unavoidable part of human life that required adherence to Christian principles of humility, sacrifice, and forgiveness before the promises of the gospel became available. Evil was only one of the two paths a man could choose.

This was exactly what the Elizabethan audience would have seen in Shakespeare's presentation of Macbeth, a man whose wife convinces him to murder the good king Duncan, only to lose sleep, peace of mind, wife, kingdom, and society's goodwill. He dies bravely, as is his nature, but empty of everything except despair. As death approaches, his conclusion that life is nothing more "than a tale told by an idiot" is certainly nihilistic, but, like Solomon's, the sentiment belongs to a character who is living out the consequence of his own ill-fated choices. The peace that follows Macbeth's demise promises to restore the harmony that belonged to a Scotland once ruled by the murdered Duncan. Though briefly interrupted by Macbeth's sin, providential nature eventually redresses a temporarily disrupted but resilient moral order. For the Elizabethans, the real truth about such matters could be found in *Romans 8:28*: "And we know that in all things God works for the good of those who love Him, who have been called according to his purpose." Based on scripture, God's purpose for the world was always good, and he was actively working through human relationships, even those broken and crippled by wrong choices, to bring that about.

Consequently, throughout Shakespeare's canon, his characters confront the choice between right and wrong behavior, between good and evil, and the consequences that follow a decision identify which choice was right, which one pleased the just but loving God of the Bible who stood, invisible, behind these plays. But that's as close as Shakespeare dare get to a religious statement. While Christian morality is the foundation upon which these plays rest, sectarian religious ideas of any sort, whether Catholic or Protestant, find no home there at all. To avoid unwanted religious controversy and censorship, Shakespeare was very careful to imply that the divine is only dimly perceivable, a nameless force that reasserts order and harmony through human personalities, decisions, and actions. He was very aware of which boundaries were too dangerous to cross.

For many moderns, medieval Christianity has an unfortunate reputation for ascetic self-denial, for uncomfortable restrictions on the presumed right of self-fulfillment. Shakespeare's plays should lay that misconception about Elizabethan Christianity to rest. If mankind were merely a leaky boat in an ocean of potential sinfulness, left without any hope of rescue, that would indeed be a situation justifying Bloom's nihilism and despair. But as Tillyard indicates and as Shakespeare's plays make clear, mankind has an escape. Christianity claims that Christ's atoning death paid the price for every man's sin, that a loving God was willing to incarnate his son to save those people who believed that to be true and who enacted the same, sacrificial love toward others. Though Shakespeare understandably never dared to venture into theological controversy, his plays still pay homage to the hope of Christian salvation, to the idea that God provides some means to overcome evil. As Shakespeare's artistic vision matures, love in all its myriad forms becomes the human and necessarily flawed

21

manifestation of God's essential nature. For him, the commonalities shared between divine and human love are enormously significant. Both promise union, harmony, fruitfulness, and purpose, all of which stand in opposition to evil's hopeless despair, its isolation, and its spiritual and emotional emptiness. By reading Shakespeare's plays in roughly chronological order his conviction of this truth becomes increasingly obvious. No biographical evidence exists to explain Shakespeare's abiding interest in love as the most important subject for his art, but from his very first poem, *Venus and Adonis*, to late Romances like *The Tempest*, the many human expressions of love, from the platonic to the sexual, engaged his creative spirit. While it certainly could be argued that all drama is about human relationships and therefore about love, Shakespeare addresses this subject ever more directly and explicitly, and he does so because he eventually concludes that our only available antidote to sin is love.

Just as Shakespeare's treatment of sin becomes increasingly complex, the same is true of his treatment of love. At first, his ideas are shaped almost entirely by two literary influences: his exposure to Ovid and his familiarity with the conventions of courtly love. The first of these influences, the Roman poet, Ovid, was part of his childhood education. In his book, *The Classical Tradition*, Gilbert Highet detects multiple classical influences on Shakespeare's intellectual life that make their presence known in his work:

> He knew three classical authors well, a fourth partially, and a number of other fragmentarily. Ovid, Seneca, and Plutarch enriched his mind and his imagination. Plautus gave him material for one play and trained him for others. From Vergil and other authors he took stories, isolated thoughts, and similes, sometimes of great beauty. . .[But his] favorite classical author was Ovid. (203)

Like almost all his peers, Shakespeare was, relatively speaking, far more familiar with Latin literature than he was with anything Greek. In his poem dedicating the First Folio, the self-educated classical scholar, Jonson, remarked rather smugly that Shakespeare "hadst small Latin and less Greek." But Shakespeare was not unusual in that regard, and his glancing exposure to the classics eventually proved to be a blessing. Jonson, whose classical training rendered him rule-bound to the classical unities of time, place, and action, was the educational exception to the norm. Shakespeare's classical naiveté, on the other hand, allowed him to rely on theatrical experience rather than ancient models to determine what worked well in the English theaters. Still, it is also clear that he read widely and voraciously, too. The Roman Seneca's closet dramas, meant for recitation rather than the stage, provided a model for his early tragedies. Plutarch provided detail for his Roman histories, including *Antony and Cleopatra*. Plautus, the Roman comic playwright whose influence on the early *Comedy of Errors* is readily apparent, taught him much about effective comic devices and structure. What Shakespeare knew about the classics was wisely and effectively used.

But it was Ovid's *Metamorphoses*, those fanciful tales of gods falling in love with mortals and transforming them afterward into plants or animals, that influenced him in profound but subtle ways. Providing captivating stories for reluctant students of Latin, the *Metamorphoses* was widely taught in grammar schools, including Shakespeare's. He clearly took these tales to heart. Besides providing a ready source of decorative allusions, Shakespeare's imagination seems to have been deeply struck by Ovid's stories of love's random, irrational, sometimes ludicrous, sometimes tragic power. Ovid's message, that love's power inevitably changes those who are infected, was hard to miss. A comedy like *A Midsummer Night's Dream* makes light of love's seemingly random couplings, its ridiculous blindness, all in good fun.

23

But by the end of the play's comic action, disappointment and anguish have been vanquished, desires have been fulfilled and marriages are in the offing. In this early comedy, moving from love denied to love fulfilled transforms everyone's pain into joy. Similar emotional transformations are also evident in the tragedies and the late romances as well, though the tragic movement is usually from ignorance of love's nature and value to a more accurate assessment of its worth. Sometimes the lovers earn that new wisdom, sometimes the society around them does. Whichever form it takes, the transformation in tragedy is always one of improved insight. From Ovid, then, Shakespeare learned that mankind is subject to the power of transforming love.

Sir Philip Sydney's sonnets and poems probably introduced Shakespeare to the traditions of courtly love, the second literary influence on his presentation of this topic. Though essentially a medieval invention, the remnants of the courtly love traditions filtered down through Renaissance literature. Initially, courtly love appeared in French and, somewhat later, Italian and then English poetry. It emphasized humility, courtesy, adulterous but unfulfilled desire, and a mock religion of love (Lewis 2). Entirely literary in its origins, many of its conventions merged with compatible classical elements from stories about Venus, Cupid, and other Greek and Roman pastoral figures. This mixture was eventually absorbed into common cultural assumptions about love that still affect behavior and expectations even today. When a man describes being struck blind by the beauty of his beloved, about knowing immediately this was the love of his life, this is the vocabulary of courtly love. The influence is similar for women who hope to be revered, treated respectfully, and made to feel more special than any other woman. Emotionally, power within the relationship belongs to her, making the man her humble and obedient servant in the offices of love. As he waits for her to requite his desire, he inevitably suffers alternating bouts of despair and hope. These common descriptions of the experience have all been shaped by courtly love.

At first, the influence of courtly love on Shakespeare is largely rhetorical. Courtly love's literary conventions had already become the common vocabulary of love. Throughout his writing, Shakespeare sometimes uses these tropes traditionally; sometimes he gently mocks them; but, like us, he cannot escape them. *Romeo and Juliet* is so delightful in large part because he uses courtly love language to elevate his lovers above the cynicism and hatred that fuel the discord between the feuding families. In *As You Like It*, he gently mocks love's absurd manifestations as Orlando roams Arden Forest, tacking fevered sonnets to his beloved on every tree. But when Shakespeare began one of his sonnets with "My mistress's eyes are nothing like the sun," he was consciously distancing himself from the artificiality of courtly love's conventional phrases. Throughout his plays, he continues to make distinctions between artificial and genuine love, which are distinguishable by both word and deed. Ever sensitive to language, he saw and demonstrated the ability of linguistic style to either hide or to express genuine emotion. Beginning with *Romeo and Juliet*, the relationship between language and truth becomes a prevalent theme in both comedy and tragedy. Even in his last great tragedy of love, *Antony and Cleopatra*, the Roman Antony's exaggerated protestations of love give way to language that is far more emotionally genuine and personal. The way characters speak about love, whether they use conventional or genuinely emotional language as they describe their experience, comes to reflect the depth of their understanding of their relationship.

As Shakespeare's treatment of love matures, he seems to recognize that the words used to speak about love can either reveal or hide whatever exists within the heart. It is never easy for people to get to those truths. The distinctions Shakespeare makes between artificial and genuine love gradually lead him to an understanding of reason's limitations and the significant value of the emotional connections that bind people to each other. Beginning most clearly with *Hamlet*, reason is shown to be a morally neutral aptitude that can exercise its sway over situations with either good or evil intention. In the right individual, reason can fathom truth and distinguish good from evil, but the impenetrable nature of the world and of human motivations make that exceedingly difficult. In the wrong personality, reason and the language that expresses its syllogisms can become tools to deceive those who are overly confident of reason's acuity. This is the dynamic that is dramatized in *Othello,* where the demonic Iago uses his relentless insinuations to deceive the Moor into believing that his completely innocent wife, Desdemona, has been unfaithful. Iago's words pervert what's true into what's false and create an illusion that belies what is obvious to everyone except the deceived husband. As Robert Heilman concludes in his analysis of the play, *Magic in the Web*:

> . . . in Iago he has dramatized Dante's summary analysis: "For where the instrument of the mind is joined to evil will and potency, men can make no defence against it." But he has also dramatized the hidden springs of evil action, the urgency and the immediacy and the passion of it. He contemplates, too, the evildoer's potency and men's defenselessness: but these he interprets tragically by making them, not absolute, but partly dependent on the flaws and desires of the victims themselves. In the *Othello* world, Iago is not a required teacher. Whoever would, could learn from Desdemona. (229)

Because humans are by nature incapable of seeing the world, including their own motives, with complete objectivity, reason and judgment function with ambivalent force, sometimes accurately assessing the world but prone to being easily deceived by the appearances of things. Once these deceptions take hold and the rational mind comes to accept the spurious as true, those same visceral emotions that can bind

26

people to each other now serve to intensify the deception. Paradoxically, the depth of Othello's connection to Desdemona blinds him to the obvious and fires the jealous rage that leads to murder. Hamlet demonstrates a similar emotional dynamic. Wracked by guilt and churning emotions, Hamlet clings heroically to the conviction that finding the truth is somehow possible, despite the many obstacles that deter the play's lesser intellects. But even Hamlet finds the journey to the origins of Denmark's malaise arduous. Over and over, the plays demonstrate the absolute frailty of human judgment, its susceptibility to falsehoods and overwrought emotions. These are the mechanisms that allow evil to subvert whatever is good within our human nature. As Heilman notes, however, it is Desdemona who offers an alternative to Iago's diabolical plotting. As passing time wove the disparate literary threads of Ovid, courtly love, and Christian orthodoxy into the fabric of Shakespeare's art, women like Desdemona, remarkably, are given special recognition.

For Shakespeare's Christian audience, the difficulties resulting from evil were introduced into the world by the sin of their first parents which corrupted the perfection of Eden. The ugly fruit of sin, however, seems to have made Shakespeare acutely aware of the sometimes resilient, sometimes fragile beauty of feminine love. That sentiment is certainly visible in Hamlet's love interest, Ophelia, in the faithful wife, Desdemona, in Lear's forgiving daughter, Cordelia, and in Prospero's joyful daughter, Miranda. Conspicuously, Shakespeare's women are the ones who most often exhibit sacrificial love, though some men, like Gloucester's son, Edgar, are citizens of that country also. If the presence of evil sometimes strikes its victims as mysterious, so, likewise, is this illogical, wonderful, necessary experience called love. This kind of love defies logic. Why two separate individuals possess a desire to commit their lives in sacrificial love to one another eludes rational comprehension. From a purely rational perspective, sacrificial love makes little sense. But Shakespeare's most admirable women live it out with unwavering faithfulness, without complaint. They remain absolutely steadfast in their love for the men in their lives. They understand that, ultimately, overcoming human resistance to the responsibilities and obligations of love is a matter of the heart, the voiceless, metaphorical organ that represents the human desire for acceptance and union. Over and over in the plays, it is the men who struggle to comprehend and express their love adequately, resorting to pat phrases derived from courtly love poetry, never fully understanding what the words refer to until they've learned the truth about love from their patient, forgiving women.

The major plays provide ample evidence of this. Standing in calm opposition to those demonic forces warping her husband's vision is Desdemona, trusting as well as trustworthy, faithful, and loving. Assuredly, some will see only her naiveté, but like other admirable Shakespearean heroines, beginning with Juliet and ending with Cleopatra, her love remains steadfast, regardless of circumstances. And in the happier world of comedy, it is Rosalind who tries to disabuse Orlando of any unrealistic expectations. This strength of character and purpose is absent from many of their male counterparts until they are able to perceive and appreciate such virtues in the women they profess to love. Like Othello, all of Shakespeare's tragic heroes suffer because of their overconfident assessment of the heart's emotions. Hamlet mistreats Ophelia for an innocent lie; Lear rejects the one daughter who truly loves him because she won't lie; Macbeth succumbs to his wife's verbal provocations and murders his royal mentor; and, like all the other Romans, Antony is so blinded by Cleopatra's sexual allure that he nearly fails to recognize the genuine love that is available to him. In both comedy and tragedy, Shakespeare's women play a crucial role in the emotional education of their men. In the former, they are rewarded for their effort with a marriage feast. In the latter, they largely become hapless victims of the emotional incompetence of their men. In both genres, women play significant and consequential roles in the transformation of the male characters, and Shakespeare pays magnificent homage to such sacrificial love with his portrait of Cleopatra.

This perspective on women, however, should not be confused with the idealization of the feminine found in early courtly love literature. Like every other perspective he absorbed, Shakespeare's portrayal of women was deliberately nuanced. The sacrificial love of a Cordelia is set off against the selfishness of her sisters. The contrast is meant to be instructive: good and evil are choices. As a gender, women are not idealized, but individual female characters exhibit behavior that reflects the best ideals of Christian culture. The love of virtuous women becomes the clearest vision we get of what divine love is like. Shakespeare's plays explore the many complexities, problems, and joys of human love. And as he does this, he conveys a recognition that this quintessentially human experience originates from and is a dim reflection of something mysterious and wonderful beyond the self. If love rightly understood is acknowledged, accepted fully, and enjoyed as intended, it can guide every aspect of human behavior; it inspires what's good and noble; and it never wavers as it confronts trials or obstacles. Shakespeare clearly understood that love is the essence of our purpose in the world. Christianity asks believers to love others as God loves individual men and women. How to do this is evident from the parable of the prodigal son, a story that identifies genuine love by its unwavering faithfulness and its generous mercy and forgiveness. These same virtues are evident in Shakespeare's best women.

In the literary domain, such a uniquely balanced perspective on women was unusual. Culturally, legally, and politically, their rights were limited. Theologically, the status of women was further diminished by the prevalent thinking about sex and marriage. Acknowledging the strength of sexual desire, medieval theologians taught that marriage was preferable to indulging such appetites gratuitously, but the best choice of all was to remain celibate, a position they extracted from the Pauline epistles. Whether or not that's what Paul intended, women came to represent temptations of the flesh. Some of that sexual disgust is prominent in both *Hamlet* and *King Lear*, but, as the text will show, that disgust is part of the emotional sickness that infects both protagonists, whose minds have been poisoned by their circumstances. In those plays, sexual disgust has a thematic purpose. But *Antony and Cleopatra* indicates that Shakespeare recognized that the problematic issue of sex was part of that mysterious but God-given desire for union with another into oneness. Because of that mysterious, quasi-mystical quality of her love, Cleopatra, his remarkable tribute to feminine strength and constancy, literally transforms death into a celebration of her longed-for union with Antony as both wife and mother.

But in crucial ways, human love is only a pale reflection of divine love. With her prodigious emotional strength, Cleopatra helps the Roman Antony comprehend the value of her Egyptian love; with allusions to Christ's sacrificial love, Cordelia is able to rescue an aged father from the cruelty inflicted by his elder daughters. Both redemptions come at a cost, for both women forfeit their lives in this effort to manifest the kind of sacrificial, redemptive, forgiving love that the gospels demand. To our secular age, this effort may seem pathetically wasteful. On more than one occasion, however, the Jesus of the New Testament reminds people that to gain what's truly valuable they must be willing to forgo the glittering temptations of the world. This Biblical paradox of losing what the world considers valuable to gain what's eternal is an unmistakable feature of Shakespeare's thinking, especially in the later plays, and it is his women, rather than his men, who live out this paradox with their constancy to the men they love. Drawing on the memory of Ovid, the plays demonstrate that the power of their patient, sacrificial love can transform their men, and that power is the most visible evidence available of the divine working within human affairs. Though unfamiliar to a secular culture, this is a very Biblical perspective of human life since both Old and New Testaments recount numerous stories of a benevolent God working through people to fulfill His promise to Israel and to the rest of the world. The miraculous nature of love is visible in these plays if we are trained to see it.

For the uninitiated, getting to such insights through the plays is, admittedly, not easy. The language is difficult, the references to people and events of the Elizabethan period are unfamiliar, and the cultural assumptions, as previous paragraphs have shown, are quite different from ours. But it is both possible and worthwhile. As an artist, Shakespeare's mission was to convert life's fascinating emotional and moral complexity into forms that made dramatic sense. Though he begins that journey by imitating existing models to learn the techniques of the major genres, Shakespeare quickly learned their limitations and, gaining confidence through experience, began modifying his forms to suit his audience. He was immensely inventive, willing to experiment with genre and dramatic technique to determine what would please those willing to spend their pennies to see his plays. But throughout his dramas, he employed a few techniques consistently. Three of these are particularly useful tools for analyzing the most prevalent themes: the selection, development, and arrangement of characters into opposing moral positions; the double plot to invite and enhance the implicit comparison of characters; and the use of sometimes elaborate tissues of imagery to guide our responses during those comparisons.

While Shakespeare's first mandate was to entertain, the culture expected a balance between entertainment and moral instruction. The essential difficulty was to do so while avoiding the deadly artistic trap of moral didacticism. Consequently, exposition of ideas, moral or otherwise, is relatively rare throughout the plays, and where such passages do occur they usually provide necessary background information to advance the story. The rather long opening scene of *Hamlet*, with its discussion of the ghost's appearance in the shape of the old king, is one example. Experience probably taught Shakespeare the limitations of this strategy, and, with his uncanny grasp of the theatrical, he came to rely more on sets of characters with opposing values to establish an authorial point of view. As the consequences of the choices made by different characters unfold, that authorial point of view gradually emerges. In *Twelfth Night*, for example, Duke Orsino's courting of Olivia is parodied by Andrew Aguecheek's bumbling courtship of the same lady. The pairing invites comparison between their motives and methods of courtship. In *Lear*, the king's blindness to Cordelia's value is re-enacted by Gloucester's blindness to his son Edgar's noble honesty, a mistake he later pays for with his eyes. There are many more examples of this throughout the plays.

A second stratagem is Shakespeare's use of double plots. Though prevalent in Shakespeare, the double plot is not universally employed. *Antony and Cleopatra*, for example, doesn't have a mirroring action. But when parallel plots are present, they encourage additional comparisons between various characters. The double plot in *1Henry 4* presents Prince Hal's two choices: fun with the wastrel Falstaff, a man who wastes time feeding his appetites; or the honor of saving England from rebellion. Similarly, the two plots of *King Lear* invite comparisons between Lear and Gloucester, between Edmund and Edgar, and between Cordelia and her sisters. The comparisons develop themes of sight and insight, head and heart, good and evil. Through such comparisons, main ideas or themes are enriched in complex ways that avoid dull exposition or obvious didacticism.

The use of imagery is a third structural method Shakespeare uses to develop the complexities of a character's moral stance. As used here, imagery is a group of similar words or phrases, each one of which has a slightly different connotation, but, together, form a symbolic pattern with a complex set of meanings. As early as *Romeo and Juliet*, for example, he emphasizes the urgent desire of young love with imagery of fire and gunpowder, which will, the good friar ominously warns Romeo, "as they kiss, consume." In *Hamlet*, the imagery of disease and decay indicate that both the prince and the world around him have been infected by the moral rot initiated by Claudius's decision to murder. The moral opposites in *Macbeth* are highlighted by the "procreant" nature of good king Duncan's reign, on one hand, and the sleepless anxieties of the murderous couple on the other. At the height of his artistic powers, Shakespeare is able to integrate both event and imagery to emphasize the ambiguities of a particular moral viewpoint. In *King Lear*, for example, the blinding of Gloucester is both an event and a thematic idea that underscores the paradox of seeing more clearly when a person is blind to the misleading appearances of the world. And, finally, in the late romance, *The Tempest*, nature's variety, from its storms to its abundant fruitfulness, highlights opposing moral qualities in the remote island's inhabitants.

These structural techniques of Shakespeare's art become the very tools available to examine individual plays in more detail. Because of Shakespeare's language and the remoteness of his culture, that journey may seem daunting. But the effort to understand his work teaches a lot about values that always remain relevant and about life's complex and wonderful richness. And it helps us understand a remarkable artist and human being. In the initial pages of the First Folio, which preserved these plays for future generations, Ben Jonson's fine valediction to his friend reminds us that the author can be seen and known through his plays:

.... Look how the father's face
Lives in his issue; even so the race
Of Shakespeare's mind and manners brightly shines
In his well-turned and true-filed lines. . . .(65-68)

According to Jonson, Shakespeare's creations, his issue or children, reflect as much about the author's mind as they do about the world and its inhabitants. His claim should quash any interesting but ultimately useless speculation about the author of these thirty-six plays. The tributes of Jonson, Hemmings, and Condell, editors of the First Folio, have made Shakespeare's authorship of the plays abundantly clear. What is far more important is coming to some appreciation of who that man was, what his mind was like, what issues engaged that mind, and why his thinking is still relevant. For better or for worse, the only way to get a better appreciation of those concepts is, as Jonson implies, through engaging with his plays.

Though details of Shakespeare's life are relatively few, Jonson is correct: the plays give us a sense of what he must have been like. Perhaps more than any other reason for reading these plays, one truth remains absolutely clear: the psychological and emotional authenticity of Shakespeare's characters emerge from the author's unusual ability to empathize and judge others objectively. Even when a moral preference is implied, there's always an exquisite sense of balance, of fairness, even with Shylock, the villain of the comedy *The Merchant of Venice*. An encounter with a major character like Rosalind from *As You Like It*, or with Lear, or with Cleopatra becomes persuasive evidence of their author's unshakeable humaneness. Those who come to his works willingly do so for many reasons, but it is invariably his ability to capture the essential foundations of our humanity that keeps them returning for more. He never simplifies but looks with unflinching objectivity at the complexities of experience. In his stories, laughter provoked by human folly is tempered by the recognition of our shared foolishness. Common frailty always deserves forgiveness, but providence eventually rectifies grievous sins against the vulnerable. Suffering is often the only way out of ignorance and into joy. And most

34

importantly, his stories demonstrate how genuine, sacrificial love provides a glimpse of the full potential of our divinely created identities. Fearlessly, he admits that characters who grasp these truths don't always escape the world's tribulations unscathed, but they always earn the respect, admiration, and love of those who witness and understand their efforts. And if they happen to be socially or politically influential, their efforts to love better or value what's good often leave their society more peaceful and ordered than they found it. Despite their faults as characters, their efforts, do make a difference. They demonstrate how such efforts to understand and implement their most humane attributes make life better for themselves and for those characters willing to be influenced by their experience.

While the discussion of Bloom's book has developed important background information for the plays, it is now time to demonstrate the value of Shakespeare's artistic effort in greater detail. The first play, *Romeo and Juliet*, establishes a baseline from which to judge the progress he makes as he learns his craft. With its story of young love sacrificed so that Verona's civil harmony can be restored, it is a truly remarkable beginning to a remarkable stage career. Like all his plays, the story is built on the conflict between good and evil. The villain here is not a person, however, but the complacent acceptance of hatred between two families, the Montagues and the Capulets. That complacency ensnares two remarkable young people, one from each of the feuding families, who willingly, delightfully respond to the random power of love.

Romeo and Juliet

The influence of courtly love conventions is seen more clearly in *Romeo and Juliet* than in any other Shakespearean play. That influence shapes the language, the characterizations, the events, even the way a scene like the balcony encounter is staged. Just as in the sonnets, he sometimes observes those conventions and sometimes chooses to violate them, but the decision is always made for a desired effect. Thematically, the most significant courtly love convention in this early tragedy, though, is the traditional tension generated by male desire for a virtuous and, therefore, physically unavailable lady. A familiar example is Lancelot's love for King Arthur's wife, Guinevere, which was expressed but never acted upon. Though left unspoken in many of these stories, the impetus behind all of this unrequited emotional longing is the desire for sexual union, acknowledged symbolically, for example, in the medieval French poem, *The Romance of the Rose*. Never prurient in these contexts, sexual desire is simply accepted as a natural component of the human condition, a force which feminine virtue was able to convert into romance. Similarly, *Romeo and Juliet* acknowledges sexual attraction as a natural part of love. But rather than denying physical union in the name of virtue, sexual fulfillment within marriage is shown to strengthen, in profound ways, the bonds that form between the lovers. As such, it is not antithetical to virtue but, under the right circumstances and with the right people, an extension of it. When fully realized, the play argues, love is sufficiently powerful to transform not only individual lives but society as well.

Although *Romeo and Juliet* has never received the academic approval that Shakespeare's later tragedies have, it is more widely known and appreciated by audiences than many of his other plays. This may be due partly to its prevalence in junior and high school classrooms, despite its sometimes rather frank sexual innuendo, and partly to its many excellent presentations in film. Handling the play's subject matter with utmost respect, Franco Zeffirelli's 1968 film version is stunning proof of just how effective and moving the story can be. Set in Renaissance Verona, the story is a familiar tale of two feuding families, the Montagues and the Capulets, who fail to heal their differences until they have lost this "pair of star-crossed lovers" to their intransigent quarreling. Full of conflict, lyrical poetry, and passion, the story passes through hope into pathos, never failing to leave its audience moved by the tragic loss of what might have been.

Given that this is Shakespeare's second attempt at tragedy, *Romeo and Juliet* shows a remarkable advance over the earlier, very derivative *Titus Andronicus*, a far more difficult play to like. Instead of *Titus*'s bloody, vengeful protagonist, this play presents two young and innocent people, children, really, who refuse to take sides in their families' feud because they have fallen in love. In the play's moral and emotional opposition of civil strife and love, no one doubts that Romeo and Juliet have made the better choice, and because of their commitment to each other, as the chastened father of Juliet eventually acknowledges, they become "poor sacrifices [to] our enmity." Though the play alludes to the dangerous haste that results from passion, it mitigates that assessment of their culpability by laying most of the blame for their deaths on fate and the family feud. Motivated by wholesome and natural emotions rather than a morally repugnant desire for revenge, the play's two protagonists are effectively absolved of any wrongdoing and garner, therefore, a full measure of the audience's sympathy. Though the impulsive clash of teens on the streets of Verona does create exciting dramatic tension, the romance between these young innocents proves far more appealing than the play's violence. Absent any definable cause, the family quarreling makes no sense. Their love, which implies a possibility of healing and civic harmony, does.

37

Besides the dramatic and lyrical presentation of pleasing subject matter, the play is also a structurally bold experiment that adapts a familiar comic formula for tragedy. The premise for many comedies is an authority figure who obstructs the desires of a young individual who somehow overcomes the hindrance by ingenuity or sheer persistence. Doing so releases everyone from unreasonable oppression so that joy and freedom are once again possible. Northrop Frye summarizes this structural principle of comedy as follows:

> What normally happens is that a young man wants a young woman, that his desire is resisted by some opposition, usually paternal, and that near the end of the play some twist in the plot enables the hero to have his will. In this simple pattern, there are several complex elements. In the first place, the movement of comedy is usually a movement from one kind of society to another. At the beginning, the obstructing characters are in charge of the play's society. At the end, the device in the plot that brings hero and heroine together causes a new society to crystallize around the hero, and the moment when this crystallization occurs is the point of resolution in the action, the comic discovery. (*Anatomy* 163)

Here in *Romeo and Juliet,* youthful desire is hindered in several ways. First, the older generation's tolerance of the feud divides Montague from Capulet, Romeo from Juliet. In the famous balcony scene, both regret their surnames until Juliet resolves the dilemma by declaring that "a rose by any other word would smell as sweet" (2.2.44). Despite the lovers' optimism, however, the divide is not easily bridged. The second obstruction is Capulet's effort to marry his daughter Juliet to the County Paris despite her resistance. The more she resists, the more belligerent he becomes. Both obstacles impede what everyone in the audience sees as the legitimacy of young, innocent but still secret love. That the lovers become sacrificial victims of these obstructions magnifies the pathos of their deaths. The moment of what

38

could have been a comic resolution comes when, shamed by such a waste of youth, beauty, and love, the family elders recognize their fault and agree to reconcile. This adaptation of an essentially comic structure for a tragic purpose proved to be a brilliant and enduring modification. In only his second attempt at tragedy, Shakespeare is already moving beyond the Senecan formula that shaped *Titus* and trusting his instincts about what would please his audience.

But most pertinently, *Romeo and Juliet* is noteworthy for its use of the courtly love conventions of the Elizabethan sonneteers, a poetic form popularized by Sir Phillip Sydney's collection, *Astrophel and Stella* but explored by many others as well, including Wyatt, Surrey, Sir Walter Raleigh, and Shakespeare himself. Addressing the achievements of the early English sonneteers, Gerald Bullett describes what had happened to these conventions by the time Shakespeare incorporated them into his art:

> As for the content of their work, until we reach Raleigh, we have little but variations, though in different styles, upon the same everlasting theme: romantic love. The spirit of the Renaissance, its idealization of the beloved (despite or because of her almost monotonous 'cruelty', often a synonym, it would seem, for 'virtue'), its frank delight in bodily beauty, its blend of soaring fancy with touches of homely realism, and, through all, its eager ingenuous curiosity: these are clearly visible in the 'exuberant specimens of genuine though young poetry' . . . .
> (The Silver Poets xiii)

All of these elements of English sonnet sequences derive from courtly love conventions and are part of the fabric of *Romeo and Juliet*. But the influence is by no means unadulterated. After Sydney's sonnet collection, written in the 1580's, a certain monotony, to use Bullett's word, infected his many English imitators, and the challenge for Shakespeare, who explored the form some years after the sonnet fad had waned, was to inject it with fresh vitality. As a result, Shakespeare's sonnets will deliberately deviate from those conventions to revitalize the poetry. Where Sydney could extol Stella's "fair skin, beamy eyes, like morning sun on snow," Shakespeare's sonnet 130 overturns such shopworn, conventional flattery of his mistress's beauty. "My mistress' eyes are nothing like the sun," it begins, and "Coral is far more red than her lips' red. . . ." To convey his disenchantment, the speaker breaks from conventional obsequiousness completely with the next line: "If snow be white, why then her breasts are dun."

Shakespeare is even willing to break with the most basic sonnet conventions to achieve the freshness he is looking for. Where other poets address their verse to a coldly virtuous lady, Shakespeare addresses his to a charming but aloof man who refuses to get emotionally involved with women. Shakespeare complicates the picture further by introducing a dark lady who is anything but chaste and whose attractions create tension between the two men. But all these deviations from established poetic convention only make sense because of the familiarity of the well-established rules of the courtly tradition. Written about the same time as *Romeo and Juliet,* the experience of writing sonnets, which require great care in choosing words and metaphors to condense meanings into fourteen lines, certainly influenced this second tragedy, as evidenced by the attention to words, images, and language throughout.

That careful attention to language can be seen in the variety of rhetorical styles, particularly with Romeo, where it indicates his emotional development. Early in the play, before he sees Juliet and when he is still infatuated with Rosalind, he tries to define love to his friend, Benvolio, who wants to console him. Love, Romeo begins,

> . . . is a smoke made with the fume of sighs,
> Being purg'd, a fire sparkling in lovers' eyes,
> Being vex'd, a sea nourish'd with loving tears.
> What is it else? a madness most discreet,

40

A choking gall, and a preserving sweet. . . . (1.1.190-194)

Romeo is speaking like a courtly lover, and his very conventional, poetic, and therefore recognizably literary definition of love is made solely in terms of the associated feelings. Because the speech is limited to that, Rosalind recedes far into the background. The artificiality of his language ends up undercutting the grandiose feelings. At this point, he is young, emotionally infatuated, and knows nothing about the kind of self-sacrificing commitment that genuine love will eventually demand.

The language of love begins to change, however, when he first meets Juliet at the Capulet banquet. As the revelers dance, the lovers find a private moment. Now their exchange is poetry of an entirely different kind:

Rom.	If I profane with my unworthiest hand
	This holy shrine, the gentle sin is this,
	My lips, two blushing pilgrims, ready stand
	To smooth that rough touch with a tender kiss.
Jul.	Good pilgrim, you do wrong your hand too much,
	Which mannerly devotion shows in this:
	For saints have hands that pilgrims' hands do
	touch,
	And palm to palm is holy palmers' kiss.
Rom.	Have not saints lips, and holy palmers too?
Jul.	Ay, pilgrim, lips that they must use in pray'r.
Rom.	O then, dear saint, let lips do what hands do,
	They pray—grant thou, lest faith turn to despair.
Jul.	Saints do not move, though grant for prayers'
	sake.
Rom.	Then move not while my prayer's effect I take.
	[kissing her] (1.5.93-106)

Zeffirelli's movie, it must be said, captures the magic of this exquisite moment perfectly. Note that their dialogue is an embedded English sonnet, making the passage no less literary than Romeo's first definition of love, but it develops a

41

religious metaphor of pilgrims and prayers that reflects the deeply felt reverence these two already have for each other. Romeo still assumes the courtly love role of the suitor humbled by all his mistress's many virtues into unworthiness, but the language has moved far beyond conventional infatuation. The emotions of awe and reverence and warmth evolve out of the anticipated relationship. Moreover, despite the artificiality of the language, it correlates seamlessly with the physical actions of the pair as they touch hands and take their first kiss. Language, action and sentiment exquisitely combine to create emotional authenticity out of literary artifice. With complete assurance, Shakespeare uses courtly love conventions in two very different contexts to support dramatic intent. The contrast generates the meaning.

While the language of the play reflects the influence of courtly love, in other ways, *Romeo and Juliet* deviates boldly from other rules of courtly love, particularly the cold, unattainable lady. Although the feud and her father's desire to have Juliet marry the County Paris threaten to make her unattainable, as courtly love requires, the famous balcony scene demonstrates that Juliet is anything but reticent about her feelings for Romeo, who, standing below her balcony in the dark, has overheard what was intended to be a private profession of love. Her heart's secret revealed, she no longer has anything to hide. To help decipher the following passage, the word "fain" means "gladly" and the word "compliment" means "customary behavior."

> Thou knowest the mask of night is on my face,
> Else would a maiden blush bepaint my cheek
> For that which thou hast heard me speak to-night.
> Fain would I dwell on form, fain, fain deny
> What I have spoke, but farewell compliment!
> Dost thou love me? I know thou wilt say, "Ay,"
> And I will take thy word. . . . O gentle Romeo
> If thou dost love, pronounce it faithfully;
> Or if thou thinkest I am too quickly won,
> I'll frown and be perverse, and say thee nay,

So thou wilt woo, but else not for the world. (2.2.85-97)

Juliet is very different from the distant and unattainable Rosalind who frustrated Romeo earlier. Rather than resist, she is completely open to the prospect of being loved and giving love in return. The reluctant Rosalind contrasts with the eager Juliet who shares the innocent secrets of a young girl's heart, revealing a frank desire to be loved. Because of Rosalind's very conventional portrayal, Juliet's personality breathes with life and romantic enchantment. She is no cold, virtuous lady who spurns the advances of her lover.

It seems absolutely natural, therefore, that Shakespeare makes room for the lovers' physical passion for union while still very deftly maintaining their emotional innocence. He helps us appreciate that innocent sexuality by providing two additional, very bawdy perspectives on love. One comes from Romeo's friend, Mercutio, a relative of Verona's prince, and the second from Juliet's nurse, whose first speech quickly reveals her delightfully earthy personality. Lady Capulet, Juliet's mother, has entered her daughter's chambers where the nurse is attending her young charge. The nurse launches into a long speech where she recalls an incident from Juliet's early childhood when the girl could barely walk:

> . . . then she could stand high-lone; nay, by th' rood,
> She could have run and waddled all about;
> For even the day before, she broke her brow,
> And then my husband—God be with his soul!
> 'A was a merry man–took up the child.
> "Yea," quoth he, "dost thou fall upon thy face?
> Thou wilt fall backward when thou hast more wit,
> Wilt thou not, Jule?" and by my holidam,
> The pretty wretch left crying and said, "Ay."
> To see now how a jest shall come about!
> I warrant, and I should live a thousand years,
> I never should forget it. . . . (1.3.36-47)

Touching in its frank domesticity, the nurse clearly relishes her husband's earthy joke. Honest, good-hearted, and completely comfortable with the sexual aspects of life, there is nothing pretentious about Juliet's nurse. Her mature, matronly humor provides one perspective on Juliet's innocent desire.

Similarly, Mercutio often spars verbally with Romeo, and, typical of young men, the humor is often about sex. After the nighttime banquet where Romeo first sees Juliet, he eludes his friends so he can get a glimpse of his new love. In the quiet darkness of the city streets, they call out his name in vain. Mercutio's voice is the loudest and most profane. He begins, of course, by mocking the conventions of courtly lovers:

> Romeo! humors! madman! passion! lover!
> Appear thou in the likeness of a sigh!
> Speak but one rhyme, and I am satisfied. . . .
> Speak to my gossip Venus one fair word,
> One nickname for her purblind son and heir,
> Young Abraham Cupid, he that shot so trim. . . .
> He heareth not, he stirreth not, he moveth not,
> The ape is dead, and I must conjure him.
> I conjure thee by Rosalind's bright eyes,
> By her high forehead and her scarlet lip,
> By her fine foot, straight leg, and quivering thigh,
> And the demesnes that there adjacent lie. . . .
> Ben. And if he hear thee, thou wilt anger him.
> Mer. This cannot anger him; 'twould anger him
> To raise a spirit in his mistress' circle,
> Of some strange nature, letting it there stand
> Till she had laid it and conjur'd it down.
> (2.1.7-26)

Like Juliet's nurse, such naughtiness offsets the purity of Romeo and Juliet's love, and that distinction is further emphasized in the balcony scene which follows Mercutio's lewd humor. There, the lovers meet enclosed very privately within garden walls with Juliet, quite appropriately for the mistress of a courtly lover, elevated up on her balcony.

By contrasting a noisy, bawdy street scene with a quiet, moonlit garden where two young lovers exchange vows, the setting itself becomes emblematic of the two, very disparate views of romantic love in Verona. For the nurse and for Mercutio, love is largely a matter of the flesh or, as evidenced later on by the nurse's shifting support of first Romeo and then Paris, a pragmatic matter of security. But the young lovers operate on a much different, far more elevated plane that is supported rhetorically as well as symbolically. The positioning of the lovers, he below, she up above, becomes a physical emblem of the relationship established by courtly love, which demands male reverence for his unattainable beloved. But, as always with courtly love, the presence of physical longing is not denied. Instead, the emblematic setting gives their frank desire for union a patina of literary and moral legitimacy.

With marvelous dramatic control, the entirety of the encounter in the garden indicates the limitations of Mercutio's purely sexual perspective on love. Quickly transitioning away from his bawdy jokes, the garden scene uses courtly love's reverence for feminine virtue to suggest the innocence of that first Biblical garden without denying any of love's passion. The emotional balance is striking. Just as their garden is worlds apart from the street, their love is not at all like Mercutio's or the nurse's. Reinforcing the imagery of pilgrims and prayers in their first exchange at the banquet, the garden setting and the language establish an atmosphere of reverence for this love and set it apart from the bawdy, violent world outside the garden walls.

It is precisely because of this separation, in fact, that their love manages to sanctify even the physical aspect of romantic love that Mercutio used to mock his friend. Just as courtly love always acknowledged a tension between respect for feminine virtue and male desire, the balcony scene does not avoid their passion.   But because of the reverent atmosphere created by language and setting, the lovers' physical desire, ever so lightly acknowledged, seems both natural and morally acceptable.   A bit frightened by her boldness, Juliet gently tries to bring the encounter to a conclusion, but Romeo persists with just the slightest hint of sexual desire before retreating to emotionally safer quarters:

> Rom.   O, wilt thou leave me so unsatisfied?
> Jul.   What satisfaction canst thou have to-night?
> Rom.   Th' exchange of thy love's faithful vow for mine.
> Jul.   I gave thee mine before thou didst request it;
> And yet I would it were to give again.
> Rom.   Wouldst thou withdraw it? for what purpose,
> love?
> Jul.   But to be frank and give it thee again,
> And yet I wish but for the thing I have.
> (2.2.125-132)

Though both seem aware of the physical implications of their love, they quickly turn away from that so they can first cement their commitment to each other.   Whatever their emotional state, these young lovers never question that marriage provides the rationale for physical intimacy.

In a garden sanctified by genuine love and separated from the world of the flesh, emotional bonding and marriage become the rightful premise for physical union.   Unlike French, Italian and even most of the earlier English flavors of courtly love, which used the woman's marriage to justify her reluctance, Shakespeare's lovers accept marriage as proof of their devotion to each other.   Breaking convention once again, Shakespeare marries his young lovers so that the joy of physical union replaces the conventional pain of unrequited love.

And Shakespeare is quite frank about Juliet's sexual desire.   Secretly married but before their wedding night, she eagerly awaits the arrival of her husband, whom the prince exiled for the revenge killing of Tybalt, Juliet's cousin and the murderer of Mercutio. Her anticipation of physical passion is unequivocal:

> And Romeo
> Leap to these arms untalk'd of and unseen!
> Lovers can see to do their amorous rites
> By their own beauties. . . .
>   Come, civil night,
> Thou sober-suited matron all in black
> And learn me how to lose a winning match,
> Play'd for a pair of stainless maidenhoods.
> Hood my unmann'd blood, bating in my cheeks,
> With thy black mantle, till strange love grow bold,
> Think true love acted simple modesty. (3.2.6-16).

In their world, true love is simple modesty. Married passion is not incompatible with virtue. The speech is an acknowledgment that married love facilitates every dimension of love, fulfilling nature's design. Her words express the wondrous transformation that sexual passion has already wrought. No longer just a girlish, obedient daughter, Juliet understands that Romeo's love has uncovered a nascent trove of hidden wealth. Because of his love, she experiences a desire, not just for physical union, but a desire to give herself to him completely:

> My bounty is as boundless as the sea,
> My love as deep; the more I give to thee,
> The more I have, for both are infinite. (2.2.133-135)

Here as elsewhere in Shakespeare, abundance is the child of genuine love, which is a form of physical, emotional, and spiritual generosity. This is a theme that begins with his sonnets but appears in some form in multiple plays thereafter. Repeatedly, from these early plays all the way through to his last effort, the paradoxical nature of love is that giving away everything that constitutes the self multiplies the many blessings that are showered upon the giver. Conversely, selfishness or an obsessive regard for self leads to crippling, spiritual poverty. This notion, a theme of Shakespeare's first eighteen so-called procreation sonnets, is only briefly alluded to here but gets much fuller treatment in *The Merchant of Venice*.

Having made his young protagonists largely innocent of any wrongdoing except, perhaps, undue haste, the sad demise of Romeo and Juliet could only be attributed to fate, as the prologue makes clear. Very succinctly, it establishes the play's tragic premise:

> Two households, both alike in dignity,
> In fair Verona, where we lay our scene,
> From ancient grudge break to new mutiny,
> Where civil blood makes civil hands unclean.
> From forth the fatal loins of these two foes,
> A pair of star-cross'd lovers take their life;
> Whose misadventur'd piteous overthrows
> Doth with their death bury their parents' strife. (1.1.1-8)

Anathema to New Testament Christianity, the revenge motif of a play like *Titus* was a dramatic vein that Shakespeare mined but quickly exhausted. Revenge and counter-revenge are the premises for the feud in this play too, and he would return to it one final time with *Hamlet* and for far sounder reasons. But *Romeo and Juliet* represents the beginning of his effort to find a more workable premise for tragedy. Here, the amorphous power of disaster victimizes the two young lovers, who remain largely innocent throughout. While this approach to the issues of tragic experience generates considerable pathos in *Romeo and Juliet*, the play falls short, as the discussion of *King Lear* will show, of what is possible when suffering and death are more directly attributed to human culpability. In this play, Shakespeare seems content to wring as much pathos as possible from the opposition of a disruptive, evil feud with his innocent lovers.

As the prologue makes clear, a remote, nebulous fate is largely responsible for the play's tragic denouement. The hand of fate is evident when Capulet gives the guest list for his party to a servant who cannot read. By chance, he crosses paths with Romeo whose friends have just convinced him he should socialize more to get over the cold-hearted Rosalind. Perusing the guest list for Capulet's servant, Romeo decides to attend the banquet in disguise where he first sees the lovely and far more receptive Juliet. Fate steps in again when Juliet's cousin, Tybalt, kills Mercutio and is then killed by Romeo to avenge the murder of his friend. After the prince banishes Romeo, another mischance occurs when Friar Lawrence's letter explaining his plan to reunite the newly married couple never reaches Romeo who, based on his friend Benvolio's misinterpretation of events, believes Juliet is now dead. Resolute for death himself, he returns to Verona where the final misfortune occurs. Finding Juliet unconscious in the tomb, he drinks the poison he obtained just moments before Juliet awakens, and when she realizes what has happened she takes her own life as well. Except for the chance meeting at the banquet, which initiated their love, everything that could go wrong did go wrong. In the most uncomplicated but mysterious fashion, fate seems to have manipulated the outcome.

Though later tragedies make irony and paradox far more prevalent than they are here, fate's numerous interventions in *Romeo and Juliet* still create ironic disparities between intention and consequence that are an identifying characteristic of all tragedy. After spending her wedding night with Romeo, for example, Juliet's refusal to marry Paris enrages her father, and he utters an ultimatum to her that, sadly enough, proves to be prophetic:

> . . . disobedient wretch!
> I tell thee what: get thee to church a' Thursday,
> Or never after look me in the face.
> Speak not, reply not, do not answer me!

My fingers itch. Wife, we scarce thought us blest
That God had lent us but this only child,
But now I see this one is one too much,
And that we have a curse in having her. (3.5.160-167)

Spoken out of the same kind of anger that fuels the warfare in
Verona's streets, these are ugly words indeed and they show
the ugly, destructive side of human passion. If the lovers are
propelled toward disaster by their emotions, at least those
emotions carry the unfulfilled promise of new life and
abundance and joy. Though he dearly loves his daughter, Old
Capulet's anger pushes Juliet toward Friar Lawrence's cell
and the fateful plot that ends in death.

The next time the father sees his daughter, she has
consumed the friar's potion and, though still alive, appears to
be cold, lifeless, and ready for the grave. At the discovery of
her body on the morning of her wedding to Paris, old
Capulet's lament introduces the paradoxical conjunction of
love and death. In shock and horror, he speaks to the
prospective husband:

O son, the night before thy wedding-day,
Hath Death lain with thy wife. There she lies,
Flower as she was, deflowered by him.
Death is my son-in-law, Death is my heir,
My daughter hath he wedded. I will die,
And leave him all; life, living, all is Death's. (4.5.35-40)

Though Capulet's rhetorical conceit may seem artificial, it
reinforces the idea, established earlier in the garden scene, that
this love, so pure and innocent, could only exist set apart from
the norms currently operating in Verona, a place of violence
and of earthly, sinful flesh, a world where anger and
vengeance constantly work against what is possible. In a
world marked by hate and dissension, the youth, beauty, love,
and promise of these star-crossed lovers have all been lost,
swallowed up by death, never to return. Normally, the comic
structure underlying *Romeo and Juliet* would have concluded

50

with their marriage, but Shakespeare emphasizes the tragic pathos of lost and irrecoverable joy with this metaphorical marriage of the lovers and Death.

But the persistent association in these final scenes between love and death suggests that this is probably more than an odd rhetorical flourish to heighten the pathos of loss. The image keeps appearing. After their wedding night, for example, Romeo and Juliet indicate their reluctance to part with a beautiful courtly love *aubade*, a poetic set-piece that announces the arrival of morning. It is a tender and joyous moment tainted by the sadness of Romeo's banishment. Juliet is torn between her desire for his company and her concern that tarrying too long might endanger her husband. Romeo, also reluctant to leave, bravely proclaims his desire to fulfill her wish:

> Let me be ta'en, let me be put to death,
> I am content, so thou wilt have it so.
> I'll say yon grey is not the morning's eye. . .
> Nor that is not the lark whose notes do beat
> The vaulty heaven so high above our heads.
> I have more care to stay than will to go.
> Come, death, and welcome! Juliet wills it so.
> How is't, my soul? Let's talk, it is not day.
> Jul.   It is, it is! Hie hence, be gone, away!
> It is the lark that sings so out of tune. . . .
> (3.5.17-27)

This strangely beautiful mixture of joy amidst the lurking presence of death foreshadows what is to come. Romeo does return to exile in Mantua, but like Old Capulet, the next time he sees Juliet, he will view what he assumes is her lifeless body, and the vision, though faulty, will lead directly to his suicide. His final words in the tomb continue to emphasize this conjunction of love and death:

> Shall I believe
> That insubstantial Death is amorous,

51

> And that the lean abhorred monster keeps
> Thee here in the dark to be his paramour?
> For fear of that, I still will stay with thee
> And never from this palace of dim night
> Depart again. (5.3.102-108)

Upon waking and seeing Romeo's lifeless body, Juliet tries to follow her husband, first kissing his lips for any poison that might remain, and, failing that, plunging his dagger into her breast to join him in death. The tragic denouement within the sepulcher becomes a physical re-enactment of Old Capulet's rhetorical flourish of death as a loving paramour. These young lovers no longer fear death because their wedding night together crystalizes the hypothetical into the actual, the verbal declaration into physical and emotional bonds that nothing, not even the fear of death, can untie. Having experienced love in both its emotional and its physical dimensions, Romeo and his wife, Juliet, have become inseparable, a bond that lasts "even to the edge of doom," to borrow a phrase from the great 116th sonnet.

That the wedding night was critical to this transformation is borne out by the sequence of the play's events. Though the death scene is absolute proof of the bond between the lovers, that commitment was by no means automatic. Banishment tests Romeo's commitment to the relationship, and, at first, he is overcome by despair. It isn't until Friar Lawrence reminds him of all the reasons for hope that he puts his self-indulgent feeling aside for something greater:

> What, rouse thee, man! Thy Juliet is alive,
> For whose dear sake thou wast but lately dead;
> There art thou happy. Tybalt would kill thee,
> But thou slewest Tybalt; there art thou happy.
> The law that threat'ned death becomes thy friend,
> And turns it to exile: there thou art happy.
> A pack of blessings light upon thy back. . . .
> Get thee to thy love as was decreed,

Ascend to her chamber, hence and comfort her.
(3.3.135-147)

Convinced by the good friar's argument, Romeo returns to her chambers for their wedding night, where, as their touching *aubade* indicates, he successfully comforts her. Very maturely, he relinquishes self-pity, accepts Friar Lawrence's advice, and addresses her sorrow with his presence. But their physical union confirms their emotional union, and from that moment on, his commitment to her never wavers. Misinformed about Juliet's supposed demise, his response is swift and decisive: "Is it e'en so? Then I defy you, stars!" And a few lines later, he makes a grim but irrevocable vow with language newly available to him from their one night together: "Well, Juliet, I will lie with thee tonight."

Similarly, Juliet is tested when she hears that her cousin Tybalt has been killed by Romeo. Momentarily, her attachment to Romeo weakens. But when the nurse advises her to forget her husband and marry Paris, the prospect of such disloyalty to the man she has just slept with clarifies her resolve. After the nurse leaves, she vents her displeasure with the advice given. Though her words about the delightful nurse may seem overblown and harsh, they indicate her steely resolve to choose Romeo:

Ancient damnation! O most wicked fiend!
Is it more sin to wish me thus forsworn,
Or to dispraise my lord with that same tongue
Which she hath prais'd him with above compare
So many thousand times? Go, counsellor,
Thou and my bosom henceforth shall be twain.
(3.5.235-240)

Later, alone in her chambers, she confronts and bravely overcomes a long list of her fears about taking Father Lawrence's sleeping potion. Thoughts of her husband steady her nerves. "Romeo, Romeo, Romeo! Here's drink—I drink to thee." And finally, like Romeo, her determination to join her husband in death beside his now lifeless body is unwavering, immediate, and absolute. In two short lines, the deed is done.

Both Romeo and Juliet pass from life into death as if death embodied their beloved spouse. Fear has been replaced by a longing for union that would have been unnatural and impossible before that fateful wedding night. Imagery, motivation, and action—like the kiss to find enough poison to die—all reinforce this association of death and love. Married, in love, and committed to each other body and soul, these two "star-cross'd lovers" in these circumstances could only end like this. As the play's prologue warned, their "death-mark'd love" was fated for a tragic end. With barely controlled anger, the prince has the final word:

> Where be these enemies? Capulet! Montague!
> See what a scourge is laid upon your hate,
> That heaven finds means to kill your joys with love.
> And I for winking at your discords too
> Have lost a brace of kinsmen. All are punish'd.
> (5.3.291-295)

A steep price has been paid for the sins of anger, pride, and negligence of what truly matters. The reconciliation between the families has come at the cost of two emotionally precocious children together with several of their kinsmen. As the families agree to erect golden statues of their dead son and daughter, the monuments are cold reminders of what has been lost and the pathetic futility of their commemoration.

Though an early play, *Romeo and Juliet* represents an important step forward in the evolution of Shakespeare's art. Firmly rooted in the poetry and conventions of courtly love, it demonstrates the author's growing confidence in the potential of love as a subject for tragedy as well as comedy. It identifies multiple assumptions about love, from the reductively sexual, to the pragmatic, to the genuinely compelling, and these distinctions shape his presentation of love going forward, providing the moral clarity that adds depth to both comedy and tragedy. Though this early tragedy occasionally exhibits rhetorically artificial moments, it also contains many examples of very compelling human speech and characterization. And it initiates that metaphorical association of love and death that appears in every subsequent tragedy, a metaphor that strengthens into an argument that love maintains a constancy that endures beyond the grave and, as a consequence, is evidence of a connection between the human and the divine. As Zeffirelli's version of the play shows, *Romeo and Juliet* works marvelously well on stage and in film, and it continues to delight audiences.

Before addressing *Hamlet*, Shakespeare's first mature tragedy, it is important to look at one of Shakespeare's history plays. For many, *1Henry4* would deserve its own chapter based on Sir John Falstaff's enormous and enormously entertaining personality alone, which represents a major advancement in Shakespeare's presentation of character. Though he is related to the medieval comic type of the vice, a stage type that personifies the magnetic lure of sin, Falstaff's character absolutely obliterates such a restrictive classification while still managing to serve the same thematic purpose. His childlike delight in all things humorous makes him completely irresistible. That, however, is precisely the problem that Falstaff represents: the allure of sin. But to recognize him simply as a literary type with a thematic purpose does him, and Shakespeare, a real disservice. Falstaff multiplies the realism that was evident in Juliet's nurse and in Mercutio into an unforgettable personality that very nearly overwhelms the other characters in the play. That kind of extraordinary individuality moves Shakespeare's art away from the literary into the drama of real life. As attractive as they are, the characters of Romeo and Juliet are rooted in the traditions of courtly love. They cannot exist in our imaginations outside of that. Falstaff overflows his literary type and makes us forget where his roots are.

But this play is far more significant for Shakespeare's theatrical development than a single character. During his examination of various British monarchs, he seems to have concluded that what separates successful reigns from their opposites is a king's recognition that the welfare of the entire populace must take precedence over personal interest, and that a good monarch must exemplify this value clearly enough that others in positions of authority are inspired to do the same. This very personal decision ends up having political ramifications because the demand for self-sacrifice often defines what is truly right or wrong, what unifies rather than what divides. In this regard, it mimics on the political level what love requires on a personal level, an indication of the universality of valid moral principles. As this play will show, Prince Hal is caught between a life in the Boar's Head Inn with his reprobate friend, Falstaff, and a life of responsibility and honor as the successor to his royal father, Henry 4. Will Hal follow Falstaff into a never-ending life of pleasure and fun? Or will he assist his aging father in putting down a dangerous uprising where the lives of many, including his own, are at stake? While neither of these men, Falstaff or Henry, are perfect, they function as Hal's good and bad angels, struggling for influence over his future. That interior battle mirrors the exterior, political struggle to defeat rebellion in the realm. Both conflicts test Hal's ability to manage desire properly. Falstaff's life is about feeding a selfish inclination for pleasure. The other choice is about sacrificing those selfish inclinations for the welfare of something larger than self.

Besides the development of character and the conviction that all decisions, both personal and political, have a moral basis, *1Henry4* is worth a chapter for a third reason: the recognition that the same mysterious forces that impact personal destinies, evident in the lives of Romeo and Juliet, play a role in the fate of nations. On one level, *1Henry4* partakes of what has been called the Tudor Myth, the idea perpetrated by the Tudors that they alone resolved the

56

aftereffects of the protracted War of the Roses and brought peace to a weary realm. On a parallel level, it also partakes of a similar Christian perspective on English history. Perhaps this had to do with the miraculous defeat of the Spanish Armada, but in dealing with larger swaths of time than a single comic or tragic episode, Shakespeare found validation for his deepening conviction that a good and loving God works everything, including circumstances that look very much like evil, for the good of his faithful people. That conviction becomes a bedrock principle in every genre that he explores. Though, like the Bible, he never minimizes the reality of suffering and death, it is precisely this principle that prevents him from sliding into the sin of despair and nihilism. As later plays like *King Lear* will show, he balances an awareness of pervasive sin with a conviction of God's protective grace, and that balance gives his tragedies enormous poignancy. Shakespeare's explorations of English history, including *1Henry 4*, play an important role in developing those insights.

1 Henry 4

During the very busy six years between Shakespeare's two Senecan revenge plays, *Titus* and *Hamlet,* he wrote several first-rate comedies, including *Love's Labor's Lost, A Midsummer Night's Dream, The Merchant of Venice,* and *Much Ado About Nothing.* He also wrote that play about young love, *Romeo and Juliet*, the subject of the previous chapter. But the bulk of his effort was expended on plays about English history, including the final sequel of *Henry VI, Richard III, Richard II, King John*, and the so-called Henriad. That series of four plays covers the deposing of Richard II, the reign of Henry IV (split into two parts), and the first years on the throne of his son, Henry V. Twelve plays in six years attests to the feverish pace of writing, rehearsing, and performing that was required to keep Elizabethan audiences satisfied. Perhaps because of this incessant pressure, it was an amazing period of creative energy and innovation that developed his instincts for what did and what didn't work on stage. Out of this frenetic period came his ability to create distinctive voices and personalities onstage, what Bloom rightly identified as characters imbued with unmistakable vitality. His talent for this was evident as early as *Titus* where Aaron the Moor's understandable sense of outraged dignity differentiates him from characters whose limited emotional integrity is undercut by the grotesque, almost farcical quality of their retribution. Aaron was a hint of what was to come.

This ability reaches a watershed moment with Sir John Falstaff, which Bloom, again, rightly identifies as a supreme achievement in characterization. He makes his first appearance in a play about Henry IV, who struggles to quash a rebellion that threatens his kingdom. Meanwhile, his son, Prince Hal, has been distracted by this fat, witty, playful companion, Sir John, who inhabits the local tavern and is completely dependent upon the prince's generosity. Boldly asserting that Falstaff "teaches us not to moralize," Bloom continues:

> . . .Falstaff wants childlike (not childish) play, which exists in another order than that of morality. . . . he is neither immoral nor amoral but of another realm, the order of play. Hal entered that order as Falstaff's disciple. . . . Hal struggles all through Henry IV, Part One, against the fascination exercised by the great wit. It seems just to observe that Falstaff charms the tough and resistant prince for many of the same reasons that Falstaff, properly played, dominates any audience. (298)

And dominate an audience he does. Queen Elizabeth, it is said, requested a sequel to *1Henry 4*, which had been performed for her at court, just so she could see more of the fat rogue, Jack Falstaff. Shakespeare complied, featuring Falstaff in *2Henry 4*, *Henry 5*, and the comedy, *The Merry Wives of Windsor*.

Despite Bloom's claim that Falstaff rises above moral legalities into the realm of play, however, his dramatic presence carries moral implications that deserve attention. In fact, to fully appreciate Shakespeare's perspective on these historical events, Falstaff's indulgence of every conceivable appetite stands as a moral indictment of each aristocrat, including Henry Bolingbroke, similarly motivated by personal desire. The lone exception to this is the supposedly reprobate Prince Hal, who, under the tutelage of Fat Jack, appears to let desire rule behavior. As enjoyable a creation as Falstaff is, therefore, his thematic significance goes far beyond his role as royal entertainer. His place in the overall design of these three histories comes into sharper focus as Shakespeare interprets events beginning with the reign of Richard II and culminating with Prince Hal's ascension to the throne as Henry V, the events covered in this group of plays known as the Henriad.

Shakespeare's cycle of four plays describes the tumultuous War of the Roses during which the houses of York and Lancaster vied for the English throne. Lasting sixty-three years, it squandered treasure, lives, and political patience. As the conflict drew to a close, an exhausted England celebrated the Tudors for the order and stability they restored to the land. The protracted war profoundly changed England. Part of a national self-examination into the origins of that rebellion and its consequences, Shakespeare's Henriad acknowledges that England had gone through a significant transformation. As Alvin B. Kernan observed in his essay, "The Henriad: Shakespeare's Major History Plays":

> In the Henriad, the action is the passage from the England of Richard II to the England of Henry V. This dynastic shift serves as the supporting framework for a great many cultural and psychological transitions which run parallel to the main action, giving it body and meaning. In historical terms, the movement from the world of Richard II to that of Henry V is the passage from the Middle Ages to the Renaissance and the modern world. In political and social terms, it is a movement from feudalism and hierarchy to the national state and individualism. In psychological terms, it is the passage from a situation in which man knows with certainty who he is to an existential condition in which any identity is only a temporary role. (245-46)

Bloom's emphasis on Shakespeare's gift for creating vibrant personalities like Falstaff is certainly true, but it is far from the whole truth, or even the most interesting truth, for the Henriad exhibits a keen awareness of the transformations mentioned by Kernan.

The pivotal moment in the transition from medieval to modern comes with *Richard II*, the first play of the Henriad. As that play begins, Richard arbitrates a quarrel between Henry Bolingbroke, a Lancastrian, and the Duke of Mowbry. Interrupting their medieval trial by combat, Richard banishes both men from England. His reason for doing so is unclear until later, when needing additional funds for his ill-conceived Irish wars, he rents out Henry Bolingbroke's lands without the banished duke's permission. To defend his property rights, Henry returns from exile where he is joined by other nobles who see Richard's actions as a threat to their own rights. Confronted by overwhelming opposition, Richard at first appeals to the medieval doctrine known as the divine right of kings in a feeble attempt to retain power. But religious principle provides meager refuge from aristocratic fear and outrage. Full of self-pity and long overdue introspection, he reluctantly relinquishes his throne to Henry and is taken off to prison where he is eventually murdered by one of Henry's supporters. Throughout, Henry is portrayed as a strong, decisive, authoritative figure, while Richard comes off as both weak and ineffectual. The next play in the Henriad, *1Henry 4*, picks up from this point.

Even though the men involved give these events a degree of inevitability, Shakespeare understood that Henry's decision to defend his claim to land rents came at a price. Self-interest, given political dignity as rights, had suddenly come into conflict with the traditional, church-sanctioned powers of the state. Perhaps this was a necessary step in the evolution of a politics that protected individual liberty. But Shakespeare already recognized the dangers of this new individualism, dangers that almost a century later would be sharply decried in Thomas Hobbes' *Leviathan*. Written after the English Civil War ended with the execution of Charles I, a shocking event that prompted the author to describe life as "nasty, brutish, and short," that political treatise envisioned a strong central government able to prevail against the dangers of the unbridled pursuit of liberty and personal needs. Shakespeare would probably have appreciated Hobbes' premise.

Large in body and appetite, the whale-sized Falstaff stands as a similar warning. But Falstaff is not so much a political critique of individualism as a condemnation of its underlying moral problem. Lovable, witty, and playful as he is, he is also irrevocably self-indulgent, embodying the very child-like propensity to give personal desires more attention than they ought to have. Throughout, the underlying premise for Falstaff's friendship with Hal is that the present association will gain future favor with the prince once he becomes king. That unspoken assumption finds verbal expression at Hal's coronation parade near the end of *1Henry 4*. Before that moment, though, Jack's freedom to do as he pleases depends upon the willing cooperation of others who, to use the play's symbolism, are robbed of their treasure. Because his playfulness is so seductive, Falstaff dominates the emotional transaction that he establishes with everyone he entertains. The truth is, participation in Jack's world requires the willing surrender of every aspect of a person's adulthood, including his judgment.

The moral hazards of individualism necessitated changes in the political sphere as well. As feudal assumptions about unquestioned state power receded, a new type of leadership would be required. Until an understanding of what that might look like evolved, a period of social and moral confusion was inevitable. Even as early as *Richard II*, the good Duke of Lancaster, who described the England he loved dearly as "this other Eden, demi-paradise," had difficulty understanding where his loyalties belonged after Henry seized the throne by force. Did fealty belong with Richard, the anointed king? Or with Henry, the more effective and decisive man? With tradition or with pragmatic power? This confusion not only weakened loyalties but had the potential to unleash the dogs of perpetual war. After all, ambitious men could use Bolingbroke's arguments to justify their own opposition to royal prerogatives that threatened to encroach on their perceived rights. After Henry's usurpation, rights would need to be negotiated before being codified into legal tradition. Until this new world took definitive shape, political power and stability would depend upon the shifting sands of personal loyalty. This is the moral and political background that explains Sir John Falstaff's large and quite unforgettable presence in *1Henry 4*.

Much of the plot conforms closely to Shakespeare's sources, Holinshed and North. Sir John Falstaff, however, is Shakespeare's own creation. But no prose description does him adequate justice. Falstaff has to be experienced on stage, where he comes dangerously close to subverting the main political themes altogether and making the play entirely about himself. Fat, perpetually hungry, addicted to sack and capons, Falstaff has endeared himself to Henry Bolingbroke's son, Prince Hal, and together with other assorted ne'er-do-wells, they haunt the Boar's Head Inn and play at being petty thieves. With child-like delight, he is forever playing with both words and truth; he puts on mock plays where he pretends to be Hal's royal father evaluating—favorably, of course–his influence on the young prince; when challenged, he will improvise an explanation for his many failures and lapses with virtuoso creativity. But throughout his escapades, one thing is certain: Falstaff is never serious. As Bloom says, he is perpetually in the mode of play. It begins the moment he sets foot on stage:

> Fal. Now, Hal, what time of day is it, lad?
> Hal. Thou art so fat-witted with drinking of old sack, and
>   unbuttoning thee after supper, and sleeping upon
>   benches after noon, that thou hast forgotten to demand
>   that truly which thou would'st truly know. What a devil
>   hast thou to do with the time of day? Unless hours were
>   cups of sack, and minutes capons, and clocks the
>   tongues of bawds, and dials the signs of leaping-houses,
>   and the blessed sun himself a fair hot wench in flame-
>   colored taffeta; I see no reason why thou shouldst be so
>   superfluous to demand the time of the day.
> Fal. Indeed, you come near me now, Hal, for we that take
>   purses go by the moon and the seven stars, and not by
>   Phoebus, he, "that wand'ring knight so fair." And I
>   prithee, sweet wag, when thou art a king, as God save
>   thy Grace—Majesty I should say, for grace thou wilt

have none—
Hal. What, none?
Fal. No, by my troth, not so much as will serve to be
prologue to an egg and butter. (1.2.1-21)

From beginning to end, this is the Falstaffian octave. He refuses to be daunted by Hal's litany of bad behavior. In the familiar spirit of male friendship, Falstaff transforms Hal's good-natured insults into opportunities to display his wit. The wordplay on "grace," used either as a royal title or the prayer before a meal, flows effortlessly from his brain. It is this natural, agile, perpetual playfulness that proves both irresistible and lovable. Infinitely inventive, Falstaff is always at play, exercising his imagination to feed his huge appetite for fun.

But the witty banter about time also implies two distinct perspectives on the passing hours, a fundamental topic of concern in a history play. Just as children caught up in play quickly lose any concept of what hour it is, Falstaff's limitless imagination creates abundant opportunities for amusement that obliterate any awareness of time. For a child, fun matters far more than the hour. The inner child in all of us willfully indulges Falstaff's behavior, despite his blissful denial of life's more serious requirements. He obeys only one, very simple rule: life exists to satisfy that child-like appetite for pleasure. Falstaff's prodigious waistline is a constant reminder that his appetites exist to be fed. That gormandizing is why Hal excoriates Fat Jack Falstaff for his obsession with food:

Hal.   How now, my sweet creature of bombast, how
        long is't ago, Jack, since thou sawest thine own knee?
Fal.   My own knee? When I was about thy years, Hal,
        I was not an eagle's talent in the waist, I could have
        crept into an alderman's thumb-ring. (2.4.326-331)

Completely impervious to humor aimed at his size, Falstaff makes no pretensions to either ego or virtue, and that

64

guilelessness captures our hearts, whets our appetite for more Falstaff, and erases any awareness of the passing hours.

All that ignores an essentially Christian perspective of time which sees life's passing hours as the theater wherein God works out His plan for the world, where each individual has a responsible role to play in the outcome. Each person, in fact, has been provided with gifts that, to be a responsible party to God's plan, he must employ for the benefit of others. Success, both in worldly as well as in moral and spiritual terms, means accepting that divinely appointed purpose. Abjuring that responsibility altogether, Falstaff reminds those in his company of his one purpose. "I am not only witty in myself," he confesses in *2Henry 4*, but am "the cause of wit in others." Bloom is right about Falstaff: he is play personified. But, like most children, he remains oblivious to the inevitable consequences of advancing time, and that moral obliviousness represents a temptation to others.

Because Falstaff has no self-awareness, Hal, who knows exactly what Jack represents, will bluntly refer to him as that fat, sack-swilling, whore-mongering rogue who lies for amusement and who robs his fellow citizens to subsidize his appetites. As much fun as Falstaff is, Hal recognizes a collection of the seven deadly sins when he sees one. That one huge body is a walking temptation to anyone lacking sufficient self-discipline to resist. The measure of truth in Hal's verbal abuse is always a bit shocking: he is not above referring to his companion as "that villainous abominable misleader of youth, Falstaff, that old white-bearded Satan" (2.4.440-463). Though the reference to Satan at first seems unwarranted, the devil, as the Bible cautions, is well versed in making sin look far more appealing than virtue.

In reality, Hal is besieged on one side by a father who expects something more from a son and, on the other, by a fun-loving companion who eventually expects a favor. Both are trying to shape Hal's identity for personal reasons. While play-acting Hal's impending confrontation with his father, the king, Falstaff describes himself as "a good, portly man. . ., of a cheerful look, a pleasing eye, and a most noble carriage" (2.4.422-424). But, taking the part of his father, Hal's assessment of Falstaff is far different, presaging the eventual rejection of his lovable companion. Pretending to be a father speaking to his prodigal son, he condemns Falstaff in terms absolute:

> Thou art violently carried away from grace, there is a devil haunts thee in the likeness of an old fat man. . . . Why dost thou converse with that trunk of humors, that bolting-hutch of beastliness, that huge bombard of sack. . . that reverent Vice, that grey Iniquity, that father ruffian, that vanity in years? Wherein is he good, but to taste sack and drink it? Wherein neat and cleanly, but to carve a capon and eat it? Wherein cunning but in craft? Wherein crafty, but in villainy? Wherein villainous, but in all things? Wherein worthy, but in nothing? (2.4.446-459)

Bloom dislikes Hal for such cold-hearted assessments of a companion so likable and full of vitality. This misreads the play, however, and is a consequence of overemphasizing character at the expense of the dramatic structure's moral implications. Falstaff is the externalization of unbridled human desire, and his eventual rejection as the governing force in Hal's life is a necessary step toward both duty and honor. Eventually, political responsibilities will require Hal to give up much of what he loves, but the reasons why become increasingly self-evident.

Several of the play's events show how Falstaff's self-absorption renders him untrustworthy in moments of crisis. When duty or loyalty is urgently required, he lapses into uproariously funny but irresponsible cowardice. In the battle against the rebels, he draws a bottle of sack out of his holster, then takes credit for defeating Hotspur, whose lifeless body he ingloriously stabs. Earlier, the same shameful behavior was evident when he fled the Gadshill robbery after being confronted by a disguised prince and his partner, Poins.

Because he is unwilling to distinguish play from its opposite, Falstaff's need for safety and glory easily overwhelms any sense of duty or honor. As the heir to England's throne, Hal cannot possibly emulate Falstaff and still lead his country. Inevitably, his responsibilities will make him incompatible with Jack.

So Hal's lovable companion also functions as a "reverent Vice." Somehow Shakespeare makes both views of Falstaff feel equally true, a conundrum which should indicate that Hal's assumption of his royal identity entails considerable personal sacrifice. Yet the brewing dissatisfaction and rebellion leave the prince no other choice. As the king's son, his loyalty must be to England and his father, not to Falstaff. Relinquishing the pleasures of the Boar's Head Tavern is the price he must pay for the responsibilities his father incurred by deposing Richard, what Hal terms "the debt I never owed." It is worth noting that the phrase contains the slightest hint of Christ's sacrifice for the sins of the world. When Hal magnanimously pays Falstaff's debt at the inn and to the travelers Falstaff robs at Gadshill, his generous spirit in small things indicates that he will also make good on the moral and political debt his father incurred. That generosity of life and spirit distinguishes Hal from the fat companion who lives to satisfy his appetites. The self-centered Falstaff takes while the generous Hal gives. The distinction is both moral and spiritual.

Enthralled by the seductive nature of sin, it is all too easy to get caught up in the pleasure of Falstaff's company, to forget responsibility, to ignore the passage of time. But while inventive and amusing, Falstaff's imaginative stories and witty dialogue mask one very relentless truth: everything mortal is subject to time. Time passes, age increases, and mortality awaits. Falstaff's unwillingness to admit his rightful age in *2Henry 4* greatly offends the Lord Chief Justice, who represents the law that Fat Jack was born to violate:

Do you set down your name in the scroll of youth, that are written down old with all the characters of age? Have you not a moist eye, a dry hand, a yellow cheek, a white beard, a decreasing leg, an increasing belly? Is not your voice broken, your wind short, your chin double, your wit single, and every part about you blasted with antiquity? and will you yet call yourself young? Fie, fie, fie, Sir John. (*2H4* 1.2.181-189)

Hal's first question to Falstaff, then, turns out to be rhetorical: "What a devil hast thou to do with the time of day?" The devil's answer, of course, is nothing because time needs to be ignored until judgment comes. While Falstaff has lost any conception of time in his world of play, time is a reality that not even Falstaff can evade, try as he might. Because Fat Jack does not use it wisely, the gift of time eventually exposes the folly of his frivolous obsession with pleasure. His physical decline as the Henriad progresses is a reminder of what awaits every sinner. And time is something that Hal, as heir apparent, cannot afford to waste.

Falstaff's physical decline is paralleled by his moral degeneration. That decline stands as a comment on how England itself has changed. One measure of that is the play's discussion of honor, which normally encompasses the values of respect, duty, loyalty, selfless service, integrity, as well as personal courage. England's nobility adhered to these values until Richard and Henry Bolingbroke asserted their rights at the expense of a nation's peaceful order. Always looking for an advantage that favors him, Falstaff's preparations for war savage the identical sin of the aristocrats. Asked to recruit soldiers for the fight against the rebels, he accepts bribes from rich citizens looking to escape the general conscription, filling the ranks of his battalion with the desperate and unfortunate military castoffs who lack money to buy their way out of service:

If I be not asham'd of my soldiers, I am a sous'd gurnet. I have misus'd the King's press damnably. I have got, in exchange of a hundred and fifty soldiers, three hundred and odd pounds. I press me none but good householders, yeomen's sons. . . such a commodity of warm slaves, as had as lieve hear the devil as a drum. . . . I press'd me none but such toasts-and-butter, with hearts in their bellies no bigger than pins' heads, and they have bought out their services; and now my whole charge consists of ancients, corporals, lieutenants. . . slaves as ragged as Lazarus in the painted cloth. . . such as indeed were never soldiers but discarded servingmen, . . the cankers of a calm world and a long peace, ten times more dishonorable ragged than an old feaz'd ancient. . . A mad fellow met me on the way and told me I had unloaded all the gibbets and press'd the dead bodies. No eye hath seen such scarecrows. (4.2.11-38)

Like Falstaff, the cowardly rich who avoid the king's press are ruled by a similar appetite for safety. This is the fallen state of the nation's honor. And when Prince Hal questions the appearance of Falstaff's men, Jack callously acknowledges that they are but "food for powder; they'll fit a pit as well as better."

The attitude has infected everything. A bit later in the play, while alone on stage, Falstaff admits to another appalling lack of principle in his speech about honor. His friend, Prince Hal, meets him briefly before the battle against the rebels commences:

Hal. . . . Say thy prayers and farewell.
Fal. I would it were bed-time, Hal, and all well.
Hal. Why, thou owest God a death.   [Exit]
Fal 'Tis not due yet, I would be loath to pay him before his day. What need I be so forward with him that calls not on me? Well, 'tis no matter, honor pricks me on. Yea, but how if honor prick me off when I come on? How then? Can honor set to a leg? No, or an arm? No. Or take away the grief of a wound? No. Honor hath no skill in surgery then? No. What is honor? A word. What is in that word honor? What is that honor? Air. A trim reckoning! Who hath it? He that died a' Wednesday. Doth he feel it? No. Doth he hear it? No. 'Tis insensible then? Yea, to the dead. But will't not live

with the living? No. Why? Detraction will not suffer it.
Therefore, I'll none of it, honor is a mere scutcheon.
And so ends my catechism. (5.1.124-141)

Throughout, Falstaff has always rationalized his behavior in the most endearing ways. His imaginative explanations for fleeing Hal and Poins when they confront him during the Gadshill robbery are great fun. But now his service to the king is a responsibility, and in that very foreign realm, he fails miserably. Truly fearing for his life this time, his catechism justifying cowardice is one more rationalization.

Bolingbroke's illegal seizure of a crown that didn't belong to him required a similar justification of honor. Falstaff's catechism merely reflects the moral decline of which honor's debasement is but one measure. As the rebellion indicates, Falstaff and Henry Bolingbroke both struggle in the same moral quagmire in different ways, and both men rationalize decisions that have been based largely on satisfying personal need. That original sin taints the entire realm now. Everyone, not just Falstaff, has lost sight of what honor really means. In his essay, "The Economy of the Closed Heart," Edward Hubler suggests that, after Richard was deposed, the English nobility was ruled by self-protection. The character that demonstrates this closed heart is Northumberland, Hotspur's father:

> The purest instance is Northumberland, Hotspur's father, who is motivated by "advised respects" throughout *Richard II* and remains unchanged throughout the two parts of *Henry IV*. He sends his son to death in a vain attempt to secure his own position and later, when still another rebellion is failing, he writes to his fellow rebels letters of "cold intent" announcing his retirement to Scotland. It is his whole character. (473-74)

Protecting self, allowing others to assume risk instead, as Nothumberland does, is the essence of the cowardice Falstaff defends with his catechism. The opposite approach, Hubler notes, is the open heart, which exhibits a courageous willingness to risk oneself for a larger cause. The former strategy is essentially selfish while its opposite, the open heart, originates from the spirit of generosity always evident in Prince Hal. That generosity—evident not only in his willingness to pay off Falstaff's debts but also in his willingness to let Falstaff take credit for subduing Hotspur in battle–stands in stark contrast to both Northumberland's self-concern and Falstaff's self-indulgence. Both of these characters embrace self-interest at the expense of significant moral, political, or social values that operate for the greater good.

In a way, however, Falstaff's admission that honor is "a mere scutcheon" is perhaps more honest than Henry's assumption that the English nation owes him any fealty at all. Usurping Richard's throne dispels any feudal notion of a royal's divine anointing and his consequent political infallibility. As a result of that fateful moment, the ancient, feudal expectations about honor have been thrown into question, and loyalty to king no longer depends on unchangeable principles of conduct like honor. Instead of a virtue that accrued to a particular status within the medieval hierarchy, honor would now depend on the adherence to a standard of behavior that a ruler must convince his subjects to share with him. And because virtue is now subject to the vicissitudes of time and public opinion, a ruler must be charismatic enough to inspire loyalty to king, nation, and worthy principles of conduct. After Richard is deposed, no ruler could possibly succeed without exhibiting the kind of self-sacrifice he expects from others.

By rejecting the self-absorbed, pleasure-seeking life of the Boar's Head Tavern and accepting, in its stead, a life of service to his country, Prince Hal eventually earns the right to become the leader his transformed country needs. From the very beginning of the play, Hal knows that this choice is inevitable. When his fun-loving companions exit the stage after the discussion of time, Hal reveals what lies hidden beneath his dissolute appearance:

> I . . .will a while uphold
> The unyok'd humor of your idleness,
> Yet herein will I imitate the sun,
> Who doth permit the base contagious clouds
> To smother up his beauty from the world,
> That when he please again to be himself,
> Being wanted, he may be more wond'red at. . . .
> If all the year were playing holidays,
> To sport would be as tedious as to work. . . .
> So when this loose behavior I throw off
> And pay the debt I never promised. . .
> My reformation. . .
> Shall show more goodly and attract more eyes. (1.2.195-214)

The contrasts between moon and sun, darkness and light, capriciousness and steadfastness, are deliberate preparation for the moral distinctions that the play is developing between the values of Falstaff and Hal. Many, including Bloom, are bothered by Hal's deliberate manipulation of public perceptions and the apparent shallowness of his connection to the loveable Falstaff, whose "loose behavior" the prince knows he must eventually "throw off." But the play makes very clear why this must be so. Hal must "pay the debt I never promised" because his father, now Henry IV of England, incurred a political debt by dethroning Richard II.

Along with Falstaff's catechism, that usurpation has unleashed the very rebellion that tests the royal father's patience with his dissolute son. Upon hearing of the bravery exhibited by Northumberland's son, Hotspur, the king is moved to compare those valiant deeds with Hal's irresponsible behavior:

> West.   In faith,
>   It is a conquest for a prince to boast of.
> King.   Yea, there thou mak'st me sad, and mak'st me sin
>   In envy that my Lord Northumberland

72

Should be father to so blest a son—
A son who is the theme of honor's tongue. . .
Whilst I, by looking on the praise of him,
See riot and dishonor stain the brow
Of my young Harry. (1.1.76-86)

Though he envies Northumberland for fathering so valiant a
son as Hotspur, Henry is wrong about both young men. Later,
Hotspur emerges as one of the rebel leaders to oppose Henry's
reign, while his own son will defeat Hotspur in battle and
allow his disreputable companion, Falstaff, to take the credit.
It will be his son, Prince Hal, who will become "the theme of
honor's tongue."

 Hotspur, the charming, choleric rebel who cannot
control his hair-trigger temper, provides a second view of
honor that adds further nuance to the one Falstaff presents. In
the lead-up to the attempted coup, Hotspur receives a letter
from his father, who has changed his mind and is backing out
of the plot. Alone, Hotspur comes onstage reading from that
letter:

> "But, for mine own part, my lord, I could be well contented to
> be there, in   respect of the love I bear your house." He could
> be contented: why is he not then? In the respect of the love he
> bears our house: he shows in this, he loves his own barn better
> than he loves our house. Let me see some more. "The
> purpose you undertake is dangerous." --why, that's certain.
> 'Tis dangerous to take a cold, to sleep, to drink, but I tell you,
> my lord fool, out of this nettle,   danger, we pluck the flower
> safety. "The purpose you undertake is dangerous, the friends
> you have nam'd uncertain, the time itself unsorted, and your
> whole plot too light for the counterpoise of so great an
> opposition." Say you so, say you so? I say unto you again,
> you are a shallow, cowardly hind, and you lie. . . . Why, my
> Lord of York commends the plot and the general course of the
> action. 'Zounds, and I were now by this rascal, I could brain
> him with my lady's fan. (2.3.1-23)

Like Falstaff, Hotspur has an unforgettable personality that buzzes with authenticity. But the letter he reads from shows that, in this newly transformed England, loyalty and courage are no longer absolute values. They are mutable and subject to circumstance, which confounds a man like Hotspur, who claims to value honor greatly. But he has misconceptions very similar to Falstaff's, whose view on any matter is debased by self-interest, for Hotspur's concept of honor is little more than loyalty to whatever cause he deems just. He can be incredibly charming, even self-aware at times, as shown by the sweet way he parts from his wife as he heads off to battle. Playfully, she asks:

> Lady. Do you not love me? Do you not indeed? Well,
>   do not, then, for since you love me not, I will not
>   love myself. Do you not love me? Nay, tell me if
>   you speak in jest or no.
> Hot.   Come, wilt thou see me ride?
>   And when I'm a' horseback, I will swear I love thee
>   infinitely. (2.3.96-102)

This intimate encounter reveals the battle-hardened Hotspur's capacity for tender love. But where Falstaff is ruled by a desire for pleasure, Hotspur is ruled by a temper that easily gets the better of his judgment. Like the Henry who returned from exile to protect his lands and revenue, and like the food-obsessed Falstaff, Hotspur is easily swayed by irrational needs.

Once again, it was the pivotal usurpation of Richard's crown that instigates Hotspur's differences with Henry. When Bolingbroke rushed home from France, all the nobles, including Hotspur, had come to Henry's aid to defend his property rights against the willful Richard. The coalition of nobles quickly disintegrates, however, when Henry and Hotspur disagree over which of them should hold prisoners of war for ransom. Pride wounded, Hotspur continues to fret over other perceived slights to the honor of the disaffected aristocrats. In his eyes, Henry has forgotten the debt he owes the nobles for their support against Richard. Hotspur's anger with Henry starts from a wounded sense of justice, and he uses that to rationalize his rebellion against "this canker, Bullingbrook." Delightfully entertaining, both Falstaff and Hotspur rationalize personal gain, and it is Bolingbroke's usurpation that has justified this self-indulgence.

Hal's perspective on honor, however, is grounded in the generous spirit of service he shows throughout, whether he is in the Boar's Head Tavern paying Falstaff's tab, in his father's presence at court, or on the battlefield. At court, he humbly apologizes for the faults of his youth and tries to allay the anxiety of a distraught father who fears his errant son might even "fight against me under Percy's pay." Hal's response to this is forthright and apologetic:

> . . . God forgive them that so much have sway'd
> Your Majesty's good thoughts away from me!
> I will redeem all this on Percy's head,
> And in the closing of some glorious day
> Be bold to tell you that I am your son. . . .
> And that shall be the day, when e'er it lights,
> That this same child of honor and renown,
> This gallant Hotspur. . .
> And your unthought-of Harry chance to meet.
>   (3.2.130-141)

Hal's pledge to redeem himself on the battlefield by defeating Hotspur very dramatically ties his fate to the outcome of that confrontation. At this point, his words must be proven by actions, but Hal has seen his father's fear and sorrow and has responded, not with Falstaff's irreverent wit or Hotspur's angry self-defense, but with a respectful and gracious promise to reform. Earlier, he had promised to emerge from the dark clouds that hid his noble intentions for the future. Now that his time has finally come, he is prepared to honor both his royal father and his earlier promise. As his actions align with his words, he is reviving the true meaning of honor.

Before the opposed sides join in battle, the same grace and respect he showed to his father are extended to Hotspur. While the leaders of both armies confer, Hal tries to prevent the confrontation where "many a soul shall pay dearly for this encounter."

> The Prince of Wales doth join with all the world
> In praise of Henry Percy. By my hopes,
> This present enterprise set off his head,
> I do not think a braver gentleman . . . is now alive
> To grace this latter age with noble deeds.
>   (5.1.86-92)

Admitting that he has "a truant been to chivalry," an indication of his humility, the prince follows this gracious tribute to an enemy with a challenge to fight Hotspur in single combat so no soldiers would have to die. Though the rebels mistrust this and reject the challenge, Hal's willingness to risk his life for the good of others reflects the same generous heart that paid those debts in the tavern. And it is this generosity of spirit that reasserts the kind of honor that will inspire his nation. Unlike Falstaff or Hotspur or even his father, Henry IV, King of England, Prince Hal does not give his personal needs and desires primacy. This is what distinguishes him and what will make him the one able "to pay the debt I never promised." In *Henry V*, Shakespeare's play about Hal's reign as king, he becomes the inspiring battlefield leader that reunites England and France and brings peace to the two nations.

At the end of *1Henry 4,* however, Hal not only defeats Hotspur but performs one additional act of respect. The prince comes upon Falstaff, who has feigned death to avoid a fight with one of the rebels, and he is moved to offer what he thinks is a final tribute to his friend:

> What, old acquaintance! Could not all this flesh
> Keep in a little life? Poor Jack, farewell!
> I could have better spar'd a better man.
> O, I should have a heavy miss of thee

If I were much in love with vanity! (5.4.102-106)

Hal has no illusions about his friend, whose sin was vanity, the overindulgence of self. Yet even though he is well aware of the temptations that Falstaff embodies, his brief but heartfelt homage indicates an appreciation for Jack's playful spirit. He was never immune to it. But Hotspur's rebellion and his father's fears require his attention, and he redeems those misused hours with a demonstration of his devotion to duty and honor. Not only has he been generous with his praise and his effort to prevent the needless deaths of his subjects, who are not, as Falstaff quipped, merely fodder for the pit, but he has been gracious and tolerant of the very man whose inventive playfulness tempted him away from his duties.

Throughout Falstaff's appearances in all three plays comprising the Henriad, he retains a similar though evolving moral and thematic purpose. Falstaff, of course, is not dead when Prince Hal leaves him at the end of *1Henry 4*, but when he reappears in *2Henry 4* he is portrayed as an older and a very different man in essential ways. He retains his irreverent and inventive wit, but as he enters the stage with his servant, his first words are a question about the health of his urine:

Fal. . . . what says the doctor to my water?
Page. He said, sir, the water itself was a good healthy
Water, but for the party that ow'd it, he might have
more diseases than he knew for. (1.2.1-5)

After *1Henry 4*, age and disease plague Fat Jack, and his declining physical condition reflects a world where honor has now fallen even further from what was once genuine virtue. When mutineers again raise their swords against the king, Prince Hal's brother, John, tricks them into surrendering, after which they are arrested and sent to prison for "present execution," a sharp contrast with Hal's chivalrous behavior before the battle with Hotspur. The now feeble Henry Bolingbroke, King of England, promises to sponsor a crusade

77

as penance for the acts that initiated this moral decline. But as that second play about the reign of Henry IV draws to a close, the expectation is raised that Hal, now King Henry V, is the only one able to reverse England's political and moral decay.

The first step in that direction is the very painful but necessary rejection of Falstaff. As Hal's coronation procession passes nearby, Fat Jack calls out in delirious joy that his patron from the Boar's Head will now accommodate every desire. "God save thy Grace, King Hal! My royal Hal!" But when Hal recognizes his old friend, his pronouncement is stern:

> I know thee not, old man, fall to thy prayers,
> How ill white hairs becomes a fool and jester!
> I have long dreamt of such a kind of man,
> So surfeit-swell'd, so old, so profane;
> But being awak'd, I do despise my dream.
> Make less thy body (hence) and more thy grace,
> Leave gormandizing, know the grave doth gape
> For thee thrice wider than for other men.
> Reply not to me with a fool-born jest,
> Presume not that I am the thing I was,
> For God doth know, so shall the world perceive,
> That I have turn'd away my former self. . . .(5.5.47-58)

Harsh as Bloom finds this, any conscientious parent knows love's compassion must be mixed with correction. The fault is Falstaff's. Always ignorant of the way time changes circumstances, Falstaff assumes his Hal will be the same man he was at the inn. He cannot be, of course, and Hal's rejection is meant to educate this recalcitrant child about the inescapable realities of time. His rejection is unmistakably moral and spiritual, his speech imbued with the language of the pulpit. The reference to white hairs and graves is a pointed reminder to Falstaff that, with his time nearing an end, he has few hours left to reform his life before eternal judgment comes upon him.

The theme of time began with Falstaff's first words to Hal, and the new king's rejection of Falstaff brings it to its recognizably Christian conclusion. Shakespeare has prepared us for this moment with multiple references to the Biblical story of the rich man and the beggar Lazarus from Luke 16:19-26. In this parable, the rich man, known to the Elizabethans through Chaucer as Dives, will only share the crumbs from his table with the poor leper, Lazarus. But when both men have left this world, Lazarus resides in heaven with Abraham while Dives suffers the fires of eternal damnation, begging a single drop of water from Lazarus to relieve his parched tongue. But the divide between heaven and hell is too great and his suffering is both inescapable and eternal. Falstaff himself makes such a reference when he insults his red-faced friend, Bardolph, in *1 Henry 4*. "I never see thy face," he says, "but I think upon hell-fire and Dives that lived in purple" (3.3.30-33). He refers to Lazarus a second time when describing those scarecrow-like military recruits drafted into service in place of men rich enough to bribe their way out of Falstaff's impress. Each time, the reference is applied to those who are victimized by Falstaff's indifference to anything but his own welfare. Falstaff knows the story of Lazarus but ignores its lesson about generosity, the opposite of his habitual self-regard. Judgment can be a necessary form of love, and so Hal drives that lesson home.

In his stern rejection, Hal reminds Falstaff that there is a penalty for ignoring time. Hal understood that lesson when he realized his wasted hours almost cost him his father's respect and his kingdom. Since the story of Lazarus emphasizes the importance of time in the face of impending judgment, it makes one more appearance in the Henriad. It comes in *Henry V*, a play that recounts Henry's glorious victory over the French, where we learn of the death of Falstaff. The hostess of the Boar's Head Tavern recounts the fateful last minutes of his passing, and it is there that we return one final time to the parable from Luke's gospel of Dives in hell, looking up at Lazarus, resting in Abraham's bosom. His tavern friends discuss whether Falstaff is bound for heaven or for hell:

> Bard. Would I were with him, wheresome'er he is, either in heaven or in hell!
> Host. Nay sure, he's not in hell; he's in Arthur's bosom, if ever man went to Arthur's bosom. 'A made a finer end, and went away and it had been any christom child. 'A parted ev'n just between twelve and one, ev'n at the turning o' the tide; for after I saw him fumble with the sheets, and play with the flowers, and smile upon his finger's end, I knew there was but one way; for his nose was a sharp as a pen, and 'a babbl'd of green fields. "How now, Sir John?" quoth I, "what, man? Be a' good cheer." So 'a cried out, "God, God, God!" three or four times. Now I, to comfort him, bid him 'a should not think of God; I hop'd there was no need to trouble himself with any such thoughts yet. So 'a bade me lay more clothes on his feet. I put my hand into the bed and felt them, and they were as cold as any stone; then I felt to his knees, and so up'ard and up'ard and all was as cold as any stone. (*H5*, 2.3.6-26)

Although the hostess's reference to Arthur's bosom is wrong, that very merry and loveable rogue, Falstaff, may very well reside in the bosom of Arthur's England. As a literary character, he has endeared himself across the ensuing four centuries. But, despite its many virtues, the England of the legendary Arthur is, in these plays, a long way from paradise, and the hostess's allusion to the Lazarus story, where the leper, now in Abraham's bosom, looks down from heaven on the very ungenerous Dives in hell, implicates the pleasure-seeking self-absorption of Fat Jack. Never repenting of his greed before death, Dives suffers eternal damnation. Though she knows the reference, its meaning seems to be lost on the good proprietor of the Boar's Head, for in her mind, Falstaff must surely be in heaven. But when she recounts how Falstaff babbled about the green fields of Psalm 23, it seems he may very well have been looking for spiritual comfort on his deathbed. This fond recounting of Falstaff's death suggests that his thoughts have finally turned to his spiritual and moral condition, but there is no textual evidence to suggest, as his loving friends do, that he has repented in time.

Because Falstaff embodies the seductive nature of sin, his admirers all too easily get caught up in the pleasure of his company. With him, it is easy to forget duty and responsibility, to ignore the passage of time. But, the play argues, there is a risk in choosing never to grow up, in choosing to avoid and neglect responsibility, and the passing of Falstaff is meant to remind us of that risk. Except for Hal, no one else in the play ever accepts full responsibility for their shortcomings, and no one else ever reforms their behavior. Falstaff's witty vitality may be entertaining, but by clinging to youth and ignoring the passage of time, he forsakes any ability to evolve into his better self. Fulfilling personal desire above more important choices is the essence of sin, and Shakespeare will demonstrate in subsequent plays, both comic and tragic, what consequences flow from this mistake.

The generosity manifest in a heart open rather than closed to duty and service as well as concomitant virtues like love and respect will continue to inform many of the subsequent plays in Shakespeare's canon, particularly comedies like *The Merchant of Venice* and *Twelfth Night*. But the four plays that make up the Henriad —*Richard II*, the two parts of *Henry IV*, and *Henry V*— initiate Shakespeare's exploration of two important aspects of human experience that eventually make tragedy possible. The first has to do with the origins of evil, which is the result of letting unrestrained personal desire dictate behavior. As appealing as Falstaff certainly is, he appears in the Henriad to remind us that it was this sin that spawned discord and rebellion in England.

These four histories also confirm a second aspect of experience that will influence his tragedies: while the consequences of sin may intrude into peoples' lives, inflicting disorder, conflict, even death, those who initiate such evils cannot escape retributive justice. Shakespeare's histories suggest that Prince Hal's emerging leadership was proof that nature had been endowed by its creator with an orderly and benevolent design. Though Falstaff and Hotspur are not intentionally evil, their imaginative and energetic personalities disrupt normal familial, social, and political expectations, and it isn't until Prince Hal becomes king that the chaos his father's moral debt incurred can be repaid.

For Shakespeare, these two insights—the human origins of evil and the evidence of a providential nature—usher in an entirely different type of tragic drama. With *Hamlet*, Shakespeare's second revenge tragedy, the Senecan conventions that shape the very derivative *Titus Andronicus* are transcended by the piercing intelligence of its protagonist. Hamlet, the Danish prince and philosophy student who must confront his uncle's evil, plumbs the moral ambiguities of that task and the world around him. Virtues like duty, justice, even love that once seemed clear are transformed by sin, obscuring the proper way forward. In Hamlet's great soliloquies, Shakespeare presents the psychological and moral turmoil of a man coming to terms with the corrupting effects of sin. For many reasons, Shakespeare's story about Hamlet's revenge completely transforms Elizabethan drama.

But none of Shakespeare's mature tragedies, including *Hamlet*, will make much sense without a clear understanding of how he viewed human nature, and it is for that reason that we now turn to an analysis of perhaps his most optimistic comedy, *As You Like It*. But even in this most optimistic play, sin finds a home in the hearts of several characters, and, as it was in *Romeo and Juliet*, it is only in the genuine love shared by a young man and an iridescently charming woman that the redemption of flawed human nature becomes possible.

As You Like It

Though, for Christians like Shakespeare, the world has been indelibly marked by sin, his youthful optimism also allowed him to see considerable evidence of redemptive grace. His plays reflect that conviction, which is evident in the love of two innocent adolescents whose unfortunate deaths redeem their city. And it is evident in Hal's decision to abjure Falstaff's influence and take up the mantle of England's king. That same conviction is evident here, in *As You Like It*, where an iridescent heroine, Rosalind, prepares her suitor, Orlando, for the challenges and the blessings of love. Though she has evolved quite naturally from the fair Juliet who saves her Romeo from Mercutio's cynicism, her character reflects the high regard Shakespeare has for the redemptive power of feminine love. Though not all of his women characters share Rosalind's aptitude, multiple examples throughout the plays substantiate such a reading. She is, therefore, not only the first but also one of the purer examples of this blessing.

An example of pastoral comedy, *As You Like It* makes that genre's traditional distinction between corrupt city life and the moral simplicity of the country. As such, it quite naturally incorporates the archetypal conflict between good and evil, represented here by Orlando's older brother, though the danger of that evil is necessarily reduced by the play's comic atmosphere. The implications of that dichotomy are elaborated by the play's multiple characters as they express a wide variety of views about love.

In a play where much is said but not much really happens, the play's charming main character nearly overshadows the purpose of those multiple viewpoints. Notable for her emotional strength and maturity, Rosalind earns high praise from Bloom:

> Rosalind is unique in Shakespeare, perhaps indeed in Western drama, because it is so difficult to achieve a perspective upon her that she herself does not anticipate and share. A stage play

is virtually impossible without some degree of irony, that is the audience's privilege. We enjoy such an irony in regard to Touchstone, Jaques, and every other character in *As You Like It*, except for Rosalind. We forgive her for knowing what matters more than we do, because she has no will to power over us, except to exercise our most humane faculties in appreciation of her performance. (204)

From her very first lines until the final syllables of the epilogue where she politely asks for applause, Rosalind remains a unique character, Bloom suggests, because she sees herself and the world around her with disarming objectivity and self-awareness. That capacity is evident, for example, when she makes fun of her own habitual loquaciousness: "Do you not know I am a woman?" she coyly asks her cousin and closest friend, Celia, "When I think, I must speak" (3.2.249). This good-natured honesty, Bloom observes, frees her from the dramatic irony of characters who only see themselves partially. With exquisite wit and charm, she demonstrates the truth that a person is most lovable when she herself is transparently loving, which is only possible with that kind of objective self-assessment. Although language cannot convey the complexities of love, this, Shakespeare seems to be saying through his remarkable heroine, is what genuine love looks like. Every other perspective on love expressed by the play's other characters pales in comparison to what Rosalind lives out with wit, charm, humor, self-awareness, and unmistakably genuine emotion.

Without the distractions of a complicated plot, the play's clever use of pastoral traditions adds depth to Rosalind's character. Shakespeare did not invent pastoral literature, of course, but draws on literary conventions that found their way into English poetry and drama from Greek and Latin predecessors. Essentially a literature of wish-fulfillment, the pastoral genre originated sometime around 300 B.C. with the Sicilian poet, Theocritus, and developed deeper roots in western literature as a result of Vergil's

Bucolics.   As Gilbert Highet puts it, pastoral writers characterize rural life by its

> . . . simple love-making, folk-music (especially singing and piping), purity of morals, simplicity of manners, healthy diet, plain clothing, and an unspoilt way of living, in strong contrast to the anxiety and corruption of existence in great cities and royal courts.   The coarseness of country life is neither emphasized nor concealed, but is offset by its essential purity. (162)

By juxtaposing civilization's corruption with the regenerative powers of rural life, the pastoral genre gives the very human longing for simplicity and lost innocence a geographical location.

That desire for an escape from difficulty merged, at times, with other themes from Latin romances like Longus' *Daphne and Chloe,* a tale of young lovers experiencing long separations and trials in exotic settings that test their fidelity. Both of these pastoral influences are evident in *As You Like It,* which, despite containing precious little drama, is designed to show how the best traits in human nature are obscured by the world's unholy preoccupation with advantage.   This is the sin of Orlando's brother, who demonstrates that, wherever selfishness prevails, family and society succumb to hatred and discord.   Because rural innocence understands that love and desire are natural parts of life, it can restore the kind of personal, marital, and civic harmony that defines human nature at its best.   Pastoral's dichotomy between city and country demonstrates why life's full abundance is unavailable where love is absent or only partially embraced.

As Juliet's anticipation of her wedding night indicates, Shakespeare's literary treatment of sex is often surprisingly frank without any of the prurience that has accrued to this topic over the intervening centuries.   This accords well with the premise of pastoral literature which, because it prefers what is natural and simple, comfortably affords a place for physical love. Shakespeare would have been aware of similar attitudes in the Bible, which promises Abraham and other believers descendants as numerous as the stars. Contrary to modern assumptions, this acceptance of sexuality as perfectly natural finds ample support in Scripture, which sees the proper expression of sexuality as one of God's many blessings. These converging assumptions form the basis for the play's treatment of the erotic. Yet while nature's abundance would be impossible without that procreative force, Shakespeare also saw that it could take two morally opposed directions. Throughout Ovid's stories, which he read as a young boy, it is the amoral, bestial, irrational side of nature that exposes love's transformative power, but life surely taught him that love can also create bonds that endure "even to the edge of doom." Both potentialities exist and both have consequences. Left unadulterated, the bestial, self-indulgent side of desire corrodes personal and social bonds, bringing disorder and chaos with it. Love that incorporates and reflects the full complexity of human nature, however, generates an emotionally and spiritually satisfying harmony that is at the center of who we are. For Christians, this is the purpose for which man was created. Since desire can be either self-centered or the opposite of that, therefore, what is valued determines whether those very natural desires become manifest as good or as evil. And what should be valued, according to *As You Like It*, is love rightly understood. On that subject, Rosalind is the master teacher.

This difference between fully and partially realized human nature is what *As You Like It* explores. In discussing other comic figures from Shakespeare, John Russel Brown makes the following observation about a prevalent Ovidian metaphor, the transformative power of love:

> Both Falstaff [*1Henry 4*] and Benedick [*Much Ado About Nothing*] remember Jove's transformation into a bull; the difference between these two lovers lies not in the presence or absence of bestiality, but in the use—the order or disorder–to

which that 'simplicity' is put. In the very conclusion of his comedies, Shakespeare did not care to celebrate 'platonic' love which ignores or supersedes man's 'hearkening after the flesh'; the love which triumphs is a full one, established at the risk of disorder and compounded of beast, man, and spirit. (136)

Neither self-indulgence nor ascetic self-denial finds approval in any of these plays. For Shakespeare, man's created nature included all three elements: the flesh, the mind, and the spirit; or, if more secular terms are preferred, the id, the ego, and the superego. Mankind was created a certain way for a reason, and until that tripartite nature is acknowledged as essentially good and therefore necessary, the full potential of human nature remains unrealized. And as the play's court scenes will show, disorder and evil are consequences of human nature only partially achieved.

If the distinction between a partially and fully realized human nature is mirrored by the oppositions between city and country, the play's pastoral structure also highlights another dichotomy. Beginning in Duke Frederick's corrupt court but moving to the Forest of Arden where Rosalind educates her beloved, the pastoral structure of *As You Like It* also makes distinctions between male and female that seem rooted in biology, particularly a woman's ability to create, birth, and physically and emotionally nurture new life, all of which are indicative of created nature's essential goodness. In contrast to that natural goodness, the court is a masculine world where the assertion of rights and power establish an appearance of order that ultimately proves untenable. It is in the forest, then, that Rosalind is most at home, most herself. Bloom is right: Rosalind, the play's central figure, is a woman who exhibits "no will to power over us," the audience, or anyone else in the play, for that matter. That is not the nature of love, which, in the play's moral environment, is antithetical to the kind of force or control that prevails at court. In Rosalind's world, love is the only power that exists, and its ways are inclusive and, under her tutelage at least, far more benevolent than the masculine ways of the court, which divide and exclude. The dichotomies of court and country find a parallel in the distinction between male and female.

If the pastoral reminds us of the value of simplicity and innocence, Rosalind demonstrates what is required to get there. Her sane, balanced view of loving relationships flourishes in Arden precisely because of its metaphorical distance from the court and everything it represents. An orphan in Duke Frederick's court, she is most at home in a place where innocence and purity and simplicity are still available, where sophistication is not allowed to obscure simple truths. And because the feminine is closely aligned with the creative potential of nature, the world she fashions in Arden is a place without conflict, a place built on truth, love, and harmony, the exact opposite of the masculine court where duplicity, hatred, and division thrive. In Arden, she teaches her beloved about relationships that endure, that encourage, that sustain and build rather than frustrate and destroy.

Rosalind is one prominent member of a line of Shakespearean women who help their men understand what it means to be truly loving and therefore fully human. Her likeness will appear again in women like Othello's Desdemona, Lear's Cordelia, and, most magnificently, in Antony's Cleopatra. Here, in *As You Like It*, the allure of rural simplicity represents not only a desire to escape life's worst difficulties but stands as a reminder of the possibility of a natural, moral innocence that man, distracted by civilized society's wealth, power, and prestige, forgets at his peril. Man cannot choose the better possibility if he has forgotten what that is. In this play, nature exists as a passive opportunity for the kind of moral virtue that makes genuine love possible. It is a possibility that some characters, like Rosalind, embrace fully, that others learn from before returning to the court renewed, and that others are still too detached from or too sophisticated to comprehend fully. The freedom available in

Arden is not the freedom to do whatever pleases but the freedom to become fully loving and, therefore, fully human.

The plot of *As You Like It*, which is remarkable for its lack of both significant event or dramatic tension, can be divided into three sections: scenes within supposedly civilized society (1.1 through 2.2), two scenes depicting Orlando's and Rosalind's separate entries into the forest (2.3 and 2.4), and then the remaining scenes which examine life within Arden (2.5 through 5.4). The first section depicts what makes civil society hazardous for those whose virtues make them vulnerable. The second shows how the play's main characters, Orlando and Rosalind, must adapt for their transition into the forest. The final section, taking place entirely in Arden, shows how love, though vulnerable to both man and nature, can realize man's fullest potential far better than civilization's false promises of wealth, power, and status. What little dramatic tension there is occurs in the first section where discord quickly becomes evident in both family and court.

The world of the first two acts is beset by conflict and teeters on the verge of disruption. Because a substantial inheritance from their father is still controlled by his miserly older brother and guardian, Oliver, Orlando begins the play with a lengthy complaint about the inadequacies of his education and financial support. Not only does another brother, Jaques, receive preferential treatment, but even Oliver's horses are better trained and fed, Orlando claims, while he languishes untutored and marginalized. As the elderly servant, Adam, listens intently, the young man explains why he can no longer abide such mistreatment:

> As I remember, Adam, it was upon this fashion bequeath'd me by will but poor a   thousand crowns, and, as thou say'st, charg'd my brother, on his blessing, to breed me well; and there begins my sadness. My brother Jaques he keeps at school, and report speaks goldenly of his profit. For my part, he keeps me rustically at home, or (to speak more properly)

stays me here at home unkept; for call you that keeping for a gentleman of my birth, that differs not from the stalling of an ox? His horses are bred better, for besides that they are fair with their feeding, they are taught their manage, and to that end riders dearly hir'd; but I (his brother) gain nothing under him but growth, for the which his animals on his dunghills are as much bound to him as I. (1.1.1-16)

The origin of the conflict between the brothers remains vague. Though Oliver privately acknowledges that Orlando is "gentle, never school'd and yet learned, full of noble device . . [and] enchantingly belov'd," he dislikes the young man intensely. He admits he doesn't know why his very soul "hates nothing more" than this younger brother (1.1.165-66). Lacking any definable cause, the nebulous admission makes Oliver's wickedness all the more evident. Orlando, of course, chafes at his brother's unloving treatment, and, inevitably, discord breaks out as soon as the two brothers meet:

Oli. Now, sir, what make you here?
Orl. Nothing. I am not taught to make any thing.
Oli. What mar you then, sir?
Orl. Marry, sir, I am helping you to mar that which God made, a poor unworthy brother of yours, with idleness.
Oli. Marry, sir, be better employ'd, and be naught a while.
Orl. Shall I keep your hogs and eat husks with them? What prodigal portion have I spent, that I should come to such penury?
Oli. Know you where you are, sir?
Orl. O, sir, very well; here in your orchard.
Oli. Know you before whom, sir?
Orl. Ay, better that him I am before knows me. I know you are my eldest brother. . . . The courtesy of nations allows you my better, in that you are the first born, but the same tradition takes not away my blood, were there twenty brothers betwixt us. I have as much of my father in me as you. . . . (1.1.29-50)

90

Where Oliver stands on the "courtesy of nations" to deprive a younger brother of his rightful due, Orlando defends his position based on a father's "blood" shared by both brothers. By twisting tradition and law to his advantage, Oliver subverts the natural bonds that should exist between kin. The deep animosity between these two brothers eventually leads to a physical altercation. Orlando's part in this is quite understandable. Smug and superior, Oliver makes no effort to deny his ungenerous behavior. Though he verges on the defiant, Orlando exhibits a certain nobility of character, never losing his dignity despite a dismissive brother.

The simmering conflict takes a savage turn when Oliver secretly enlists Charles the wrestler to dispatch the troublemaker once and for all during a proposed match with Orlando. Physically strong but naïve, Charles easily succumbs to Oliver's lies. Contradicting his private observations about Orlando, the older brother now conveniently describes him as "the stubbornest young fellow. . ., full of ambition, an envious emulator of every man's good parts, a secret and villainous contriver against me. . . ." and, thus, worthy of death. Believing Oliver's lie, Charles agrees to accept Orlando's challenge so that he can "give him his payment." Ignorant of his brother's evil plot against his life, the unsuspecting Orlando is now in mortal danger.

But Charles also provides the first glimpse of another, far different world, free of intrigue, conflict, and moral hazard. When Oliver asks for news from the court, the wrestler recounts how its current ruler, Duke Frederick, has usurped his older brother, Duke Senior, who now lives as an exile in Arden Forest. Though Oliver hears this as a warning of a younger brother's dangerous ambition, it is also a second example of how brotherly discord disrupts social order and divides what could be a unified world into halves, the corrupt court and an ancient and far more innocent garden:

Oli. Where will the old Duke live?
Cha. They say he is already in the forest of Arden, and a

many merry men with him; and there they live like the old Robin Hood of England. They say many young gentlemen flock to him every day, and fleet the time carelessly, as they did in the golden world.
(1.1.113-119)

Here, the golden world of primal innocence and ease is conflated with the very English forest of Robin Hood who was known for his generosity to the poor. The description is meant to invoke a mythical time very much like the Biblical Eden. In stark contrast to the discord of the present moment, this golden age invokes a time when people lived happily and peacefully. In this brief description, exile in Arden seems far more attractive than the court's intrigues, so young nobles gravitate toward Arden. Something in man, it seems, makes the good preferable to sin and corruption. This "something" is the essential human nature that the play seeks to define through events in Arden.

The vulnerability of those without power or privilege, like Orlando, is exposed a second time with the introduction of the play's two female characters: Rosalind, the daughter of the deposed Duke Senior, and his niece, Celia, the daughter of his wicked younger brother, Duke Frederick, who usurped civil authority from his elder brother. In contrast to the play's feuding sets of brothers, the two female cousins share a deep, unshakeable friendship. When they witness the match between Charles and Orlando, who not only survives but defeats his opponent, Rosalind tells the young gallant "you have wrestled well and overthrown more than your enemies (1.2.253ff). Though she has fallen quickly herself, Duke Frederick learns that Orlando is the son of Sir Rowland de Boys, who "the world esteem'd . . . honorable," but whom Frederick "did find. . . still mine enemy" (1.2.225ff). As a result, Orlando is forced to flee the court, leaving his beloved Rosalind behind. Clearly, he too has been deeply smitten, referring to her as he exits the scene as the "heavenly Rosalind."

The two women prove just as vulnerable as Orlando. Having now banished the victorious but unfortunate young wrestler, Frederick's ignoble jealousy and distrust threaten to poison the close relationship between the two female cousins, Celia and Rosalind. He worries that Rosalind could further inflame his subjects, who already dislike the pain inflicted upon the exiled duke's family. "Her very silence, and her patience," he fears, "speak to the people, and they pity her" (1.3.78-79). For the incipient danger posed by her obvious virtue, Rosalind too must leave. Family and palace intrigue divide the young lovers who are sent off on separate journeys into the forest. The court has nothing substantial enough to nourish this new love. Though there is an appearance of order, Frederick's court is sterile and rotting from the inside. Someone has to redeem the situation, and that person is Rosalind.

The second section of the play is comprised of two scenes, one for each of the seemingly powerless people who have now been banished from Duke Frederick's court. Rejection tests the character of the evicted, and how they respond to their plight differentiates Orlando and the two female cousins from those who choose to remain behind in the deceptively civilized world of the court. As for the girls, banishment could easily have severed their relationship, but the love between these very vulnerable women remains steadfast. Facing a potentially hostile world by herself, Rosalind's normally cheerful disposition evaporates and, with her thoughts racing, she responds to Celia's sympathy in short, clipped phrases that reveal her fear.

> Cel. O my poor Rosalind, whither wilt thou go? Wilt thou
>   change fathers? I will give thee mine. I charge thee be
>   not thou more griev'd than I am.
> Ros.   I have more cause.
> Cel. Thou hast not, cousin,
>   Prithee be cheerful. Know'st thou not the Duke
>   Hath banished me, his daughter?

Ros.	That he hath not.
Cel.	No, hath not? Rosalind lacks then the love
	Which teacheth thee that thou and I am one.
	Shall we be sund'red? Shall we part, sweet girl?
	No, let my father seek another heir. (1.3.90 – 99)

Where Frederick sows division, Celia reminds her disconsolate cousin "that thou and I [are] one."

Celia's unwavering devotion to her cousin goes far beyond mere words, too. For their protection, the two women flee the court, disguised as brother and sister. Rosalind assumes the identity of the young man, Ganymede; Celia will take the name Aliena, indicating her estrangement from an unworthy father. But the obvious love these two women share also proves their readiness for the commitments romantic love will eventually require. Their natural affection has already prepared them for what is possible only in Arden.

For the women, a hint of that comes quickly. Once there, they purchase a small cottage from a friendly shepherd who was in the midst of a debate about the proper way to woo his beloved. From conflict and division, they have arrived where the ways of love are common subject matter. The concerns of the forest are vastly different from those of the court. In this new world, it is possible to create a life that accurately reflects who they truly are. The forest brings a sense of freedom, of new possibility, something the cheerful Celia recognizes. As they prepare to leave the court, she remarks, "Now go we in content to liberty, and not to banishment" (1.3.137-38). As events in the forest will show, this is indeed a place where they are free to define the love they desire for themselves. But that can mean either the freedom to indulge every desire or it can mean the freedom to become fully human. These, the play will show, are two very different goals.

Because he is a man escaping from the masculine world of the court, Orlando's preparation for what Arden has to offer takes quite a bit longer. As long as he remains in Duke Frederick's world, there's an unmistakable prickliness about him. Just as his bold assertion of what Oliver owes him reveals no fear of confrontation, Orlando's participation in the wrestling match is symbolic of his comfort with the ongoing power struggles that occur in this male-dominated court. Because it is a world that demands assertiveness, courage, and strength, the weak, the powerless, and the vulnerable are all subject to the stronger. No pushover, Orlando nevertheless lacks the necessary resources to resist the amoral authority that operates in this realm, so he, too, is forced to flee a brother who, as Adam warns, is prepared to "burn the lodging where you use to lie, and you within it" (2.3.23-24).

On his journey into the forest, however, Orlando's other attributes come to the fore. The prickly self-assertion is replaced by kindness and concern for Adam, the family's elderly servant, who sees Orlando's best side and offers to accompany him on his travels. That transformation is initiated by Adam's generous offers of his life saving for the arduous journey ahead of them. He shows no fear of the future. Drawing on the wisdom of Matthew 10:29, Adam confidently expresses his belief that all will be well. Providence, which graciously feeds the birds of the air, will supply whatever they need:

> . . . He that doth the ravens feed,
> Yea, providently caters for the sparrow,
> Be comfort to my age! Here is the gold,
> All this I give to you, let me be your servant. . . .
> Let me go with you,
> I'll do the service of a younger man. . . . (2.3.43-54)

The two men belong together because they share a natural nobility that has no necessary relationship to birth, wealth, power, or authority. Adam's generosity reflects the same overflowing abundance visible in a divinely created nature that provides. Life, not death, thrives in Arden, and

Rosalind's joyful openness to that same procreative power is equally visible in her gentle, loving nature. It is that connection to that power that makes her so fully at home in Arden where, as Corin the shepherd explains, his greatest pride is "to see my ewes graze and my lambs suck" (3.2.76).

Adam's prayer reflects a trust in created God's abundant goodness, and that trust anchors his charitable kindness, his willingness to serve, and his patient endurance in the face of adversity. And typical of all things good, the old man's kindness multiplies. As a result of Adam's generosity and faith, Orlando is inspired to reciprocate when the old man falters on their journey. Hungry and exhausted, Orlando makes the old man comfortable and then sets off to search for food. When he comes upon the deposed Duke Senior at his supper, Orlando habitually employs the same male belligerence that operates at court to obtain the food he needs, but his good-natured host reminds the intruder that "your gentleness shall force, more than your force move us to gentleness" (2.7.102-03). Just as the two female cousins quickly find that Arden makes fear unnecessary, Orlando discovers that the aggressive self-assertion so normal in Duke Frederick's world is also unnecessary in this enchanting garden. The general absence of threatening aggression, the assertion of rights, is precisely what makes fear unnecessary. As the men enter Arden, the better way is coming into focus.

A far different place than Duke Frederick's court, Arden makes possible a completely different approach to human relationships than Orlando's previous circumstances required. But Arden isn't completely benign either, a view of nature that, for Shakespeare, ignores the obvious difficulties of a cold rain. As the first lines of one of the play's mournful songs remind us, both nature and human nature can sometimes inflict pain: "Blow, blow, thou winter wind, thou art not so unkind as man's ingratitude" (2.7.174ff). The original, unblemished garden is gone.

Unfortunately, both types of nature have been corrupted by original sin. But exposure to nature's elemental forces can also resurrect an awareness of man's common vulnerability and a concomitant sense of compassion for others. Duke Senior elaborates and deepens Adam's view of a providential nature that benevolently answers every human need:

> Are not these woods
> More free from peril than the envious court?
> Here feel we not the penalty of Adam,
> The season's difference, as the icy fang
> And churlish chiding of the winter's wind,
> Which when it bites and blows upon my body
> Even till I shrink with cold, I smile and say,
> "This is no flattery: these are counsellors
> That feelingly persuade me what I am."
> Sweet are the uses of adversity. . . .
> And this our life, exempt from public haunt,
> Finds tongues in trees, books in the running brooks,
> Sermons in stones, and good in every thing. (2.1.3-17)

The first man's sin ruined the unalloyed benevolence of the original world, introducing adversity, suffering, and death. As several of the play's songs remind us, Arden is no Eden. Forced to endure banishment and exile, the duke has accommodated himself to a nature that has been changed by "the penalty of Adam." His distinction between court and forest might initially seem naïvely romanticized, but that misses the point of his speech. He admits, for example, that nature has "feelingly persuade[d] me what I am." And who he is is a man who has learned from "icy fang" and the "churlish chiding of the winter's wind" to recognize his own helplessness, a perspective that changes his relationship to similar others.

Enduring this confrontation with elemental nature has renewed Duke Senior's awareness of humanity's shared vulnerability. Given the right attitude, a benevolent purpose is discernable, even in this suffering. This is the sermon he has heard in the trees, the brooks, and the stones. This faith, this recognition of the essential goodness within every aspect of created nature, even the suffering, is a prerequisite for the contentment Arden makes available. Because Arden's nature is completely unadorned and unencumbered by the self-centered misconceptions of a corrupt civilization, its simple pleasures and freedoms as well as its "icy fang" cultivate an appreciation for everything truly good about life. Despite its origins in pastoral literature, Shakespeare's Arden has no remnant of that genre's romanticized nature.

While the uses of suffering are one lesson nature preaches, love's sweetness is another. But *As You Like It* very carefully delineates what genuine love looks like by providing perspectives from four sets of characters. A description of love is provided by the self-indulgent, sex-obsessed Touchstone; by the cynical Jaques; by the mismatched lovers, Silvius and Phebe; and, of course, by Rosalind and Orlando. Taken together, these four views of love help define what love isn't and what, by contrast, it actually should look like

Like the wicked Oliver and Duke Frederick, Touchstone, the court jester Rosalind and Celia bring along with them into Arden, is largely driven by his selfish desires. Once in Arden, he quickly finds and pursues Audrey, a country wench who is completely without guile. Unfortunately for her, Touchstone's view of love is mired in the physical, and he sets about seducing the gullible young lady with wit and cynical attention. For Touchstone, she is merely a means to an end, food for his sexual appetite. Ironically named after the stone used to distinguish real gold from dross, Touchstone's courtly wit and bawdy insinuations remain largely incomprehensible to this innocent young girl. In one exchange, his coarse dialogue hinges on the double meaning of "honest," which meant both speaking the truth and sexually purity. Hamlet will use the same double-entendre in the nunnery scene:

Touch.   Truly, I would the gods had made thee poetical.

98

Aud.	I do not know what "poetical" is. Is it honest in deed and word? Is it a true thing?
Touch.	No, truly; for the truest poetry is the most feigning, and lovers are given to poetry; and what they swear in poetry may be said as lovers they do feign.
Aud.	And would you not have me honest?
Touch.	No, truly, unless thou wert hard-favor'd; for honesty coupled to beauty is to have honey a sauce to sugar. . . .
Aud.	Well, I am not fair, and therefore I pray the gods make me honest.
Touch.	Truly, and to cast away honesty upon a foul slut were to put good meat into an unclean dish.
Aud.	I am not a slut, though I thank the gods I am foul.
Touch.	Well, prais'd be the gods for thy foulness! Sluttishness may come hereafter. But be it as it may, I will marry thee. . . . (3.3.16-42)

Though he does propose marriage, he engages a minister of dubious reputation, Sir Oliver Martext, because, as he admits in an aside to the audience,

> . . .I were better married of him than of another, for he is not like to marry me well; and not being well married, it will be a good excuse for me hereafter to leave my wife. (3.3.90-94)

Oblivious to her simple goodness, Touchstone abuses her trust and innocence to satisfy his sexual appetites. His primal sin mirrors the selfishness that has corrupted the world of the court where neither Oliver nor Frederick values the obvious virtues of others. Though they are entirely mismatched, Touchstone's sexual appetite diminishes whatever potential there might be in his relationship with Audrey.

The longer Touchstone stays in Arden, however, the simple honesty of the locals begins to reduce whatever appeal his sophisticated wit once held. In another exchange with the shepherd Corin, Touchstone's sophistication is deflated by the young man's honesty about the simple demands and pleasures of his life:

Touch.   . . . . Wast ever in court, shepherd?
Cor.   No, truly.
Touch.   Then thou art damn'd.
Cor.   Nay, I hope [not].
Touch.   Truly, thou art damn'd, like an ill-roasted egg, all on one side.
Cor.   For not being at court? Your reason.
Touch.   Why, if thou never wast at court, thou never saw good manners, then thy manners must be wicked, and wickedness is a sin, and sin is damnation. Thou art in parlous state, shepherd.
Cor.   Not a whit, Touchstone. Those that are good manners at court are as ridiculous in the country as the behavior of the country is most mockable at the court. . . .
Touch.   Shallow, shallow. A better instance, I say; come. . . .
Cor.   You have too courtly a wit for me. I'll rest.
Touch.   Wilt thou rest damn'd? God help thee, shallow man! . . . .
Cor.   Sir, I am a true laborer: I earn that I eat, get that I wear, owe no man hate, envy no man's happiness, glad of other men's good, content with my harm, and the greatest of my pride is to see my ewes graze and my lambs suck. (3.2.32-77)

Measured against the values Corin lives by, values like hard work, promoting peace between neighbors, cultivating gratitude, tolerant endurance, and appreciation for nature's abundant gifts, Touchstone's civilized manners and wit end up looking exceedingly shallow. In the end, his name seems

100

an ironic misnomer, for by over-valuing his own wit he fails to see the gold that exists all around him.

The second perspective on love comes from Jaques, the play's melancholic commentator, who reveals his natural disposition in a reported encounter with Touchstone. After witnessing Touchstone railing against fortune and time, Jaques desires the "liberty" of a court fool so that he too can "speak my mind. . .[to] cleanse the foul body of the infected world" (2.7.51ff). What Jaques sees, however, is as limited a perspective as Touchstone's. In his famous seven ages of man speech, he concludes that man's "strange eventful history [ends in] second childishness, and mere oblivion, sans teeth, sans eyes, sans taste, sans every thing" (2.7.164ff). Despite any joy in the previous six stages of life, the sad end of human endeavors, according to Jaques, is a pointless stupor devoid of all sensibility and pleasure. Even the sweet ardor of youth is reduced to the foolishness of a "lover sighing like [a] furnace, with a woeful ballad to his mistress' eyebrow" (2.7.147ff).

Like Touchstone, Jaques is a reductionist, a person who simplifies the complex for his own purposes. The court jester's purpose is to satisfy the natural desires of the flesh, whereas the melancholic reduces the complex to expose whatever he considers human folly. He reduces the lover in his seven ages speech to an absurdity, for instance, because all he chooses to see in love is its irrational foolishness, the Orlando's of the world driven mad by desire and tacking poems "to his mistress' eyebrow" on every tree. Little wonder, then, that his encounter with the love-struck Orlando does not go well:

> Jaq.   I pray you mar no more trees with writing love-songs in their barks.
> Orl.   I pray you mar no moe of my verses with reading them ill-favoredly.
> Jaq.   Rosalind is your love's name?
> Orl.   Yes, just.
> Jaq.   I do not like her name.
> Orl.   There was no thought of pleasing you when she

	was christen'd. . . .
Jaq.	You have a nimble wit. . . . Will you sit down
	with me? And we two will rail against our
	mistress the world and all our misery.
Orl.	I will chide no breather in the world but myself,
	against whom I know most faults.
Jaq.	The worst fault you have is to be in love.
	(3.2.259-282)

Just as Touchstone's oversimplification of love misses the true value of a girl like Audrey, Jaques's oversimplifications of human motives and behaviors obscure whatever isn't foolish about those. Desire is good and natural and necessary. And foolishness should be exposed and corrected, as Jaques does when he overhears Touchstone's plan to desert Audrey as soon as he gets what he wants from her. There is certainly virtue in his decision to intercede, dismissing the fake minister, Oliver Martext, and insisting the couple go to a legitimate churchman to be properly married. But love isn't just physical desire or absurd poetry published for the cynical amusement of others. Whatever may be true in these views, both views are still incomplete.

The third perspective on love comes from those mismatched lovers, Silvius and Phebe. Like Orlando, Silvius is completely overwhelmed by his feelings for Phebe, who, unlike Rosalind, can barely tolerate her lover's adoring presence. "Now I do frown on thee with all my heart," she begins, "and if mine eyes can wound, now let them kill thee" (3.5.15-16). When Rosalind, still disguised as Ganymede, witnesses the cruelty of Phebe's words, she interjects herself into this exchange to remind the shepherdess of her hard heart and the fleeting opportunity for love:

Ros.	. . . Who might be your mother,
	That you insult, exult, and all at once,
	Over the wretched? What though you have no
	beauty—
	As, by my faith, I see no more in you

102

Than without candle may go dark to bed—
Must you be therefore proud and pitiless?

Being anything but "proud and pitiless" with her Orlando, she tries mightily to correct Silvius' thinking:

You foolish shepherd, wherefore do you follow
        her,
Like foggy south, puffing with wind and rain?
You are a thousand times a properer man
Than she a woman. 'Tis such fools as you
That make the world full of ill-favor'd children.
'Tis not her glass, but you that flatters her.

And she concludes by reminding Phebe how fortunate she is to have someone who loves her so unequivocally:

But, mistress, know yourself, down on your
        knees,
And thank heaven, fasting, for a good man's love;
For I must tell you friendly in your ear,'
Sell when you can, you are not for all markets. . ..
(3.5.35-60)

The diatribe is fraught with comic irony, however, because Phebe has instantaneously fallen in love with Rosalind-Ganymede, who must now treat the suddenly smitten shepherdess with the same cruel honesty that she has just censured. Even for the glorious Rosalind, love has a way of humbling every shred of human pride. While the complete irrationality of love has become obvious to all, Rosalind's empathy for Silvius increases her appreciation of Orlando's unshakeable devotion to her and, therefore, the gratitude she owes him for that love. This initiates the movement away from deceptive disguise and toward the revelation of every hidden truth.

If Touchstone's acquiescence to the flesh, and Jaques' rejection of all forms of worldly corruption, and Phebe's

103

ingratitude for genuine devotion represent three of the play's limited perspectives on love, the relationship between Rosalind and Orlando provides a sane alternative. Unfortunately for Rosalind, however, the precautionary disguise she assumed before entering Arden now prevents Orlando from courting her directly. "Alas the day, what shall I do with my doublet and hose?" she laments (3.2.219). Logically there's no reason for her to conceal her identity any longer, so her decision to maintain the role of Ganymede only makes sense as an effort to verify Orlando's love, which so far has only been expressed in the exaggerated rhetoric of courtly love poetry. From the foolish adoration of a Silvius, she understands that that is insufficient.

Arden's inhabitants have been amused by the fevered sonnets the love-smitten Orlando has been tacking to every tree. "From the east to western Inde," begins one, "No jewel is like Rosalind" (3.2.88-9). Touchstone, of course, can't resist ridiculing these rhymes by reducing a lover's attraction to its lowest denominator. "If the cat will after kind," he mimics, "So be sure will Rosalind" (3.2.103-4). His reduction of love to the merely physical overlooks love's potential richness that includes sexual desire but also much more as well. To verify that Orlando's love is genuine, therefore, the disguised Rosalind proposes to instruct him on the proper way to woo a girl. Rosalind's catechism demonstrates exactly what the emotional richness of love looks and feels like. For what transpires between these two in Arden is magical, addressing all the shortcomings that plague the civilized world they left behind. Ironically contradicting a situation where a woman is disguised, the catechism is intended to reveal what women are really like.

Because Orlando's sonnets are full of common poetic tropes, Rosalind immediately understands that her lessons need to impart a more realistic view of women and their mercurial emotions. Orlando, however, is incorrigible. He refuses to dilute his romanticized vision of love:

Ros.	But are you so much in love as your rhymes speak?
Orl.	Neither rhyme nor reason can express how much.
Ros.	Love is merely a madness, and I tell you, deserves as well a dark house and a whip as madmen do; and the reason why they are not so punish'd and cur'd is, that the lunacy is so ordinary that the whippers are in love too. Yet I profess curing it by counsel.
Orl.	Did you ever cure any so?
Ros.	Yes, one, and in this manner. He was to imagine me his love, his mistress; and I set him every day to woo me. At which time would I, being but a moonish youth, grieve, be effeminate, changeable, longing and liking, proud, fantastical, apish, shallow, inconstant, full of tears, full of smiles; for every passion, something, and for no passion truly any thing, as boys and women are for the most part cattle of this color; would now like him, now loathe him; then entertain him, then forswear him; now weep for him, then spit at him; that I drave my suitor from his mad humor of love to a living humor of madness, which was, to forswear the full stream of the world, and to live in a nook merely monastic. . . .
Orl.	I would not be cur'd, youth.
Ros.	I would cure you if you would but call me Rosalind. (3.3.396-426)

Humorously acknowledging the volatility of female emotions, Rosalind displays an awareness of the craziness that love inflicts on both women and men, but their exchange contains layers of emotional subtlety. Because he truly enjoys being in love, Orlando resists exchanging his naïve romanticism for Ganymede's exaggerated realism. He refuses to believe that Rosalind could be anything less than perfectly good and consistently loving. He agrees to practice wooing Ganymede-Rosalind, not because he wants to be cured, but because he wants to relive the process of wooing daily. She, on the other hand, pretends to be curing him, not so much to minister to his emotional lunacy but to have a reason to spend precious time with him. Despite the quasi-educational premise for these meetings, the audience is aware that, underneath the dialogue, the flame of love is already roaring-hot, and together they live out some of the very contradictions she mocks. When he is late the next time they meet, for example, she pretends to be cross with him. Later, however, when she learns he's been wounded saving his wicked brother, Oliver, from the jaws of a lion, she faints, all the while trying to explain to her puzzled onlookers why a masculine Ganymede would receive the news as a woman might. The emotional chemistry at work in all this is unmistakable. On stage, it is really quite amusing.

And part of that chemistry is avowedly sexual. In a second session of burlesque wooing, Rosalind mercilessly teases her young charge. When he again pledges unwavering loyalty to his beloved Rosalind, she matter-of-factly suggests that women are just as subject to infidelity as men. And, worse, she warns him, they'll never admit they were wrong:

Ros.	Now tell me how long you would have her after you have possess'd her.
Orl.	Forever and a day.
Ros.	Say "a day" without the "ever." No, no, Orlando, men are April when they woo, December when they wed; maids are May when they are maids, but the sky changes when they are wives. I will be more jealous of thee than a Barbary cock. . ., more clamorous than a parrot against rain. . . . I will weep for nothing, like Diana in the fountain, and I will do that when you are dispos'd to be merry. I will laugh like a hyen, and that when thou art inclin'd to sleep.
Orl.	But will my Rosalind do so?
Ros.	By my life, she will do as I do.
Orl.	O, but she is wise.
Ros.	. . . the wiser, the waywarder. Make the doors upon a woman's wit,

	and it will out the casement; shut that, and 'twill out at the key-hole. . . .
Orl.	A man that had a wife with such a wit, he might say "Wit, whither wilt?"
Ros.	Nay, you might keep that check for it, till you met your wife's wit going to your neighbor's bed.
Orl.	And what wit could wit have to excuse that?
Ros.	Marry, to say she came to seek you there. You shall never take her without her answer, unless you take her without her tongue. O that woman who cannot make her fault her husband's occasion, let her never nurse her child herself, for she will breed it like a fool! (4.1.143-176)

Much of Rosalind's enduring charm is this witty ability to ridicule the frailties of her sex, which she purposely sets in opposition to Orlando's romantic idealism. If he pledges unchangeable love, she promises maddening contrariness; or a weakness for her neighbor's bed; or the uncanny ability to transform her faults into her husband's. Any woman unable to turn the tables on her hapless husband, she concludes, will raise a fool for her child. But in the process of itemizing feminine weaknesses, she convinces all of us that her self-awareness will make her the exception. Everything about her suggests that knowing where the faultlines are is exactly what will help her avoid them.

Orlando's unshakeable sincerity together with Rosalind's witty self-awareness creates a picture of two well-adjusted characters who truly enjoy each other's company. Very quickly, the audience sees that they really do belong together. Though she can mock love as thoroughly as Touchstone or Jaques, Rosalind is entirely different from these other two. No sooner has she ridiculed wedded bliss than she makes her confession to Celia after Orlando has left her company. "O coz, coz, coz, my pretty little coz," she begins, "that thou didst know how many fathom deep I am in love! But it cannot be sounded; my affection hath an unknown bottom, like the Bay of Portugal. . . . I tell thee, Aliena, I cannot be out of the sight of Orlando. I'll go find a shadow, and sigh till he come" (4.1.205-217). Having just delivered a thoroughly anti-romantic catechism to Orlando, Rosalind has established herself as a realistic and therefore reliable observer of human nature, a stature that makes her confession of love all the more believable and genuine. When Touchstone and Jaques provide their very limited perspectives on love, those views help to establish the validity of Rosalind's feelings for Orlando. Hers is clearly the only valid perspective on the topic. So it is entirely fitting that Touchstone comes to meekly accept the value of his wife's simple honesty, that "pearl in a foul oyster." And it is equally fitting that Jaques joins the reformed Duke Frederick who, in the final scenes, retreats to a "life monastic."

Rosalind's balance of realism and genuine emotion stands as a corrective for these two partial and incomplete perspectives, which lack her joy, her vitality, her ability to comprehend and accept all of love's crazy contradictions. Though none of the contradictions she uses to describe love are entirely true at any given time, they are inarguably true in the aggregate. That is the nature of love: crazy, contradictory, inescapable, necessary, and an essential part of human experience. She sees love wholly and objectively without losing any of the joy that love should bring to life. That is her gift, her magic, and neither Touchstone nor Jaques have the character to duplicate it. That is what differentiates her from the others, and it is what makes her entirely and completely loveable. Because Orlando sees that, accepts it, and loves her for it, he is entirely worthy to be her partner. They belong together because, unlike any of the other characters, they are both fully capable of inspiring each other's love and devotion. This, we come to realize, is romance.

In typical comic fashion, the last scenes of the play bring all the potential couples together: Touchstone accepts his country life with Audrey; Phebe, who learns that Ganymede is really Rosalind, accepts Silvius's love; and, of course, Rosalind and Orlando are finally able to openly pledge their mutual devotion to each other. Frederick, who had set out to arrest and execute his brother, Duke Senior, meets an old religious man who dissuades him from this final wicked enterprise and convinces him to retreat from the world altogether after restoring civil authority to his deposed brother. Aggression, discord, and selfish desire have all been tamed by love; deception and disguise by plain truth; and wickedness by virtue. Though man will always be vulnerable to the winter winds, both real and metaphorical, life can still be sweet and lovely if simple goodness retains its value. This is, indeed, as it should be and, therefore, as we like it.

As You Like It continues to charm audiences with its captivating heroine, its balanced view of life and love, and its promotion of simple pleasures and basic virtues as antidotes to the corrupting influence of the desire for power, prestige, or pleasure. The ambiguity of Falstaff, where self-indulgence is inextricably packaged with an irresistible promise of endless play, has been separated into two distinguishable localities: the wicked court and the virtuous countryside. Although *As You Like It* presents nature as a passive choice that allows the good in people to flourish, this delineation of moral opposites evolves and sharpens, beginning with *Hamlet*, the subject of the next chapter. And that process begins to change the mood of Shakespeare's work, moving in its more urgent seriousness toward the tragic. Comedy is still possible, of course, as *The Merchant of Venice* and *Twelfth Night* will show, but, even there, the threat posed by evil intentions is more pronounced and only narrowly avoided.

But underneath both the tragic and the comic visions, Shakespeare never relinquishes his conviction that all nature, including human nature, has been purposefully created for everything that is definably good. In *As You Like It,* that side of nature is a choice freely available to those, like Orlando and Rosalind, whose innate virtue allows them to recognize and embrace that goodness. That's what makes them different from the play's lesser characters, who must learn, if at all possible, the reason to choose what's good. But the inherent risk of free will is that those so endowed can choose what's good or what's not. In *Hamlet*, the obstinate presence of evil is inescapable, the inevitable consequence of characters driven by their desires instead of by their better natures. But there is also a concomitant recognition that the natural world is home to an essentially unknowable divine power that abhors evil and constantly works to reassert the good. After *As You Like It*, the good in nature is not only passively available but is actively promulgated by a power that works within both nature and the affairs of human history. Though a subtle shift in dramatic emphasis, this awareness of the supernatural working within nature makes Shakespeare's great tragedies possible.

In a compelling little book, Northrop Frye makes the following very astute observation about the difference between Ben Jonson's and Shakespeare's views of nature, particularly the invisible forces that threaten to disrupt its visible orderliness. In his late masques, Jonson would refer to that force as a form of magic:

> This conception of nature as an order threatened, but not essentially disturbed, by witchcraft is in Shakespearean romance too. What Shakespeare has that Jonson neither has nor wants is the sense of nature as comprising not merely an order but a power, at once supernatural and connatural, expressed most eloquently in the dance and controlled either by benevolent human magic or by divine will. . . . [T]he myth of nature in Shakespeare [puts the emphasis] not on the visible rational order that obeys, but on the mysterious personal force that commands. (*The Natural Perspective*, 71)

Shakespeare is very aware that not every command is heeded, but the mature plays make very clear what the consequences of doing so are. Contrary to the prevalent assumption that Christianity's optimistic belief in redemption makes tragedy unviable, it is precisely because Shakespeare's work exhibits

110

this awareness of a metaphysical power at work in human affairs that tragedy is possible, and it is why his plays possess the kind of intellectual and emotional depth that eludes lesser artists. In Greek tragedy, the suffering experienced by the protagonists drives them to a recognition of forces largely indifferent to their fates. Suffering in the face of mortality, they question and plead with the gods who never answer. Tragedy reminds us that whatever name a particular culture gives to the force that directs our destinies and whatever reasons may exist for the full course of an individual's experience in the world, nothing can adequately explain the essential mystery of either that force or its purposes. It is unknowable and divine and, for all our pretensions to power, we are inherently limited mortals completely inadequate to plumb those mysteries. For Shakespeare, the moral tenets of Christianity, like free will, sin, the possibility of innocence, the necessity of forgiveness, all open a door to the very same questions about human nature, suffering, and death that Greek tragedy explores so effectively. *Hamlet*, a play that shows how covetous desire poisons every aspect of life in Denmark, is named for its remarkable and endlessly fascinating central character. Though the ghost of his murdered father commands Hamlet to avenge that death, to call it a tragedy of revenge misrepresents the rich and complex theatrical experience we have been given, for nothing has ever quite matched that play's ability to raise questions about what it means to be human.

Hamlet

Despite its familiarity and reputation, *Hamlet* stubbornly defies every effort to provide a cohesive description of the play's experience. Whether it's in the comfort of a favorite reading chair, in a darkened theater, or even with the assistance of an astute critic, every encounter feels a bit like an unsolved puzzle. Still, while every commentator struggles to construct a framework large enough to capture the play's many details and multitudinous themes, most critics respectfully acknowledge its dramatic power, its intelligent and articulate protagonist, and its willingness to address important existential themes. The incongruence between the play's raw dramatic power and any comprehensive explanation for how exactly it achieves that effect is, in fact, a large part of *Hamlet*'s fascination.

The details of the story are familiar enough. Hamlet's father, the legitimate king of Denmark, has been secretly poisoned by his brother, Claudius, who then quickly marries Hamlet's mother, Gertrude. As the Danes celebrate the marriage, the ghost of Old Hamlet appears and demands that his son, Prince Hamlet, avenge his untimely death. Having just returned from Wittenberg where he studies philosophy with his friend, Horatio, young Hamlet responds to this news with understandable outrage and vows to fulfill his father's request. But the veracity of the ghost is far from certain, so Hamlet, struggling to control his emotions, arranges for a troupe of traveling players to re-enact the murder on stage. Recognizing this as an accusation of his crime, Claudius abruptly interrupts the performance, giving Hamlet the confirmation of guilt he's been seeking. But when the prince happens upon Claudius at his prayers, the ambiguity of what he sees quickly dissipates his new-found resolve. Indecision prevails until Claudius, fully aware now that his nephew is dangerous, sends Hamlet off to England where execution awaits. On that trip, however, providence intervenes to save the prince's life and he returns to Denmark unharmed. Noticeably changed by his escape, Hamlet calmly faces his future only to be caught up in another devious royal plot which ends in the deaths of king, queen, and prince. The Norwegian, Fortinbras, who has crisscrossed through Denmark at various times during the play, steps in to fill the political void, and order is once again secured.

In its necessary oversimplification, this synopsis not only hides the rich experience of the play but also overlooks key difficulties. The first issue is the delay. Although it incorporates the obvious conventions of revenge tragedy (a ghost who announces a secret murder that must be exposed, the pretension of madness to disguise the hero's plans, the criminal's subversive attempts to evade justice, the bloody denouement), the play inverts this uniquely Elizabethan genre's central proposition: that a relative's murder must be repaid in kind. Instead, Shakespeare's protagonist spends almost the entire play lamenting his flagging motivation to avenge his murdered father. The difference is apparent from a comparison with Shakespeare's first revenge tragedy, *Titus Andronicus*, where the protagonist never doubts that the rape and mutilation of his daughter deserve his relentless pursuit of the perpetrators. Hamlet, though, is a completely different avenger, and until his delay is accounted for, this profoundly moving but difficult play will defy every effort at clarification.

But *Hamlet* has a second, even more puzzling problem: what to make of his transformation from a state of persistent agitation to a preternatural calm after the aborted trip to England, averting his execution. Every critic admits that something changes in Hamlet as a result, but there is little unanimity about the significance of that change or whether his new tranquility about the prospect of impending death relates to his inability to avenge his father's murder. While Hamlet spends considerable time talking about death, the text provides no evidence that his obsession with it is in any way connected to his delay. Consequently, the aborted England

113

trip feels more like a haphazard device to bring his procrastination to an end rather than a well-integrated thematic inflection point.

The final problem is how to interpret the last act's bloody denouement where the king's treachery finally provokes Hamlet to kill his nemesis. Both *Titus* and *Romeo and Juliet* make sense as arguments against revenge. Has Shakespeare's position on revenge changed since those previous plays? Or does his earlier moral repugnance simply give way here to the conventions of this sub-genre? If not, how is the death of Claudius qualitatively different from revenge? If the preceding four and a half acts are intended to demonstrate Hamlet's cautious, skeptical approach to the purgation of Denmark's evil, does that caution provide moral justification for the killing? If not, is Hamlet really any different from other avengers like Shakespeare's Titus or Kyd's Hieronimo, neither of whom exhibit any reluctance while pursuing their opponent?

While these issues are indeed worthy of critical attention, the enduring fascination with *Hamlet* suggests that they do very little to detract from the play's effect. Despite its difficulties, it remains profoundly interesting and exciting, just as it apparently was for its original London audience. Elizabethan imitations of the Roman playwright Seneca's revenge drama predate Shakespeare's *Hamlet* by several decades but reappear on the English stage in the waning years of the sixteenth century with a dramatic splash. This revived interest was documented by the London entrepreneur, Phillip Henslowe, who made a fortune lending money to playwrights in exchange for the right to publish their scripts. He kept a careful record of all his transactions in a diary, which mentions a 1597 revival of Thomas Kyd's *The Spanish Tragedy*. An old play probably written and first performed in the late 1580's, this hugely successful revival reignited public interest in revenge tragedies. Speculation has it that Shakespeare based his own *Hamlet*, written just three years

114

later in 1600, on a lost version of a similar story by Kyd, now referred to as the *ur-Hamlet*.

Though the text of Kyd's *Hamlet* has been lost, several contemporary accounts suggest that it was either badly acted, badly written or both. Shakespeare's version of this familiar story, therefore, must have completely surprised Elizabethan audiences with its unmistakable dramatic power. Oddly, the play's very first line poses a question from those coming to relieve the night watchman on the outer walls of Elsinore castle. "Who's there?" one of them asks, reversing roles with the guard, who should be the one challenging anyone approaching him. That odd exchange indicates that something is badly off-kilter in Denmark, and in that first question, the play creates a tense atmosphere of mystery that never wanes. In the first act alone, the ghost of Hamlet's murdered father appears three times, twice without saying a word to anyone, a device that intentionally heightens curiosity. While the play's dramatic power is immediately evident, the lead role is, paradoxically, both an opportunity and a challenge for actors because of the wide range of emotions and multiple passionate soliloquies. In its current form, this play of over four thousand lines, which would take between four and five hours to perform in its entirety, remains a watershed of dramatic literature. More books and academic articles have been written about *Hamlet* than about any other play, by far. On stage and in our cultural fabric, *Hamlet* has set an indelible standard for effective, thought-provoking drama.

Sharing the same literary roots, Kyd's *The Spanish Tragedy* and *Hamlet* include those by now familiar Senecan conventions. In *Hamlet*, however, those similarities are largely superficial. The experience of Shakespeare's play is completely different from the experience of *The Spanish Tragedy*, which is propelled forward largely by its story line: how Hieronimo will implement his revenge. Shakespeare's tragedy shifts dramatic focus from plot to protagonist, from external event to psychological process. *Hamlet*'s emphasis is no longer on how the protagonist will overcome the obstacles thrown up by the murderer but on the intellectual, emotional, and moral struggles the protagonist endures as he confronts the dilemmas raised by revenge. The plot of Shakespeare's play cannot possibly make sense, therefore, without first coming to terms with the evolution of Hamlet's character as the play progresses.

As a result of this shift in emphasis, Hamlet changed dramatic literature and stagecraft forever. Hamlet's imaginative and intelligent encounter with a role he does not want in a world he no longer understands becomes the real story. Revenge is simply the vehicle for this psychological and spiritual journey which, as he encounters the various moral issues posed by personal retribution, reflects Elizabethan culture's basic Christian assumptions. By creating a character with such a vividly realized psychological life, Shakespeare not only completely transforms dramatic presentations but creates an immensely moving and tragic story of one man's journey through the heart of darkness.

Rather than a problem, then, Hamlet's delay is actually a feature, for it is the avoidance of revenge, the inexplicable delay, that transforms Shakespeare's tragic drama by shifting focus from plot to psychological process. Despite many attempts over the past four centuries to explain why Hamlet avoids avenging his father's murder, both the play's protagonist and the story in which he finds himself remain enigmas, even to the prince himself. It isn't just that the many plot details refuse to fit comfortably together, like a hastily designed puzzle. The play defies any attempt at a cohesive explanation because Hamlet himself cannot articulate why he lacks the initiative to implement the task he has been assigned. Nor is it for lack of trying to explain this delay. If anything, as A.C. Bradley once observed, he provides a surplus of explanations. He delays, he says at one point in the action, because the ghost demanding vengeance may actually

116

be a demon luring him toward eternal damnation. Later, he fears he may simply be a coward. Then the itinerant actor's speech on Hecuba prompts the speculation that passing time has dulled his initial passion for revenge. Later, finding Claudius at his prayers, he wonders if killing him at such a moment would send the murderer's soul to heaven while his father's tortured spirit still lingers in purgatory. Hamlet's relentless questioning of virtually every aspect of his experience, including his own motivation, throws a deep shadow onto the play, which Maynard Mack, in an influential essay, has labeled a play "in the interrogative mood." Because of this incessant questioning by both prince and critics, no one analysis has ever satisfied completely. Nor will this attempt provide completely satisfying cohesion to this rich, complicated, mysterious, frustrating, and fascinating play, which stands as an exercise in humility. As others have noted, Hamlet the prince is right to chastise his friends, Rosencrantz and Guildenstern, for their ineffectual attempt to pluck out the heart of his mystery.

But uncovering a well-hidden cause for Hamlet's delay may simply be the wrong goal. Instead, it may be far more useful to describe a thematic purpose for his confusion and the many critical mistakes he makes as a result of that uncertainty. After all, every one of Shakespeare's tragic protagonists exhibits a similar state of confusion where a great many equally unanswerable questions are posed. Misled by Iago, for example, Othello is tortured by the uncertain fidelity of his obviously loving wife, Desdemona. Duped by the flattery of his two selfish daughters, Lear is abandoned to the elements where he questions indifferent nature, human ingratitude, justice, and love. Based on impenetrable and misleading equivocations, Macbeth murders a generous mentor and forfeits every available blessing, and, as his life disintegrates, he laments the forces that led him to this confusion. Even Antony, Shakespeare's final tragic protagonist, never fully comprehends his connection to

Cleopatra until, mistakenly believing she is dead, he nearly botches his suicide. Though the aging lovers are briefly reunited before he dies, he pays the ultimate price for doubting her commitment to him, which is magnificently confirmed by her death in the play's final act. Beginning with Hamlet, every one of Shakespeare's tragic protagonists endures a period of mental anguish and questioning. This is the essence, in fact, of tragic suffering.

This confusion, which is the consequence of Claudius's primal sin against a brother, Hamlet's father, is precisely the point. Though everyone else in the play also swims in this dark ocean of uncertainty, they do so blithely unaware of its dangers. Refusing to succumb to Claudius's duplicity, Hamlet is the only one who pays a significant intellectual, emotional, and spiritual price for another man's sin. Sin, the play demonstrates, undoes everything that once was both certain and good. In the not-too-distant past, Hamlet was a university student, with friends like Horatio and the oddly entwined Rosencrantz and Guildenstern. He was betrothed to the sweet and vulnerable Ophelia, daughter to the royal counselor, Polonius, and sister to Laertes. His father, Old Hamlet, was Denmark's king, a man who entrusted his own life to divine providence as he confronted adversaries in single combat, emblematic of where Hamlet the prince will eventually arrive spiritually. And the disappointment he feels for his mother Gertrude's disloyalty to her husband, Hamlet's royal father, is a measure of the depth of the love mother and son once shared. All of this has suddenly vanished from Hamlet's life as a result of Claudius's sin. And when the ghost implores the young prince to avenge the old king's murder, all the certainties he once took for granted–parental love, friendships, primogeniture, political stability, philosophical and spiritual assumptions about the world—are suddenly suspect. What can possibly be deemed trustworthy when nothing seems to be what it once was? Though the audience only gradually becomes aware of these

118

circumstances, this is Denmark's situation as the play opens. When the ghost confronts the night watchmen, some mysterious metaphysical force has entered the land of the living, and there is no longer any certainty about its message, its intent, or about any other circumstance in Denmark.

The very nature of revenge is at the center of Hamlet's conundrum. As Helen Gardner has shown, any contemplated act of revenge would have raised many difficult moral questions. A personal rather than a church or state-sanctioned form of punishment, revenge was not only a recognized source of social disorder but also a morally and spiritually repugnant measure, for it was susceptible to all the errors of judgment to which flawed individuals are prone. Since the condemnation of revenge had a moral, political, social, literary, and religious basis, all of Shakespeare's early tragedies, including *Hamlet,* consistently reject revenge as an acceptable response to sin. In his confusion and anguish, in fact, Hamlet commits many of his own sins and actually becomes, as a result, the clearest argument against revenge. Though surrounded by the conventions of revenge tragedy, then, Hamlet never actually enacts personal justice on his father's murderer. Initially, he assumes this is his purpose, but how and why that original intention changes becomes the play's real subject.

Traditionally, revenge tragedy involves the protagonist in a psychological struggle with a suspected murderer who strives mightily to evade his well-deserved punishment. That opposition of protagonist and antagonist is no different in *Hamlet,* but the prince's delay is marked by an atypical preoccupation with the reasons for this procrastination. That he gives many different explanations, none of which satisfy him or the play's critics is an indication of a valiant effort to understand his circumstances before taking any action. After an impromptu rehearsal for the play-within-the-play, where Hamlet observes the itinerant player's emotional speech about Hecuba, the wife of a Trojan brutally killed by the vengeful Pyrrhus in retaliation for the death of Achilles, the prince reprimands his own lack of motivation:

> Is it not monstrous that this player here,
> But in a fiction, in a dream of passion,
> Could force his soul so to his own conceit
> That from her working all the visage wann'd,
> Tears in his eyes. . . . And all for nothing,
> For Hecuba! . . . Yet I,
> A dull and muddy-mettled rascal, peak
> Like John-a-dreams, unpregnant of my cause,
> And can say nothing. . . Am I a coward? (2.2.551-571)

He examines this lack of motivation repeatedly but never finds an answer that quashes his anxiety. As late as Act V, he is still bewildered by his inaction. Talking with his friend, Horatio, he says:

> Does it not, think thee, stand me now upon—
> He that hath kill'd my king and whor'd my mother,
> Popp'd in between th' election and my hopes,
> Thrown out his angle for my proper life,
> And with such coz'nage—is't not perfect conscience
> To quit him with this arm? (5.1.63-68)

Just as Lear will futilely hammer against his predicament, questioning justice, nature, and the cause of his daughter's hard hearts, Hamlet endures a similar process of incessant, relentless questioning about why action isn't forthcoming as easily as he thinks it should. Some of the play's circumstances partially explain why revenge is delayed, but none of those satisfy Hamlet himself. Until the last scenes of the play, his inaction is a source of immense personal dismay that he is unable to resolve on his own. It is only the interrupted trip to England that provides an answer sufficient to end his confusion.

What the text does make abundantly clear is that, because of the murder of Hamlet's father, the Danish kingdom has succumbed to a pervasive sickness that, events will show, is moral in nature. Imagery of bodily corruption and disease is ubiquitous. Upon seeing the ghost and hearing its story, one of the night watchmen concludes that "something is rotten in the state of Denmark" (1.4.89). A few lines later, Hamlet laments that "the time is out of joint" (1.5.188). Similar disease imagery appears again when Hamlet visits his mother's chamber to convict her of her iniquities. When she tries to deflect the truth of his harsh words by blaming his "antic disposition," he quickly corrects her:

> Mother, for love of grace,
> Lay not that flattering unction to your soul,
> That not your trespass but my madness speaks;
> It will but skin and film the ulcerous place,
> Whiles rank corruption, mining all within,
> Infects unseen. (3.4.144-149)

From Hamlet's perspective, the physical and emotional desires that brought his mother and Claudius together are at the very heart of Denmark's moral corruption. Though the details of her complicity are never entirely clear, her union with Claudius is at the root of Denmark's illness and led to a brother's primal sin against a brother. Whether Gertrude was complicit in the murder of her first husband is irrelevant. Ignoring every suspicious circumstance and social impropriety, she is at the very least morally and intellectually lazy. And because she now shares the fruits of Claudius's covetous heart, Gertrude cannot escape being tainted by the crime that now infects her country.

Nor can anyone else escape it either, including Hamlet, who suffers its effects differently. His anguish following the ghost's revelation has extinguished all the goodness that a previous life once offered. Those were possible in an orderly, rational world, but confidence in such things has disappeared. Meeting Rosencrantz and Guildenstern, childhood acquaintances Claudius has

121

employed to uncover Hamlet's intentions, he describes how his former delight in things human has evaporated:

> What a piece of work is a man, how noble in reason, how infinite in faculties, in form and moving, how express and admirable in action, how like an angel in apprehension, how like a god! The beauty of the world; the paragon of animals; and yet to me what is this quintessence of dust? Man delights not me—nor woman neither. (2.2.303-309)

Before the horrible reality of sin intruded into Hamlet's awareness, man was at the very apex of God's creation, the very "paragon of animals" and an "angel in apprehension." Murder and an incestuous marriage changed all that. Now the once certain world he confronts has become muddled. Everything that once seemed clear and certain has become ambiguous. Absent any adequate moral structure, Hamlet is adrift.

The infection emanating from royal sin is inescapable. The royal couple has polluted every aspect of life. Having returned from his studies to attend the funeral and the wedding, he encounters his university friend, Horatio. The two young men discuss the confusion of values they encounter in Claudius' Denmark:

> Ham. . . . what is your affair in Elsinore?
>   We'll teach you to drink deep ere you depart.
> Hor. My lord, I came to see your father's funeral.
> Ham. I prithee do not mock me, fellow student,
>   I think it was to see my mother's wedding.
> Hor. Indeed, my lord, it followed hard upon.
> Ham. Thrift, thrift, Horatio, the funeral bak'd-meats
>   Did coldly furnish forth the marriage tables.
>   (1.2.174-181)

As the play opens, Hamlet returns to a realm where nothing is as it once was. An appearance of normalcy barely hides something as yet unidentified but decidedly rank underneath. In this new Denmark, the normal boundaries between death

122

and marriage, funeral and wedding have disappeared. The sins of the recently married royals have debased the emotional and moral truths that these ceremonies formalize into ritual. Grief over a loved one lost has been diluted and sullied by the supposed joy of an over-hasty marriage, rendering both ceremonies devoid of genuine meaning and therefore rancid. They become mere show. Funeral and wedding now serve, in fact, to hide sin and shame with a pretense of legitimacy.

The moral disorder even affects language, which struggles to contain the obvious incongruities. As they enter the stage for the first time, the royal pair attempt to paper over their shameful behavior with a cascade of contradictions. "Though yet of Hamlet our dear brother's death the memory be green," Claudius begins,

> Yet so far hath discretion fought with nature
> That we with wisest sorrow think on him
> Together with remembrance of ourselves.
> Therefore our sometime sister, now our queen. . .
> Have we, as 'twere with defeated joy. . .
> With mirth in funeral, and with dirge in marriage
> In equal scale weighing delight and dole,
> Taken to wife. . . . (1.2.1-14)

After one short month, sorrow for a recently dead brother-husband is delicately balanced by "remembrance of ourselves," but the quick marriage proves which event was valued more highly. Then comes the crucial verb phrase, "Taken to wife," which is buried beneath an avalanche of descriptive prepositional phrases, each one containing a startling oxymoron like "mirth in funeral," that reflects this deliberate obfuscation. Where any distinction between moral opposites has disintegrated, contradictions no longer seem odd or unnatural, especially when spoken from a position of power and authority. As the assembled court digests this announcement without objection, their complacent acceptance of such deceitful language amplifies the original sin, indicating the extent and the depth of Elsinore's moral

123

corruption. Even language becomes a tool to obscure the corruption.

Hamlet's initial response to Denmark's corruption is understandable rage. When the ghost makes known its request for vengeance, Hamlet, the philosopher-prince, assumes the role of the physician responsible for purging Denmark of its illness. His first response to the ghost's pitiful story makes his spiritual starting point quite clear:

> O all you host of heaven! O earth! What else?
> And shall I couple hell? O fie, hold, hold, my heart,
> And you, my sinows, grow not instant old,
> But bear me stiffly up. Remember thee!
> Ay, thou poor ghost, whiles memory holds a seat
> In this distracted globe. Remember thee!
> Yea, from the table of my memory
> I'll wipe away all trivial fond records. . .
> And thy commandment all alone shall live
> Within the book and volume of my brain. . .
> O most pernicious woman!
> O villain, villain, smiling, damned villain!
> (1.5.92-106)

Although a student of philosophy, where reason and logic are employed in the search for truth, Hamlet's first reaction is anger, and this battle between emotion and reason will not only undermine his sense of identity but complicate his ability to perceive truth. This passionate desire to implement justice for a murdered father begins his disintegration, for it requires a transformation of Hamlet into something he is not. "[F]rom the table of my memory," he pledges, "I'll wipe away all trivial fond records." From this moment on, the only notion that will occupy his thoughts will be the ghost's "commandment." Hamlet, once a son, prince, student, friend, now has a new identity: avenger. All his other roles, he concludes, need to be discarded. From the perspective of Christian morality, however, this newly assumed identity of avenger imperils Hamlet's soul. That he questions every

124

aspect of the world he finds himself in and avoids this commission differentiates him from the far more vengeful impulses of Laertes, who, late in the play, blindly falls for Claudius's subterfuges and is instrumental in the play's final bloody denouement.

Just as the shameful nakedness of original sin needed to be hidden under fig leaves, Claudius's sophisticated rhetoric attempts to gloss over the apparent contradictions spawned by murder and adultery. From Hamlet's perspective, mother and father-uncle are hiding behind an appearance of normalcy. They too are playing roles. To counteract the duplicity of the royal pair, Hamlet will assume an "antic disposition," a disguise of mental distraction or madness, to hide his intentions. But hiding behind a false role, as Claudius does, is not Hamlet's preferred mode. Earlier, when he first appeared in court to greet his mother and his uncle-father as king, Gertrude chides him for seeming to mourn his father longer than required. Dressed in mourning black, Hamlet declares that, unlike the royal couple, his outward appearance is an accurate reflection of what he truly feels inside:

Gert.   Do not for ever with thy vailed lids
         Seek for thy noble father in the dust.
         Thou know'st 'tis common, all that lives must die.
         . . .

Ham.   Ay, madam, it is common.
Gert.   If it be,
         Why seems it so particular with thee?
Ham.   Seems, madam? Nay, it is, I know not "seems."
         'Tis not alone my inky cloak, good mother,
         Nor customary suits of solemn black . . .
         That can denote me truly. These indeed seem,
         For they are actions that a man might play,
         But I have that within which passes show,
         These but the trappings and the suits of woe.
           (1.2.72-86)

Hamlet's first words are a declaration of transparency. Though circumstances force him to forsake this to everyone but his friend, Horatio, integrity and truth matter to him, and so Hamlet the philosopher will refuse to act until Denmark's secrets are verified and brought into the light. Unfortunately, getting to Elsinore's truth is not only difficult but quickly becomes a matter of life and death. His psychological disguise, he hopes, will provide opportunities to confirm his suspicions safely. Like all Shakespearean disguises, though, his antic disposition becomes an additional moral complication that embroils Hamlet ever more deeply in Denmark's moral confusion, becoming the mystery that his antagonist, circumscribed by his own sins, chooses to solve with increased duplicity.

The ghost, which, for Hamlet, initiates this descent into confusion, embodies the intersection between the supernatural and natural, and, as such, it exemplifies the all but unbridgeable gulf that exists between ordinary mortals and the supernatural, between the knowable life in this world and the mysterious and therefore terrifying state that follows death. Throughout the play, Hamlet seems obsessed with the gruesome details of the passage into the hereafter. After hearing the ghost's story, he contemplates suicide but rejects that avenue because of this fear of what comes after the end of life.

> To die, to sleep---
> To sleep, perchance to dream--- ay, there's the rub,
> For in that sleep of death what dreams may come,
> When we have shuffled off this mortal coil,
> Must give us pause; there's the respect
> That makes calamity of so long life;
> For who would bear the whips and scorns of time. . .
> But that the dread of something after death
>   . . . puzzles the will,
> And makes us rather bear those ills we have,
> Than fly to others that we know not of?   (3.1.63-81)

126

This is no longer mere philosophical speculation. Murder and an ambiguous being from the hereafter have brought a new immediacy to the question of death, and, as he does with every other issue, Hamlet applies his intellectual gifts to them. From the beginning of the play where he chastises a mother unwilling to properly mourn a dead husband until the play's last act where he contemplates the progress of a dead king's dust through the stopper of a beer barrel and, more personally, the death of a once-beloved Ophelia, Hamlet seems haunted by the prospect of this inevitability. Like young men with most of life's promises still ahead of them, Hamlet probably perceived death as less imminent and therefore less consequential than more pressing concerns, but his father's death, the deaths of Polonius and Ophelia, as well as the prospect of his own demise suddenly make this topic a pervasive aspect of his life.

Is it possible that these trappings of woe are there simply to foster an atmosphere of dreadful mystery? Or is that atmosphere more purposeful? As Mack argues, perhaps this brooding, interrogative mood is included to reflect our common struggle to come to terms with that greatest of all mysteries, mortality. "There are more things in heaven and earth," Hamlet reminds his friend, Horatio, after speaking to the ghost, "Than are dreamt of in your philosophy" (1.5.166ff). The one question that matters, the existentialist author Camus once said, is what prevents us from committing suicide. For Camus, it was a question about the purpose and meaning of life in a universe where God no longer existed, where man was alone and fully responsible for his actions. This comes fairly close to describing where Hamlet is spiritually after hearing the ghost of his father, and, for a moment, suicide offers a tempting escape.

But, unlike Camus, Hamlet never denies the reality of the metaphysical. Instead, the sin identified by the ghost makes any certain interpretation of whatever lies beyond this life an impossibility. Spiritually, this is a very precarious state

127

where the moral ambiguity of revenge could lead to unintended consequences for all eternity. Murder and infidelity have shattered every one of Hamlet's old assumptions, including any he might have had about death, which is now not only a boundary between life and its opposite but between what's known and what can never be fully known in life. A young man who recently had a young man's preoccupations, Hamlet is now face to face with all the implications of mortality, including the consequences of any sin he might commit in pursuit of rough justice. Because he can no longer assume that what follows death will necessarily be better, he understands with new clarity that the choices he now makes will have significant and eternal consequences.

This is why Hamlet must carefully parse the moral difference between revenge and justice, and it is his persistent effort to do so that differentiates him from other avengers. Since self-inflicted death cannot provide an escape from this responsibility, Hamlet is effectively trapped in the roles that have been thrust upon him. There is no other choice but to fulfill his duty to a murdered father to the best of his ability. What the implementation of that duty looks like, however, is anything but clear. Though he intends to use his "antic disposition" to find a way toward justice, he does not relish the unnatural roles conventionally required by vengeance. Acknowledging that "the time is out of joint," he still fears what the remedy will cost him. "O cursed spite," he bemoans, "that ever I was born to set it right."

If suicide is an unacceptable risk, punishing Claudius also endangers Hamlet's life and immortal soul, whose guardian is a conscience that relies on truth. As a result, Hamlet's first task is to solve the puzzle of the ghost, a figure of considerable ambiguity. It appears to be real enough since Hamlet is not the only character who sees it. But later, in Gertrude's room when it appears for the final time, Hamlet sees and speaks to it but the queen sees nothing. Moreover, Elizabethans themselves would hold confused notions about ghosts of dead relatives communicating with the living. Catholic notions of purgatory, a status between heaven and hell where sins could still be purged away, could explain such apparitions as tormented souls seeking prayers to shorten their suffering and release them into heaven. The ghost of Old Hamlet, in fact, describes himself as "doom'd for a certain term to walk the night and for the day confin'd to fast in fires, till the foul crimes done in my days of nature are burnt and purg'd away" (1.5.10-13). Protestants who rejected the idea of purgatory altogether would more likely see a ghost as a disguised demon tempting the living toward the fiery pit, a danger Hamlet recognizes. "The spirit that I have seen may be a devil, and the devil hath power to assume a pleasing shape. . .and perhaps abuses me to damn me" (2.2.598-603). As a result of this uncertainty, Hamlet suffers considerable anxiety about the ghost, about what's true and what's false, about his mission, and about the death and its aftermath that his confrontation with Claudius's could easily bring.

To help him verify the ghost's story, Hamlet employs the itinerant players to re-enact Old Hamlet's murder. When they perform the scene before the assembled court, Hamlet will be observing the king's reaction:

> If 'a do blench,
> I know my course. The spirit I have seen
> May be a dev'l, and the dev'l hath power
> T' assume a pleasing shape, yea, and perhaps,
> Out of my weakness and my melancholy. . .
> Abuses me to damn me. I'll have grounds
> More relative than this—the play's the thing
> Wherein I'll catch the conscience of the King.
> (2.2.597-605)

As these words suggest, Hamlet's original impassioned reaction to the ghost's story has now been replaced by a more cautious and rational search for truth. In Mark Rose's very interesting *Shakespearean Design*, an analysis of the scenic structure of Hamlet, he argues that "The Mousetrap" occupies the vital center of the five acts and thus carries considerable thematic weight (109). Speaking to the players, Hamlet asks to hear an impromptu speech about Pyrrhus, who brutally murders Priam and his wife, Hecuba, in retribution for the death of the Greek hero, Achilles. What Hamlet hears describes the roles he imagines each member of his own family should have played during this crisis: the noble, fallen father, the sorrowful mother-wife, and the undeterred avenger. Moved by the player's tears for the imaginary Hecuba, though, he can never really be Pyrrhus because something in Hamlet's nature will not permit irrational, unthinking brutality, let alone justice without verification of guilt. So as Hamlet prepares the players for the mousetrap, he instructs them to exercise discipline and self-control in their speeches, which should not be clumsily "mouthed" like the town crier. The necessity of rejecting this false ideal of impassioned, reflexive brutality and regaining self-control is verified by his encounter with Ophelia in the nunnery scene and, later, by events in his mother's chambers. The two scenes with women serve as a measure of his spiritual progress. With Ophelia, his disappointment and rage at her apparent duplicity lead to the harsh condemnation and rejection of a largely innocent young woman. Later, in his mother's chambers, he is blunt but implores her to repent of her sins. Even before that fateful trip to England, Hamlet has begun to change.

Although Hamlet is beginning to comprehend the dangers of making decisions in a morally confused world, his passions at times still get the better of his judgment. Polonius's innocent young daughter, Ophelia, who has been the object of Hamlet's affection, is the first to pay a price for that. As a counselor to Claudius, Polonius all too eagerly accommodates the king's requests for information about Hamlet. His first assumption is that Hamlet's gloomy mood "is the very ecstasy of love" (2.1.99), but he soon chooses to verify this by using the "bait of falsehood" to "take this carp of truth" (2.1.60). After placing his daughter where he knows

Hamlet will find her, Polonius hides nearby to overhear their conversation. Reading a prayer book, she is the picture of innocence, but when Hamlet appears, she obeys her father's request to reject Hamlet's interest. She too assumes a role, this time playing the part of the injured woman. "My lord," she begins, "I have remembrances of yours that I have longed long to redeliver. I pray you now receive them." But when Hamlet denies ever giving these gifts, perhaps concerned this might be a trap, she provokes him further with her reply:

> My honor'd lord, you know right well you did,
> And with them words of so sweet breath compos'd
> As made these things more rich. Their perfume lost,
> Take these again, for to the noble mind
> Rich gifts wax poor when givers prove unkind.
> (3.1.96-100)

Though "words of so sweet breath composed" contradict this claim of Hamlet's unkindness, Ophelia is separating herself from a prince who, her father had warned, "you must fear" because "on his choice depends the safety and health of this whole state" (1.2.16-21). Denying her love out of dutiful obedience to her family, Ophelia lies. But, as it is often staged, Hamlet seems to detect Polonius hidden nearby, and he abruptly asks, "Where's thy father?" Ophelia lies a second time, replying, "At home, my lord." At this, Hamlet's anger erupts, and all his disgust at feminine weakness—his mother's, Ophelia's–pours out in a torrent of bitter vitriol:

> Ham.   Let the doors be shut upon him, that he may play
>   the fool no where but in 's own house. Farewell.
> Oph.   O, help him, you sweet heavens!
> Ham.   If thou dost marry, I'll give thee this plague for
>   thy dowry: be thou as chaste as ice, as pure as
>   snow, thou shalt not escape calumny. Get thee to
>   a nunn'ry, farewell. Or if thou wilt needs marry,
>   marry a fool, for wise men know well enough
>   what monsters you make of them. To a nunn'ry,
>   go, and quickly too. Farewell.

131

| Oph. | Heavenly powers, restore him! |
| Ham. | I have heard of your paintings, well enough. God hath given you one face, and you make yourselves another. You jig and amble, and you lisp, you nickname God's creatures and make your wantonness your ignorance. Go to, I'll no more on't, it hath made me mad. I say we will have no moe marriage. Those that are married already, all but one shall live, the rest shall keep as they are. To a nunn'ry, go. (3.1.131-149) |

Though addressed to Ophelia, the anger originates from Hamlet's disgust with his own mother. But unlike Gertrude, Ophelia lies out of an obedient, child-like, largely innocent spirit that willingly sacrifices her own love for what she believes is Hamlet's good and the good of the state.

After Hamlet's exit, she professes a profound sorrow for everything that has been lost:

> O, what a noble mind is here o'erthrown!
> The courtier's, soldier's, scholar's, eye, tongue,
>   sword,
> Th' expectation and rose of the fair state,
> The glass of fashion and the mould of form,
> Th' observ'd of all observers, quite, quite down!
> And I, of ladies most deject and wretched,
> That suck'd the honey of his music vows,
> Now see that noble and most sovereign reason
> Like sweet bells jangled out of time, and harsh. . .
> Blasted with ecstasy. O, woe is me
> T' have seen what I have seen, see what I see.
> (3.1.150-161)

The words declare her genuine love for Hamlet as well as her willingness to sacrifice personal desire for what she assumed was his good. Unfortunately, Ophelia has been caught up in something much larger than she understands, and she is victimized by the general atmosphere of deception and intrigue that swirls around her.

But Hamlet is not altogether wrong about Ophelia either. Her innocence allows her to be used by far more duplicitous characters, an unfortunate circumstance in a fallen world that appears again in characters like the Edgar of *King Lear*. Nor is Hamlet himself immune to those same forces, for his anger severs him from all the love that had once seemed possible. Based on what his eyes see, he assumes Ophelia is morally identical to Gertrude. Every woman is included in this denunciation, beginning with Eve, who named "God's creatures," and ending with Gertrude, who made her "wantonness" her "ignorance." Part of their very nature, deception is evident when they paint over God's face with another. Their deceitfulness transforms men into monstrous fools, capable of murdering a brother. Angered by Ophelia's lies, Hamlet cannot help but reveal the disgust he feels for his mother and the intention that "all but one" married couple shall live. Witnessed by Polonius, his secret intent is now out in the open. Upon hearing of this exchange, Claudius knows. "Love?" he scoffs, "his affections do not that way tend," and he plans to send Hamlet away to execution in England.

Neither Ophelia nor Hamlet are responsible for the world they find themselves in, but it manages to taint them anyway. No one can escape calumny. At times, Hamlet's awareness of this general guilt generates an appreciation of the need for mercy. When Polonius says he will treat the players "according to their desert" (2.2.527), Hamlet is mildly incensed. "God's bodkin, man, much better: use every man after his desert, and who shall scape whipping?" But that inclination toward Christian mercy is difficult, if not impossible, to apply to Claudius, whose heinous crime seems to place him beyond the pale of redemption.

This is exactly the question raised when Hamlet, who is on his way to his mother's bedchamber, witnesses Claudius at his prayers. As far as Hamlet is concerned, the king's shocked reaction to the play-within-the-play has confirmed his guilt, but, once again, the prince is unable to discern truth from appearance as he contemplates the kneeling penitent. Unbeknownst to Hamlet, who is too distant to hear, Claudius understands that God cannot forgive him yet "since I am still possess'd of those effects for which I did the murther: my crown, mine own ambition, and my queen" (3.3. 52-55). The moral ambiguities so prevalent in Claudius's Denmark prevent Hamlet from penetrating beneath surface appearances to the truth that lies hidden underneath, and so, once again, he delays his revenge until there's a moment "that has no relish of salvation in't":

> Now might I do it pat, now 'a is a-praying;
> And now I'll do't---and so 'a goes to heaven,
> And so am I reveng'd. That would be scann'd:
> A villain kills my father, and for that
> I, his sole son, do this same villain send
> To heaven.
> Why, this is hire and salary, not revenge. (3.2.73-79)

Though the moral brutality of planning another man's eternal damnation may shock, his decision to leave a praying king unscathed continues his transformation away from reflexive, emotional responses back toward reasoned judgment. For the first time since the ghost, he understands that, despite his mother's sins, the two of them are joined by the same natural bonds that exist between a son and a murdered father. As angry and disgusted as he has been with Gertrude, he decides not to punish her and heads toward her bedchamber with a more benign purpose.

During the nunnery scene when he was enraged by what seemed to be Ophelia's duplicity, Hamlet had strongly hinted that he would kill the royal couple, but his intentions toward his mother have changed. While his purpose for confronting his mother is no longer revenge but conviction of sin, it is important to acknowledge what motivates this change. "Soft, now to my mother," he begins before continuing:

O, heart, lose not thy nature! Let not ever
The soul of Nero enter this firm bosom,
Let me be cruel, not unnatural;
I will speak daggers to her but use none. (3.2.393-396)

If Hamlet's encounter with the praying king proves that mere mortals are ill-equipped to ascertain the guilt or innocence of even a murderer's soul, then he knows he is in no position to judge the heart of the woman who gave him life. To avoid the cruelty of a Nero, perhaps the most heartless of Rome's emperors, he invokes those natural bonds between a parent and a child that will become the subject of Shakespeare's greatest tragedy, *King Lear*. If human justice is inherently flawed by man's inability to penetrate appearance down into truth, those elemental connections of love that are part of human nature provide some alternative basis for dealing with sin. Though he will be honest to the point of cruelty, he vows not to harm her. Unfortunately, the conversation takes a bloody turn anyway when Hamlet, thinking he hears the king, mistakenly kills Polonius who has been hiding behind the arras, once again to overhear a conversation that deserved to be private.

With the old man's death, Hamlet's fate is now sealed. He has given Claudius reason to punish this rash act, so, quickly moving to save her soul, Denmark's physician proceeds to lance the corruption in his mother's heart. Taking out separate miniatures of her two husbands, he begins:

Look here upon this picture, and on this,
The counterfeit presentment of two brothers.
See what a grace was seated on this brow:
Hyperion's curls, the front of Jove himself,
An eye like Mars, to threaten and command. . . .
This was your husband. Look you now what follows:
Here is your husband, like a mildewed ear,
Blasting his wholesome brother. Have you eyes?
Could you on this fair mountain leave to feed,
And batten on this moor? Ha, have you eyes?

135

You cannot call it love, for at your age
The heyday in the blood is tame, it's humble,
And waits upon the judgment, and what judgment
Would step from this to this?   (3.4.54-71)

The repetition of the phrase "have you eyes" hammers upon her emotional and moral blindness. Since she is old enough to know better, the choice between two qualitatively different husbands cannot be due merely to sexual passion. Her judgment is faulty, a sin his new-found self-discipline helped him avoid just before coming to her room. Finally recognizing her complicity in Denmark's corruption, Gertrude pledges, at Hamlet's requests, not "to let the bloat king tempt you again to bed" where he might "make you ravel all this matter out, that I essentially am not in madness, but mad in craft." Instead of revenge, Hamlet has succeeded in bringing his mother to the doorstep of repentance.

The bedroom scene is a particularly clear example of Hamlet's desire to bring hidden truth into the light, a characteristic that separates him from those, like his two parent-sinners, who try vainly to keep their wickedness secret. To her credit, Gertrude seems truly shocked to learn of the murder of her first husband by her second. After Hamlet has stabbed Polonius, she exclaims in horror:

Queen. O, what a rash and bloody deed is this!
Ham.   A bloody deed! Almost as bad, good mother,
           As kill a king, and marry with his brother.
Queen. As kill a king!
Ham.   Ay, lady, it was my word. (3.4.27-30)

Her surprise seems genuine enough, but that insight happens because Hamlet values truth more than deference, a trait that distinguishes him from a man like Polonius, who easily accepts and reports what only appears to be true. Wanting to be useful, he is far too eager to please authority. At times, he can seem quite fatherly and even sympathetic, expressing

136

some regret for instructing Ophelia to discontinue her relationship with the prince:

> I fear'd he did but trifle
> And meant to wrack thee, but beshrow my jealousy!
> By heaven, it is as proper to our age
> To cast beyond ourselves in our opinions,
> As it is common for the younger sort
> To lack discretion.   (2.1.109-110)

And his long list of cautions indicates genuine concern for the welfare of his son, Laertes, when the young man is about to leave for Paris.

What Polonius lacks, however, is Hamlet's skepticism and imaginative curiosity. Both men hope to discover or verify certain facts about another individual, and both are willing to use deception to learn those facts. In this they are similar. But what differentiates them is Hamlet's persistent effort to evaluate the moral legitimacy of what he sees. Polonius accepts things at face value. What he sees is assumed to be true. It is the corrupt king who evaluates the facts Polonius brings him. Throughout, Polonius remains remarkably incurious about why the king would care to know these things about Hamlet. Like the others inhabiting Claudius's court, he gives no thought to the peculiar circumstances of Old Hamlet's death and the sudden remarriage of Gertrude. Lacking sufficient curiosity to dig below surface appearances, Polonius sails glibly through life without a functional moral compass, which makes him a useful tool for a man like Claudius. Hamlet understands such men, which allows him to toy, at times, with Polonius, with Rosencrantz and Guildenstern, and with Osric, that fop who appears at the end to lure the prince into the fateful duel with Laertes. Osric has removed his hat during an ostentatious bow to Hamlet:

> Osr.   Sweet lord, if your lordship were at leisure, I
>   should impart a thing to you from his Majesty.

137

Ham.	I will receive it, sir, with all diligence of spirit. Put your bonnet to his right use, 'tis for the head.
Osr.	I thank your lordship, it is very hot.
Ham.	No, believe me, 'tis very cold, the wind is northerly.
Osr.	It is indifferent cold, my lord, indeed.
Ham.	But yet methinks it is very sultry and hot for my complexion.
Osr.	Exceedingly, my lord, it is very sultry—as 'twere—I cannot tell how. (5.2.89-99)

Hamlet has seen fit to mock Polonius in the same manner as they look at clouds together. He also mocks Rosencrantz and Guildenstern with the musical pipe whose stops they are unable to play. He does so because all of them willingly show deference to authority regardless of its moral legitimacy. They turn whichever way the wind blows. Men like Claudius have no problem manipulating truth to their advantage, and it is men like Polonius, Rosencrantz and Guildenstern, and Osric who, eager for favor or advancement or importance, enable those manipulators.

None of this applies to Hamlet, whose imaginative curiosity and whose skepticism not only make him suspicious of his father's death and his mother's remarriage but is evident in all his ruminations about the ghost, man's nature, death, and the hereafter. That intelligent curiosity is married to a healthy skepticism about what is true, and this combination is precisely why Claudius cannot bend Hamlet to his will, why Hamlet is such a serious danger to the king. Not only will Hamlet not manipulate truth but he is steadfast and relentless in searching for the genuine. Like all men in a fallen world, he is susceptible to his emotions. He makes mistakes and misjudgments. But there is an authenticity to his search and in his passionate arguments, as shown by his effort to reform his mother's behavior, that Polonius will never have. Because of his unwavering devotion to the truth, Hamlet will succeed in bringing what was once hidden out into the open. Though both men have similar missions, Polonius lacks the necessary character to uncover anything beneath surface appearances.

The king, of course, is at the center of what's hidden. Cognizant of his sin and therefore insecure about his moral authority, Claudius is unable to openly punish Hamlet for Polonius' murder as a legitimate king would. So he continues to resort to subterfuge, sending the prince off to England along with a sealed letter that instructs the recipients to execute Hamlet upon his arrival. Part way into the voyage, however, Hamlet discovers the letter, rewrites it so that his escorts, Rosencrantz and Guildenstern, would be executed in his stead, and then reseals the letter with the royal stamp he happened to have with him. Pirates then intercept his ship and with their help he makes his way back to Denmark. The impact of these miraculous events, which alleviate all of Hamlet's anxieties about revenge, is enormously significant.

The change in his demeanor is unmistakable. Back in Denmark, he reveals these events to his friend, Horatio, who warns Hamlet to be vigilant during the supposedly friendly duel with Laertes. Unaware that Claudius and Laertes have conspired to use the duel to eliminate him once and for all, Hamlet expresses a new sense of peace:

> Hor: If your mind dislike anything, obey it. I will
>   forestall their repair hither, and say you are not fit.
> Ham: Not a whit, we defy augury. There is special
>   providence in the fall of a sparrow. If it be [now],
>   'tis not to come; if it be not to come, it will be
>   now; if it be not now, yet it will come—the
>   readiness is all. Since no man, of aught he leaves,
>   knows what is't to leave betimes, let be.
>   (5.2.217-24)

Almost all interpretations agree that Hamlet is somehow different after the aborted trip to England, but the exact nature of that change is a matter of much debate. Bloom, who acknowledges the gospel allusion, suggests that for "Hamlet there is nothing but the readiness, which translates as a willingness to let everything be, not out of trust in Yahweh but through a confidence in a final consciousness. That consciousness sets aside both Jesus's Pharisaic trust in the resurrection of the body and also the skeptical reality principle of annihilation" (422). Occupying a state of neither "denial nor affirmation," Hamlet, Bloom continues, has nothing left but readiness. What this explanation means, however, seems especially obscure and does little to help us decipher Hamlet's state of mind.

Other accounts avoid Bloom's mysticism and find more pragmatic explanations. In his *The Question of Hamlet*, for example, Harry Levin concludes that, though the sparrow reference from the gospels suggests an awareness of "divine immanence," Hamlet "waxes increasingly fatalistic as he approaches the crisis, and the same speech culminates with one of his stoical echoes from Montaigne: '. . . what is't to leave betimes?' His speculative questions have been reduced to the practical question of timing. . . ." (101). In effect, Levin says, the passage implies Hamlet's acceptance of his imminent death and that, as a result, any excuse for not imposing the justice Claudius deserves has vanished. All that remains is figuring out how to implement that justice. Because Hamlet does not have nor seek any control over subsequent events, however, Levin's explanation does not satisfactorily account for the events that unfold.

For Shakespeare's Christian audience, however, the meaning of the text would have been obvious as well as profound. Emblematic of every living being's journey through life, the predestined end of the voyage to England was death, which Hamlet temporarily avoids because of the intercession of divine providence. And what God provided was His sovereign protection, exactly what the reference to the sparrows in Matthew 10:29 promises. In that passage, Jesus reassures his followers of his heavenly father's faithful protection as they go out into the world to spread his message. "Are not two sparrows sold for a penny?" he asks rhetorically.

140

"Yet not one of them will fall to the ground outside your Father's care." That the sparrow still falls implies that the protection isn't from physical death but from spiritual harm, precisely the fear that kept Hamlet from crossing that boundary earlier in the play. Proof of divine protection was evident in the way that the hidden plot for his execution was revealed. Without any effort from Hamlet, the truth was exposed, the means to thwart the plot were available, and the intercession of the pirates assured his safety. None of this, Hamlet realizes, was mere chance or coincidence. Ultimately inescapable, death remains the final destination of every person's journey. All anyone can do on that journey is trust in God's provident care, trust that the sovereign God will lead him into the right decisions, and be spiritually ready for the inevitable.

The gospel reference is a reminder, then, that a sovereign God is cognizant of every detail of His creation, that He will guide and protect those who can discern the difference between what's good and what isn't. Assured of God's presence in his life, assured of His care and protection, assured that God himself would uncover Denmark's hidden truth, and assured that that revelation wouldn't require his effort, Hamlet is released from the prison of his anxiety, from the necessity of playing multiple roles, and from the administration of a justice that he was, by naturally limited insight and judgment, ill-equipped to enforce on his own. Like that image of Old Hamlet at the beginning of the play, a king who trusted in God's provident care as he fought the enemies of his realm in single combat, risking his own life in the process, Hamlet understands that he can trust the good intentions of a loving Father.

With anxiety about mistakes and lack of success dispelled, Hamlet is himself once more. Objecting to Laertes's extravagant sorrow at Ophelia's grave, he comes forward boldly, proclaiming, "This is I, Hamlet the Dane." Having handed over his problem to God in complete trust,

Hamlet regains his given identity and becomes God's instrument to impose the very justice he had previously assumed was his responsibility alone. That his death might now be imminent is no longer a cause for fear. He knows from whence his security and confidence come.

That Hamlet was saved from death once is a proof of a certain kind of salvation, of God's favor on his life, but that never meant that suffering or death could be avoided forever. Because of the event on the voyage to England, Hamlet's earlier fear of death and what follows have dissipated. Passing through the graveyard with Horatio, he encounters the gravedigger who unearths the skull of Yorick, once a court jester. "Where be your gibes now, your gambols, your songs, your flashes of merriment. . .?" he begins, before continuing. "Now get you to my lady's chamber, and tell her, let her paint an inch thick, to this favor she must come; make her laugh at that" (5.1.89-195). This sentiment is captured in the Medieval Latin phrase *memento mori*, which translates as "remember death," for it is coming. Prepare body and soul because death cannot be escaped. "The readiness," as Hamlet has said, "is all." The only recourse is to live according to the Creator's will and trust in God's overall plan for the life that has been given. If justice belongs to God alone, Hamlet is available to be His instrument. Nothing more is required of him. In this state of mind, he accepts the challenge to meet Laertes in what he thinks is a friendly competition with rapier and dagger. Calm, rational, and self-controlled, he is no longer afraid of mistakes, failure, or death. This is the peace that passes understanding.

Laertes's reaction to the deaths in his family contrasts sharply with Hamlet's far more Christian perspective. Hamlet questions, probes, makes mistakes, learns, and then changes when he understands that divine providence has favored him. Rushing home from France to avenge his father's murder, however, Laertes discovers that his sister has also drowned in a nearby lake, unable or unwilling to save herself. Like his

142

father, Laertes accepts Claudius's explanation for all this at face value and, in his rage, he vows to kill Hamlet, the man he believes is responsible for both pitiful deaths. Ever the shrewd opportunist, Claudius invokes the love of a son for a dead father to incite Laertes' anger:

> King. Laertes, was your father dear to you?
> Or are you like the painting of sorrow,
> A face without a heart?
> Laer. Why ask you this?
> King. Not that I think you did not love your father,
> But that I know love is begun by time,
> And that I see, in passages of proof,
> Time qualifies the spark and fire of it. . . .
> But to the quick of th' ulcer:
> Hamlet comes back. What would you undertake
> To show yourself indeed your father's son
> More than in words?
> Laer. To cut his throat i' th' church.
> King. No place indeed should murther sanctuarize,
> Revenge should have no bounds. (5.2.108-128)

Justifying an act of revenge he himself assiduously tried to avoid, the ironic hypocrisy of Claudius's argument is truly astounding, but it is enough to convince an impassioned Laertes, and, to hide their murderous intentions, the two men agree to poison a rapier and a cup of wine for the fencing match.

Inflamed by his passion for revenge, Laertes assumes he knows the truth of what happened and acts impulsively on that partial knowledge. It's the same mistake Hamlet made in the nunnery scene with Ophelia and in his mother's chambers when he accidentally dispatched Polonius. Unlike the prince, who learns from the rashness of these mistakes, Laertes's unthinking fury makes him the perfect revenger as well as a willing tool to implement the king's purposes. Hamlet also allows himself to become an instrument of justice, but his experience has taught him to choose the right master.

143

Enslaved by his passion and unwilling to observe and reason, Laertes is exactly what Hamlet is not, so he chooses to serve Claudius rather than a providential God. Hamlet's skepticism and learned self-control allow him to regain his natural identity, Laertes loses his to an unfettered desire for vengeance. He forsakes the role of son, brother, traveler, youth and, instead, thoughtlessly embraces the role of avenger and, consequently, becomes a wicked king's tool. He forsakes both his life and his very soul to satisfy that appetite for vengeance. As Hamlet's experience proves, it was a choice he didn't have to make.

In a universe where Providence continually works to implement its justice, the match between Laertes and Hamlet does not go as Claudius had planned. The queen drinks from the poisoned chalice before her husband can prevent her, and a wounded Hamlet, realizing his opponent's rapier is tainted, manages to return the favor to Laertes who, dying, confesses the entire devious plot to the assembled court. What was hidden is now known to all. Mortally wounded, poisoned, and face-to-face with death because of the king's treachery, Hamlet turns on his uncle-father, wounds him with the poisoned rapier, and forces him to drink from the poisoned cup. "Here, thou incestuous, murd'rous, damned Dane, drink off this potion! Is thy union here? Follow my mother!" Hamlet's pun on "union," a word that refers to the pearl used to poison the chalice of wine and to the marriage union, conjoins the notions of Denmark's poisonous infection, the illicit love between husband and wife, and this moment of death. The love that once bound the royal couple in a marriage founded on murder ironically binds them now in death, continuing the metaphorical conjunction of love and death already seen in *Romeo and Juliet* and which will appear in every Shakespearean tragedy thereafter.

So the royal pair who enjoyed their ill-gotten earthly gains are united once again in death, victims of the revenge that Laertes tried to carry out. Claudius, the man who uses

144

others to covertly implement his evil purposes, has finally been exposed, "hoist by his own petard." Besides the murder of a brother, he is responsible for the deaths of his wife and queen, his nephew-son, as well as his appointed assassin. With his secret sin finally exposed, the death of Claudius is less revenge than the enforcement of God's justice on a wicked and unrepentant man. As the final confirmation of God's favor on the prince, Hamlet's earlier desire to catch Claudius at a moment "that has no relish of salvation in't" has been answered affirmatively. Where the wages of sin are death, Hamlet's trust in a caring, protective God proves to be his salvation, and his friend Horatio proclaims that "flights of angels sing" the prince to his final rest.

Left behind to protect Hamlet's "wounded name," Horatio, the prince's steadfast friend who never had to play a false part, summarizes what led to this carnage:

> . . .Let me speak to th' yet unknowing world
> How these things came about. So shall you hear
> Of carnal, bloody, and unnatural acts,
> Of accidental judgments, casual slaughters,
> Of deaths put on by cunning and forc'd cause,
> And in this upshot, purposes mistook
> Fall'n on th' inventors' heads. . . . . (5.2.379-385)

Treachery was everywhere, Horatio asserts, but Hamlet's relentless questioning, his skepticism, his reluctance to act rashly, his steadfast search for truth, everything, in short, that makes him Hamlet, was anticipated in Providence's divinely ordained plan. While the wicked Claudius chose to murder a brother, Providence used Hamlet's many gifts in the service of divine justice, which the young, sometimes confused prince reluctantly did. Though Hamlet couldn't always avoid mistakes, he was willing to acknowledge them for what they were. After bringing his mother to repentance, he regrets the murder of Polonius:

> For this same lord,   [pointing at Polonius]

145

I do repent; but heaven hath pleas'd it so
To punish me with this, and this with me,
That I must be their scourge and minister.
(3.4.172-175)

And he regrets his mockery of Laertes's excessive grief at the grave of Ophelia. "I am very sorry, good Horatio, that to Laertes I forgot myself, for by the image of my cause I see the portraiture of his" (5.2.75-77). Though he has been assigned the difficult role of scourge and minister to purge Denmark of its corruption, he still manages to find ways to be objective about himself. All of this indicates why providential protection and grace fell upon him.

Chosen to be the divine instrument to punish Claudius for his sins, Hamlet perishes in that effort, but that does not mean Providence disappears from Denmark's affairs. With no one left to restore civil order in Denmark, Fortinbras, a relatively minor character in the play, is named king of Denmark. Like Hamlet, he had lost a father in the single combat with Old Hamlet mentioned in the first act, and his first inclination was to avenge that defeat by raising an army and invading Denmark. Ironically, he is dissuaded from that purpose by Claudius's very able diplomacy. But Fortinbras reappears midway through the play marching through Denmark on his way to some other battle. And he is present, on his way back from that campaign when the wholesale slaughter of the last act occurs. Therefore, when Fortinbras is named king of Denmark, the very objective of his initial inclination to avenge a father's death has also been achieved without his intervention. Providence had arranged events to bring about a desired end for him, just as it had for Hamlet.

Considered the first of Shakespeare's mature tragedies, *Hamlet* is also his last extended examination of revenge after *Titus* and *Rome and Juliet*, neither of which exhibit anything like the emotional and intellectual depth of this third, much better attempt. Whether *Hamlet* deserves to be included in the tragic genre, however, is not a settled matter.   Based on Aristotle's analysis of Greek tragedy in the *Poetics*, some might argue that Hamlet's fate does inspire the requisite pity and fear necessary for tragedy: pity for his prolonged confusion and suffering; fear that providence can sacrifice a man of his gifts to purge Denmark of another man's sin.   For some literary analysts, however, Christianity's promise of something better after this life's difficulties is incompatible with tragedy.   But so much of Shakespeare's background—his Latin-based education which introduced him to Seneca, his ignorance of far-better Greek tragedy, his investment in the company that performed his plays— suggests that, far more important than any literary theory, entertaining his audience was Shakespeare's paramount interest.   That *Hamlet* continues to puzzle, intrigue, challenge, and delight audiences four centuries later says something about the validity of that motivation.

At the same time, however, the plays that follow *Hamlet*, his comedy and his tragedy, show the influence of its moral and spiritual depth.   As the Christian influences already visible in *Hamlet* continue to mature, they allow Shakespeare to make increasingly subtle distinctions between characters and the emotional, moral, and spiritual values that drive their actions.   And rather than inhibiting the tragic, his awareness of a power working within characters to counteract the consequences of sin actually provides a foundation for the tragic, something that lesser artists of his era failed to grasp. The Greeks wrote very moving tragedies about people caught up unawares in the machinations of fate or the gods. Shakespeare's best tragedies, including *Hamlet*, show a similar awareness of man's intersection with a God whose plans and purposes are largely beyond human comprehension. It is that confrontation with the mysterious, the confusion and consequent suffering that follows from our inability to explain the predicaments of mortality, that make tragedy possible.

Though his trust in divine Providence resolves Hamlet's confusion and anguish, it is still difficult to distinguish between his very lethal actions in that final scene and revenge. Clearly, he accepts the role of Denmark's physician and surrenders his own will to the larger, mysterious force of divine justice, but for many, it's a distinction without a real difference. This, however, is precisely the problem that revenge embodies, and it is why crime and punishment have become the responsibility of the state rather than of individuals. That Shakespeare was unable to address this issue satisfactorily in a genre that obligated his protagonist to act unilaterally is perhaps understandable, but the dilemma may explain why he never revisited the genre.

As we move on to other plays, many of the same themes that make Hamlet's experience so rich and complex continue to be explored, among them the difficulty of distinguishing between what is true and what is not, the role of language in any effort to distinguish truth, the nature and consequences of human desire, the conflict between reason and emotion, between head and heart. *Hamlet* is indeed a watershed in dramatic literature and a watershed in Shakespeare's professional development. Immensely dramatic and suspenseful, nothing like it had ever appeared on the stage before, and with it came one of the most intriguing characters ever created. The play triumphs because nothing is avoided during its thoughtful examination of the human confrontation with sin, evil, and death. With this difficult, sometimes confusing, but always remarkable play, Shakespeare's genius had come into its own.

The Merchant of Venice

In 1592, theater-going Londoners were cramming into playhouses to see Christopher Marlowe's exciting offering, *The Jew of Malta.* Several years before, Marlowe's *Tamburlaine,* a two-part story about a Scythian shepherd who took up a sword to conquer the world, had delighted them with its rhetorical fireworks, and they were ready for more. Intriguing rumors swept through the city about his latest villain-hero, Barabas, whose name sounded eerily like the Jewish murderer freed in place of the condemned Jesus. When theater-goers finally entered the playhouse, they were thrilled to see Marlowe's protagonist introduced by the hated Italian, Machiavel, purveyor of conspiracy and poison. This was a villain they knew well. Convinced they were in for a delicious treat, they witnessed how Marlowe's Jew went on to manipulate his Christian and Turkish antagonists into various mortal intrigues until he was pushed into a boiling cauldron intended for his last set of victims. Throughout, Barabas's many enemies endure his melodramatic vitriol delivered with bombastic oratory. The Londoners absolutely loved it all. An immediate success, Marlowe's play appeared onstage many more times that decade and remained popular for the next fifty years.

The assumption that Marlowe's play influenced Shakespeare's *The Merchant of Venice* with its Jewish moneylender antagonist is difficult to avoid. While there are some superficial similarities, however, the two characters are quite different in essential ways. As Havelock Ellis indicates in his introduction to Marlowe's play, *The Jew of Malta* exhibits a

> vigorous design and rich free verse [that] show a technical advance on *Faustus.* . . . . But after the second act the play declines; the large conception of the Jew with his immense lust of wealth only rivaled by his love for his daughter, topples over into harsh and extravagant caricature. Marlowe seems to have

worked hastily here, and when Shakespeare, a few years later, took up the same subject. . . [in] *The Merchant of Venice* . . . his sweetness, humanity and humour, easily rises to a much higher pitch of art.   (xxvii)

As a dramatic character, Marlowe's Barabas begins well but declines into a cartoonish portrait of extreme and devious cruelty.   While parallels exist between both Jewish antagonists–the obsession with money, the insistence on the letter of the law, the dismay when a beloved daughter elopes with a Christian, and the desire to avenge perceived Christian grievances–Shakespeare's play is far more complex thematically and structurally, relying once again on a double plot.

Even though Shakespeare's story will prove to be far more sophisticated than Marlowe's, it still presents several problems that must be addressed. The first is the anti-Semitic aspects of Shylock's characterization. While offensive to modern audiences, those cultural attitudes cannot and should not be judged outside of the Elizabethan context from which neither Marlowe nor Shakespeare could escape. From a historical standpoint, neither playwright would have had any personal interaction with someone like Shylock since all Jews had been expelled from England in 1290. So, while bothersome, the anti-Semitic tropes in Shakespeare's play would have originated from widespread cultural or religious assumptions that had no chance of ever being modified by personal experience. Whatever their origins, however, those anti-Semitic elements of Shakespeare's story all too easily obscure Shylock's important thematic purpose, for the moneylender's attitudes toward money, toward the charging of interest, toward generosity elaborate Shakespeare's concept of romantic love, the subject of the play.

The second problem is what appears to be the absence of any clear relationship between the play's two disparate plots. In the main story, the poor but honorable Bassanio has heard of a beautiful, rich heiress in the distant city of Belmont

150

who can only marry when a man chooses correctly between three different metal chests, a lottery established by her late father to weed out unacceptable suitors. With the financial help of his friend, Antonio, the merchant of the play's title, he sets off to try his luck. Bassanio wins the lady's hand only to learn that his merchant friend back in Venice has defaulted on the loan that funded his successful courtship. Before the lovers have a chance to marry, they return to Venice to assist in Antonio's defense. Meanwhile, the subplot develops the story of the merchant's contract with the Jewish moneylender, Shylock, who loaned Antonio the funds for Bassanio's courtship of Portia, the rich heiress. When the merchant cannot repay his debt, Shylock wants to enforce the contract's provision to take a pound of the merchant's flesh. Shylock's insistence on the letter of the law horrifies the Christian community, but the dispute is resolved in a tense courtroom scene, Shylock is humiliated, Antonio is saved, and the play's various couples are free to celebrate their nuptials.

For many people, the main plot, where the wooing of the lady in Belmont occurs, seems quite unrelated to the subplot's contractual dispute between a merchant and a moneylender. Thematically, however, the play's cohesion derives from the notion of usury, which is the contractual obligation to repay the loaned amount with additional funds as a cost of borrowing. Though it may seem unnatural to think of love in transactional terms, the play's double plot establishes a contrast between usury, a form of giving to get, with the open-handed generosity that is the foundation of genuine love. It is a concept that has already made an appearance in two previous plays: Juliet wished she had more to give to her Romeo; and Hal willing paid both Falstaff's and his father's debt. Both instances demonstrate the paradox that giving away returns an abundance of unexpected riches that dwarfs the original gift. This is the concept explored in greater detail in *The Merchant*.

But the contrast has additional nuances that the play explores as well. For Shakespeare, it seems, an act of loving kindness can be seen as imposing a kind of emotional obligation on the receiver of that act. Now the giver may do so with or without expectation of a similar act of kindness in return. To expect something back diminishes the original act of kindness and is a form of emotional usury that differentiates this from genuine love. In contrast, genuine love will never expect anything in return for its kindness, which is given freely and without obligation. Throughout Shakespeare's plays, the very foundation of genuine love is a generous heart. It is why choosing the lead casket, identified by the phrase "Who chooseth me must give and hazard all he hath," is the correct choice for Portia's future husband. Offering something out of genuine love, without any expectation, entails the risk that the act may never be returned in kind. But that is what true love does repeatedly. It is constant in generous giving. But the miracle of love, if both partners share this understanding, is that their generosity multiplies the joys of love that both receive. The inevitable consequence of the right attitude in a loving relationship is abundant joy for both. Conversely, the inevitable consequence of the wrong attitude toward giving, embodied in the usurious moneylender, Shylock, is the absence of joy. It is this complex perspective of usury that ties the two plots of *The Merchant* together.

The Merchant, then, is another significant theatrical milestone in Shakespeare's development because it begins to work out ideas about love that had already appeared in many of his previous literary efforts. The underlying premise about generosity is derived from a familiar parable in Matthew 25: 14, which may have been a far more important influence on Shakespeare's play than Marlowe's *The Jew of Malta*. In that New Testament passage, a rich man gives gold to three different servants according to their abilities. The first two put their gold to work and increase what they were given. The third, however, buries his in the ground. After some time, when the master asks each servant the result, the first two are rewarded for their industry while the third is chastised for his fearful timidity. After his gold has been redistributed, the third servant is then cast out of the household. Though the punishment may seem harsh, the parable is meant to show that each person is generously provided with emotional and spiritual gifts that must be used rather than kept hidden. Blessings will multiply only when those God-given talents, including the ability to love, are put to use and the resulting profits —be those monetary, emotional, or spiritual— generously shared with others.

The morally problematic lack of generosity has already appeared in Falstaff, the self-indulgent child of *1 Henry 4*, who steals both time and treasure from the generous Prince Hal, who robs travelers of their purses, and who feeds the large appetites of his corpulent body. Though there isn't a malicious bone in his body, he consumes rather than gives. He refuses to function in any way that the world might profit from his talents. By indulging every desire for pleasure, Falstaff makes himself incompatible with love, duty, honor, and responsibility. Like the third servant in the parable, he squanders his true gifts.

As Shylock's story unfolds in *The Merchant*, his ungenerous money lending becomes a metaphor for a similar kind of self-love, which seeks to be enriched rather than to enrich. His greed is meant to be evaluated by the generosity of the Christian community in which he exists. While this contrast looks anti-Semitic over four hundred years later, the point being made about the nature of love is certainly not. As John Russel Brown notes:

> *The Merchant of Venice* presents in human and dramatic terms Shakespeare's ideal of love's wealth, its abundant and sometimes embarrassing riches; it shows how this wealth is gained and possessed by giving freely and joyfully; it shows also how destructive the opposing possessiveness can become,

and how it can cause those who . . . love to fight . . . for their existence. (74)

The subplot with Antonio, the merchant who borrows from Shylock and almost loses a pound of flesh as a result, indicates that generosity involves a very real risk that is only resolved by Christian mercy, a type of moral and spiritual generosity that establishes a reliable foundation for love. The two plots, one concerned with love, the other focused on money, make the consequences of these different attitudes toward generosity clear. Rather than being disparate and unconnected, therefore, the play's two plots develop a cohesion that depends on this confrontation between the generous and the ungenerous, between Antonio, Portia and Bassanio on one side and Shylock on the other.

This association between money and love had already appeared in Shakespeare's sonnets, among his earliest literary efforts. The first seventeen so-called procreation sonnets form an extended plea to a young man who reserves his beauty and virtue, losing the rewards that are only possible through love—marriage, children, companionship. The narrative voice in these poems is someone with a deeply felt need for the friendship of a man who feels no such need himself, either with the speaker or with the sonnets' nameless dark lady who also vies for the attention of this cold-hearted man. The dynamics of this relationship pose a problem for the narrator, who can either acknowledge his vulnerability or hide that away, like the treasure given to the parable's third servant. Ironically, the other, nameless man to whom the sonnets are addressed already lives precisely like that third servant:

> When the sonnets are aware that the friend's faults constitute a threat to the friendship, there is the recurrent accompaniment of ironic self-consciousness, arising, it appears, from a knowledge of the waywardness with which affection, in order to maintain its being in an imperfect world, bestows itself with imperfect cause. It must, at times, debase its currency in order to exist. The alternative to this dilemma is the economy of the

154

> closed heart. . . . The closed heart may be poor, but it is at ease. Those men are most content who, though they inspire affection in others, have no need of it themselves. . . . They have the power to hurt, but they are not hurt. Their happiness is their ignorance of their incompleteness. (Hubler 469-470)

This need to protect the self from any emotional harm is what Hubler means by the economy of the closed heart. Both the speaker and the dark lady are willing to accept this insular man just as he is, to debase the much purer currency of their own love, to use Hubler's phrase, because love simply demands this kind of self-sacrifice. It is the nature of genuine love. The other man, however, knows nothing about such generous giving of self. He is self-contained, self-absorbed, and thus insulated from love's risks as well as its rewards. Shakespeare seems to accept that, in a fallen world where sin is inevitable, choosing to love generously is a risk for many reasons, not the least of which is that the object of love may not be perfectly worthy. Love requires a courageous step into the unknown that some, like the other man addressed in the sonnets, hesitate to make. But the attempt to remain safe from love's risks is sinful because, rather than enhancing, it diminishes life. Like the third servant in the Matthew parable, the fear of loss, of risk, causes such men to wastes both life and time. They remain both ignorant and incomplete.

In *The Merchant,* money provides a symbolic objectification of both attitudes: either an open spirit of generosity that can give as well as receive love; or the desire to acquire and hoard a gift in hand, like the parable's third servant, out of a fear of losing what is already possessed. As metaphor, money elucidates the assumptions that correctly value love's wealth. To quote John Russel Brown again:

> It is sometimes argued that Shylock's affairs are so far removed in kind from the affairs of the lovers in Belmont that the play falls into two parts. But in one way the play is very closely knit, for, besides contrasting Shylock with Antonio, the discussion about usury is yet another contrast between him and

155

Portia and Bassanio. As we have seen from the sonnets . . ., Shakespeare saw love as a kind of usury, and so in their marriage Bassanio and Portia put Nature's bounty to its proper 'use'. Shylock practices a usury for the sake of gain and is prepared to enforce his rights; the lovers practice their usury without compulsion, for the joy of giving. (64)

In a play far more morally nuanced than Marlowe's, *The Merchant* continues to elaborate the financial metaphor first seen in the sonnets. It must be admitted, however, that Shakespeare's reliance on such an esoteric symbol does indeed threaten the play's cohesion. Perhaps it is not surprising, then, that the play has been variously labeled a melodrama, a "problem play," or worse, a failed comedy.

Both of the play's lovers, Bassanio and Portia, must learn to properly evaluate what they desire and why they desire it. While neither of them initially enters the experience unblemished, the casket lottery begins to untangle the moral complexities of romantic love for both. Bassanio, the beleaguered male lover, has traveled to Belmont to woo Portia, a beautiful and rich young heiress. Originally, his motive for this venture was to revitalize his "disabled estate" which he had squandered "by . . . showing a more swelling port than [his] faint means would grant continuance" (1.1.123-125). Whether he was overly generous or, like Falstaff, an extravagant, self-indulgent spendthrift isn't clear, but Portia's wealth is what draws him toward Belmont. So at first, his motivation is at least partly gain, not unadulterated, selfless love.

But Bassanio is changed by his encounter with Portia. No longer motivated by her financial wealth, he quickly grasps the essential point of the lottery's relatively straightforward rules. Each prospective husband has one chance to make the right choice among the three chests: one of gold, one of silver, one of lead. Each casket has a cryptic hint suggesting what is hidden inside. For the gold, the hint is "Who chooseth me shall gain what many men desire." For the silver, it is "Who chooseth me shall get as much as he deserves." For the third, lead chest, it reads "Who chooseth me must give and hazard all he hath." After the Prince of Morocco, who selects the gold chest, and the Prince of Aragon, who chooses the silver both fail, we see Bassanio (who is ignorant of the other suitors' choices) select the lead casket and win Portia's love. The first two suitors fail because they choose based on what they believe they will get or gain from the marriage. Bassanio succeeds because he alone recognizes the truth embodied in the lead chest, that, to win at love, a person must give and hazard all. The prospect of love changes him. Inspired by Antonio's generosity, he too is now ready to risk giving selflessly and unreservedly. By the merchant's example, he has learned the essential quality of a truly loving heart. His comfort with that kind of generosity is the reason he is the right husband for Portia.

Like Bassanio, Portia will also be transformed by genuine love. Not a single gallant from the parade of suitors that came before Bassanio understood love well enough to solve the lottery puzzle, and their failures make her irritable and disconsolate. Not understanding the purpose of her father's lottery, she sees it as an unnecessary hindrance to her right to choose a mate. Before Bassanio, she is "aweary of this great world" because she "may neither choose who [she] would nor refuse who [she] dislike[s]" (1.2.24-25). In conversations with her handmaiden, Nerissa, she mocks her failed suitors, indicating that "there is not one among them" whom she would miss. Unwilling, at first, to trust nature's benevolent power working through love, she succumbs to bitter resentment of the men who seem to control her fate.

Bassanio changes all that. As he contemplates which casket to choose, she reveals her overflowing feelings in an aside to the audience that is very much like the Juliet who has come to fully appreciates Romeo's love. Portia feels the excess of her own emotions:

O love, be moderate, allay thy ecstasy,

> In measure, rain thy joy, scant this excess!
> I feel too much thy blessing; make it less,
> For fear I surfeit. (3.2.111-114)

Now, instead of dearth, Portia's words reflect abundant emotion, blessings in excess of expectations. This is the nature of the love she hopes to share with the man who has already captured her heart, even before he participates in the casket lottery. Like a cloud heavy with life-giving moisture, she can barely contain her desire to shower this love upon him. And when he chooses correctly, she promises to pour down abundant love into his life. The language of accounting and finance links this speech to the play's central metaphor. The language is very much like Juliet's:

> You see me, Lord Bassanio, where I stand,
> Such as I am. Though for myself alone
> I would not be ambitious in my wish
> To wish myself much better, yet for you,
> I would be trebled twenty times myself,
> A thousand times more fair, ten thousand times more rich,
> That only to stand high in your account,
> I might in virtues, beauties, livings, friends,
> Exceed account. But the full sum of me . . .
> Is an unlesson'd girl, uschool'd, unpractic'd,
> Happy in this, she is not yet so old
> But she may learn. . . .
> Myself, and what is mine, to you and yours
> Is now converted. (3.2.149-167)

The financial imagery she employs emphasizes an unimaginable multiplication of tangible and emotional wealth that she would gladly deposit into her future husband's account. In contrast to the interest Shylock charges on his loans, this is the paradoxical usury of true love. Rather than ignored, or demanded, or seized, or taken, or somehow forced, genuine love is instead given away freely. The miracle is that, as a result of giving it away freely, without expectation, the

158

fruits of love continue to multiply. With it comes the promise of friendship, joy, commitment, marriage, union, and children. Like Bassanio and Antonio both, Portia personifies the open heart, the one willing to use all her gifts to enrich the beloved without any expectation of recompense.

These lovers, then, have come to an experience of and an appreciation for what John Russell Brown terms love's wealth, which Portia eagerly wants to give away to her beloved. The lavish richness of Portia's joy following Bassanio's lottery success has its metaphorical equivalent in the financial well-being of the Venetian merchant, Antonio, whom Shakespeare has honored in the play's title. Because the intrigue between Shylock and Antonio becomes a demonstration of both kinds of wealth, the financial and the emotional, it very neatly unifies the play's two plots. Despite having all his assets tied up with multiple commercial voyages, Antonio agrees to assist his friend Bassanio's effort to win Portia's love, and he offers this assistance with no assurance or expectation of compensation in return.

The sincerity of that generosity becomes clear when, after his default, he appears to have lost his legal case to Shylock. Prepared for the death that surely would follow the extraction of that contractual pound of flesh, he refuses to blame Bassanio for his predicament:

> Bassanio, fare you well,
> Grieve not that I am fall'n to this for you;
> For herein Fortune shows herself more kind
> Than is her custom. It is still her use
> To let the wretched man outlive his wealth,
> To view with hollow eye and wrinkled brow
> An age of poverty; from which ling'ring penance
> Of such misery doth she cut me off. (4.1.265-272)

This refusal to blame his friend is Antonio's final gesture of generosity. Because he is a "wretched man" who has "outlive[d] his wealth," he argues, death is preferable to years of poverty. Antonio's generosity never expected any reciprocity and carries with it, therefore, no hint of his friend's culpability. His gift has been freely given. And, in Shakespeare's very Christian world, that generosity is rewarded. A loving gift grounded in selfless generosity, it inspires an unlooked-for and unexpected return on his investment. Portia, whose life has been transformed as a result of the merchant's generosity, will now offer all the treasure in her possession to save Antonio's life. In contrast to the Shylock transaction, usury plays no part in the generosity exhibited by either Antonio or Portia. They are willing to give all without any expectation of return.

Once the issue of their mutual love is settled by the casket lottery, news of Antonio's predicament reaches the two lovers in Belmont. His ships now lost at sea, he has defaulted on Shylock's loan and stands at death's doorstep because the moneylender demands his pound of flesh. When Portia learns of the reason for Antonio's contract with the moneylender, she vows to pay off the merchant's debt, even if it takes treble the original amount to satisfy Shylock's demands. Because the merchant's generosity led to true love, the financial and emotional debt Bassanio incurred is now being abundantly repaid in kind. Postponing their wedding night, Portia sends her new husband to save Antonio with the anticipated funds and a ring he vows never to lose. To ensure Antonio will survive his trial, though, Portia and her maidservant Nerissa disguise themselves as young law clerks and set off for Venice. Both her money and her time are now invested in the effort to save Bassanio's benefactor. Not only has Antonio's generosity opened Portia's heart to love, it inspires her to return his original largesse with even more lavish generosity. The generosity she extends to her husband's benefactor confirms that she has fully grasped the importance of love's wealth. Her transformation is complete.

Shylock, however, operates by an entirely different calculus. Any money he lends out must be increased by the interest he charges. His assets, used solely for his own benefit, include no measure of generosity. For him, wealth is determined by the number of ducats in his account. Like Portia's failed suitors, he is motivated by gain, and he relies on the law, his contracts, to mitigate any risk.

That same lack of generosity is also evident in his attitude toward food, which is Falstaff's currency as well. Launcelot, his servant, complains that he is constantly famished while in Shylock's employ. Shylock, in turn, warns Launcelot, who is about to change masters and become the servant of the nearly penniless Bassanio, that he will no longer be able to "gormandize, as thou hast done with me." In one of the play's many paradoxes, Shylock's material wealth leads to emotional and spiritual privation while Bassanio's poverty is rewarded with Portia's abundant wealth. Within the play's elaborate financial metaphor, Shylock's covetousness is a kind of spiritual scarcity that leaves him, in the end, poor, defeated, and alone.

Christian reactions to the practice of usury, in fact, have ignited his hatred of the merchant Antonio. A creature of the closed heart, he hid that hatred during the contract negotiations with the merchant. The provision of that agreement is so absurd and Shylock's assurances so equivocal that Antonio signs the contract. But the contract's terms have been structured to satisfy Shylock's appetite for revenge on the Christian whose generosity assisted other debtors and thus precluded any of Shylock's profit from usury. As Antonio himself acknowledges, he often helped others who defaulted on Shylock's loans:

> I oft deliver'd from his forfeitures
> Many that have at times made moan to me;
> Therefore he hates. (3.3.22-24)

But Shylock's hatred has another source, one that implicates the supposedly virtuous Christians. While opposition to usury is the proximate cause of the Jew's hatred, that animosity is multiplied further by Christian mistreatment of the moneylender, which Antonio does not deny. "You call'd me dog for lending with interest," Shylock concludes. To which the merchant replies, "I am as like to call thee so again, to spet on thee again, to spurn thee too." While the words shock, Shylock's grievances in a purportedly Christian society are real enough, and Antonio's predicament should remind his audience of the dangers of such moral complacency.

Still, the moneylender uses the bad behavior of his Christian neighbors to rationalize his desire for vengeance, and that desire precludes any inclination he might have toward mercy or forgiveness. His desire to acquire more for himself, to become enriched at the expense of others, or to satisfy his hunger for revenge are all evidence of an ungenerous spirit. Both sins are cut from the same cloth. And without that spirit of generosity, Shylock cannot possibly fathom the universal need for mercy. The pound of flesh, therefore, cannot be construed simply as valid repayment for a debt owed. It becomes a test of Shylock's willingness to generously extend to others without expectation of repayment, and, unlike Antonio, he utterly fails the test. And Shylock fails because, as Paul reminds his Jewish brethren throughout the New Testament, he is bound to the law without grasping the spirit of the law.

For Shylock, the repayment of debts is purely transactional. Where a dispute arises, the original contractual obligation must be supported by the implementation of lawful justice. Like his version of religion, he is prone to a legalism that has no room for error or forgiveness. The law is the letter of the law, no more nor no less. Failure to meet its obligations brings condemnation. Confident of his rights, he brings his case against Antonio before the Duke of Venice, a Christian, for resolution. Everyone close to the merchant pleads his case, but Shylock is adamant, and he begins pointing out the hypocrisy of his Christian audience:

What judgment shall I dread, doing no wrong?

162

> You have among you many a purchas'd slave,
> Which like your asses, and your dogs and mules,
> You use in abject and in slavish parts,
> Because you bought them. Shall I say to you,
> "Let them be free! Marry them to your heirs!
> Why sweat they under burthens? Let their beds
> Be made as soft as yours, and let their palates
> Be seasoned with such viands"? You will answer,
> "The slaves are ours." So do I answer you:
> The pound of flesh which I demand of him
> Is dearly bought as mine, and I will have it.
> If you deny me, fie upon your law! (4.1.89-101)

In Shylock's mind, possession and ownership of wealth incurs inalienable rights over what is owned, be those possessions slaves or ducats or usurious interest. The same logic applies to the implied wealth of his contract with Antonio or any other debtor. What he is owed belongs to him. If the debt cannot be repaid, the law should remedy the loss according to the agreed-upon contract. In this case, the remedy is a pound of the merchant's flesh.

Part of Shylock's charm, if it can be called that, is his willingness to confront his Christian accusers with their hypocrisy, to extend the skewed logic of their worst behavior to his advantage. Viewed as property, the "slaves" they hold have no rights, so neither does Antonio outside the obligations of the contract. Moreover, Christian insults have grievously offended the moneylender:

> Signior Antonio, many a time and oft
> In the Rialto you have rated me
> About my moneys and my usances.
> Still have I borne it with a patient shrug
> (for suff'rance is the badge of all our tribe).
> You call me misbeliever, cut-throat dog,
> And spat upon my Jewish gabardine,
> And all for use of that which is mine own. . . .
>   (1.3.106-113)

Shakespeare deliberately humanizes Shylock by acknowledging legitimate causes for his anger toward Antonio and other like-minded Christians. Though Shylock wants to protect and enhance "that which is mine own," Shakespeare also refuses to hide his perpetual humiliation at Christian hands. Soon after the contract has been signed, one of Antonio's friends questions Shylock about the odd prospect of taking a pound of flesh for a defaulted loan. The moneylender's reply is both ominous and understandable, presaging his arguments later in court:

> I am a Jew. Hath not a Jew eyes? Hath not a Jew hands, organs, dimensions, senses, affections, passions; fed with the same food, hurt with the same weapons, subject to the same diseases, healed by the same means, warmed and cooled by the same winter and summer as a Christian is? If you prick us do we not bleed? If you tickle us do we not laugh? If you poison us do we not die? And if you wrong us shall we not revenge? If we are like you in the rest, we will resemble you in that. If a Jew wrong a Christian, what is his humility? Revenge. If a Christian wrong a Jew, what should his sufferance be by Christian example? Why, revenge. The villainy you teach me I will execute, and it shall go hard but I will better the instruction. (3.1.49–61)

Along with the hammering cadence of basic human qualities shared by both Jew and Christian alike, the simmering anger, the wounded sense of chronic injustice is unmistakable. The injury of his eye must be redressed by an equivalent injury to the eye of the perpetrator. The legalistic logic of equivalency fuels his desire for revenge.

But, ultimately, the play refuses to excuse Shylock's unwillingness to convert his ungenerous heart, though it allows him to do so. As presented, Shylock's character validates the truth of Matthew 6:21 which is a reminder that wherever a person's treasure lies, there his heart will be also. When Shylock's daughter, Jessica, runs away with the Christian, Lorenzo, the Jew's response is reported by the minor character Solanio. Shylock's dismay indicates what he truly values. "I never heard a passion so confus'd," Solanio begins,

> So strange, outrageous, and so variable
> As the . . . Jew did utter in the streets.
> "My daughter! Oh, my ducats! O, my daughter!
> Fled with a Christian! O, my Christian ducats!
> Justice! The law! My ducats, and my daughter!
> A sealed bag, two sealed bags of ducats,
> Of double ducats, stol'n from me by my daughter!
> And jewels, two stones, two rich and precious stones,
> Stol'n by my daughter! (2.8.12-21)

Though grief for the loss of a daughter and for the loss of his ducats and jewels are comingled, more importance is given to the financial loss. Jessica leaves a greedy father for love. Though the ducats were inexcusably stolen, the transfer of wealth from an avaricious father to a daughter willing to risk his ire for love becomes a symbolic statement of the moral values that operate in each of their lives. As the hoarder, Shylock laments lost wealth. As the lover, Jessica takes wealth to share with her beloved. Even when Shylock loses a daughter to love, his primary concern is for his stolen treasure. That's what his avaricious heart really values.

In the world of commerce and finance, notions of ownership and possession require the implementation of justice, for whatever is possessed can be stolen, and whatever is stolen must somehow be redressed. Unlike the logic of love, where mutual giving and taking interact both freely and symbiotically, Shylock's transactional thinking requires the law's strict implementation of justice to protect what is contractually his. Because of contract and law, he takes no risks. Unlike a relationship of genuine love, which expects no compensation for emotional risk, Shylock is protected. His argument at Antonio's trial rests on the notion that, without the law, the contracts that form the basis of Venetian wealth would prove worthless. On that basis alone, he argues, his contract with Antonio should be honored. He deserves his pound of flesh. His perspective of the world is transactional and materialistic. Thwarted greed, in fact, provoked his original anger with Antonio, and that avariciousness allows no room for generosity and, consequently, no room for mercy, since both risk giving something away freely.

Dejected by the Jew's strict transactional logic, Antonio prepares himself for an agonizing death. But now comes the counter-argument. Disguised as the law clerk, Bellario, Portia reminds the assembled court that the law and justice are not the only considerations here:

> The quality of mercy is not strain'd,
> It droppeth as the gentle rain from heaven
> Upon the place beneath. It is twice blest:
> It blesseth him that gives and him that takes,
> 'Tis mightiest in the mighty, it becomes
> The throned monarch better than his crown.
> His sceptre shows the force of temporal power,
> The attribute to awe and majesty,
> Wherein doth sit the dread and fear of kings;
> But mercy is above the sceptered sway,
> It is enthroned in the heart of kings,
> It is an attribute to God himself;
> And earthly power doth then show likest God's
> When mercy seasons justice. Therefore, Jew,
> Though justice be thy plea, consider this,
> That in the course of justice, none of us
> Should see salvation. We do pray for mercy,
> And that same prayer doth teach us all to render
> The deeds of mercy. (4.1.184-202)

From the Christian perspective, the law is never sufficient. "Treat every man according to his deserts," says Hamlet, "and who shall 'scape whipping?" Everyone is guilty. Everyone needs mercy. When "mercy seasons justice," Portia argues, the resulting compassion will reflect the nature of God himself. If only justice mattered to God, no one would ever

166

deserve salvation, so to reflect God's true nature, mankind, created in His image, must also judge with mercy. Because sin can never be removed without God's forgiveness, any demand for earthly justice must be leavened with similar mercy. Like the rain from heaven, she argues, mercy is a gift that, when given away, blesses both the giver and the receiver. In this, generosity, mercy and love are all part of the same spirit.

None of this makes much sense to a man like Shylock whose usury benefits him alone. Because mercy, like love, flows from a generous heart, Shylock cannot fathom her argument. Seeing that the moneylender refuses to alter his position, the disguised Portia proceeds to apply justice in strict accordance with Shylock's contract. According to Bellario's interpretation, the agreement allows Shylock, fittingly enough, to take his pound of flesh from "nearest the merchant's heart." Ironically, the ungenerous money lender is legally entitled to, quite literally, dishearten the generous, open-hearted merchant. Encouraged, Shylock praises the wise law clerk, clinging stubbornly to the justice that promises Antonio's pound of flesh.

With vengeance tantalizingly close to fulfillment, Shylock cannot resist temptation. The desire to avenge Antonio's habit of lending to friends without interest blinds Shylock to even the smallest demonstration of mercy. When the Duke asks Shylock to employ a surgeon to staunch the flow of blood after the grim implementation of his contract, the moneylender objects even to this small gesture of mercy because it is "not in the bond." But it is this insistence on the absolute letter of the law that provides Bellario with the solution to save Antonio's life. After agreeing that Shylock's bond allows him to take a pound of flesh, the law clerk goes on:

> Tarry a little, there is something else.
> This bond doth give thee here no jot of blood;
> The words expressly are "a pound of flesh."

Take then thy bond, take thou thy pound of flesh,
But in cutting it, if thou dost shed
One drop of Christian blood, thy lands and goods
Are by the law of Venice confiscate
Unto the state of Venice. (4.1.305-312)

Faced with this insoluble dilemma, Shylock finally relents, but now it is Bellario who insists on the letter of the bond. It is the bond, she insists, or nothing. When the moneylender is ready to leave the court empty-handed, the disguised Portia levels the next charge: Shylock plotted the death of a Venetian citizen, a crime punishable by forfeiture of his wealth to the victim and the possibility of a death sentence. Though the duke mercifully spares the Jew's life, he rules that Shylock must immediately give away half his wealth to his runaway daughter and her Christian husband. He must also promise to make them his heirs after his death. But the final humiliation is that Shylock must convert to the Christian faith. By insisting on the letter of the bond and refusing to supply any mercy to a detested foe, Shylock loses everything he once held so dear. Because hatred for his Christian antagonists had sealed his heart against love and mercy, virtues dependent on a spirit of generosity, Shylock relentlessly feeds his desire for vengeance and loses everything in that quest. He is exactly like the princes who choose the gold and silver caskets, believing they would obtain what they desired or deserved. All of these failures demonstrate the sad consequence of such self-indulgent avariciousness.

The anti-Semitism in such a thorough humiliation of the Jew is, as Bloom suggests, impossible to ignore (171). But Shakespeare is actually quite even-handed throughout the play, including this courtroom drama where Christian arguments are tinged with a hint of additional hypocrisy. In the past, Shylock has been wronged by people who now profess a belief in the value of mercy and forgiveness. How the trial unfolds qualifies the virtues of the courtroom victors and their application of Christian values. For just as the play's villain rationalizes his desire for vengeance by reminding his fellow citizens of their sins, these Christians apply morally sound arguments to rationalize saving the life of a Christian who, according to Shylock, probably owns slaves and spits on a Jew he despises. No one in this courtroom is above reproach. Though Shylock's greed and his desire for revenge are rooted in comic villainy, he is presented in a way that reminds us of his basic humanity. That his Christian neighbors are blind to that fact and to their culpability in his anger and his desire for vengeance is intended to temper any delight their triumph over the ungenerous moneylender might inspire.

The *Merchant* presents us with one additional problem: what to make of the ring intrigue. While this last puzzle gently pulls the audience back into the mode of comedy, it is a problem for both plot and theme. The resolution of Shylock's threat occurs in Act IV, after which he disappears. The remainder of the play, Act V, is used to resolve the issue of Portia's ring, given to her husband, Bassanio, who swears to never part with it. Her maid, Nerissa, receives the same vow from her new husband, Gratiano, to whom she has also given a ring. But after Shylock's trial, the two women, disguised as law clerks, refuse any other payment for their legal wisdom except the rings, which both men have pledged to keep forever. Full of gratitude for their friend Antonio's narrow escape, the men can hardly refuse this request, which sets up the play's final conflict. With the play's only villain already dispatched, the final act can seem both thematically unrelated and anticlimactic. It is neither, of course. As John Russell Brown observes:

> Not recognizing Portia in the young lawyer, Antonio and Bassanio cannot know how deeply he [Bellario, the disguised Portia] is satisfied, how 'dearly' he has given; they do not know that he has acted with love's bounty. Portia chooses to bring this to their knowledge by the trick of asking Bassanio for the ring she gave him at their betrothal. At first he refuses because of his vow, but when he is left alone with Antonio, his love for this friend persuades him to send the ring to the young

169

> lawyer. This twist in the plot is resolved in the last act, and still further illustrates the kind of possession which is appropriate for love's wealth. (69)

The ring issue in the final act serves as a fitting coda to the theme of the open heart, which needs to be willing to risk and hazard all. As we have seen already, love's paradoxical logic proves that greed and possessiveness lead to deprivation, whereas giving and generosity are blessed with nature's full bounty. The husbands break their vows and give away their rings from a sense of gratitude and generosity. Since they give them to their wives disguised as law clerks, only the audience recognizes the false dilemma of the apparently broken vow.

That dilemma is dispelled when the two men return to their wives in Belmont where their little treachery is playfully uncovered with much bawdy innuendo from the women, which serves as a subtle promise of marriage's full richness. It also serves as a comment on the necessary balance required to preserve the marriage bond, again hearkening back to the Shylock subplot where a strict, legalistic adherence to the letter of a contract needs to be tempered by mercy and forgiveness. The husbands' sin of generosity to the law clerks who saved their friend deserves to be forgiven. Portia's speech on mercy ties Shylock's trial scene to this resolution of the ring intrigue. As John Russell Brown suggests, ". . . this last act is a fitting sequel to the discord of the trial scene where love and generosity confront hatred and possessiveness; it suggests the way in which love's wealth may be enjoyed continually" (70). That is, through forgiveness.

The Merchant is a good enough play that it can stand on its own, even without the money metaphor. Shylock, a sufficiently menacing villain, never topples over into the cartoonish, melodramatic figure that Marlowe's Barabas becomes. Shakespeare takes great pains to give him a recognizable human face. And the love story, with its crucial casket scene, has enough suspense to hold the attention of an

170

audience that doesn't care all that much about thematic cohesion. On stage, the two plots work well on their own. The play is entertaining and delightful. But the money metaphor greatly enriches the play's meaning and provides a thematic consistency that is otherwise lacking. A familiarity with Shakespeare's use of that metaphor earlier in his career lends credence to its use here, but he took a risk in making it the play's unifying concept.

Shakespeare seems to have understood that such an intensely personal metaphor could prevent an audience from grasping his purpose in using it, for it never appears again quite so explicitly. But genuine love is always associated with abundance and joy and remains a central concept in all subsequent plays. In the context of his entire canon, *The Merchant* is a seminal effort, exhibiting Shakespeare's ability to integrate image or metaphor into drama, pushing it into the realm of literature. As he does here, he continues experimenting with imagery to provide thematic unity without diminishing dramatic intensity. Because it demonstrates the inherent conflict between the kind of love that risks sacrificing self for another and the insular, selfish nature of sin, *The Merchant* also lays the intellectual and artistic groundwork for his later tragedies. The sonnets initiate this exploration of the open heart's difficulty with those self-possessed individuals who remain content to live with a closed heart. Though it has the structure and feel of the comic, *The Merchant* puts that conflict at the very center of its dramatic soul. Later tragedies, like *Othello, King Lear*, and *Antony and Cleopatra* will explore that conflict between the open and the closed heart further, emphasizing with stunning insight its many paradoxes and ironies.

In the next play, *Twelfth Night*, Shakespeare exhibits a much finer, more subtle comic touch that tones down the villainy and ramps up the zaniness. Nevertheless, it provides a heroine who possesses the same open-hearted desire for genuine, sacrificial love. Her misfortune is to fall in love with

171

a self-absorbed duke, only to become the object of un-looked-for affection herself. In *Twelfth Night*, the absurd randomness of love once again takes center stage, as it did in *As You Like It*, but many of the same themes seen in *Hamlet* and *The Merchant*—appearance and reality, sight and insight, open and closed hearts, and love's wealth—also make their appearance. An example of Shakespearean comedy at its best, *Twelfth Night* is both great drama and great literature.

Twelfth Night

In the much earlier comedy, *A Midsummer Night's Dream*, the fairy king Theseus has just witnessed the emotional mayhem unleashed by his protege´ Puck, a mischievous little sprite who has been sprinkling magic dust into the eyes of six paired young friends. Unbeknownst to all the young lovers, who had entered this enchanted forest for a bit of innocent fun, the magic in Puck's dust would cause the unsuspecting victim to sleep and, upon waking, to fall in love with the first being encountered. No one is spared. Puck's misbehavior eventually touches everyone, including the fairy queen, Titania, who falls in love with the rustic Bottom, already magically disfigured with an ass's head. Hilariously, she passionately declares her love for the transfigured Bottom with complete sincerity. Stroking his donkey ears as he brays for more hay, she croons:

> I pray thee, gentle mortal, sing again:
> Mine ear is much enamour'd of thy note;
> So is mine eye enthralled to thy shape;
> And thy fair virtue's force perforce doth move me
> On the first view to say, to swear, I love thee.
> (3.1.140-144)

The disparity between the emotion behind Titania's words and what the audience sees is hugely funny and tender, for it exaggerates what every lover somehow understands: that love's power magically transforms our vision of the beloved. Regardless of the reality visible to everyone else, the lover can only see beauty and virtue in the beloved. Not necessarily or altogether unfortunate, this blindness to reality can be one of love's miracles, a truth that adds depth and poignancy to Titania's words. Only vaguely aware of his disfigurement, Bottom's reply acknowledges the irrationality that seems an inherent element of love:

173

Methinks, mistress, you should have little reason for that: and yet, to say the truth, reason and love keep little company together nowadays; the more the pity that some honest neighbors will not make them friends.   (3.1.145-149)

For better or for worse, love often allows desire to overrule reason, unleashing the imagination, which is quite capable of creating a reality that reflects what the heart desires more than what the eye sees.

In the forest of *A Midsummer Night's Dream* where irrational love makes the irrational believable, Theseus is moved to observe that "the lunatic, the lover, and the poet are of imagination all compact." In the antics he witnessed that magical summer eve, imagination proved an ambivalent gift, and that insight is at the heart of *Twelfth Night* as well. Often considered Shakespeare's most mature comedy, this later play will bring a poet, a lunatic, and a thrall of variously motivated lovers into amusing conflict, all of which is fueled by imagination run amok. It's as if Shakespeare, recalling what Theseus said, wanted to expand further on that thought.

To modern audiences, the significance of this later comedy's title is obscure. But it is also the only one in the First Folio with an intentionally helpful subtitle: *Or What You Will*, which translates roughly as "what you can desire or imagine." The subtitle identifies the very human tendency to imagine ourselves in ways that are quite different from how we actually are. To a degree, everyone in the play is victimized by some form of self-deception. And Theseus-like, the audience watches them engaging in the same absurd role-playing that amused those Twelfth Night revelers. In varying degrees of self-awareness, every character assumes a role that obscures their real identity, either from others or from themselves.

Comedy, including Shakespeare's, comes in many flavors and forms, from light-hearted romantic comedy to the bitterly satiric. They differ primarily in how they view and accept human folly, which is always comedy's subject matter.

174

Light-hearted comedy tends to tolerate folly as understandably human and either forgivable or modifiable. Satire, on the other hand, considers folly a consequence of ignorance, stupidity, or maliciousness, none of which, from the perspective of satire, is redeemable or deserving of forgiveness. Shakespeare, who experimented with both types, seems to have been more adept at the romantic and light-hearted type than the satiric. Though one of this play's characters, the puritanical Malvolio, receives some harsh treatment, *Twelfth Night*'s atmosphere is more indicative of Shakespeare's breezy comic spirit. As Bloom notes in his chapter on the play, a live performance works best if it is acted with full-throttle zaniness. Like the final hours of the Christmas holiday season alluded to in the play's titles, *Twelfth Night* is meant to be good fun.

Nevertheless, all comedy implies a judgment of human folly. Even the gentler comedy of *Twelfth Night*, built on role-playing characters, is still making implicit judgments about which of their identities is better, the assumed one or the "real" one. The validity of that implied judgment is eventually confirmed when the deluded characters finally recognize the foolishness of their false posture and reassert a more genuine and life-affirming identity. The initial state only seemed normal but was actually an illusion, hiding what is eventually proven to be far more real and lasting.

As Northrop Frye observed, certain types of comedy have a natural movement that supports the rejection of folly and the acceptance of a more pragmatic reality:

> Thus the movement from *pistis* to *gnosis*, from a society controlled by habit, ritual bondage, arbitrary law and the older characters to a society controlled by youth and pragmatic freedom is fundamentally, as the Greek words suggest,   a movement from illusion to reality. Illusion is whatever is fixed or definable, and reality is best understood as its negation: whatever reality is, it's not that. Hence the importance of the theme of creating and dispelling illusion in comedy: the

175

> illusions created by disguise, obsession, hypocrisy, or unknown parentage. (*Anatomy* 169-70)

As seen in earlier plays like *As You Like It*, comedy establishes an initial state where characters are prevented from fulfilling some legitimate desire, usually for love and marriage, that the older generation resists because of some arbitrary law or social custom. In most comedies, everyone except the play's elders understands that these desires are necessary and good. This tension between restrictive elders and a younger generation driven by healthy desire is inherently dramatic and inherently funny. Because this tension between generations is almost universal, the audience participates in and is delighted by the defeat of whatever hinders the youthful effort to find life and joy. Ignorance or blindness gives way to enlightenment. This is what Frye means by the movement from *pistis* to *gnosis*, from ignorance to knowledge, from false to true, and from illusion to reality.

While Shakespeare's early comedies adhere closely to this formula, *Twelfth Night* eliminates the external obstruction altogether. Instead, the roles characters choose to play, sometimes unconsciously, serve to impede their romantic desires. The conventional comic movement toward self-fulfillment is internal and psychological rather than external and narrative. Rather than the defeat of an obstinate elder, *Twelfth Night's* comic movement is from self-deception toward self-awareness.

Given the play's complex story, that movement requires three interrelated plots. The main plot hinges on disguise which, as Frye notes, is one form of comic illusion. Two twins, Viola and Sebastian, have been shipwrecked and separated near Illyria where Duke Orsino thinks he's in love with Olivia, a rich heiress who has pledged to mourn her recently deceased brother for the next seven years. Her vow to mourn is, of course, the first obstruction. Since both twins believe the other has perished, Viola decides that, to survive in a strange land by herself, she must assume the disguise of a male page, take the name Cesario, and gain employment with the conventionally lovelorn Duke Orsino. Since the duke's object of affection, Olivia, falls in love with his emissary, the disguised Viola, her disguise becomes the second obstruction.

While all three characters pursue love based on a false premise, then, the disguised Viola becomes the crucial linchpin of the whole house of cards that each of them has helped construct. Until her true identity is revealed, love for each of them will remain random, absurd, and unrequited. As Frye indicates, it's a rule of comedy that characters are either disguised or assume a posture that thwarts the fulfillment of their desires. Because the false roles they play hide what is genuine, those postures must be exposed, mocked, and discarded before society can be renewed by love. Passing time eventually brings what's hidden out into the open, proving that love cannot flourish where pretense is tolerated.

This process is set in motion by Duke Orsino, who fancies himself the courtly lover pursuing an unattainable lady despite her consistent rejections of his fervent appeals. It is a pretense because Orsino is far more in love with the words and the posture of a courtly lover than he is with the women herself, a fact bourne out by his employment of an emissary to deliver his missives. He doesn't need to see her or to listen to her denials. In fact, her continual rejection of his overtures, which would eventually dissuade a normal person, actually serves to sustain his role-playing. In Theseus' triumvirate of mortal fools, Orsino imagines himself the poet.

The first subplot is designed to expose and mock the absurdity of these courtly lovers. It introduces Olivia's uncle, Sir Toby Belch, whose name implies his proclivity to an excess of food and drink, a predisposition that should remind us of another rogue hanger-on, Sir John Falstaff. Besides living off his rich niece's generosity, Sir Toby's principal occupation is swindling Sir Andrew Aguecheek, a companion willing to pay for advice that might help win Olivia's hand.

The witty, sophisticated Olivia, however, clearly has no conceivable interest in a bumbling, socially incompetent man like Sir Andrew, whose surname implies his tendency to flush a feverish red at the slightest provocation. Sir Toby, then, is a man who inhabits the same carefree, self-indulgent, morally oblivious universe that shelters Falstaff. It is a world, if Sir Toby had his way, of perpetual holiday like the one alluded to in the play's title. He is the vice figure who deceives his gull to fill his purse. He plays upon Sir Andrew's absurd dream of becoming Olivia's lover. This subplot mocks the foolish pretensions of Duke Orsino.

But into this happy world comes Sir Toby's nemesis, Olivia's puritanical steward, Malvolio, whose name purposely resembles the word "malevolent." Because he is responsible for running her household in an orderly manner, these two clash repeatedly until Sir Toby and his companions hatch a plot to convince Malvolio that Olivia, his wealthy employer, is secretly in love with him, an improbable impossibility. Both plots, therefore, contain characters whose passions spur their imaginations to pursue women who couldn't possibly return their affections. The absurdity of Malvolio's passion for his employer is also meant to mimic and mock the foolishness of the main plot's lovers. In Theseus' triumvirate of mortal fools, Malvolio is the lunatic, and his foolish pursuit of Olivia ends when Sir Toby and his screwball friends throw the steward into a darkened cellar, an Elizabethan remedy for the mad.

The final plot introduces Viola-Cesario's male twin, Sebastian, and his friend Antonio, who hides from the authorities because of a past military altercation with Duke Orsino's army. Unlike his ship-wrecked and disguised sister, Sebastian freely roams the city, which he does with the help of Antonio's financial generosity. That generosity establishes his thematic purpose, which is similar to the character of the same name in *The Merchant of Venice*. As in that play, a spirit of generosity becomes a necessary condition for genuine love.

It should be no surprise, then, that on one of Sebastian's excursions, he happens to cross paths with Olivia, the object of Orsino's affection. As Viola-Cesario's identical twin, he is astonished but receptive when the rich heiress, mistaking Sebastian for the duke's disguised page with whom she is in love, boldly confesses her affection. This is the irresistible, Ovidian power of love, and it is pointless to resist its power. But these events begin the process of discovery, and the three plots are brought to a comically satisfying resolution, replete with the necessary pairings of appropriate lovers. In Theseus' triumvirate of mortal fools, therefore, Sebastian functions as the lover, a man surprised and dazed by a beloved's unexpected declaration of devotion. The authenticity of what he experiences exposes the play's other lovers as pallid imitations of the real thing.

The sad irony of Orino's assumed role as poet is that, despite his obvious love for classical allusions and poetic tropes, he's an abject failure at achieving the goal he claims to want. From his very first speech, the pretense is evident in the language he uses, which is so artificial that any genuine feelings of love are crowded out. With a somewhat obscure and convoluted passage, he verbalizes those conventional but well-deserved feelings of despair. To relieve his melancholy, musicians are playing in the background, an auditory reference to music's power to soothe emotional discord:

> If music be the food of love, play on,
> Give me excess of it; that surfeiting,
> The appetite may sicken, and so die.
> That strain again, it had a dying fall;
> O, it came o'er my ear like the sweet sound
> That breathes upon a bank of violets. . . . Enough, no
>   more,
> 'Tis not so sweet now as it was before.
> O spirit of love, how quick and fresh art thou,
> That notwithstanding thy capacity
> Receiveth as the sea, nought enters there,
> Of what validity and pitch soe'er,

179

But falls into abatement and low price
Even in a minute. So full of shapes is fancy
That it alone is high fantastical. (1.1.1-15)

Because Orsino loves a metaphor, the passage needs a bit of careful parsing. Desire is first compared to a persistent hunger for food or music that will continue to intensify until satisfied by an excess of what it seeks. That image then reminds him of the vast seas, capable of swallowing whole ships, reducing the value of their rich cargo to nothing. It is excess alone, he goes on to suggest, that will eventually slake this kind of relentless appetite.

Now this may sound a bit like the language used by such admirable women as Juliet and Rosalind, but the difference between the metaphors of excess they use and this passage is that Orsino himself is the consumer of the surfeit. Whereas the women want to give the abundance that overwhelms them to the men they love, the despair, the appetite, the loss are all his alone. It's all quite dramatic, as if there is pleasure to be mined in the role of courtly lover being played. But Shakespeare is already preparing us for the right perspective on Orsino: when he compares his romantic desire to an insatiable appetite that must be fed, a thematic correlation to Sir Toby's compulsion for food and drink begins to take shape, and it becomes clear that compulsive, irrational desires rule both men. Self-absorbed and too easily pleased by the role of poet, Orsino mistakes the grand experience of his own passions for the far more fulfilling experience of genuine love.

As if to prove his poetic *bona fides*, Orsino concludes with a highly literary image from Ovid. The reference is to the hunter, Acteon, who had the misfortune of falling in love with Diana, the goddess of chastity, whom he accidentally saw bathing in a pool. Upset by the intrusion, she transforms him into a stag that is pursued and brought down by his own hounds. Similarly, Orsino's first sight of Olivia has transformed him into a victim of his own desires:

180

> O, when mine eyes did see Olivia first. . .
> That instant was I turn'd into a hart,
> And my desires, like fell and cruel hounds,
> E'er since pursue me. (1.1.18-22)

Even though Orsino sounds like a man tormented by love, his description of that experience is completely literary and artificial. If there is anything genuine here, it has been hidden beneath a veneer of poetic pretense.

As any actor would understand, the problem with playing a role is that the role can all too easily replace an authentic identity or, in the worst case, any grasp on reality. This appears to be true of Orsino, who mistakenly believes his beloved's persistent rejection reflects some problem with her rather than with the manner of his courtship.

> There is no woman's sides
> Can bide the beating of so strong a passion
> As love doth give my heart; no woman's heart
> So big, to hold so much; they lack retention. . . .
> But mine is all as hungry as the sea,
> And can digest as much. Make no compare
> Between that love a woman can bear me
> And that I owe Olivia. (2.4.93-103)

Completely lacking any self-knowledge, he arrogantly concludes women could never love with the intensity of male passion, an assertion that is thankfully confirmed by the play's female leads who, though equally susceptible to irrational love, are far more aware of what love actually looks, sounds, and feels like. The irony of his arrogant male assertion is that he says this to Viola-Cesario, who for some incomprehensible reason, has come to love him with a heart far more patient, dutiful, and consistent than his own. Blind to that truth by her disguise and his own illusions, Orsino will eventually learn that his extravagant view of male passion is completely misguided. Such male puffery will be thoroughly lampooned in the first subplot by the humiliation of Malvolio.

181

But men are not the only ones infected with pride. Olivia's vow to mourn her brother is equally artificial in its extravagance. By committing to a vow that would shape her destiny for the next seven years, she imposes an unnatural restriction upon her life that makes it impossible to respond to the unexpected. Believing she can completely control future events shows an unacknowledged pride that is slyly mocked by the simmering conflict between her freewheeling uncle, Sir Toby, and her puritanical steward Malvolio. In both circumstances, the urge to control creates the comic tension between an existing order and the pragmatic freedom, to use Frye's term, that tries mightily to subvert it. During one of Toby's rowdy, late-night sessions with his companions, Malvolio enters indignantly:

> My masters, are you mad? Have you no wit, manners, nor honesty but to gabble like tinkers at this time of night? Do you make an alehouse of my lady's house? . . . . Sir Toby, I must be round with you. My lady bade me tell you, that though she harbors you as her kinsman, she's nothing allied to your disorders. (2.3.86-97)

That accusation of madness will come back to haunt Malvolio, but Toby's reply to the steward's admonition identifies the tension between Malvolio's need for order and their exuberant freedom. "Art any more than a steward," he asks rather impertinently. "Dost thou think that because thou art virtuous there shall be no more cakes and ale?" Though he misunderstands the limitations of holiday freedom, the exact opposite of Olivia's assumption about control, Toby is at least partially right: Malvolio has confused order with virtue, and his effort to control their antics mimics his mistress's effort to control events in her life. Olivia's household, then, is emblematic of the tension that exists between order and the freedom to enjoy life, and, as such, it mirrors the incipient opposition between Olivia's effort to control her future and the disruptive force of romantic love that will soon engulf her.

182

Feste, one of Shakespeare's wise fools, tries to illuminate the absurdity of her vow. Like the fool in *King Lear*, his role in the play is to speak wisdom to the foolishness so prevalent in the play. When he first appears, he humorously tries to provoke Olivia into rethinking her vow to disengage from the world. She plays along:

> Fe. Good Madonna, give me leave to prove you a fool. . . .
> Oli. Make your proof.
> Fe. I must catechize you for it, Madonna. Good my mouse of virtue, answer me.
> Oli. Well, sir, for want of other idleness, I'll bide your proof.
> Fe. Good Madonna, why mourn'st thou?
> Oli. Good fool, for my brother's death.
> Fe. I think his soul is in hell, Madonna.
> Oli. I know his soul is in heaven, fool.
> Fe. The more fool, Madonna, to mourn for your brother's soul, being in heaven. Take away the fool, gentlemen.
> (1.5.57-71)

Feste's logic uncovers the absurdity of the vow: while it isn't wrong to mourn a dead brother, it risks making her look foolish, for what she doesn't see or understand yet can easily overturn good intention. Fortunately, Olivia accepts this catechism graciously. The wisdom of it becomes evident when love unexpectedly disrupts her effort to control her future.

The foolish vow begins to crack when Orsino's page comes to woo. Although Viola-Cesario has memorized the speech Orsino has prepared to win Olivia's love, his very conventional expressions of love fail to change her heart. Olivia implores the messenger to skip those trite phrases entirely:

> Oli. Whence came you, sir?
> Vio. I can say little more than I have studied, and that question's out of my part. . . . Are you the lady of the house?
> Oli. If I do not usurp myself, I am.

183

Vio.	Most certain, if you are she, you do usurp yourself; for what is yours to bestow is not yours to reserve. But this is from my commission. I will on with my speech in your praise, and then show you the heart of my message.
Oli.	Come to what is important in't. I forgive you the Praise. (1.5.177-193)

Olivia clearly has no interest in the duke's overly conventional expressions of love. Though his passion may or may not be real, his expressions of it never break through the vow made to her brother's memory.

Though employed to court Olivia on the duke's behalf, Viola-Cesario is clearly bothered by Olivia's indifference to Orsino's expressions of love. The indifference puzzles her because, having fallen for Orsino herself, she has proclaimed a willingness to risk all to "be his wife." Despite the seeming impossibility of her present circumstances, Viola's patience and trust demonstrate her faith in love's power. For the moment, Olivia seems quite impervious to that. Initially, neither of them recognize they are both trapped in self-imposed roles that prevent them from fulfilling a worthy desire, but because Viola has already fallen in love herself, she leads Olivia into the unexpected.

The conversation between these two women now shifts to the dangers of withholding nature's gifts from the world. Subject to time, beauty demonstrates the fragility of these gifts. Though she continues to coyly mock Orsino's conventional praises of her beauty, the heiress agrees to remove the veil hiding her face. Her face fully visible at last, she asks:

Oli.	Is't not well done?
Vio.	Excellently done, if God did all.
Oli.	'Tis in grain, sir, 'twill endure wind and weather.
Vio.	Tis beauty truly blent, whose red and white Nature's own sweet and cunning hand laid on. Lady, you are the cruell'st she alive

184

> If you will lead these graces to the grave,
> And leave the world no copy.
>
> Oli.   O, sir, I will not be so hard-hearted; I will give out
> Divers schedules of my beauty. It shall be inventoried
> and every particle and utensil labell'd to my will: as,
> *item*, two lips, indifferent red; *item*, two grey eyes with
> lids to them; *item*, one neck, one chin, and so forth.
> Were you sent hither to praise me?
>
> Vio.   I see what you are, you are too proud. But if you
> were the devil, you are fair. (1.5.235-251)

Introducing the complex theme of beauty, Olivia mocks the conventional praise courtly lovers like Orsino pay to feminine appearance. Viola, however, is more self-aware. That a woman's beauty is subject to corrupting time is a common refrain in Elizabethan sonnets, including Shakespeare's. But this theme receives additional depth from Viola's observation that Olivia's beauty is a gift that needs to be used, that "what is yours to bestow is not yours to reserve." Once again, it is a reference to the Matthew parable about the servant who buries the coins he's been given rather than investing them wisely. In this context, the vow is sinful as well as foolish because Olivia is hiding rather than using what has been provided to her for love. Her vow would squander the natural and divinely ordained gifts of beauty and desire that, when properly used, multiply love's wealth.

Time, embodied in that seven-year vow, is the enemy. Olivia's conviction of beauty's invincibility is an illusion as false and dangerous as Orsino's conviction of the superiority of male love. "'Twill," she claims, "endure wind and weather," a phrase echoed later in the play's mournful final song, similar to songs heard in *As You Like It*. Just as Orsino is ignorant of the artifice in his language, Olivia is ignorant of beauty's fragility. Her sin, Viola-Cesario reminds her, is that she is "too proud" to be aware of time's effects, which are rarely kind to feminine beauty, a notion common in seduction poetry. No matter how temporary, her rejection of love endangers that gift. In the next scene, in fact, Feste sings about the cruelty of time and the necessity to act quickly when love appears:

> What is love? 'Tis not hereafter;
> Present mirth hath present laughter;
> What's to come is still unsure.
> In delay there lies no plenty,
> Then come kiss me sweet and twenty;
> Youth's a stuff will not endure. (2.3.47-52)

Carpe diem: beauty and love are gifts that do not last forever, so seize the day and use them as nature intended. "In delay," Feste reminds us, "there lies no plenty. . . ." Nature's bounty will slip away from those who put off love. Something has to shatter Olivia's mistaken conviction that she has time enough for love. As gifts divinely ordained for the good of mankind, love and desire do just that. And so in the most unexpected way, love will shortly intrude to disrupt her false illusion of control over life's events.

Quite subtly, the play identifies an additional issue about feminine beauty, which, like Viola's male doublet and hose, can function as a disguise. Olivia's witty mockery of Orsino's obsession with external appearance subtly hints at a desire to be known and understood more deeply. Though she knows she has been gifted with external beauty, she also understands that it distracts from what is far more important and meaningful. Because courtly lovers are so obsessed with female beauty, that wonderful attribute can blind such men to what's valuable and real. Thus, disguise of any kind, be it clothing, beauty, or an artificial role, becomes a prison restricting a person's freedom to experience love fully.

But escape is at hand. Seeing that the duke's rhetoric is unwelcome, Viola abandons his trite phrases entirely and begins to speak in a far more personal and genuine language that reflects her own desire for Orsino. As artifice gives way to something more real, those words begin to transform

Olivia's heart, but the effect that the speaker desired is not the one she gets:

> Vio. If I did love you in my master's flame. . .
>   In your denial I would find no sense,
>   I would not understand it.
> Oli.   Why, what would you?
> Vio. Make me a willow cabin at your gate,
>   And call upon my soul within the house;
>   Write loyal cantons of contemned love,
>   And sing them loud even in the dead of night . . .
>   O, you should not rest
>   Between the elements of air and earth
>   But you should pity me!
> Oli. You might do much. (1.5.264-276)

Caught up in the romance of what sounds very much like genuine longing, Olivia is clearly moved. Viola's words become the irresistible food feeding a heart that, until this moment, was completely unaware of its own hunger. Where Orsino is love's dilettante, playing a role without any direct involvement in the actual courtship, Viola's presence and her words are the thing itself. Ironically, of course, the emotion Olivia responds to was actually meant for someone else. That Olivia was deceived by that, however, is proof of love's random but undeniable Ovidian power. It strikes where least expected and in ways that shatter any pretensions of control. The blind bow-boy, Cupid, to use Mercutio's mocking description, is the very appropriate symbol of this irrational force.

This rhetorical change has unintended consequences. Moved by Viola's genuine passion, Olivia muses alone after the page has left: "How now? Even so quickly may one catch the plague?" Stricken, she realizes that her fate is no longer in her control. "Fate, show thy force: ourselves we do not ow[n]; what is decreed must be; and be this so." Acknowledging love's undeniable force, Olivia has finally submitted to something greater and more powerful than her

187

own volition. While this openness to love's power is precisely what distinguishes the two women, Olivia and Viola, from Orsino, who remains enslaved to his chosen role, circumstances make the objects of their feelings unavailable to them. Tasting the same bitter medicine she fed Orsino, Olivia loves a disguised woman who can never requite her affections; Viola, to her misfortune, loves a man who thinks he desires someone else. Though both women are captive to desires with uncertain outcomes, their acceptance of these natural feelings proves their worthiness for love. They wait, "like Patience on a monument," to use Viola's phrase, for whatever the future brings. There is no guarantee, for anyone, that desire will be fulfilled as they envision. This is the risk that must be assumed when submitting to love's mysterious ways, but trusting love's wisdom and essential goodness is part of the lesson that all the players must learn.

Although Viola assumes her disguise for reasons that seem valid, she eventually concludes that it is a 'wickedness wherein the pregnant enemy does much.' She comes to see that deception of any kind is the handiwork of the devil because the illusions created by disguise, artifice, and beauty hide whatever is genuine and true. For her, it is not a new insight. She had acknowledged as much early in the play when a sea captain provides useful advice about surviving in Illyria. Grateful for his help, she compliments him:

> There is fair behavior in thee, captain,
> And though that nature with a beauteous wall
> Doth oft close in pollution, yet of thee
> I will believe thou hast a mind that suits
> With this thy fair and outward character. (1.2.47-51)

The outer "beauteous wall," what the eye beholds, can disguise whatever is hidden inside. The only visible proof of what might be hidden is a person's "fair behavior." Aware that her current disguise can hide her true self from others, Viola sees that getting rid of it is the only way to resolve her predicaments with a love she doesn't want and a love she cannot have. Disguise, self-deception, role-playing all serve to hide what must eventually come out into the light of truth.

Twelfth Night's first subplot makes a similar point about the problems caused by the disparity between an imagined and a true identity, but here the humor is edgier. Annoyed by Malvolio's constant reprimands, Sir Toby, Sir Andrew, and Maria, Olivia's maid, devise a plot to embarrass her steward. They compose a letter purportedly from Olivia implying that she is in love with Malvolio, who is quickly captivated by the wholly improbable prospect of her love. The masterfully comic scene where Malvolio finds and reads this letter aloud shows just how a desire for wealth and status fires his imagination, leaving reason and propriety behind. As the hidden schemers listen and comment, he fantasizes about what marriage might mean for his position within Olivia's household:

Mal.	To be Count Malvolio!
Sir To.	Ah, rogue!
Mal.	There is example for't: the Lady of the Strachy married the yeoman of the wardrobe. . . .
Sir And.	Fie on him, Jezebel!
Mal.	Calling my officers about me, in my branch'd velvet gown; having come from a day-bed, where I have left Olivia sleeping—
Sir To.	Fire and brimstone!
Mal.	And then to have the humor of state; and after a demure travel of regard---telling them I know my place as I would they should do theirs---to ask for my kinsman Toby---
Sir To.	Bolts and shackles!
Mal.	Seven of my people, with an obedient start, make out for him. I frown the while, and perchance wind up my watch, or play with my—some rich jewel. Toby approaches; curtsies there to me---
Sir To.	Shall this fellow live?
Mal.	I extend my hand to him thus, quenching my

189

familiar smile with an austere regard of control---

. . . .

Saying, "Cousin Toby, my fortunes, having cast
me on your niece, give me this prerogative of
speech"—

Sir To.   What, what?
Mal.   "You must amend your drunkenness."
           (2.5.35-73)

Just as Titania's passion mistakes an ass for her beloved,
Malvolio's excited emotions obliterate his usual sense of
propriety, and, to the hilarious dismay of the plotters, he
envisions himself the master of her household, able, finally, to
command rather than earn Sir Toby's respect and compliance.
Malvolio's imagined scenario reveals his self-absorption, his
desire for power, control, and status.   Like Portia's suitors
who choose the wrong caskets, Malvolio loves, not because it
requires something from him, but because it provides what he
thinks he deserves.   His lack of self-knowledge is almost as
profound as Orsino's.

That self-concern contrasts sharply with Viola's
sensitive understanding of others.   When she realizes that
Olivia has fallen for her outward appearance, she muses aloud:

Poor lady, she were better love a dream.
Disguise, I see thou art a wickedness
Wherein the pregnant enemy does much. . . .
How will this fadge? My master loves her dearly,
And I (poor monster) fond as much on him;
And she (mistaken) seems to dote on me.
What will become of this? As I am man,
My state is desperate for my master's love;
As I am woman (now alas the day!),
What thriftless sighs shall poor Olivia breathe!
O time! Thou must untangle this, not I,
It is too hard a knot for me t' untie. (2.2.26 – 41)

Like many of Shakespeare's women, Viola exhibits the kind of sensitivity, emotional strength and confidence that the men around her cannot. Though struggling with her own desire, she understands the inevitable disappointment Olivia's love for her disguised self will cause. Despite her tender age, no one else in *Twelfth Night* exhibits such emotional maturity. And like Olivia, she is strong enough to trust that time will eventually work out an acceptable outcome. Viola's selfless devotion to the mission Orsino gave her, along with her steadfast faith in love's eventual goodness, demonstrate her worthiness for any husband she desires.

Viola-Cesario's dedication to the virtues of service, trust, and patience sets the standard by which Malvolio's selfish desire for wealth, status, and power should be measured. He is nothing like her. His allusion to Olivia lingering on their daybed, exhausted by his sexual prowess, is pure egotism. It is a shortcoming Olivia impatiently observes when her puritanical steward criticizes Feste, the fool she employs to remind everyone of their shortcomings:

> O, you are sick of self-love, Malvolio, and taste with a distemper'd appetite. To be generous, guiltless, and of free disposition, is to take those things for bird-bolts that you deem cannon-bullets. (1.5.90-92)

Her reprimand is entirely accurate: Malvolio is anything but generous, free, or, consequently, guiltless. Dour and humorless, he makes more of small matters than he ought. His insistence on order shows a lack of flexibility and tolerance. Self-righteous and unwilling to forgive, he lacks any capacity for mercy, and without this, joy eludes him, which is why he can never participate in Toby's holiday world. His only consolations, ironically, are the trappings of wealth and status: the titles, the velvet gowns, the "rich jewel," and the wealthy, beautiful, sexually satisfied wife who, he imagines, allows him free reign over their household.

Though he believes he is in love, Malvolio's vision of the future contains no emotional, moral or spiritual transformation whatsoever. Instead, the role his imagination created has devolved into absurd delusion. Lacking any self-awareness, he follows the false advice in the letter and dons a perpetual smile and cross-gartered yellow stocking, both of which are known to irritate Olivia immensely. Because of this apparent madness, Sir Toby and his friends cast Malvolio into a dark cell from which he sends furtive pleas for mercy and release to his intended mistress. As his pitiful pleas are thwarted by the conspirators, the terrifying darkness of his prison mirrors his emotional and spiritual state. Toby, the king of misrule, has subverted the tyranny of Malvolio's imposed order. That defeat ushers in a world revitalized by holiday.

But Toby's joyful world of holiday freedom is not unsullied. His exploitation of Sir Andrew, a man so unaware of his limitations that, like Malvolio, he easily imagines Olivia could be in love with him, is a troubling feature of *Twelfth Night*'s holiday world. The illusion of hope allows Toby to steal from Andrew's purse, to enrich himself at his friend's expense, the very opposite of what love and friendship should do. By taking advantage of his niece's liberality and Andrew's stupidity, Toby demonstrates a troubling lack of generosity, mercy, or kindness. That moral deficiency allows him to gull his friend, who, like Orsino and Malvolio, falls victim to his own delusions. It is Andrew's feverish dream of love that allows the amoral Toby to steal his friend's treasure. *Othello* repeats this metaphor of the pilfered purse when Iago takes Roderigo's money in exchange for advice about seducing the moor's completely devoted wife. These examples make two points: first, the desires generated by imagination very easily deceive reason into believing what's false; and, second, those illusions persist at a cost. The penalty for the pretenses of Orsino, Olivia, Andrew, Malvolio, and even Viola, our intrepid heroine, is lost time and opportunity.

Like the third servant in the Matthew parable, they have buried their gift instead of investing it. Each of these characters allowed disguise, role-playing, or a lack of self-awareness to impede the fulfillment of that very natural need for love, for honesty, for connection. The poet, the lunatic, and the lovers are all victimized by the roles imagination created.

Dispelling illusion is the primary purpose of the third and final plot. The main plot's knotty confusions begin to unravel with the appearance of Viola-Cesario's twin brother, Sebastian, whose excursions around Illyria are made possible through the generosity of his friend, Antonio. On one of those outings, Sebastian's path happens to cross Olivia's. Mistaking him for his identical twin in the guise of Orsino's page, Cesario, Olivia confesses her love, pledges their betrothal which she seals with a pearl ring, and heads off with her entourage to prepare for their wedding. Completely confused but delighted by this overture, Sebastian is enchanted by a city where a rich, beautiful stranger showers her love on him at first sight. He struggles to comprehend this magical turn of events:

> This is the air, that is the glorious sun,
> This pearl that she gave me, I do feel't and see't,
> And though 'tis wonder that enwraps me thus,
> Yet 'tis not madness. . . .
> Yet doth this accident and flood of fortune
> So far exceed all instance, all discourse,
> That I am ready to distrust mine eyes,
> And wrangle with my reason that persuades me
> To any other trust but that I am mad,
> Or else the lady's mad; yet if 'twere so,
> She could not sway her house, command her followers. . . .
> With such smooth, discreet, and stable bearing
> As I perceive she does. (4.3.1-20)

In twenty compact but truly wonderful lines, the play's main ideas about illusion and reality, reason and madness, blindness and insight coalesce. Together, they re-create that magical moment when a person understands down to his soul that he is truly loved. Sebastian's amazement and wonder sound so genuine because he understands that where he is shipwrecked is also where he is loved. It came upon him suddenly and was received with joy. Somehow, the language here captures everything that is special about love's intrusion into a life. There is nothing artificial here. Nothing is hidden or disguised. Desire is genuine and is answered with love. There is no restrictive, self-imposed barrier to what is honest and true. There is no calculation, greed, or self-aggrandizement. What we see and hear in his response is love's truth, and it stands in sharp contrast to everything in the other two plots, and it is this experience that artifice, illusion, and self-deception hinder. Metaphorically, this is what Toby steals from Sir Andrew and what illusion and disguise steal from the other main characters.

Sebastian's response to Olivia's amazing overture is completely genuine because he lives the definition of love's value from the Matthew parable, referenced earlier by his sister, Viola. Though his friend, Antonio, must hide from the Illyrian authorities, he has freely given Sebastian funds to explore the city, and Sebastian's use of that gift has enriched his own as well as Olivia's life. Rather than hoard his gift, like the fearful servant reprimanded in the Matthew parable, Sebastian wisely puts it to use. Without fear and its consequent need to hide or to disguise himself for protection, he engages with life. Because of his courage and determination, he earns love's wealth, symbolized by Olivia's gift of a pearl ring.

Sebastian's experience signals the restoration of a renewed harmony that is a consequence of his free and unfettered openness to love. But in *Twelfth Night* that vision of love's ideal result is not unblemished, for the normal comic ending of happily paired couples and promises of marriage is marred by threats of revenge. The three male lovers, Orsino,

194

Malvolio, and Sebastian stand as a precaution to the dangers of illusion. Confusing one twin with the other, Orsino at first threatens harm to his page, Viola-Cesario, when he witnesses Olivia's love for her brother. Once that confusion dissipates, he somewhat reluctantly accepts the love of the patient and forgiving Viola, whose true identity has finally been revealed. Malvolio threatens revenge, not only because he has been humiliated, but also because Olivia, thinking him mad, never came to his rescue. His illusion of a romantic relationship has created expectations that cannot possibly be fulfilled. The reactions of both men to the vicissitudes of love have been compromised by their reluctance to fully let go of illusion. Viola, in particular, will pay a price simply because she is not Olivia, the original object of Orsino's affections, and she will need all of her patience to win her beloved's heart. Only Sebastian, who fully appreciates the wondrous miracle of love, will enter into a promising relationship with his fortunate Olivia. Bottom was right: reason and love hold little company in this world.

Unlike Shakespeare's earlier comedies, the ending of *Twelfth Night* is a mixture of joyful delight and an almost melancholy awareness of the very human inability to see and accept what is genuine. Given this perspective, it is fitting, that the play ends with a song from the one character whose eyesight was always clear, who was tasked with speaking the truth that others were reluctant to hear. Alone on stage at the end of the play, Feste, Olivia's fool, sings this jaunty but melancholy little limerick:

> When that I was and a little tine boy,
> With a hey ho, the wind and the rain,
> A foolish thing was but a toy,
> For the rain it raineth every day.
>
> But when I came to man's estate,
> With a hey ho, the wind and the rain,
> 'Gainst knaves and thieves men shut their gate

For the rain it raineth every day.

But when I came, alas, to wive,
With a hey ho, the wind and the rain,
By swaggering could I never thrive,
For the rain it raineth every day.

In romance, a man's "swaggering" pride leads nowhere. It is fitting that Orsino and Malvolio are both mocked for that sin. But the recurring refrain of "the wind and the rain" should also remind us of Olivia's foolish pride in beauty's resilience. Her illusion of control had to dissipate before love was possible. What was real to her then is not what is real in the end. Nature, which Feste's song equates with the inevitable storms that come with wind and rain, will have its way with our pride and our illusions. As nature's way of dealing with beauty, time is double-edged: it steals the bloom off the rose, but it also ushers in another spring. When Olivia and Viola choose to trust time to untie the Gordian knot that binds them, they have chosen to participate in this natural process that is hindered by foolish illusions, illusions that hide love's truth and the fruitful bounty that it promises.

Whatever joy the play's ending holds, *Twelfth Night* has this unmistakable, somber undertone that signals a shift toward Shakespeare's great tragedies. Love triumphs here, as it should, but the complexity of its comic vision also reflects an awareness of evil's persistence in a fallen world. Here, nothing is entirely pure. Even holiday fun is somehow blemished. Malvolio's pride is far more insidious than Olivia's or even Orsino's, but there's cruelty in his humiliation and punishment too. And though Sir Toby's marriage to Maria is his reward for exposing Malvolio's hypocrisy, he also steals from his friend, Sir Andrew. No part of human existence is free from sin, and in the tragedies the wages of sin are suffering and death. That awareness of persistent evil brings us to the very doorstep of the tragedies.

But the somber undertones of *Twelfth Night* are not the only indications of Shakespeare's readiness for tragedy. To repeat the Northrop Frye quote, comedy demonstrates a movement from "a society controlled by habit, ritual bondage, arbitrary law and the older characters to a society controlled by youth and pragmatic freedom." Fundamentally, comedy is social rather than psychological in nature. The habit or ritual bondage or law that prohibits youth and pragmatic freedom is a normal assumption within the play's cultural setting. That Shylock can charge interest and invoke Venetian law to protect his bond seems perfectly reasonable to both the characters in the play and the audience watching. But villainy endures. Shylock, like Malvolio, is defeated, not changed.

Considered by many to be Shakespeare's finest comedy, *Twelfth Night* indicates just how much his presentation of love has changed since plays like *Romeo and Juliet*, *A Midsummer Night's Dream*, and *As You Like It*. In all three of these early plays, love is very much an Ovidian or courtly love experience. Love intrudes into life instantly and magically. It comes like an arrow shot from Cupid's bow, changing the way the wounded speaks and thinks. In *Twelfth Night,* love is more of a process, a transformation that cannot happen until the illusions that hinder genuine love have been stripped away. It demonstrates, humorously, the origins of such illusions in fear and self-absorbed selfishness. And it demonstrates what makes a person worthy of genuine love, which is impossible without the full, honest acceptance of the best aspects of human nature, those that encourage a spirit of generosity and sacrificial service. Not everyone succeeds at such honesty, but those who do are rewarded with every kind of wealth and abundance that life can offer. Others, like Malvolio, who remain mired in their self-centered illusions, are rightfully deprived of those riches, and that deprivation is often the proximal cause of anger and revenge.

Twelfth Night, therefore, shows its author's deepening insights into the nature and experience of love. That hard-won perspective of essential human qualities under nearly constant threat from contrary behaviors brings him to the very doorstep of his mature tragedies, which gaze steadily at this conflict between good and evil. Everything that went into those earlier plays—Ovid, courtly love, his interest in English history, the structural principles of comedy, and, perhaps most importantly, the very Christian awareness of sin and its consequences–have prepared him for this venture into the tragic, which was by no means inevitable. How all these psychological, emotional, intellectual, and moral elements come together in Shakespeare's hands is something of a miracle itself. And contrary to the belief that tragedy and Christianity are incompatible, those Christian principles deepen his sensitivity to the ironies and paradoxes of human existence that tragedy asks us to remember, particularly the notion that suffering is sometimes the only way to important insights. Without his understanding of basic Christian principles about the nature of love and sin, his great tragedies would never have happened. Certainly, the very seminal tragedy, *Othello,* the next play examined, is a case in point.

Othello

Because *Othello* culminates with the protagonist murdering his innocent wife in their marriage bed, which many consider an exceptionally morbid denouement, the reasons for Shakespeare's fascination with Cinthio's tale of domestic violence are often hard to fathom. A bewildering tragic character, this mercenary general garners little sympathy primarily because his nemesis, Iago, convinces him that the woman he recently married has been unfaithful when everyone in the audience knows she hasn't been. Based on a lost handkerchief, the circumstantial evidence is entirely without merit, making his revenge even more unreasonable. Since forgiving such poor judgment is understandably problematic, it makes the play both difficult to watch and difficult to like. Moreover, a story about a black African soldier misled by a white subordinate to commit a crime against his white wife raises troubling questions about cultural identity, violence and power, race, and misogyny. As a result, the play is a rich banquet for proponents of the New Historicism, the critical approach that has dominated literary discussions for almost four decades. In *Shakespeare, Race, and Colonialism* (2002), for instance, Ania Loomba suggests that, as Western European civilization became increasingly aware of countries and cultures far different from its own, it gradually developed a sense of "otherness." Citing Harvard professor Stephen Greenblatt, the founding voice of New Historicism, she continues:

> Suggesting that 'Self-fashioning is achieved in relation to something perceived as alien, strange or hostile,' Stephen Greenblatt has shown how Renaissance aristocratic and upper classes fashioned their identities at least partly against the images of the newly discovered 'natives' of the New World. . . . Of course, the English differentiated

themselves not only from the New World 'savages' or dark-skinned Africans but also from Iberian Catholics. (9)

During her subsequent discussion of *Othello*, Loomba goes on to detail the complex interrelationships between race, religion, and colonialism in the play, suggesting that *this story* is best understood as the product of a historical moment which understood ethnic identity as fluid. "Despite being a Christian soldier," she suggests, "Othello cannot shed either his blackness or his 'Turkish' attributes, and it is his sexual and emotional self, expressed through his relationship with Desdemona, which interrupts and finally disrupts his newly acquired Christian and Venetian identity" (96). In this reading, Othello's race, his sexuality, and his vague connection to Islamic culture separate him from a European civilization which Shakespeare, as a product of his increasingly imperialistic society, perceived as racially, religiously, and culturally superior. As he becomes increasingly isolated from everything Venetian, including his wife, Othello resolves this racial and cultural tension by killing a wife he once loved and reclaiming his truer identity. Given the theoretical framework of New Historicism, this could sound reasonable enough until we recall that it is Iago, a Venetian, who is the villain of the play. Since none of the Venetians exhibit any recognizable cultural superiority, it is hard to see how this reading makes sense of the text.

Despite being strongly embraced by many college English departments, New Historicism's underlying syllogism limits the rich ambiguities of many of literature's greatest texts. Loomba, for example, spends considerable effort establishing the development of Western Europe's sense of cultural superiority and the consequent otherness of foreign civilizations. Since western authors participate in those developments, their argument goes, the nascent racism, sexism, homophobia, and gender discrimination New Historicism sees emerging from this sense of cultural otherness are inevitably present in their literary texts as well. Unfortunately, the significance of any text under examination is thereby effectively predetermined, which cannot be the purpose of any literary analysis that purports to be objective. Shakespeare's treatment of Othello's race is a case in point. Certainly, the emphasis given to Othello's blackness in the play's first scenes fits quite comfortably into these New Historical paradigms. Yet since neither Othello nor Desdemona expresses any doubts about who they are, racially or otherwise, Loomba's conclusion that the play demonstrates the difficult experience of fluid racial and cultural identity not only fails to convince but actually overlooks familiar themes visible in several of Shakespeare's earlier plays.

Firmly in control of his material, Shakespeare employs many of his usual themes in the play's initial scenes, including the distinction between sight and insight, superficial and deeper truths, and selfishness and generosity. As the focus of the sight theme, Othello's blackness in the very center of white Venice makes its presence felt early in the play. To sow discord in the Moor's new family, Iago, the play's villain, and his dupe, Roderigo, rouse Brabantio, Desdemona's father, from his sleep to inform the old man that his daughter has secretly married Othello.

> Bra.   What's the reason for this terrible summons?
>   What is the matter there?
> Rod.   Signior, is all your family within?
> Iago.   Are your doors lock'd?
> Bra.   Why? Wherefore ask you this?
> Iago.   Zounds, sir, y' are robbed! For shame, put on your gown;
>   Your heart is burst, you have lost half your soul;
>   Even now, now, very now, an old black ram
>   Is tupping your white ewe. (1.1.82-89)

Along with Othello's blackness, the first scenes immediately introduce the theme of robbery, which we've seen before in the Falstaff of *1Henry 4*, another vice figure, and more recently in *Twelfth Night*. Just as Sir Toby steals from his fool, Andrew Aguecheek, Iago is emptying Roderigo's purse as compensation for advice given to encourage his friend's romantic interest in Desdemona, and this early morning ruckus is a last-ditch pretense of saving the maiden for his fool. While this ongoing theft from a supposed friend establishes the villain's essentially selfish, acquisitive nature, Iago's profane description of the newlyweds' nuptials reveals a similar contempt for Othello, from whom he intends to steal peace of mind, joy, and, if at all possible, his newly wedded wife. Because he lacks any redeeming generosity, spiritual or otherwise, Iago's view of love cannot help but be reductive. For him, it is nothing more than a physical, bestial encounter, brief and meaningless. His association of the Moor's blackness with bestial sexuality, therefore, is both uncomfortable and striking. Among the Venetians, he is not alone in his view.

A bit later, as the incensed father confronts his new son-in-law before the Venetian council, hastily assembled that same night to discuss the threat of a Turkish invasion, the old man resorts to similar racially charged language.

> If she in chains of magic were not bound,
> Whether a maid so tender, fair, and happy,
> So opposite to marriage that she shunn'd
> The wealthy curled darlings of our nation,
> Would ever have, t' incur a general mock,
> Run from her guardage to the sooty bosom
> Of such a thing as thou—to fear, not to delight! (1.2.65-71)

Introducing the theme of magic, increasingly significant in this and subsequent plays, Brabantio claims that Othello must have employed some sort of magic to seduce his daughter since she not only rejected other eligible (and white) Venetian suitors but never would have chosen so a person as foreign as the Moor. That sense of otherness that Loomba's book and other New Historicist critiques find in this kind of language seems to validate their hypothesis, but, in this play, any socio-political emphasis on race overlooks the thematic importance of magic and its relationship to Othello's color. That blackness does indeed make him very different from everyone else around him, but it functions exactly like the odd features of another alien figure encountered in an early comedy.

Recall that, in *A Midsummer Night's Dream*, the fairy king Theseus witnesses the chaos unleashed by Puck, who has been sprinkling magic dust into the eyes of six paired young friends. Unbeknownst to all the young lovers, Puck's magic dust puts the unsuspecting victim to sleep only to fall in love with the first being encountered when eyes reopen. Puck's misbehavior eventually touches everyone, including the fairy queen, Titania, who falls in love with the rustic Bottom, already magically disfigured with an ass's head. Hilariously, she passionately declares her love for the transfigured Bottom. Stroking his donkey ears as he brays for more hay, she croons:

> I pray thee, gentle mortal, sing again:
> Mine ear is much enamour'd of thy note;
> So is mine eye enthralled to thy shape;
> And thy fair virtue's force perforce doth move me
> On the first view to say, to swear, I love thee.
> (3.1.140-144)

While the disparity between the emotion in Titania's words and what the audience sees is hugely funny and tender, it exaggerates what every lover somehow understands: that love's power magically transforms our vision of the beloved. Regardless of what is visible to everyone else, the lover can only see beauty and virtue in the beloved. Not necessarily or altogether unfortunate, this blindness to certain obvious realities can be one of love's miracles, a truth that adds depth and poignancy to the fairy queen's words.

Humorous though this wooing is, Titania's inability to see Bottom's transformed head is the prototype for

Desdemona's blindness to Othello's skin. For the uninitiated or unaffected, love is beyond rational and certainly looks a bit like madness, but the emotional dynamic between Othello and Desdemona is identical to the one between the fairy queen and Bottom. Both scenes convey love's miraculous ability to ignore the obvious and to focus on deeper, more important emotional realities. These realities become apparent to Brabantio's daughter through the stories Othello tells about his past. A soldier by occupation, the plain-spoken Moor recounts how he and the fair Desdemona fell in love.

> Her father lov'd me, oft invited me;
> Still question'd me the story of my life
> . . .—the battles, sieges, fortunes,
> That I have pass'd.
> . . .I spoke of most disastrous chances:
> Of moving accidents by flood and field,
> Of hair-breadth 'scapes i' th' imminent deadly breach,
> Of being taken by the insolent foe
> And sold to slavery, of my redemption thence
> And portance in my travel's history
> . . . . These things to hear
> Would Desdemona seriously incline
> . . . . and with a greedy ear
> Devour up my discourse. Which I observing
> . . .found good means
> To draw from her a prayer of earnest heart. . . .
> My story being done,
> She gave me for my pains a world of sighs. . . .
> And bade me, if I had a friend that lov'd her,
> I should but teach him how to tell my story,
> And that would woo her. (1.3.128-166)

For a young, sophisticated but comparatively sheltered Venetian lady, Othello's story provides a glimpse into the exotic and dangerous life of a military adventurer. Through his account, she sees the courage, the strength, the perseverance, the hardships, the physical and psychic pain endured by this man for a cause greater than himself. Her admiration evolves into the kind of love that values these qualities and willingly, joyfully overlooks any differences that might matter to others. Just as Titania accepts Bottom's transfigured visage as perfectly normal, Othello's blackness dissolves and vanishes in the elixir of Desdemona's love. Throughout the story, she alone never mentions it. Whatever sense of otherness colors the language of lesser characters like Iago and Brabantio, the color of her husband's skin carries no significance for Desdemona. Always referring to him as her lord, she sees only his nobility, and she willingly and consistently submits to it without sacrificing any of her dignity. Unlike her judges who have been asked to evaluate her relationship to the Moor, her regard for his character is completely genuine. Hoping to enlist Othello's military prowess for the imminent Turkish assault on their fortification in Cyprus, the Venetian council may accept this marriage for hypocritical reasons, but Desdemona's love for the Moor is never blemished by similarly selfish motives or by the animus that infects Iago. Not even when he confronts her in that final scene where she is face to face with death.

Since none of the other Venetians comprehends this miraculous bond, they can only ascribe the union of these two lovers to magic. Brabantio, Desdemona's irate father, continues to harp on it:

> O thou foul thief, where hast thou stow'd my daughter?
> Damn'd as thou art, thou hast enchanted her . . . .
> (1.2.61-62)

A few lines later, he alludes to it again, saying "if she in chains of magic were not bound" sweet Desdemona would never have married the Moor. And again, "if 'tis not gross in sense, That thou hast practic'd on her with foul charms, Abused her delicate youth with drugs or minerals. . ." A bit later while pleading his case in front of the council, he returns to that theme again: "She is abus'd, stol'n from me, and corrupted By spells and medicines bought of mountebands. . . ." One of the attending Venetian senators picks up the idea: "But, Othello, speak. Did you by indirect and forced courses Subdue and poison this young maid's affections?" But while mention of charms, spells, drugs, and witchcraft pervades these first scenes, the play very carefully distinguishes between two different kinds of magic. For the Venetians, magic is a power employed by an unscrupulous individual to subdue another person's will to their own. This magic is coercive. Befuddled by the affection that blossomed between these two unlikely people, they settle on this kind of magic as the probable cause. As such, it blames Othello for victimizing Desdemona.

But the play establishes a second meaning for the word, a meaning that eliminates any notion of perpetrator and victim. After explaining how his stories affected Desdemona, Othello answers:

> She lov'd me for the dangers I had pass'd,
> And I lov'd her that she did pity them.
> This only is the witchcraft I have us'd. (1.3.167-170)

As in *A Midsummer Night's Dream*, the love between this black man and this white woman is itself a form of magic, an inexplicable willingness to both ignore and accept at the same time, to value what's important and minimize what isn't. This is not so much a decision as an attitude of generosity, however. It is a form of magic because, defying all rational sense, it cheerfully accepts the other as is and overlooks flaws and forgives lapses. And the effects of this magic prove to be powerful as well as profound.

Throughout the play, Desdemona operates under its spell. When Brabantio asks her to choose between father and husband, her answer, very much like Cordelia's in *Lear*, is clear. She addresses her father:

> To you I am bound for life and education;
> . . . both do learn me

206

How to respect you; you are the lord of duty;
I am hitherto your daughter. But here's my husband;
And so much duty as my mother show'd
To you, preferring you before her father,
So much I challenge that I may profess
Due to the Moor, my lord. (1.3.182-188)

Regardless of circumstances, this commitment to her husband never wavers. As Iago's provocations make Othello increasingly irritable toward her, she never relinquishes the image of the man who won her love. After confronting his wife about her lost handkerchief, the first token of his affection and evidence, he thinks, of her illicit affair with Cassio, he exits, leaving her bewildered. Still, she refuses to blame him. "Something sure of state," she muses, ". . . hath puddled his clear spirit; and in such cases men's natures wrangle with inferior things though great ones are their object" (3.4.140-145). And when Othello begins talking of revenge for her supposed infidelity, her faithful maid and the wife of Iago, Emelia, tries to console her, saying "I would you had never seen him!" Desdemona's gives the only answer her steadfast character could:

So would not I. My love doth so approve him
That even his stubbornness, his checks, his frowns. . .
Have grace and favor in them. (4.3.19-21)

Like Shakespeare's other positive female characters, Desdemona has imbibed deeply of love's magic. As her spirited defense of her innocence later in the play indicates, this is much more than romantic naiveté. It is an integral part of a loving nature that knows no other way to see the world.

After Othello and his entourage arrive in Cyprus to fend off the Turkish threat, which never materializes, Iago begins to undermine the Moor's faith in Desdemona's purity. The majority of the play is actually a very detailed depiction of Othello's temptation, with Iago taking the devil's part. Like his mentor, the Father of Lies, Iago's methodology is deception. The goal is to transform the vision Othello holds of an innocent, faithful Desdemona into its opposite, a cunning, sexually promiscuous lady who has already tired of her black paramour and has chosen a man, Cassio, more to her liking. Quite ironically, the man who won Desdemona's love with a narrative of his life is undone by Iago's false narrative of an affair that never happened. Both men are poets, weaving fantastical images out of airy words that have the power to transform people's thinking and behavior. This too is a form of magic, but, increasingly, Shakespeare seems to understand that the essential mysteriousness of love cannot be explained and, as such, it defies any effort to describe or quantify it in words. Neither Othello nor Desdemona can convince her father or the Venetian council that their love is genuine, and so witchcraft becomes the accepted explanation for their union. But where Desdemona lives out her conviction that this is, in fact, love, her husband allows Iago's very carefully crafted but untruthful language to sully her reputation. By deceiving Othello into accepting a defiled vision of his wife, Iago becomes a practitioner of the wrong kind of magic, the only kind that Venetians like him seem to understand.

The deception reaches a shocking nadir during the crucial middle scene of the play. With very subtle verbal manipulations, Iago is able to discredit Othello's lieutenant, Michael Cassio, then encourages him to seek Desdemona's help to regain the Moor's favor, a liaison that our villain then uses to make Othello jealous of his wife's affection. As Iago's insinuations incite vivid pictures of their illicit lovemaking, the same imagination that had once secured his wife's heart now inflames his jealousy, that "green-ey'd monster" (3.3.166), until the Moor is hungry for revenge.

> Oth. Like to the Pontic Sea,
> Whose icy current and compulsive course
> Nev'r feels retiring ebb, but keeps due on
> To the Propontic and the Hellespont,

Even so my bloody thoughts, with violent pace
Shall nev'r look back, nev'r ebb to humble love
Till that a capable and wide revenge
Swallow them up. [He kneels.] Now by yond marble
    heaven,
In the due reverence of a sacred vow
There engage my words.

Iago.   Do not rise up yet. [Iago kneels.]
Witness, you ever-burning lights above. . .
Witness that here Iago doth give up
  The execution of his wit, hands, heart,
To wrong'd Othello's service! Let him command,
And to obey shall be in me remorse,
What bloody business ever. [They rise.]

Oth.   I greet thy love,
Not with vain thanks, but with acceptance
    bounteous. . . . .
Within these three days let me hear thee say
That Cassio's not alive.

Iago. My friend is dead; 'tis done at your request.
But let her live.

Oth.   Damn her, lewd minx! O, damn her, damn her!
Come, go with me apart, I will withdraw
To furnish me with some swift means of death
For the fair devil. Now art thou my lieutenant.

Iago. I am yours for ever. (3.3.453-480)

The image of the surging sea on its "compulsive course" captures the intensity of Othello's resolve. Desdemona's fate is now clearly sealed. But a second look at this scene intensifies the shock of this desire for revenge, for we are witness to a grim mockery of a wedding, replete with a commitment, solemn vows, and words of love. Following their pledge of fealty, the two men are hooped together in their desire to assuage a perceived wrong. If anyone in the play betrays his wedding vows to have and to hold until death comes to separate them, however, it is Othello, not Desdemona. Though she has done nothing to deserve the ambiguous title of "fair devil," Othello has been deceived into an alternative union with Iago, who is far more beholden to a demon very familiar with the pathway to hell.

What drives Iago's deep hatred of Othello is never very clear. He provides multiple reasons, among them Othello's preference for Cassio's military services, a rumor that Othello has seduced his wife, Emelia, and a belief that Othello is unworthy of the trust that the Venetians have placed in him. But none of that can be taken very seriously, as Bernard Spivack has pointed out in his *Shakespeare and the Allegory of Evil* (Columbia UP, 1958). After examining the traditional vice figure in great detail, Spivack concludes that Iago, like Falstaff, is part medieval vice, a figure, who lures people away from whatever is good, and partly a character realistic enough to be believable. Nothing beyond that is required to move the story forward. The play simply needed a villain, and the success of many earlier theatrical precedents proved that Iago didn't need to be a fully developed personality. He just needed to be believable enough. The reasons he proceeds to undermine Othello's confidence in Desdemona's innocence, therefore, is not as important as that he can and does. The emphasis, then, is not on Iago's character but on the intricate process of temptation and Othello's susceptibility to it.

Putting aside his motives for hating Othello, then, Iago is still very honest about who he is at times. Early in the play, he describes himself to his supposed friend, Roderigo, who wonders why Iago pretends to serve Othello so diligently. His answer divides those who serve a master into two distinct categories:

> I follow him to serve my turn upon him.
> We cannot all be masters, nor all masters
> Cannot be truly follow'd. You shall mark
> Many a duteous and knee-crooking knave
> That . . . [w]ears out his time. . .
> For nought but provender . . . .

Whip me such honest knaves. Others there are
Who, trimm'd in forms and visages of duty,
Keep yet their hearts attending on themselves,
And throwing but shows of service on their lords,
. . . and when they have lin'd their coats
Do themselves homage. These fellows have some soul,
And such a one do I profess myself. (1.1.42-55)

What's remarkably ironic about this self-assessment is not only its accuracy but that he's so honest about his motives to a friend from whom he is stealing. Throughout the play, Iago is paradoxically associated with two attributes: honesty and wit. While the first of these is normally thought to be an ability to align what is said with what is morally true and good, in Iago it is merely an ability to assess the world around him realistically. That objectivity allows him to be keenly observant of himself as well as others. As he plots how to use Cassio to make Othello jealous, for example, he notes that the lieutenant is "a proper man" (1.3.392), which his honorable dealings with Desdemona prove. He also admits that Othello himself is "of a constant, loving, noble nature" (2.1.289), which, despite the play's tragic ending, is true at the beginning of the play.

Iago's particular brand of villainy, however, marries that objectivity with both imagination and reason to calculate whatever advantages might profit him. Like those who have "lin'd their coats [to] do themselves homage," the nature of Iago's evil is to take whatever enhances his circumstances. Cassio doesn't have his military experience, so take Cassio's position. Othello's nobility has won the heart of the desirable Desdemona, so destroy that marriage. Thievery, whether it be of Roderigo's money, of Cassio's reputation, of Othello's serenity, or of Desdemona's innocence, becomes both dramatic event and metaphor for a particular type of evil that relies on language to advantage the self. Iago's wit, manifest in his knack for innuendo, becomes a tool to promote his own honesty while undermining the honesty of others. Not long

211

after he reveals himself to an obtuse Roderigo, he pretends to side with Othello against both Roderigo and Desdemona's father, whom he has just provoked with that abhorrent image of an old black ram.

> Iago. Though in the trade of war I have slain men,
>   Yet do I hold it very stuff o' th' conscience
>   To do no contriv'd murder. I lack iniquity
>   Sometime to do me service. Nine or ten times
>   I had thought t' have yerk'd him here under the ribs.
> Oth.   'Tis better as it is.
> Iago.   Nay, but he prated,
>   And spoke such scurvy and provoking terms
>   Against your honor,
>   That with the full godliness I have
>   I did full hard forbear him. (1.2.1-10)

Imitating those who practice "throwing but shows of service on their lords," Iago is remarkably adept at this kind of duplicity. Could there be a less honest statement than his "I lack iniquity"? Yet it is precisely through such shows of service as this that he creates an illusion of honesty that he so skillfully plies to his advantage. Not only does he disabuse Othello of his faith in Desdemona but he works constantly to enhance his reputation for honesty.

Once he has gained that advantage, he uses that presumption of honesty to insinuate his perverse vision of love into Othello's imagination. After encouraging Cassio to seek Desdemona's help in winning back the Moor's favor, which he lost in a drunken brawl instigated by Iago, this villain uses that to suggest something more untoward is behind his wife's pleas.

> Oth.   What dost thou say, Iago?
> Iago.   Did Michael Cassio, when you woo'd my lady,
>   Know of your love?
> Oth.   He did, from first to last. Why dost thou ask?

Iago.	But for a satisfaction of my thought,
	No further harm.
Oth.	Why of thy thought, Iago?
Iago.	I did not think he had been acquainted with her.
Oth.	O yes, and went between us very oft.
Iago.	Indeed!
Oth.	Indeed? Ay, indeed. Discern'st thou aught in that?
	Is he not honest?
Iago.	Honest, my lord?
Oth.	Honest? ay, honest.
Iago.	My lord, for aught I know.
Oth.	What dost thou think?
Iago.	Think, my lord?
Oth.	Think, my lord? By heaven, thou echo'st me,
	As if there were some monster in thy thought
	Too hideous to be shown. Thou dost mean
	something. . . .
	What didst not like? . . . If thou dost love me,
	Show me thy thought. (3.3.93-116)

Relying on Othello's naïve presumptions about who is honest, Iago knows that he can use Othello's imagination, evident in the way he won Desdemona's love, to undermine the Moor's confidence in his wife's fidelity. Repeatedly, Iago will employ this kind of innuendo to further his intended purpose, which gradually evolves into the murder of an innocent wife by a deceived husband. Deception, the other side of the coin of blindness, uses language to transform Othello's wonderful gift of imagination into a weakness. This is the mechanism of evil.

As Othello prepares for what is now an inevitability, Desdemona's physical presence very nearly dissuades him from killing her. After kissing her as she sleeps in their marriage bed, he confesses that her "balmy breath . . . doth almost persuade Justice to break her sword" (5.1.16). While dramatically teasing the hopes of an audience, this momentary wavering also draws attention to his essential shortcoming as a husband: his focus on his feelings rather than on her. He has been wronged, he believes, so the proper recourse is revenge, a form of rough justice that he mistakenly believes will end the agony of his jealous heart. "Perdition catch my soul," he muses earlier in the play, "but I do love thee! And when I love thee not, chaos is come again" (3.3.90-91). He is so easily swayed by Iago in large part because he has never fully grasped his wife's essential value, what the play alludes to in the metaphor of magic. When he tries to explain to her why the lost handkerchief is so important, he too speaks of magic.

> Oth. Lend me your handkerchief.
> Des.   Here, my lord.
> Oth. That which I gave you.
> Des.   I have it not about me.
> Oth. Not?
> Des.   No, in faith, my lord.
> Oth. That's a fault. That handkerchief
> Did an Egyptian to my mother give;
> She was a charmer, and could almost read
> The thoughts of people. She told her, while she kept it,
> 'Twould make her amiable, and subdue my father
> Entirely to her love; but if she lost it,
> Or make a gift of it, my father's eye
> Should hold her loathed, and his spirits should hunt
> After new fancies. . . . take heed on't,
> To lose't or give't away were such perdition
> As nothing else could match.
> Des.   Is't possible?
> Oth. 'Tis true; there's magic in the web of it. (3.4.52-69)

The significance is not whether Othello believes his own description of the handkerchief's history. Instead, the vignette reveals a very Venetian misinterpretation of magic, the kind that could "subdue" a man into loving his wife but which could also vanish when the talisman containing its power is lost. Othello credits the handkerchief with magic and ignores the magic that keeps his wife unshakably devoted to his worthiness.   Like Rosalind's from *As You Like It*, Desdemona's magic is entirely different from what Othello mistakenly ascribes to the handkerchief. Her magic earns its respect and reverence through its constancy, its emotional generosity, its willingness to forgive. Because it only has the power to inspire, it never subdues. A man has to see it, believe it, choose it, then value it above all else.

It is all too easy to view Desdemona as romantically naïve, inattentive to the danger her husband's jealousy represents.   But once she understands that danger, she is absolutely clear about her innocence.

> Oth.   Think on thy sins.
> Des.   They are the loves I bear to you.
> Oth.   Aye, and for that thou di'st.
> Des.   That love's unnatural that kills for loving. . . .
> Oth.   Peace, and be still.
> Des.   I will so. What's the matter?
> Oth.   That handkerchief which I so lov'd, and gave thee,
>   Thou gav'st to Cassio.
> Des.   No, by my life and soul!
>   Send for the man and ask him. (5.1.39-49)

Nor is this the first time she has declared herself innocent of any illicit love. Unfortunately, Othello believes that Iago has already murdered Cassio. Her alibi apparently gone, Othello smothers her only to have her return briefly after Emilia, hearing the commotion, returns to their bedchamber.

> Des.   O, falsely, falsely murder'd!
> Emil.   O Lord, what cry is that?
> Oth.   That? What?
> Emil.   Out, and alas, that was my lady's voice.
>   Help, help, ho, help! O sweet mistress, speak!
> Des.   A guiltless death I die.
> Emil.   O, who hath done this deed?
> Des.   Nobody; I myself. Farewell!
>   Commend me to my kind lord. O, farewell! [dies]

(5.1.117-125)

The return from beyond the grave happens too often in Shakespeare's tragedies to be mere coincidence. Juliet is the first instance, but it occurs here and in *King Lear*, with allusions to similar associations of love and death in *Hamlet* and *Antony and Cleopatra*. Here, it reinforces the idea that love's mysterious magic is powerful enough to transcend even death. Her words from beyond the grave contrast with Iago's self-imposed silence as he's hauled off to prison and torture. Though Othello laments his mistake and takes his own life as punishment for his failure, that suicide seems insufficient proof that he has fully grasped what he has lost. His focus remains, not on his innocent wife, but on his legacy.

> Speak of me as I am, nothing extenuate,
> Nor set down aught in malice. Then must you speak
> Of one that lov'd not wisely but too well;
> Of one not easily jealous, but being wrought,
> Perplexed in the extreme; of one whose hand
> (like the base Indian) threw a pearl away
> Richer than all his tribe. . . .(5.2.342-348)

Beyond the acknowledgment that he has thrown away a pearl of great value, the speech seems strangely devoid of self-awareness so late in the play. Loved too well? Not easily jealous? This is one more reason Othello is so difficult to like as a tragic protagonist. By way of contrast, Desdemona's momentary resurrection includes the wondrous absolution of Othello, despite his obvious shortcomings. It is the essence of her love, this generous forgiveness, this ever-fixed constancy, and it is precisely why she can return from a place where her magic derives its power and meaning.

Othello's essential mistake is to assign the wrong kind of magic to an unworthy object—the handkerchief—while remaining blind to the far more valuable magic his wife embodies. He glimpsed the magic of love at work in their

216

wooing but allows Iago's wit to debase that original vision into one that acknowledges only the physical urge. That is Iago's reductive vision of love, where the old black ram is tupping the white ewe. It is a vision that has no room at all for Desdemona's magic. In his very fine analysis of the play, *Magic in the Web*, Robert Heilman addresses the use of that metaphor in the play:

> Wit and witchcraft: in this antithesis is the symbolic structure of *Othello*. By witchcraft, of course, Iago means conjuring and spells to compel desired actions and states of being. But as a whole the play dramatically develops another meaning of witchcraft which forces itself upon us: witchcraft as a metaphor for love. The magic in the web of [Desdemona's] handkerchief. . . extends into the fiber of the drama. Love is a magic bringer of harmony and may be the magic transformer of personality; its ultimate power is fittingly marked by a miraculous voice from beyond life. Such events lie outside the realm of "wit"—of the reason, cunning. . . . Wit must always strive to conquer witchcraft. . . . Whatever disasters it causes, wit fails in the end: it cuts itself off in a demonic silence before death, while witchcraft—love—speaks after death. (225)

This opposition between witchcraft and rational cunning becomes the opportunity Iago uses to implement his temptation of Othello. Love, one form of witchcraft in the play, is transformed by the villain's narrative into the lust of the flesh. This transformation is a diminishment of the full richness of love's magic, of course, but while love has great power to move people toward each other, it is also very susceptible to the imaginings of its subjects. The power of narration, which becomes a second form of witchcraft, is found in the web of a stolen handkerchief. It derives its power from language and works upon the imagination. Reason could function as a tool to verify the visions that the imagination creates, but it proves a weak instrument against the power of desire and the visions it chooses to enjoy.

217

The intricacies of temptation and sin, which are the driving forces in *Othello,* provide the subject matter for all the great plays that follow. While the Moor's susceptibility to Iago's wicked manipulations may undercut his stature, his story dramatizes the complex process, mechanisms, and consequences of evil. Opposed against this force is the mysterious, magical power of love, offered as the only available remedy for the plagues unleashed by the wicked. The following plays, *King Lear* and *Macbeth*, will stage this opposition with far greater assurance, but those plays would not have been possible without *Othello*. The first of these, *Lear*, is largely about the consequences of evil. Written almost simultaneously, *Macbeth* addresses both cause and effects. Throughout all of his later plays, however, this complex metaphor of magic is worked out in greater detail. In part, it references man's ability to envision alternative versions of himself that reflect his most deeply held values, whether those be good or evil. Internally, the mental vision that takes shape is reflected uniquely in a person's language and affects how the world is viewed. We need only think of Malvolio imagining himself as Olivia's husband, adorned in furs and jewelry and reminding Sir Toby of his proper place. Like Iago, Malvolio's experience is all about self-enrichment. Others, like Juliet, Rosalind, and Desdemona, imagine a much different type of world, one that accommodates a desire for fulfillment that has its basis in an emotional and spiritual generosity, a willingness to share to enrich another. Juliet, Rosalind, and Portia have all used this language of shared abundance and wealth to express their love. This paradoxical vision of life, which Shakespeare saw in the Matthew parable, runs counter to Iago's acquisitive logic. The evil derived from his worldview corrupts Othello's experience of Desdemona's magic, converting a pristine vision of her into its opposite. Othello understands this perversion too late to make any difference to the story's outcome or to its audience, which gives this play its bitter aftertaste. Nevertheless, his play has a significant impact on everything that follows because it begins the exploration of this strange, sometimes wonderful, sometimes terrible alchemy formed in the complex interactions of imagination, language, love, and the values that underlie a particular human character. Because of *Othello*, the wonderful complexity of love and sin and the language that shapes both is deeply embedded in each of the following plays. Using magic as the metaphor for this complexity, the Moor's story manages to capture both the glory and pain of human experience, and any interpretation of the late plays must take that metaphor into account.

King Lear

In some manner, all the previous plays examined address the essential qualities that constitute human nature, a nature that retains some traces of its originally created virtue but which has been sullied, according to Christian doctrine, by the proclivity to feed its sinful desires. *King Lear* takes a much closer look at the subject of human nature, and the result is a magnificent if searing poem of such complexity and richness that it stands alone on the stage of dramatic literature. The word "poem" is deliberate because *Lear* integrates character, theme, imagery, and event into a tightly knit artistic entity that is symphonic in scale and beauty. Here as in other plays, characters whose moral assumptions and attitudes are significantly different invite multiple lines of inquiry. More than any other play, however, those familiar themes observed in previous plays are enriched exponentially. Almost without exception, every event and line resonates with irony or paradox or thematic significance.

Written in 1606 when Shakespeare was in his early forties and at the height of his creative powers, *Lear* consists of two parallel plots that mirror each other in many ways but which also contrast significantly in others. Set in pre-Christian England, the main plot follows the last years of its title character, King Lear, who wants to step down from his duties and pass on those responsibilities to his three daughters, Goneril, Regan, and Cordelia. As the play opens, each daughter will be awarded an equal share of his kingdom once they declare how much they love him. Goneril and Regan provide the expected tributes, but when Cordelia, his favorite, gives a truthful but comparatively barren reply, Lear angrily disinherits her and gives her in marriage, dowerless, to the

King of France. With the proviso that he retain a hundred knights, Lear divides England between his eldest daughters as Cordelia and her new husband set off to their home in a foreign land. Expecting both rest and respect, Lear is shocked to discover that his eldest daughters have no intention of fulfilling their pledges to honor and love him. Their ingratitude tortures his mind. As he slips into madness, he is mercilessly cast out onto a stormy heath with Kent, his disguised loyal servant, and his relentlessly honest jester, the Fool. Full of rage and fury, his unanswered prayers for revenge gradually give way to an understanding of his complicity in this downfall from grace.

The subplot duplicates this downward trajectory with the story of the Duke of Gloucester and his two sons, the legitimate Edgar and the illegitimate but beloved son, Edmund. Of similar age to Lear, Gloucester makes an almost identical misjudgment of his two sons. To gain the family inheritance, Edmund falsely implicates Edgar in a plan to murder Gloucester who, enraged by this accusation, sets out to arrest his naïve but legitimate heir. After Edgar flees and is disinherited, Edmund takes his place as his father's favorite. But when he is shocked by Goneril and Regan's treatment of Lear, Gloucester takes action to support and comfort the old king, a decision that costs him dearly. Infuriated, Regan's husband, the Duke of Cornwall, arrests Gloucester, blinds him, and then casts him out into the stormy heath. Disguised as Poor Tom, the mad beggar, the good son Edgar finds his blind father and teaches him that endurance is better than despair.

The two plots merge when Lear and his followers meet Gloucester and Edgar on the heath. Though all are rescued by Cordelia and her French army, relief is short-lived, for she loses the ensuing battle against her evil sisters. But victory eludes the wicked as well. Forsaking their husbands for Edmund, Lear's two evil daughters succumb to jealous rage and poison each other. Meanwhile, Edmund, who has arranged the murders of both Lear and Cordelia in their prison cell, confesses his misdeeds to his brother, Edgar. But the confession is too late. The murderers manage to hang Cordelia before Lear can save her, and, in one of the most wrenching scenes in all of literature, he dies with her lifeless body in his arms. The throne and all its responsibilities pass to Edgar, who has exhibited throughout this ordeal the qualities that promise a better future.

In at least one respect, *King Lear* resembles those classics of Greek tragedy, *Oedipus Rex* and *Antigone*, for *Lear*'s protagonist is, as he laments, a man "more sinned against than sinning." Lear's suffering, however, is so real, so intense, and ultimately so disproportionate that he garners legitimate sympathy for his ordeal. When death finally releases him from "this wheel of fire," that piteous and moving moment illuminates the fragile beauty of life in a world under siege from ruinous evil. Like the best Greek tragedies, *Lear* establishes comparisons between those aspects of human nature that lead to unwarranted suffering and the good but imperfect human qualities that stand in opposition to such evil. For the Greeks, such oppositions existed as irresolvable dilemmas, but Shakespeare's Christianity, while never minimizing sin or its consequences, acknowledges that, even though evil may claim momentary victories, ultimately, providential grace will always reassert its power restoring peace. As the play examines human failings closely, it leads quite naturally to the limitations of worldly justice and, from there, to nature's essentially moral design which has been created to abhor evil and thus to restore order from the subsequent chaos. Within that terrible dynamic, the human manifestations of love provide a window, opaque though it may be, into the mysterious power that battles against evil.

Both Greek and Shakespearean tragedy recognize suffering is somehow deeply rooted in the inadequacies of human perception. This unfortunate intersection of an opaque world with men of limited reason and insight is reflected in

222

two rhetorical devices common to exemplary tragedies. Irony, a rhetorical device where a character's words convey unintended meanings, reflects the complexity of perceived reality, as does paradox, a device where two contradictory meanings may both seem to be true. Any adequate discussion of *Lear* must take note of its heavy load of both irony and paradox, which inevitably point to unanswerable mysteries of human existence. These mysteries are the subtext of tragic art. As Normand Berlin writes in *The Secret Cause:*

> Einstein, the clearest of thinkers, believed that "the most beautiful experience we can have is the mysterious. It is the fundamental emotion which stands at the cradle of true art and science." A serious examination of the tragic tradition confirms the validity of this view. It is the fundamental emotion and contains the very seed of tragedy and religion and science. However, whereas religion offers answers to the mystery, whereas science strives to comprehend answers to mystery, tragedy enhances the mystery by dramatizing portions of the mystery. (2)

Whatever else may be said about tragedy as a genre, its purpose is not to provide answers to life's mysteries but to remind us that those unanswerable mysteries exist. While the subject of the next chapter, *Macbeth*, somehow comforts because it dramatizes the restoration of natural order after a period of unrelenting brutality, *Lear* brings us face to face with an evil that is demonstrably pervasive and therefore inescapable. While its causes can be anatomized, doing so utterly fails to explain why men continue to pursue its false promises or why any deity involved in human affairs would tolerate its existence. Suffering, given symbolic confirmation in the play's relentless storm, appears to be imposed as some supernatural tool to correct the folly of pride and teach patience. Directly confronting the many paradoxes of suffering and death, tragedy poses questions about life under such preordained conditions. As Berlin implies, a Christian tradition that promises salvation might easily have eliminated the possibility of tragedy altogether. But Shakespeare, a man keenly aware of life's complexities, also recognized the inexplicable persistence of the contrary impulses of both sin and redemptive love. That these possibilities co-exist in the particular, that they are not just spiritual abstractions, opens rather than closes the window to a tragic vision that counterbalances his equally firm grasp of the comic.

Very quickly, the play shows how evil finds a foothold in particular circumstances. As the play opens, Lear is set to divide his kingdom between his three daughters. His method for doing so, however, reveals the inadequacy of his values, for the distribution of land is conditioned on his daughters' profession of filial love and gratitude. "Tell me, my daughters," he begins, ". . . which of you shall we say doth love us most, that we our largest bounty may extend where nature doth with merit challenge?" His eldest daughters, Goneril and Regan, happily oblige him with the frothy rhetoric typical of hypocritical excess. "Sir, I love you more than words can wield the matter," begins Goneril, though she continues despite this professed inadequacy of words. "Dearer than eyesight, space, and matter, Beyond what can be valued. . . ." Regan can only mimic her sister's words. "I am made of that self metal as my sister, and prize me at her worth. . . Only she comes too short." For Lear, the remainder of the play will unravel the entwined distinction between misleading rhetoric and truth.

But his expectations are highest when his favorite daughter's turn comes. Her suitors, the Duke of Burgundy and the King of France, are present to witness what follows. "Now our joy," he says, "what can you say to draw a third more opulent than your sisters'?" Because he is looking for opulence, a word denoting ostentatious wealth, her unadorned answer proves devastating:

> Cord. Nothing, my lord. . . .
> Lear. Nothing will come of nothing, speak again.

224

Cord.   Unhappy that I am, I cannot heave
        My heart into my mouth. I love your Majesty
        According to my bond, no more nor less.
Lear.   How, how, Cordelia? Mend your speech a little,
        Lest you may mar your fortunes.
Cord.   Good my lord,
        You have begot me, bred me, lov'd me; I
        Return those duties back as are right fit,
        Obey you, love you, and most honor you.
        Why have my sisters husbands, if they say
        They love you all? (1.1.87-100)

Lear inadvertently opens the door to suffering when he apportions his kingdom according to the splendor of his daughters' declarations of love. His error is twofold: first, he is willing to materially reward verbal performance without determining actual merit; and, second, he makes the false assumption that words always convey emotional truth and are never used to hide it. Since love can only be demonstrated rather than measured, Lear's false equivalency forces Cordelia to admit she is unable to "heave [her] heart into [her] mouth." And because Lear is also oblivious to the conundrum that words reveal as well as hide, he compounds his false equivalency between material and emotional value by mistaking Goneril and Regan's flattery for the truth.

Just as *Othello* does, this crucial scene addresses the complex interplay between expectations established by a person's values and language. Like Iago, the elder sister use words in ways that disguise their desire to satisfy their own needs first. Lear, on the other hand, imagines all of his daughters love him equally and expects, therefore, similar declarations. Cordelia, however, explains her devotion to Lear in terms almost identical to those Desdemona uses when she distinguishes the love owed to a father from her love for the Moor. While it is a perfectly valid distinction, it fails to satisfy Lear's inflated expectations.

Because language alone cannot easily resolve the moral conundrums raised by expectations, an old man who misunderstands the nature and value of love violates the very bonds that he seeks to verify. Orlando from *As You Like It* persists in his conviction of Rosalind's virtues and the love they inspire, despite Ganymede's best efforts to disabuse him of those feverishly romanticized sentiments. Foolish he may look to others, but he exhibits the constancy of genuine love. This is precisely what Lear lacks: that conviction that Cordelia, despite the inadequacy of her words, will honor the natural bonds that exist between parent and child, not out of mere duty, but out of genuine love. A few lines later, after everyone else has left the stage, the two shameless elder daughters quite accurately agree that Lear "hath ever but slenderly known himself" (1.1.294).

When his unrealistic expectations about the love daughters owe a father are combined with his ignorance of the spoken word's limitations, his fury can barely be contained. "So young, and so untender?" he asks Cordelia incredulously. "So young, my lord, and true," she replies. Once again, he completely misses the ambiguity of her last word, for "true" can mean both "truthful" and "devoted" or "loyal." The exchange throws Lear into a rage that clouds his judgment further.

Dividing Cordelia's portion of the kingdom between his other two daughters, Lear's angry reply amplifies his inclination to measure values wrongly: "Thy truth then be thy dow'r!" Mistaking her plain words for the absence of love, he strips her of her prenuptial wealth. Nothing, he had warned her, will come of nothing, a word that will reverberate throughout the play. Having disinherited her, he asks both of Cordelia's suitors if either will take her without her dowry. Reminiscent of the casket scene in *The Merchant of Venice*, Cordelia is valued by three men: a father who is blind now to her value, Burgundy who will only take her with a dowry, and the King of France who sees her true worth. In language reflecting the paradoxes of value, he comforts her:

> Fairest Cordelia, that art most rich being poor,
> Most choice forsaken, and most lov'd despis'd,
> Thee and thy virtues here I seize upon. . . .
> Not all the dukes of wat'rish Burgundy
> Can buy this unpriz'd precious maid of me. (1.1.249-259)

Where values are not clearly distinguished, as in Lear's kingdom, contradictions flourish. What is poor is actually rich; what is forsaken is actually prized. Like Macbeth's Scotland where fair is foul, Lear's kingdom exhibits a similar confusion of values that only France can perceive and distinguish accurately. And note that what France values is Cordelia's virtue. While every one of France's paradoxes will be played out in subsequent events, here the conflict between Lear and Cordelia draws attention to the problem of seeing and then evaluating worth correctly. In doing so, the play introduces two prominent themes: the theme of sight, which is extended and contrasted by the play's many allusions to blindness; and the theme of judgment or justice. Lear's blindness to Cordelia's true value causes him to misjudge her intentions and her words.

Evident as both symbol and plot device, Shakespeare's use of eyes and sight and blindness is part of a nuanced commentary on the problems of human perception. As Robert Heilman writes in his excellent study of *King Lear:*

> In fact, the whole content of the sight pattern is resolved into the Sophoclean paradox that the blind may see better than the proudly keen-eyed. But the play also attacks the problem of seeing and understanding from another direction: it presents elaborately the obstacles which interpose between human sight and its objects. We are made fully aware that man faces obdurate materials, efforts to deceive, and his own tendency to

reconstruct the objective world according to his own preconceptions. (67)

Lear's ability to discern internal as well as external truth, as previous plays show, is severely limited by all the factors Heilman identifies, including the very human propensity to mistake the fantasy hope and imagination create for a reality that is actually much different. Lear wants to believe all his daughters love and honor him. Though his faithful servant Kent tries to warn him that he has misjudged his youngest, his mistaken preconceptions about the verifiable qualities of love not only blind him to the obvious flattery of Goneril and Regan but blind him to Cordelia's true worth as well.

The difference between physical sight and insight, therefore, suggests that it is the quality of Lear's thinking that is deficient. His eldest daughters' opulent flattery distracts him from the unadorned truth that love cannot be known except through a demonstrated commitment to honor and respect. This is the bond Cordelia mentions. The simplicity of her reply is repeated with greater force by Kent. "Be Kent unmannerly," he begins, "when Lear is mad," an ironic foreshadowing of Lear's coming ordeal on the heath. He continues the confrontation with brutally frank language:

> What wouldest thou do, old man?
> Think'st thou that duty shall have dread to speak
> When power to flattery bows? To plainness honor's bound
> When majesty falls to folly. . . .
> Thy youngest daughter does not love thee least. . . .
> Lear. Kent, on thy life, no more.
> Kent. My life I never held but as a pawn
>   To wage against thine enemies. . . .
> Lear.   Out of my sight!
> Kent. See better, Lear. . . . (1.1.145-159)

Kent's blunt honesty contrasts with the insincere and false rhetoric of Lear's eldest daughters. Because the words of both Kent and Cordelia lack the expected opulence, however, Lear

228

tastes their plain truth as a cold dish. This inability to differentiate between extravagant flattery and the plain truth is a failure of insight, a failure of judgment that is likewise evident in his material quantification of his daughters' love. At this point, his imagination lacks sufficient insight to appreciate emotional and verbal authenticity. Without that nuanced insight into human relationships, Lear triggers a cascade of events that transforms his understanding of what truly matters.

As is the poisonous nature of evil, those events also ensnare the Duke of Gloucester, who becomes the locus of the sight theme. Just as Lear misjudges his daughters, Gloucester is similarly deceived by one of his two sons. Immediately following Lear's failure to correctly evaluate Cordelia, Gloucester mistakenly disinherits his legitimate son, Edgar. Because his illegitimate birth effectively disinherits him, Edmund slyly insinuates that Edgar plans to murder Gloucester and split the estate and its revenues between the two brothers. Since Edmund had already convinced his brother to flee, a decision that gives the appearance of guilt, an enraged Gloucester calls for Edgar's arrest. But to understand all this turmoil, Gloucester cavalierly attributes the discord to "these late eclipses of the sun and moon." Alone on stage after hearing his father's superstitious reading of events, Edmund dismisses such evasions of moral responsibility:

> This is the excellent foppery of the world, that when we are sick in fortune— often the surfeits of our own behavior— we make guilty of our disasters the Sun, the moon, and stars, as if we were villains on necessity, fools by heavenly compulsion, knaves, thieves, and treachers by spherical predominance; drunkards, liars, and adulterers by an enforc'd obedience of planetary influence, and all that we are evil in by a divine thrusting on. An admirable evasion of whoremaster man, to lay his goatish disposition on the charge of a star! . . . I should have been that I am, had the

maidenl'est star in the firmament twinkled on my bastardizing. (1.2.118-133)

Measured against Gloucester's evasion, it is hard not to like what appears to be Edmund's moral honesty, but that clear-sighted understanding of responsibility does not prevent him from taking advantage of a naïve brother or misleading a father as capable of sympathy as he is susceptible to deception. While Edmund's rationality allows him to see moral responsibility, it is not sufficient to guide his behavior. Some other quality of human nature is necessary to help evaluate what is true and worthy. Measured against Edgar, as subsequent events will show, Edmund's illegitimacy is much more than a matter of different mothers.

The emotional evolution of both Lear and Gloucester through suffering will define what that quality is. Initially a man overly deferential to those in power, Gloucester's behavior exhibits the evasion of moral responsibility mocked by Edmund. When Regan's husband, the Duke of Cornwall, for example, offends Lear by placing the king's messenger in the stocks, Gloucester attempts to pacify a justifiably outraged Lear by saying," You know the fiery quality of the duke." Aware of who really exercises power now, Gloucester tries to soothe his former king while maintaining some influence with the daughters and their husbands. He will soon learn that he cannot have it both ways. Disrespect and cruelty require taking a stand, making a judgment. In a world initially designed to reflect divine virtue, the values essential to human nature cannot be compromised without losing what differentiates man from animals.

A peacemaker who dislikes confrontation, Gloucester is eventually forced to recognize just how abhorrent the behavior of Lear's eldest daughters has become. When Lear chooses the storm and the heath over his daughters' cruelty, Gloucester confides his desire to help the old king with Edmund, who uses this information to curry favor with those in power.   Interpreting Gloucester's kindness to Lear as treason, Goneril, Regan, and Cornwall arrest the duke, and in one of the cruelest scenes in literature, Cornwall blinds Gloucester by gouging out his eyes.

Paradoxically, the loss of Gloucester's eyes marks the beginning of his insight. Blind now, Gloucester calls out for Edmund to avenge his suffering only to learn from Regan, "…thou call'st on him that hates thee. It was he that made the overture of thy treason to us. . . ." Gloucester's reply to this revelation marks the beginning of his transformation, for rather than self-pity, his first thought is of the harm he caused his good son: "O my follies! Then Edgar was abus'd. Kind gods, forgive me that, and prosper him!" The first steps toward insight are a recognition of sin and the necessity of repentance, and, like Lear, the sin Gloucester committed was doubting the natural bonds that should tie a father to his child.

The sight theme explores the inability of eyes to see the world accurately, a limitation that, as Heilman points out, has many causes. What is salient about the pattern of sight imagery is this inability to obtain and understand sufficient truth to make morally good decisions, and, in that regard, eyes and eyesight become symbols for the limitation itself. When both Lear and Gloucester reject the good child for the bad, it is clear that any human sense that interacts with the rational mind is equally fallible. Both Lear and Gloucester are misled by what they hear, by the letters they read, by words that cannot convey what the heart feels, or by words intentionally crafted to hide the truth. Ears and eyes share the same limitation. Both men must learn to be far more skeptical of their ability to discern what is true and to rely upon those basic, almost pre-verbal impulses of the heart that do not require rational interpretation. After Gloucester's blinding, Regan taunts him by suggesting he can now "smell his way to Dover." Repeatedly, the play emphasizes the difficulty of ascertaining accurate information about the world and promotes, instead, a reliance on basic truths ingrained so deeply in human nature that they are felt even before they are understood. Symbolically, eyes tie us to the world that easily misleads because of its complexity. Regan's reference to the sense of smell ironically implies that other, more basic human qualities may prove to be more reliable guides.

The first paradox, therefore, is that man may see better when he is blind to the things of this world, a paradox that is deeply Christian. But the interior world of reason and imagination is rendered equally suspect by unacknowledged selfish desires. Man, the play argues, must allow himself to be guided beyond self by feelings of connection to others so visceral that they are part of human nature itself. These are the bonds that Cordelia failed to describe clearly enough to satisfy Lear's demand for a public display of filial affection. But the inadequacy of words does not make her declaration any less true. In the Biblical story of creation, God saw that isolation was not good, that man needed a partner, a connection to some other. Unlike her sisters, Cordelia understands, cherishes, and respects that innate desire for connection that exists beyond words and is demonstrable only through acts of kindness and love. Both Gloucester and Lear must endure great suffering before they achieve her wisdom, no matter how inaccurately that truth was expressed.

The remainder of Gloucester's existence illustrates that the blind do in fact see better than those who have eyes, for the blind are no longer enthralled by the illusions of this world. Having lost the eyes that failed to see Edmund's duplicity or Edgar's worthiness, the blind Gloucester is led away by a nameless old man. Fearing that his alleged treason might endanger his guide, Gloucester tries to send him away. "Good friend, be gone," he says:

> Thy comforts can do me no good at all;
> Thee they may hurt.
> Old man.   You cannot see your way.
> Glou.   I have no way, and therefore want no eyes.
>   I stumbled when I saw. . . .O dear son Edgar,

The food of thy abused father's wrath!
Might I but live to see thee in my touch,
I'ld say I had eyes again. (4.1.14-24)

Recalling Falstaff's gluttony, the association of food with an angry father's wrath suggests that the old duke's emotion satisfied a selfish need for retribution. Though he had been emotionally and spiritually lost, Gloucester's injuries seem to have inspired him to a genuine concern for others, especially the son he wronged. His longing to correct this error is expressed, ironically, in terms of sight, which, because he has lost his eyes, merge with the more elemental sense of touch. This synesthesia, a rhetorical device that intermixes senses, suggests that human sight will remain fallible until it has been enlightened by that connection to deeper feelings that go beyond words. This emotional bond is precisely what both Gloucester and Lear overlook in their initial confrontations with the children who do understand what connects them to their fathers. While he still had eyes, Gloucester rediscovered enough sympathy for the old king exiled to storm and heath that he goes to assist Lear "bearing a torch," a light in the darkness. It is his first act of unselfish kindness, and though that kindness costs him his eyes, it begins his journey toward enlightenment.

The paradox of the sight theme is further amplified by the prevalent imagery of clothing, a symbol that also carries multiple implications. Where Lear's eldest daughters assume the mantle of authority, a rich garment that can hide sin, the absence of clothing can expose human vulnerability. Edgar, Gloucester's legitimate son, comes to exemplify that defenseless vulnerability. Naively, he believes Edmund's manipulative lies and loses Gloucester's trust. Threatened with arrest, Edgar decides to disguise himself as the mad beggar, Tom of Bedlam:

Whilst I may scape
I will preserve myself, and am bethought

233

To take the basest and most poorest shape
That ever penury, in contempt of man,
Brought near to beast. . . . Poor Turlygood! Poor Tom!
That's something yet: Edgar I nothing am. (2.3.5-21)

After discarding everything except a loincloth, knotting his hair, and besmirching himself with filth, Edgar transforms himself into elemental man. His "nothing" purposely echoes the same word in Lear's warning to Cordelia, for they are both children whose identities have been reduced to "the basest and poorest shape" in their father's eyes. Edgar makes real the sad state of those whose worth has been misread. With his flesh exposed to the elements, Edgar becomes "unaccommodated man," and heads out into the stormy heath where Lear is now wandering with his fool and the loyal Kent, disguised as the servant, Caius. Edgar's plight suggests that those who trust the innocence of others, as Lear has done with his eldest daughters, make themselves vulnerable to manipulation. Thus, Edgar personifies the part of Lear that was victimized by the deceitful flattery of Goneril and Regan. But having been brought "near to beast" by this vulnerability, Edgar, like Lear, draws ever closer to those innate feelings that must inform the rational mind of the natural bonds that unite fathers and children. This synchronization of heart with mind is the prerequisite for discerning what is true and worthy. Only with that wisdom can the relationship between justice and mercy be properly understood. But correctly understanding the problem of judgment begins with vulnerability, associated on the heath with nakedness.

Feeling more "sinned against than sinning," Lear struggles mightily with the problem of justice. Cast out by the daughters he erroneously chose to bless, Lear cannot contain his rage. But where Gloucester passively submits to both despair and the ministrations of Edgar, Lear boldly defies the raging storm he now endures, which externalizes his inner turmoil. He dares it, implores it to do its worst because the harms it inflicts are nothing compared to those of his ungrateful daughters. Both of these old men had been susceptible to deceit, but as king, his vulnerability broadens the implications of the clothing imagery beyond personal injury into the public realm of justice and mercy. But Lear cannot get to the wisdom needed for an understanding of justice until, like Edgar, he sheds the clothing that protects him from the most basic elements of nature. One of the first allusions to clothing occurs when he announces that he will "now. . . .divest us both of rule, interest of territory, cares of state" on the condition he can keep one hundred men to attend him. By taking off the robes and crown that symbolize authority, Lear naively surrenders all power to his children while retaining a meaningless semblance of royal status. Like his misjudgment of Cordelia, Lear's divestiture of authority once again is a misunderstanding of something he values far more than he realizes—the symbols of royal power. Like Gloucester, those miscalculations make both old men vulnerable to the evil intentions of more calculating individuals, but the vulnerability that comes by casting off unnecessary finery begins to connect each of them to those feelings ingrained in human nature, the truths of the heart, that make wisdom possible.

As Edgar's plight suggests, the absence of clothing is a form of vulnerability, of innocent helplessness susceptible to injustice. Exiled out onto the heath, Lear observes, "Thorough tatter'd clothes small vices do appear; Robes and furr'd gowns hide all" (4.6.163-4), a phrasing that begins to associate clothing imagery with the justice theme. Symbol and imagery merge with actual event when, imitating Tom O' Bedlam's nakedness, Lear casts off his garments to give his vulnerability a dramatic reality. Exposure to elemental nature begins Lear's instruction, a concept also expressed by Duke Senior in the forest of Arden. Using wit and jest to tutor his master, the fool, who constantly reminds Lear of his folly, often uses clothing imagery to make his point. "When thou gavs't them the rod and put'st down thine own breeches," he quips, "Then they for sudden joy did weep." His reference to clothing implicates the fateful role reversal initiated by Lear's decision to divest himself of authority and power, which transformed his daughters into the parents who never hesitate to use the rod. The unnatural reversal of roles brings Lear to question the meaning of justice.

During this first confrontation with Edgar, who, paradoxically, is disguised by his nakedness, Lear's imagination begins to focus on Mad Tom's lack of clothing:

> Thou wert better in a grave than to answer with thy uncover'd body this extremity of the skies. Is man no more than this? Consider him well. Thou ow'st the worm no silk, the beast no hide, the sheep no wool, the cat no perfume. Ha? Here's three
> on's are sophisticated.   Thou art the thing itself: unaccommodated man is no more but such a poor, bare, fork'd animal as thou art. Off, off you lendings! Come, unbutton here. [Tearing off his clothes.]
> Fool. Prithee, nuncle, be contented, 'tis a naughty night to swim.
>   in (3.2.101-110)

Like Gloucester, Lear's troubles began when he misinterpreted what his ears heard and his eyes saw, for his mind focused only on the obvious, the surface opulence, and missed what was of real value underneath all that. As Lear tries to get beneath whatever hides essential man, symbol, event, and language merge into a tightly integrated, artistic whole. Clothing makes man too "sophisticated." What clothing hides, those human attributes he failed to comprehend until circumstances forced him to, matters intensely now. He is desperately hungry for answers. Since clothing hides the essential qualities of man, they become superfluous to the matters currently under his consideration.

236

Edgar and Lear both end up unclothed and exposed to the elements for different reasons. One pretends to be mad and is using nakedness as a disguise. The other is mad and disrobes so he can find his way to wisdom. Edgar is the lesson. Lear, the student, contemplates what he sees:

> Poor naked wretches, wheresoe'er you are,
> That bide the pelting of this pitiless storm,
> How shall your houseless heads and unfed sides,
> Your loop'd and window'd raggedness, defend you
> From seasons such as these? O, I have ta'en
> Too little care of this! Take physic, pomp,
> Expose thyself to feel what wretches feel,
> That thou may'st shake the superflux to them,
> And show the heavens more just. (3.4.28-36)

Though their nakedness identifies their vulnerability, it also becomes the opportunity to understand the need for pity, the emotional foundation of a morality that demands personal kindness as well as justice. Edgar, who was deceived by his brother Edmund, will meet the blinded Gloucester and will lead him past despair into endurance. He is the personification of kindness to his tortured father. Through Edgar's actions on behalf of Gloucester, morality is manifest at the personal level. The province of their experience is the personal and the family. As a king, however, Lear begins to recognize larger social issues through the lens of his agony. Precisely because his eldest daughters have been so unkind, Lear is forced to admit his neglect of the defenseless, one of whom now stands shivering before him. Surely, Lear is "more sinned against than sinning," as he asserts in a moment of full-blown self-pity, but it was only when he realized that his daughters were wrong to reason away his hundred knights that the truth about every man's vulnerability became real to him.

In this play and the later *The Tempest*, a storm comes to symbolize the necessity of and reason for human suffering. In both, the argument seems to be that pride can only be humbled through suffering its consequences. Though Edgar and Lear's nakedness symbolizes their vulnerability, it is only through that vulnerability that both come to appreciate the bonds, to use Cordelia's word, that connect parents to children and individuals to an ordered society. Though naïve about Edmund's evil, Edgar's love never falters for the father who grievously wronged him. Suffering provides the opportunity to confirm his identity as a loving son. When circumstances require it, he comforts and honors the man who gave him life. For Edgar, suffering dissolves his naiveté about evil without diminishing his willingness to live out the duty a son has to a father.

Lear's suffering develops a brand of humility that is wider, more universal in scope. Suffering not only teaches him what would have made him a better father but also, oddly enough, what would have made him a better king. Although it is after the fact, the fool schools Lear on this subject by constantly pointing out the folly of relinquishing his crown:

> Fool. Nuncle, give me an egg, and I'll give thee two
> crowns.
> Lear. What two crowns shall they be?
> Fool. Why, after I have cut the egg I' th' middle and eat
> up the meat, the two crowns of the egg. When
> thou clovest thy crown i' th' middle and gav'st
> away both parts, thou bor'st thine ass on thy back
> o'er the dirt. Thou hadst little wit in thy bald
> crown when thou gav'st thy golden one away.
> (1.4.155-163)

Giving away the crown, an article of clothing worn to symbolize royal power, while still expecting the kind of respect due a king defies reason and logic. Though no longer a king in fact, Lear's suffering clarifies that royal part of his identity. When the blind Gloucester meets the mad king, dressed now in weeds and wildflowers, he hears Lear speak and asks," Is't not the King?" To which Lear replies with exquisite irony, "Ay, every inch a king." Though naked vulnerability has illuminated his insight, it is too late for royal authority to be of any earthly use. All that is available to him now is spiritual and emotional transformation. Reminiscent of Matthew 16:26, which questions the wisdom of gaining the world if it means losing one's soul, Lear had to lose a kingdom to gain something that, in the end, proves far more valuable. The paradox of the clothing theme, then, is that those, like Goneril and Regan, who selfishly overvalue the security of royal power and wealth, are denied the kind of deeper insight available only to the vulnerable. Their blindness to the necessity of judgment tempered by mercy, a truth that both Lear and Gloucester learn on the heath, will eventually make the wicked sisters equally vulnerable but unable to comprehend its lessons.

For Lear, that journey into wisdom passes through the ordeal of madness. The play carefully prepares us for this process. Unable to fathom the cruel disregard of his eldest daughters, Lear struggles to maintain his grip on reality. He repeatedly warns those attending him that his distress will make him mad. When the nearly naked Tom O 'Bedlam emerges from the hovel, Lear finally slips into the madness he feared. But this is madness with a purpose, for it seems to free Lear's imagination from the restrictive logic of false quantification that once ruled his decisions. He begins to freely associate bits of perceived reality with thoughts from his internal turmoil. "Didst thou give all to thy daughters?" he asks mad Tom, as if the cause of his particular mental chaos is the only explanation for all human misery. But the specific evil of these daughters leads to broader questions about human nature. Throughout his ordeal, the essential question for Lear becomes," Is there any cause in nature that make these hard hearts?" The answer to this question has little to do with reason and everything to do with things spiritual. Little wonder then, that when Lear is encouraged to enter the hovel, he points to mad Tom and responds," First, let me talk to this philosopher." Though the irony of that statement is profound, it is there, somewhere beyond the rational, that man is able to come to wisdom.

Since it was Lear's imagination and heart that were deficient, the transformation occurs outside the rational and in a very fluid realm where ideas and images collide, setting off fiery sparks of anger, bitter regret, even calls for revenge upon those "thankless daughters." But the anguish includes more than bitterness. Overhearing Lear's ramblings, Edgar says, "O, matter and impertinency mix'd. Reason in madness!" As Heilman notes:

> The madness pattern. . .is concerned with the ways in which men interpret phenomena, the meanings which they find in experience, the general truths which they consciously formulate. . . . Its materials are men's philosophic attitudes,. . . their grasp, more specifically, of the problem of evil. Lear's madness is, in one respect, a result of his inability to bring an obdurate universe under intellectual control. . . (180)

The storm that Lear endures out on the heath, of course, reflects the turmoil in his mind, but having slipped out of his old habits of thinking, his imagination is free to recast his understanding of such problems in new ways. That he doesn't flinch from the investigation of such questions nor from any of the possible answers differentiates him from Gloucester, who eventually attempts to escape his despair through suicide. Reflecting his larger sphere of influence as king, however, Lear examines issues that penetrate far deeper into the mysteries of human existence. The pain of his daughters' cruelty drives him toward a wide range of moral and emotional truths, no matter the cost. He is hungry, now, to understand everywhere he was blind.

Having already opened his heart to pity for the defenseless, Lear begins an examination of justice, a power he could have used to protect those who sorely needed it. The examination, however, is at first tinged with matters from his own experience. Inside the hovel with Kent, the fool, and the mad Tom O 'Bedlam, all of whom are assigned various legal roles, Lear conducts a mock trial of those thankless daughters. While Kent tries to calm Lear, the naked Edgar is disguised as the mad Tom. The ironies are profound:

> Lear.   I will arraign them straight.
> [To Edgar] Come sit thou here, most learned justice;
>   [To the Fool] Thou, sapient sir, sit here. Now
>   you she-foxes—
> Kent. . . . How do you sir? Stand you not so amaz'd.
>   Will you lie down and rest upon the cushions?
> Lear. I'll see their trial first, bring in their evidence.
>   [To Edgar] Thou robed man of justice, take thy
>   place,
>   [To the fool] And thou, his yoke-fellow of equity,
>   Bench by his side. [To Kent] You are o' th'
>   commission, sit you too.
> Edgar. Let us deal justly . . . . Purr, the cat is grey.
> Lear. Arraign her first, 'tis Goneril. I here take my oath
>   before this honorable
>   Assembly, she kick'd the poor king her father.
> Fool. Come hither, mistress. Is your name Goneril?
> Lear. She cannot deny it.
> Fool. Cry you mercy, I took you for a joint stool.
> Lear. And here's another, whose warp'd looks proclaim
>   What store her heart is made an. (3.6.19-54)

Cruelty is the essence of the daughters' crime: they "kick'd the poor king her father." What his daughters 'hearts are made of concerns Lear greatly. A mock trial raises profound questions about evil. "Let them anatomize Regan," he concludes, "See what breeds about her heart." What, in fact, is the nature of evil?

The answer comes quickly as Lear's mock trial is followed by Gloucester's blinding. Conducted by Regan and her husband, Cornwall, this second trial equates their brand of justice with raw power. Here, justice is corrupted by personal need. Afraid that a mad and naked Lear might awaken public sympathy, their justice is implemented to protect their interests. Motivated by a selfish regard for safety, this second trial, draped with an appearance of logic and justice, violates the truth that the mad Lear is uncovering out on the heath: justice without mercy cannot be justice. But in this second court, Gloucester's sympathy for Lear must be punished:

> Though well we may not pass upon his life
> Without the form of justice, yet our power
> Shall do a court'sy to our wrath, which men
> May blame but not control. (3.7.24-27)

Though a servant, appalled by the blinding, manages to mortally wound Cornwall, this sham trial degrades any reasonable standard of justice. Under the current regime, Gloucester cannot be executed without some semblance of a trial, but Cornwall's anger can still use the power of authority to harm the old duke nevertheless, whether or not the public approves it. While the Regan-Cornwall form of justice seems to prevail for the moment, the servant who comes to Gloucester's defense begins to suggest that a far more equitable justice may also be at work. The mechanics of that justice, however, seem to work according to some other, unfathomable schedule that allows human folly to open the door to suffering.

In a world ruled by the likes of Goneril and Regan, a world where personal vendetta is disguised as justice, the defenseless weak will inevitably suffer. When the play's two victims, the mad Lear and the blind Gloucester, finally meet on the heath, this desecration of justice is at the forefront of Lear's mind. Though the sight theme figures prominently, what's striking is how the passage blends several of the most basic human senses:

> Glou. O, let me kiss that hand!

Lear. Let me wipe it first, it smells of mortality.
Glou. O, ruined piece of nature! . . . . Dost thou know
       me?
Lear. I remember thine eyes well enough. Dost thou
       squinny at me?
       No, do thy worst, blind Cupid, I'll not love. Read
       thou this challenge, mark but the penning of it.
Glou. Were all thy letters suns, I could not see. . . .
Lear. . . . No eyes in your head, nor no money in your
       purse? Your eyes are in a heavy case, your purse
       in a light, yet you see how this world goes.
Glou. I see it feelingly.
Lear. What, art mad? A man may see how this world
       goes with no eyes. Look with thine ears; see how
       yond justice rails upon yond simple thief. Hark in
       thine ear: change places, and handy-dandy, which
       is the justice, which is the thief? (4.6.132-154)

As the sight theme implies, the efficacy of eyes is severely limited by the difficulty of seeing and understanding whatever lies underneath the impenetrable surface of an obdurate world. This is, however, the fixed and unchangeable condition of fallen man. In such a state, Gloucester is right: the blind man must see the world feelingly, with his heart open and vulnerable to pity, for all are sinners and all require mercy. But doing so is not easy where people like Goneril, Regan, Edmund, and Cornwall exist. Lear's reply, heavy with irony, acknowledges the price people who make themselves vulnerable will pay when the strong prey upon the weak: "What, art mad?" It is a kind of madness to undress into vulnerability. But the play has already shown that Lear's madness, his suffering on the heath, has opened his eyes to the values that ultimately make life tolerable. Lear is indeed a "ruined piece of nature." That he is no longer capable of much more than sharing those insights with the blind, however, does not make those insights any less valid, even in a world that tolerates evil.

The paradox of the madness theme is that what looks like madness actually leads a man like Lear to undeniable truths while what looks pragmatic and reasonable contains an element of madness. Lear's troubles began when he attempted to evaluate and measure what, ultimately, could not be measured. Not long after setting aside crown and scepter, his eldest daughters use this same quantification of love to control their suddenly powerless father, who had made the retention of a hundred knights a condition of his transfer of power. Although both daughters willingly accept the authority of their new offices, they renege on their pledge to let Lear keep his knights. Staying with Goneril until she threatens to reduce his hundred knights to fifty, he then flees to Regan's residence where the same calculus is imposed. She, however, will reduce his knights to twenty-five. Thoroughly humiliated, Lear tries to bargain only to find, when Goneril shows up and embraces her sister, that both daughters are intent on the same purpose. "What need you five and twenty? ten? or five?" asks Goneril, to which Regan asks "What need one?" Having ceded all power to these two, Lear's helplessness brings him to a recognition of his dependence on something other than opulent words of love. His daughters should not rationalize away his need for respect and love. "O, reason not the need!" he begins:

> Our basest beggars
> Are in the poorest thing superfluous.
> Allow not nature more than nature needs,
> Man's life is cheap as beast's. Thou art a lady;
> If only to go warm were gorgeous,
> Why, nature needs not what thou gorgeous wear'st,
> Which scarcely keeps thee warm. . . . (2.4.264-270)

To make his point about "true need," Lear's reply once again references clothing, which can be either gorgeous or just enough to serve nature's needs. If man were only an animal, he would not need anything beyond what would keep him warm. Anything more would be superfluous. The clothing imagery, of course, prepares us for the imminent nakedness of Edgar and Lear himself, but what he really needs here is some evidence of the love his daughters once professed for him. Of that there is none because the same calculation that discredited Cordelia is now being visited upon him.

While their arguments may sound reasonable enough, Goneril and Regan are rationalizing their desire to consolidate all power from their father, whom they blame for permitting "these not-to-be-endur'd riots" of his knights and his "all-licens'd Fool." After Lear leaves his daughters to face the pitiless storm, those who now wield the power explain their decision to Gloucester, who is very uneasy with these events:

> Corn.   Whither is he going?
> Glou.   . . . I know not whither.
> Corn.   'Tis best to give him way, he leads himself.
> Gon.   My lord, entreat him by no means stay.
> Glou.   Alack, the night comes on, and the bleak winds
>   Do sorely ruffle; for many miles about
>   There's scarcely a bush.
> Reg.   O sir, to willful men,
>   The injuries that they themselves procure
>   Must be their schoolmasters. Shut up your doors.
>   He is attended with a desperate train,
>   And what they may incense him to, being apt
>   To have his ear abus'd, wisdom bids fear.
> Corn.   . . . tis a wild night, my Regan counsels well.
>   (3.1.296-309)

Regan speaks more truth than she knows when she claims Lear's self-inflicted injuries will become his schoolmasters. But all of this is served up as an excuse for bad behavior. Where bonds of filial love and gratitude are absent, the duty and respect owed to an aged father are replaced by self-interest, which reason works to justify. Though he hesitates to help Lear, Gloucester tries to remind everyone of the relentless storm and the bleak heath that await the former king, but his very tentative pity is wasted on such hardened hearts.

But the daughters and their husbands are not the only characters who rationalize their evil. All along, Edmund has been motivated by the same self-interest that spurs Goneril and Regan. Where Lear's eldest daughters fail to earn any sympathy, however, Edmund has already shown a likable, roguish honesty by acknowledging that man cannot use superstition and astrology to escape moral responsibility. But his honesty is only applied to others, and he uses his very realistic observations of people for his own advancement. Just as Goneril and Regan hid their intentions with florid proclamations of love, Edmund describes how he deceived both father and brother:

> A credulous father and a brother noble,
> Whose nature is so far from doing harm
> That he suspects none; on whose foolish honesty
> My practices ride easy. I see the business.
> Let me, if not by birth, have lands by wit. . . .
> (1.2.179-183)

To those who calculate for their own benefit, innocent credulity and a noble nature look like "foolish honesty." They make Gloucester and Edgar vulnerable to deception and manipulation and therefore such credulousness, Edmund opines, ought to be shunned. Every decision, every encounter is weighed according to the advantage that might be gained. For those, like Edmund, who use their wits to improve their fortunes, the principles the good son Edgar follows are worse than useless. They impede advancement. It is perfectly rational, therefore, that Edmund should eventually betray his father to gain favor with Regan and Cornwall.

But this rational, self-consumed calculation for personal gain carries the seeds of its own annihilation. Though the attitude may temporarily gain control of circumstances, it is blind to the basic emotions, the bonds, that unify families and

246

communities. It is immune to the enlightenment that suffering and vulnerability bring to the play's two old men. Again, quoting Heilman regarding the Goneril-Regan-Edmund trio:

> . . .to Lear's reason-in-madness there is opposed their tainted reason, a self-confident, unshackled sharpness of mind, shrewd and penetrating as far as it goes, but incapable, ultimately, of detecting its own frailty and limitations, of formulating a workable pattern of existence, and of bringing to them the saving insights of men of imagination. (284)

The evil at work in *Lear* is, ultimately, based on a kind of madness in reason. It cannot build anything of lasting value because the nature of evil lacks the comprehensive and inclusive quality of the good. As events of the play unfold, each of the rationalizing characters succumbs to passions they fail to anticipate because they neglected to cultivate any understanding of them. Their primary concern before acting is calculating what benefits accrue to them. But their ignorance of feelings and emotions eventually undo them all. In a blind fury because of Gloucester's perceived treason, Regan's husband enacts a cruelty so shocking that it offends a servant and leads to Cornwall's death. That his cruelty begins with uncontrolled anger, that his life ends because of a servant's genuine sympathy are warnings lost on Goneril, Regan, and Edmund. Their self-enhancing rationality has no insight into the irrational forces beyond their control. Blind to the irrational power of human emotion, they mistake anger for justice and lust, in the case of Goneril and Regan, for love. Unlike the two old men suffering on the heath, they are incapable of imagining the world from any other perspective than the personal.

  If there is reason in Lear's madness, there is also madness in the evil perpetrated by those who calculate their advantage in every situation. The benefits they gain over the credulous and the noble turn out to be temporary. Those temporary benefits are not revoked, however, by Cordelia's return with a French army to relieve her suffering father. Shakespeare's tragic resolution is far richer in its complex implications than such an easy and obvious rescue. Instead, Goneril falls for the charismatic Edmund and forsakes her husband, the Duke of Albany, who has gradually come to the realization that his wife is "not worth the dust that the rude wind blows" in her face. Since Regan, whose husband succumbed to the wounds suffered during Gloucester's blinding, has also fallen in love with Edmund, the wicked sisters poison each other in an escalating war of jealousy. Ironically, irrationality disrupts the carefully laid plans of the wicked. Those who rely on rational calculation never anticipate how passion might disrupt their designs. Like the other tragic figures, Lear and Gloucester, they were blind to the necessary role feelings have in human life, but unlike those who earn their insights through suffering, all the evil characters die unenlightened. To the end, they remain blind to the full and complex truth of human nature.

By implicitly asking for a comparison between the suffering and the evil characters, the play raises important questions about human nature, about man's identity and purpose. Looking at the evil trio, it seems that men who depend on reason unenlightened by basic feelings will be reduced to the animal, undone by long-ignored passions they cannot control. With his frequent use of animal and sexual imagery, Lear is struggling to understand this aspect of human nature. After Goneril attempts to reduce the number of his attendants, he calls her "detested kite," following that with a frightful prayer:

> Hear, nature, hear, dear goddess, hear!
> Suspend thy purpose, if thou didst intend
> To make this creature fruitful.
> Into her womb convey sterility. . .
> And from her derogate body never spring
> A babe to her! If she must teem,
> Create her child of spleen, that it may live

And be a thwart disnatur'd torment to her. (1.4.275-283)

And when Regan follows her sister's lead, he points to his heart and claims she too "hath tied Sharp-toothed unkindness, like a vulture, here." Despite his ordeal, Lear is never able to resolve the question of human cruelty on his own. The association of unkindness with animal nature and the sexual impulse re-emerges in his mad discussion with the blind Gloucester:

> When I do stare, see how the subject quakes.
> I pardon that man's life. What was thy cause? Adultery?
> Thou shalt not die. Die for adultery? No,
> The wren goes to't, and the small gilded fly
> Does lecher in my sight.
> Let copulation thrive, for Gloucester's bastard son
> Was kinder to his father than my daughters
> Got 'tween the lawful sheets.
> To't, luxury, pell-mell, for I lack soldiers. (4.6.108-117)

In Lear's mind, the ironic assertion that Edmund was kinder to Gloucester than his daughters were to him justifies wanton copulation, for he needs soldiers to bring justice to those wicked daughters. The presence of a blind Gloucester gives the lie to that. But he has also been schooled in the errant ways of justice and the fact that, as he says, "none does offend, none, I say, none," prompts him to preach endurance:

> If thou wilt weep my fortunes, take my eyes.
> I know thee well enough, thy name is Gloucester.
> Thou must be patient; we came crying hither.
> Thou know'st, the first time that we smell the air
> We wawl and cry. I will preach to thee. Mark. . . .
> When we are born, we cry that we are come
> To this great stage of fools. (4.6.176-183)

Crying, Lear tells Gloucester, is man's fate from the moment of birth because none can avoid the consequences of their foolishness.   But this sanguine mood of acceptance, his promotion of patience to Gloucester, a man recently contemplating suicide, will not hold for long.   A few lines later, Lear returns once again to his desire for revenge. "When I have stol'n upon these sons-in-law, Then kill, kill, kill, kill, kill, kill!" The hurt, the anger, the helpless frustration persists. By this time, Lear has learned much about suffering, pity, justice, the limitations of sight, and responsibility, but expiation eludes him until he is reunited with Cordelia, his joy.

Balancing one of the cruelest scenes in literature, Gloucester's blinding, is one of the most tender, Cordelia's rescue of her tormented father.   The first demonstrates how self-interest degrades the best of what is human into the animal, red in tooth and claw, to borrow from Matthew Arnold.   The second demonstrates the healing balm of human kindness and love. Very efficiently, the play draws a clear distinction between the natures and the consequences of good and evil.   Motivated by self-gratification, the wicked end in violence, division, and death, as the mortal jealousy of the evil sisters show.   Cordelia's love, on the other hand, is sacrificial, risking all to comfort an abused father.   Remarkable for its affection and compassion, their reconciliation is a moving tribute to the decency of which man at his best is capable. With his ordeal on the heath finally behind him, Lear has been sleeping.   As he awakens, he recognizes Cordelia, who asks, "How does my royal lord?" to which he replies," You do me wrong to take me out o 'th 'grave."   When she asks for his blessing, he tries to kneel at her feet:

> I am a very foolish fond old man,
> Fourscore and upward. . .
> And to deal plainly,
> I fear I am not in my perfect mind.
> Methinks I should know you. . .
> Yet I am doubtful: for I am mainly ignorant
> What place this is. . . .
> Do not laugh at me,

<blockquote>
For as I am a man I think this lady
To be my child Cordelia.
Cor.   And so I am, I am.
Lear.   Be your tears wet? Yes, faith. I pray weep not.
If you have poison for me, I will drink it,
I know you do not love me, for your sisters
Have (as I remember) done me wrong;
You have some cause, they have not.
Cor.   No cause, no cause. (4.7.59-73)
</blockquote>

In remarkable symmetry with the self-deposition scene at the beginning of the play, Cordelia's very simple reply of "no cause" eliminates the misguided calculus where kingdoms are rewards for opulent but misleading words. Recalling the paradoxical implications of the financial metaphor in *The Merchant*, where giving away enhances wealth, there is no calculus in Cordelia's freely given absolution. As such, her forgiveness is the moment of Lear's expiation. Re-enacting the Christian miracle of salvation, she accomplishes what he could never achieve on his own. The Biblical connection is not at all far-fetched. The association to the sacrificial servant of the gospels is clear when Cordelia, having just arrived in England to save Lear, remarks," O dear father, It is thy business that I go about," a phrasing that echoes the explanation of a twelve-year-old Jesus for leaving his parents to teach in the temple. The allusion is particularly apt because, from a Christian perspective, that was the historical moment that God's redemptive wisdom began to illuminate a dark and spiritually ignorant world. Shakespeare clearly wants to suggest that, for Lear, Cordelia's return is equal parts salvation, expiation, and the comforting light that will finally dispel the darkness of the world's evil.

From this moment on, nothing else matters to Lear except his bond with Cordelia, the one he once angrily dismissed with the phrase "nothing will come of nothing." Now she is everything to him; he understands fully her worth. When her French army is defeated and they are taken off to prison, Cordelia calmly asks, "Shall we not see these daughters and these sisters?" But Lear has no interest in them any longer. "No, no, no, no!" he replies:

> Come, let's away to prison:
> We two alone will sing like birds i' th' cage;
> When thou dost ask me blessing, I'll kneel down
> And ask of thee forgiveness. So we'll live,
> And pray, and sing, and tell old tales, and laugh . . . .
> And take upon 's the mystery of things
> As if we were God's spies. . . . (5.3.8-16)

Reliving that moment when his one good daughter forgave him is all that matters now to Lear. Why some hearts are so hard and others are tender enough to forgive must surely be part of "the mystery of things" known only to God. In the end, such things are beyond human comprehension. Sin, evil, kindness, and forgiveness—these can be identified and classified and appreciated for their consequences, but why they are part of the human experience, ultimately, cannot be understood. In his despair, Gloucester had once said, "As flies to wanton boys are we to th 'gods, they kill us for their sport." Inexplicably, though, Edgar's kindness finds a way to mitigate that despair. Nor can the indifferent supernatural realm contemplated in Gloucester's speech explain a Cordelia. In her defiant, unwavering love, she herself is the precious mystery that is just as much a part of nature as evil. This is the truth that Lear finally understands. Unlike her sisters, something in Cordelia's nature made her choose to love and honor her father over any concern for safety or self-interest. In contrast to his rejection of her during that opening scene, Lear has come to value Cordelia according to her true worth, the virtues that France accepted in place of an expected dowry.

Cordelia's act of forgiveness is not the only proof of her love for Lear. Like Antonio from *The Merchant of Venice*, she has risked all by returning to rescue her father. But as the presence of evil indicates, this is a fallen world where forgiveness and love afford no protection from the scourge of death, an inescapable, universal consequence of sin. After Edgar, disguised this time in armor, defeats his illegitimate brother in a trial by combat, Edmund renounces his sins but not before he has set in motion the imprisoned Cordelia's murder. His confession comes too late to save her, and Lear enters carrying the lifeless body of his favorite child in his arms. The eighteenth-century critic, Samuel Johnson, found the scene too painful to watch. From the very deepest grief, far beneath the calculus of reason, Lear mimics the sound of an animal in wounded agony:

> Howl, howl, howl! O, you are men of stones!
> Had I your tongues and eyes, I'ld use them so
> That heaven's vault should crack. She's gone forever!
> I know when one is dead, and when one lives.
> She's dead as earth. Lend me a looking glass,
> If that her breath will mist or stain the stone,
> Why then she lives. . . . .
> This feather stirs, she lives! If it be so,
> It is a chance which does redeem all sorrows
> That ever I have felt. (5.3.258-268)

The sounds are animalistic because this grief cannot be rendered in human language. He looks frantically for signs of life, but the feather is not stirring. It is an illusion of desperate hope. A moment passes before he goes on. What comes next, however, gives voice to a profound ambiguity:

> And my poor fool is hanged! No, no, no life!
> Why should a dog, a horse, a rat have life,
> And thou no breath at all? Thou'lt come no more.
> Never, never, never, never, never.
> Pray you, undo this button. . . .
> Do you see this? Look on her! Look her lips.
> Look there, look there! [Lear dies] (5.3.306-312)

The play began with Lear's false equivalency between opulent speech and love. That false equivalency was proof that he knew nothing about a loyal heart. Now, with Cordelia's death, his language is reduced to the most elemental words that somehow manage to profess the profound depth of the love between them. There is no opulence here. Where animal imagery once reflected the anger and disgust he felt for his eldest daughters, here it gives voice to a grief that goes beyond rational thought, vividly aware of the bonds between father and daughter. Ironically, his predicament mirrors exactly what Cordelia faced in that first scene, but now it is Lear who finds it impossible to adequately express feelings, to heave his heart into his mouth. Evidence of life is everywhere except where he needs it most, and the finality of her passing is more than he can bear. The final truth is harsh. Suffering may result in insight. Forgiveness may produce a shared joy. Yet neither can preserve the very precious opportunity man has been given. Life is fragile. Everything beneath the heavens, both good and bad, is subject to the grave.

And yet, what is to be made of his illusion that her lips are whispering a final thought to him? It is probably no coincidence that every Shakespearean play recognized as tragedy contains a similar final scene. After taking Friar Lawrence's potion, the entombed Juliet appears to be dead, a sight that inspires Romeo to follow her beyond the grave. As Hamlet puns on their union, Claudius is poisoned by the same pearl that inadvertently kills his beloved Gertrude. Convinced of Desdemona's infidelity, a jealous Othello strangles his innocent wife on their marriage bed and then, realizing his mistake, commits suicide. Because of their sin, the Macbeths are the negation of this pattern where love cannot be defeated by death. Driven mad by guilt, Lady Macbeth's death precedes that of her distracted but despairing husband, who, by this time, is inured to any horror and therefore feels no connection to her at all. And Antony's death inspires the mercurial Queen of Egypt to commit fully to the man she loved by nursing the poisonous asps. In each instance, love seems to function as an invisible connection that transcends even death. Death may be the "bourne from which no man returns," as Hamlet says, despite the ghost's multiple appearances, but Shakespeare's tragic denouements seem to suggest that love gives meaning to the passage from life into what lies beyond. Perhaps love cannot preserve life, but somehow it endures and inspires and guides, even from beyond the grave. How and why it can do so may be the final mystery, pointing to the presence of the divine working its loving influence through the most essential quality of human nature. Despite suffering and evil, this is cause for great joy, for it provides a reason to choose what's right and good.

To some who consider tragedy the pessimistic and comedy the optimistic genre, this reading of *Lear*'s ending may seem too hopeful. On this, Heilman again has the final word:

> Pessimism does not consist in seeing evil injure good; it is instead the inability to see good; or it is to conclude only that evil is mistaken for good; or to discover total depravity, but no grace. To find the play painful or shocking is to be unable to grasp quality as quality, and to substitute success for quality; it is to think in terms of the naïve expectation that longevity, as well as invulnerability to mortal ills, is the reward of virtue. This is the error of Lear at the beginning of the play— the introduction of irrelevant quantitative standards. Quantity of life or quantity of immunity to suffering has, alas, no relationship to moral integrity. . . . To assume or to seek such relationship is to substitute reward for merit, accident for substance; it is to move from tragedy to melodrama. (290)

Where melodrama offers simple problems and simplistic resolutions, tragedy looks at human existence in all its complex but richly suggestive paradoxes and never blinks, regardless of the painful truths that emerge. But it sees more than suffering, too. In the end, tragedy is the more hopeful genre because, like *King Lear*, it recognizes grace when it sees it, even amid wickedness, and insists on its relevance to human life. Though magic is never referenced explicitly in this play, Shakespeare clearly shows in this immensely moving examination of human nature that any proper evaluation of it must account for the magic of Cordelia's love.

Macbeth

Faced with two ungrateful daughters, Lear asks one of that play's essential questions: "Is there any cause in nature that make these hard hearts" (3.6.77)? The mock trial with a fool and a madman dissolves before the question receives an answer, but the unexamined passion and sexual jealousy that eventually consumes those stony-hearted sisters identify the consequences. Still, those consequences don't actually clarify why they chose to be that way, why they were not more like Cordelia. Was the evil an inescapable part of their unique human nature, a particular implementation of their being that was somehow defective? Written almost simultaneously with *Lear*, *Macbeth* seems to be an attempt to provide an answer to Lear's question: what causes the persistent evil that plagues human existence? In accordance with traditional Christian doctrine, the answer provided by *Macbeth* has to do with man's endowment of free will and his consequent vulnerability to temptation.

Except for *Othello*, the detailed attention *Macbeth* gives to the process and consequences of temptation is unique. This consideration may have taken root from events of the time. As the first years of the seventeenth century approached, England's mood was increasingly anxious. Because of the childless queen's advanced age, the uncertainty of succession made the inevitable political change worrisome. After Elizabeth's death in late March, 1603, however, the smooth transition to her successor, King James, was met with great relief and, for a time, exuberant joy. But that elation was soon replaced by further anxiety, for his ascension to the English throne almost immediately ran into trouble. As the son of the Scottish queen, Mary, a Catholic who had been imprisoned and then executed for conspiring against the Protestant Elizabeth's reign, James embodied the hope of many in that faith for more equitable treatment. But despite his best efforts, he was unable to prevail over a reluctant and increasingly

Puritan parliament.   Bitterly disappointed by the king's perceived weakness, a group of Catholic conspirators hatched an audacious plot to murder every parliamentarian, along with King James, whose support for their cause seemed inadequate. They placed their hopes in the king's young daughter, Elizabeth, whom they felt they could control once she took her place on the English throne.

Lacking any widespread support, the ill-conceived plot was doomed to failure. In 1605, a little over a year after Elizabeth's death, nobles loyal to James intercepted a letter alluding to a Catholic conspiracy to blow up the House of Lords where the assembled members and the King himself would be attending parliament.   Understandably alarmed by the letter, James wanted the parliament building in the heart of London carefully searched.   Several attempts failed to uncover anything, but just one day before the legislature convened, a final investigation of the building's basement discovered a man, Guy Fawkes, guarding thirty-six barrels of gunpowder. The size of the charge probably would have been enough to achieve its aim. Fawkes was arrested, imprisoned, and eventually executed, but not before he revealed the details of the plot and the names of his co-conspirators. Among them was a Jesuit priest by the name of Henry Garnet, who, in 1598, had written *A Treatise on Equivocation,* which described how linguistic ambiguity could assist in the evasion of truth, principles he reportedly employed during his trial. Though he was only guilty of knowing about the plot through the confessional, Garnet's legal tactics failed to prevent his gruesome execution. Nevertheless, his attempts to equivocate during the trial were widely publicized and fueled the pervasive suspicion of anything Catholic. To those loyal to the crown, these conspirators were evil incarnate, ready to use half-truths and equivocation to justify their actions.

With the evils of equivocation on every Elizabethan mind, it may not be surprising that deceptive half-truths play a pivotal role in *Macbeth*. Most likely written in 1606, a year

258

after the Gunpowder Conspiracy and just months after the trials, the story of Macbeth's decline begins with equivocation. In the play's murky atmosphere where "fair is foul and foul is fair," half-truths and ambiguity awaken dangerous ambitions to murder a legitimate king. The parallels between art and reality were certainly no accident. First performed at King James 'court, Macbeth's ruthless path to the throne might warrant examination but certainly could not be condoned, especially with memories of Guy Fawkes and Garnet still occupying everyone's thoughts. While the Macbeths were deceived by equivocation, in the aftermath of the Gunpowder Plot, the consequences of their sin had to be completely unambiguous. The play's infamous witches certainly start Macbeth on his downward trajectory, but he alone is responsible for his choices, his lack of repentance, and for his well-deserved punishment. As it had in this historical moment, justice also had to prevail in art.

The bloodiest of Shakespeare's tragedies, *Macbeth,* is a careful examination of the reasons men succumb to temptation and the consequences of choosing evil rather than good. The play very artfully creates an atmosphere where temptation is not just a psychological process but a moral and spiritual one as well. With great precision, it demonstrates how temptation originates from a desire that is given shape and form by the imagination, how those visions intrude into the mind where they subvert reason and judgment, eventually leading to the negation of what's intrinsically good in human nature. While the action of the play very clearly occurs in this world, *Macbeth* also allows us to glimpse dark shadows of supernatural forces that operate within human events. Though Macbeth and his wife align themselves with those evil powers and temporarily control Scotland, divine retribution is eventually visited upon them through some chosen nemesis who restores order. Though the Macbeths choose their path, it is nevertheless impossible to escape the sense that mysterious and unnamed forces are also at work in these events. Those forces are embodied in the three witches.

That Macbeth consciously chooses evil violates common expectations about a tragic protagonist who, it is often assumed, should be a good but flawed individual unable to foresee the consequences of his own decisions. Sophocles's Oedipus, for example, unknowingly kills his father and marries his mother. Though circumstances prevent him from recognizing either parent until it is too late, his decisions violate cultural and ethical norms which require his punishment. Because circumstances blind Oedipus to the consequences of his decisions, however, his ignorance of those circumstances effectively removes moral culpability. In this particular Greek tragedy, moral ignorance inadvertently leads to actions that the gods or fate punish. Sophocles's *Antigone*, a second example from Greek tragedy, involves a conflict between two moral absolutes. Even though no good choice actually exists, the gods still discipline Antigone for burying her brother in violation of Creon's prohibition. In both cases, protagonists are caught in impossible predicaments that supernatural forces still choose to punish. Classical Greek tragedy depicts a world where people of limited insight have little choice except to endure unfair suffering and death. This is simply mankind's unfortunate predicament.

But as *Hamlet* already indicated, Shakespeare was forging his own definition of what constituted tragic drama. Unlike Oedipus, Antigone, or even Hamlet, Macbeth is neither a morally innocent victim nor is he ensnared by unresolvable moral conundrums. Instead, he knowingly and repeatedly makes self-serving, evil rather than morally good choices. Nor is he blind to the consequences of his decisions. He covets a position that doesn't belong to him, and he acts on that desire, hoping more than believing that bold action will bring success, that the expected earthly consequences can be avoided, that the pleasure of earthly success will help him

260

endure whatever punishment might come after death. Within the Christian context of Shakespeare's culture, Macbeth is the unrepentant sinner who suffers the inevitable consequences of a heart that become inured to whatever is good and holy. Endowed with free will, his moral culpability is absolutely clear.

Despite the seductive ambiguities of the witches' prophecies, then, he really has no excuse. Other characters don't make his choices. But neither can the influence of the witches be discounted as inconsequential. Even more than the ghost of Hamlet's murdered father, they deserve to be taken seriously. Somewhere in the play's darkest shadows, there is the sense that good and evil are engaged in a spiritual battle for Macbeth's soul. Just before he approaches the witches one final time to discover his fate in the coming battle against his amassing enemies, the hags wind up their charms in preparation for his visit:

> Great business must be wrought ere noon:
> Upon the corner of the moon
> There hangs a vap'rous drop profound,
> I'll catch it ere it come to ground;
> And that, distill'd by magic sleights,
> Shall raise such artificial sprites
> As by the strength of their illusion
> Shall draw him on to his confusion,
> He shall spurn fate, scorn death, and bear
> His hopes 'bove wisdom, grace, and fear;
> And you all know, security
> Is mortals' chiefest enemy. (3.5.22-33)

From this spell, Shakespeare's very Christian audience knew he was being seduced by a heady concoction of desire, equivocal promises, and morally specious reasoning, but Macbeth's confusion would also be seen as the result of powers beyond his control. The relationship between the witches and Macbeth is a symbiosis of respective weaknesses. Since he possesses free will, they do not have the power to force his decisions. All they can do is exploit the place where their prospect has unfulfilled desires. The weaknesses inherent in human nature would take care of the rest. Foreshadowed by *Twelfth Night's* Malvolio, the Macbeths fall victim to their ambition, a desire for wealth, power, and status. These are human weaknesses that larger, more powerful forces, personified in the witches, are able to exploit. Their magical incantations connect them to these dark powers.

Unencumbered by any subplots, *Macbeth*'s story is uniquely straightforward. As the play begins, Duncan, the victorious Scottish king, is surveying a battlefield gradually going quiet. His royal forces have prevailed. Macbeth, perhaps Scotland's bravest warrior, has fought valiantly to protect his nation from rebellion and invasion. Generous and grateful, Duncan rewards Macbeth with the title of the defeated rebel leader, an event that three witches had already shared with the valiant warrior. Though Macbeth is all but convinced the weird sisters can accurately foresee the future, their message is also troubling: while they suggest Macbeth would eventually become king, they also claimed no child of his would ever succeed him. Instead, his friend, Banquo, would father a long line of Scottish kings that, according to legend, included King James himself. Despite this puzzling ambiguity, ambition now flames hot in his own and his wife's imaginations. Since his determination wavers as the crucial moment approaches, Lady Macbeth challenges him to murder Duncan, which he does. Afraid for their own lives, Duncan's sons flee and are therefore blamed for their father's death. Consequently, Macbeth is crowned and he attempts to settle into his new role. But since the witches predicted an uncertain future, relentless anxiety about his prospects disrupts the royal couple's effort to maintain a façade of calm normalcy. Despite his wife's plea to hide his restless imaginings, their lives drift apart. Resolving to murder anyone who might jeopardize his future, Macbeth initiates a series of bloody actions that cost him peace of mind, sleep, his marriage, friends, political stability, and eventually his life. Unlike his wife, his behavior is not the result of guilt. Like an animal obsessed with survival, he no longer has sufficient emotional energy to stay connected to his wife. As her marriage disintegrates, Lady Macbeth descends into madness, quickly followed by death which comes shortly before the avenging Scottish nobles defeat and kill her husband. Duncan's son assumes the throne and peace returns to Scotland.

Because Macbeth's bloody reign is replaced by stability and peace, *Macbeth*'s moral implications are quite clear and nearly impossible to misinterpret. First performed for King James, who not only dabbled in the mythology of the occult but personally witnessed the Gunpowder Conspiracy trials, Shakespeare's play would have been received as confirmation that God often uses good men like Banquo and MacDuff to root out evil and restore a nation's harmony. Such a view of history is quite Biblical. As *1Henry 4* makes clear, Shakespeare's histories assume that time is the divine workshop where society is continually redeemed from the effects of human frailty and sin.

But the Thane of Glamis's choices put him beyond redemption. In *Macbeth*, time is redemptive only to men of good character. Because he has deliberately and repeatedly forsaken his best nature, Macbeth's experience of time is entirely different. As the avenging army advances toward the castle where he is trapped, he hears the last shriek of his dying wife, consumed by grief and despair. Preparing to engage his enemies, Macbeth reacts to the event with the nihilism of a man who has lost everything, including his soul:

> Sey. The Queen, my lord, is dead.
> Macb. She should have died hereafter;
> There would have been a time for such a word.
> To-morrow, and to-morrow, and to-morrow,
> Creeps in this petty pace from day to day,
> To the last syllable of recorded time;
> And all our yesterdays have lighted fools

The way to dusty death. Out, out, brief candle!
Life's but a walking shadow, a poor player,
That struts and frets his hour upon the stage,
And then is heard no more. It is a tale
Told by an idiot, full of sound and fury,
Signifying nothing. (5.5.16-28)

The lines capture the emotional and spiritual bleakness of a man whose life is now devoid of any significance. Ambition led to murder which led to additional bloodshed, isolation, despair, and death. This particular life has been bled dry of both purpose and meaning. Except for his wife, no one else in the play expresses such deep despair. But the despair is not universal. Since those who have suffered under his rule are fighting to restore honor and respect to their community, their efforts are blessed with significant meaning. Macbeth's enemies know what their purpose is. Macbeth's decision to murder Duncan, on the other hand, removes everything of value from the lives of both husband and wife. They have lost respect, trust, friends, community, peace, sleep, and the companionship and love of a devoted spouse.

His life was not always so bleak. As the play opens, a sergeant provides an account of his ferocious confrontation with the leader of the Scottish rebels trying to overthrow good king Duncan:

. . . brave Macbeth. . .
Disdaining Fortune, with his brandish'd steel
(Like Valor's minion) carv'd out his passage
Till he fac'd the slave;
Which nev'r shook hands, nor bade farewell to him,
Till he unseam'd him from the nave to th' chops,
And fix'd his head upon our battlements. (1.2.16-23)

Duncan, impressed by Macbeth's valiant efforts, decides to reward his captain with the defeated rebel leader's title, Thane of Cawdor. But this first description of Macbeth is itself ambiguous. On one hand, Macbeth bravely supports a noble king who is associated with generosity, abundance, and grace. But the image is also of a bloody man who "meant to bathe in reeking wounds," a foreshadowing of his coming reign of terror. Which of these is the real Macbeth? "There's no art," Duncan naively observes, "to find the mind's construction in the face." Capable of either good or evil, however, the true character of any man is hidden within, opaque to human vision, until action reveals what's truly in his mind and heart. For better or for worse, one Thane of Cawdor rebels and another takes his place. The first is defeated, confesses in "deep repentance," and bravely accepts his punishment. "Nothing in life," says Duncan's son Malcolm, "became him like the leaving it." As the death of the first Thane of Cawdor shows, the fate of those who rebel against legitimate authority is certain. It is a lesson that the second Thane of Cawdor should not ignore but does.

The difference between the valued warrior at the beginning of the play and the dry husk of a man at the end reveals Macbeth's decline. A life full of promise has been replaced by deep spiritual desolation. Like all men, Macbeth had been endowed with a variety of gifts, including his skills in blood and death which, quite remarkably, nature can use for good. A generous king willingly repays him for employing all these to preserve Scotland's order. Where Duncan's benevolence had once showered rewards upon a brave and valiant man willing to risk his life in service to his king and nation, the man at the end is encircled by the consequences of his bloody reign. Even the last vestiges of freedom have disappeared. "They have tied me to a stake," he laments. "I cannot fly but bear-like I must fight the course." The how and why of that change is the real substance of *Macbeth*. Like the lost paradise of *Genesis*, *Macbeth* recreates the oldest story of all: the fall from grace into the horrid consequences of sin.

That degeneration begins with the three witches, equivocating agents of darkness, who provide Macbeth with a blurred glimpse into the future. Their message is misleading because it is also partially true. But desire, in the form of ambition for the crown, prompts him to hear what's true and ignore the danger even he suspects. Fresh from his victorious battle against rebel forces, he encounters the three witches on the heath. The first greets him with his present title, but the remaining two greet him with titles that have yet to be bestowed:

> 1W.   All hail, Macbeth, hail to thee, Thane of Glamis!
> 2W.   All hail, Macbeth, hail to thee, Thane of Cawdor!
> 3W.   All hail, Macbeth, that shalt be king hereafter!
>   (1.3.49-52)

At this juncture, Macbeth has no insight into how this will come about. Since no mortal can see into the future, the encounter is fraught with the kind of dangerous moral ambiguity that promotes confusion, a state where "fair is foul, and foul is fair." And the sowing of confusion is exactly what the incantations of these witches anticipate. Within the uncertainty they create, the moral compass loses direction, and desire's imagined visions of royal power all too easily lead Macbeth down into the darkness of sin and damnation. Because equivocation fosters the moral confusion that renders the wrong choice more attractive than experience proves it to be, it is all too easy for desire to initiate the corruption of Macbeth's soul.

But man has also been endowed with a conscience to counter the dangers inherent in free will. At first, that conscience actively resists the idea of Duncan's murder, so the temptation, which occupies the play's first two acts, occurs in stages. When Duncan rewards Macbeth with the defeated rebel's title, Thane of Cawdor, the witches' ability to predict the future accurately seems confirmed. But both Macbeth and his companion, Banquo, recognize the moral dangers in the witches' prognostications. Turning to Macbeth, Banquo warns that these predictions "Might yet enkindle you unto the crown," which is followed by the admonition, ". . . oftentimes, to win us to our harm, the instruments of darkness tell us truths." In a private moment a few lines later, Macbeth wrestles with exactly that problem:

> This supernatural soliciting
> Cannot be ill; cannot be good. If ill,
> Why hath it given me earnest of success,
> Commencing in a truth? I am Thane of Cawdor.
> If good, why do I yield to that suggestion
> Whose horrid image doth unfix my hair,
> And make my seated heart knock at my ribs,
> Against the use of nature? (1.3.130-137)

The battlefield image of Macbeth from the play's first scene describes a man who knew that rebellion was evil and must be repelled. But the witches have already planted a seed in Macbeth's imagination, and it will take root as the same ugly weed of desire for illegitimate power that motivated the first Thane of Cawdor. As we see in Macbeth, that process begins when moral certainty has been replaced by moral indecision, a condition already evident in Macbeth's assessment that the prophecy "cannot be ill; cannot be good." Because such uncertainty craves resolution, his imagination is already creating a "horrid image" of a murder "against the use of nature." Recoiling from the thought of what he might need to do, Macbeth still exhibits a conscience delicate enough to resist such an unnatural act.

Throughout Shakespeare, human nature's potential for good is assumed to be part of the natural world's design. This very Biblical model of nature helps to define the Macbeths' depravity. Offsetting their unnatural cruelty is a nature of harmony and fecundity that the Macbeths violate in word and deed. As Duncan and his entourage approach Macbeth's castle, he comments that the fortress, nestled in the bucolic Scottish countryside, "hath a pleasant seat, the air nimbly and sweetly recommends itself/Unto our gentle senses." To which Banquo remarks:

> This guest of summer,
> The temple-haunting marlet, does approve,
> By his lov'd mansionry, that the heaven's breath
> Smells wooingly here; no jutty, frieze,
> Buttress, nor coign of vantage, but this bird
> Hath made his pendant bed and procreant cradle.
> Where they most breed and haunt, I have observ'd
> The air is delicate. (1.6.3-10)

The author of *Genesis* understood that the bleakness of sin's many consequences would stand out more sharply against the perfections of Eden. Superficially, the nature that both men observe restores nerves chafed raw by the stress of recent battle. But this seemingly superfluous exchange points to the other, more spiritual battle that is ongoing. Paradoxically, the very castle where death awaits also provides safe haven for the birds that make their nests among the battlements. The vision is emblematic of the essential moral quandary life outside the original garden presents. What the two men observe is a nature struggling to assert its abundant fertility against the encroachments of chaos and blood, the opposition between good and evil. In opposition to death, new life emerges from the beds and "procreant cradle[s]," where the marlets can "breed and haunt." It is a scene that embodies the tension between life's abundant goodness and death's various negations of life. The struggle between these forces is cyclical, and just as Macbeth repeats the mistake of the previous Thane of Cawdor, the battle between life-enhancing forces and death is the perpetual struggle of human experience.

This dichotomy is enhanced further by Duncan's affiliation with the forces of life. After hearing of Macbeth's battlefield valor, Duncan greets his champion with language that is rich with agricultural images of husbandry and new growth:

> Welcome hither!

> I have begun to plant thee, and will labor
> To make thee full of growing. (1.4.28-30)

Far from passive, a good king works to cultivate the prosperity of others. Rich with the promise of future abundance for all that serve him well, Duncan's generosity aligns him with the natural fecundity observed outside Macbeth's castle. Both the title and Duncan's liberality are the fruit of the king's "labor," for each is meant to enrich the other.   As seen in many previous plays, giving selflessly and generously multiplies love's wealth, so when both king and citizens put all God-given gifts to use, both giver and receiver are enhanced. As an extension of nature's bounty, Duncan's royal generosity reflects the will of a Creator who designed nature to overwhelm the agents of death with new life and abundance. Consequently, when Macbeth decides to murder Duncan, he alienates himself from this nature and all its promised wealth.

Though at first the witches' message intrigues him, Macbeth knows full well the moral decision he faces. In a remarkably complex soliloquy, he contemplates which path to follow. A rich amalgam of the rational and the imaginative, the argument attempts to evaluate worldly and supernatural consequences of such a heinous act before reaching its apocalyptic conclusion. As servants are preparing a table for Macbeth's royal guest, he examines one possible consequence of murder: the possibility of escaping detection altogether:

> If it were done, when 'tis done, then 'twere well
> It were done quickly. If th' assassination
> Could trammel up the consequence, and catch
> With his surcease, success; that but this blow
> Might be the be-all and the end-all---here,
> But here, upon this bank and [schoal] of time,
> We'ld jump the life to come. (1.7.1-7)

If all the consequences of murder could be gathered up and managed successfully in this world, then Macbeth would be willing to risk whatever consequences might follow in the afterlife. Ironically, these first lines contain an echo of John 13:27 where, at the Last Supper, Jesus speaks to Judas and tells him," What you are about to do, do quickly." The Biblical allusion, which subtly equates Macbeth to Judas, provides immediate moral orientation since, as it was for Jesus, this too will be Duncan's last supper. But Macbeth continues:

> But in these cases,
> We still have judgment here, that we but teach
> Bloody instructions, which, being taught, return
> To plague the inventor. This even-handed justice
> Commends th' ingredience of our poison'd chalice
> To our own lips. (1.7.7-11)

As Bolingbroke learned when he overthrew Richard II, deposing a rightful king taught others how to assert their rights in exactly the same way. Rebellion begets more rebellion. So even if supernatural consequences could be avoided, judgment in this world cannot be escaped. Since punishment is unavoidable, therefore, the passage transitions to the social preclusions against murder:

> He's here in double trust:
> First, as I am his kinsman and his subject,
> Strong both against the deed; then, as his host,
> Who should against his murtherer shut the door,
> Not bear the knife myself. (1.7.11-15)

Besides the recurring cycle of violence that regicide would incite, Macbeth knows that Duncan's murder would also violate social and cultural norms. His conscience is certainly troubled by these significant cultural arguments against murder. What follows, however, acknowledges the moral and spiritual dimensions of such a "horrid deed."

> Besides, this Duncan

270

> Hath borne his faculties so meek, hath been
> So clear in his great office, that his virtues
> Will plead like angels, trumpet-tongued, against
> The deep damnation of his taking-off;
> And pity, like a naked new-born babe,
> Striding the blast, or heaven's cherubin, hors'd
> Upon the sightless couriers of the air,
> Shall blow the horrid deed in every eye,
> That tears shall drown the wind. (1.7.15-24)

This powerful and frightening vision should give anyone pause. With its apocalyptic imagery, the concluding lines of Macbeth's soliloquy complete the transition to the spiritual consequences of the contemplated murder. Evil cannot be hidden. It will be proclaimed and punishment will inevitably be meted out. When good is measured against evil, Duncan's virtues will speak with trumpet tongues, and either pity or heaven's cherubim will stride through the coming storm of tears, announcing Macbeth's sin for all to hear. The deed will be exposed and judged, either by his kinsman or by avenging supernatural powers. Dissuaded from his contemplated purpose, his conclusion follows:

> I have no spur
> To prick the sides of my intent, but only
> Vaulting ambition, which o'erleaps itself
> And falls on th' other--- . (1.7.25-28)

Since ambition rather than any recognizably just cause is his only motive, the plan to murder Duncan will inevitably fail. At this point, Macbeth is fully cognizant of the consequences following Duncan's murder. Every aspect of human nature, including its social, moral, and spiritual norms, argues against it, and he resolves not to commit such a heinous act. For the moment, reason is sufficient to prevent a contemplated sin. Everything begins to change, however, when Lady Macbeth makes her first appearance.

As his dramatization of admirable women characters like Rosalind, Viola, Cordelia, and Cleopatra evolves, Shakespeare moves toward a conviction that they, far more than the men around them, are often uniquely sensitive to those heart-felt inclinations for union with another, be that a child, a husband, or a parent, and being so inclined, they are eager to convey what they know and feel to enrich their relationships. When present, those inclinations contribute to the stability of marriages, family, and, ultimately, to the surrounding community. As such, the nature of the feminine normally plays a significant role in every aspect of life. This is true of Lady Macbeth as well, but her influence on her husband is the very negation of this view of the feminine. While her husband's thinking and actions comprise most of the play's subject matter, Lady Macbeth plays an enormously significant part in his decline.

Though her lines are relatively few, Lady Macbeth inverts this principle of feminine nature. Once she grasps the opportunity that Duncan's arrival represents, she remains narrowly focused on what the two of them might gain by murdering their royal visitor. Keenly aware of her husband's ambition and of the conscience that she knows will dissuade him from acting on that desire, she decides that she must do everything in her power to fulfill his aspirations. She makes a crucial moral choice. While reading her husband's letter where he describes not only the witches' prophecy but the king's imminent arrival at her castle, she prepares herself for the confrontation that will decide their fates. Harboring an ambition for power stronger than his own, she offers a chilling, demonic prayer to the agents of darkness:

> The raven himself is hoarse
> That croaks the fatal entrance of Duncan
> Under my battlements. Come, you spirits
> That tend on mortal thoughts, unsex me here,
> And fill me from the crown to the toe topful
> Of direst cruelty! Make thick my blood,

Stop up th' access and passage to remorse,
That no compunctious visitings of nature
Shake my fell purpose. . . . Come to my woman's breasts,
And take my milk for gall, you murth'ring ministers,
Wherever . . . you wait on nature's mischief! (1.5.38 – 50)

In several ways, this is significantly different from her husband's very logical process to reject the idea of regicide. Where the witches seek him out, Lady Macbeth goes before the powers of "direst cruelty" to prevent any "compunctious visitings of nature" that might restrain her "fell purpose." Imploring those evil spirits to "unsex" her, to expunge those natural feminine qualities that nurture and protect, she is willing to exchange her mother's milk for bitter gall. This rejection of her own feminine identity in order to motivate a man who she fears is still "too full o 'th 'milk of human kindness" represents an ironic perversion of the self-sacrificing love seen in Shakespeare's more genuinely loving women.

Those "spirits that tend on mortal thoughts" are quick to answer Lady Macbeth's prayer, and she confronts him with all the aggressive force of a battlefield opponent. But her chosen weapons are emotional rather than logical. Where he contemplated the moral, social, and spiritual consequences of murder, the only consequences she mentions are the ones that allegedly affect her. She uses the love that exists between them to get what she thinks they both want. When they next meet, Macbeth informs her he can't and won't murder Duncan. Her response is swift and emotional:

Lady M. Was the hope drunk
        Wherein you dress'd yourself? Hath it slept
          since?
        . . . . From this time
        Such I account thy love. Art thou afeared
        To be the same in thine own act and valor
        As thou art in desire? . . . .
Macb.   Prithee peace!

> I dare do all that may become a man;
> Who dares [do] more is none.
> Lady M. What beast was't then
> That made you break this enterprise to me?
> When you durst do it, then you were a man.
> (1.7. 35-49)

Lady Macbeth attacks her husband's honesty, his sense of duty to her, his love for her, and, finally, his very manhood. She is willing to undermine the very foundation of his identity and nature to bend his will to hers. And her strategy works because the logic and reason he used to dissuade himself earlier are no match for this assault on the visceral sense of who he is as a man and a husband, especially when the assault is perpetrated by the woman he lives and sleeps with. Those spirits she invoked have transformed a loving, feminine nature into this, into a woman willing to abuse the very bonds that tie husband and wife to each other.

Macbeth's decision not to murder was based on an appreciation of man's moral nature and the supernatural consequences of sin. Those standards define what it is to be human, to be a man, both of which are grounded in the virtues Duncan rewarded but which his wife rejected. The confusion sown by the witches is intensified by Lady Macbeth's argument which consists of three main points: first, a husband shouldn't confide a shared hope to his wife that he doesn't intend to fulfill; second, if a husband loves his wife he will fulfill his promises, even if it is to murder a king; and third, a truly brave and manly husband would steel his resolve to murder Duncan. The first is a tacit admission she doesn't possess the moral clarity or strength to resist temptation. The second and third arguments pervert the nature of both love and manliness into their moral opposites. Like a fourth witch formulating her charm, she's able to employ emotionally and morally specious arguments that effectively increase her husband's confusion and motivate him to do what she believes, quite mistakenly, they both want.

In a world where "fair is foul, and foul is fair," where kindness and morality are weaknesses and cruelty is manly and good, Lady Macbeth convinces her husband by declaring her willingness to pervert feminine nature absolutely, to plumb the depths of depravity. She had already emphasized her allegiance to unnatural cruelty when she envisioned demon spirits as babes sucking gall rather than nourishing milk from her "woman's breasts." This first allusion initiates an elaborate web of associations to young, vulnerable babies that serve to define the cruelty of the Macbeths. As it had in that earlier invocation to mortal spirits, that allusion to helpless babes is used again to bolster her argument here, for she transforms a particularly maternal moment into an image of ghastly brutality:

> I have given suck, and know
> How tender 'tis to love the babe that milks me;
> I would, while it was smiling in my face,
> Have pluck'd my nipple from his boneless gums
> And dash'd the brains out, had I so sworn as you
> Have done to this. (1.7.54-59)

Although she is ultimately unable to sustain this pretense of unfeminine cruelty, Lady Macbeth's dreadful image is enough to shock her emotionally vulnerable husband into compliance. "Bring forth men-children only," he concludes, "for thy undaunted mettle should compose nothing but males." Since he too now equates such heartless cruelty to manliness, it is clear that Macbeth, morally confused and emotionally vulnerable, has succumbed to her arguments. Her temptation complete, she very diligently lays out the details of their plot.

Despite her best effort to convert those innately feminine virtues into a nature steeped in cruelty, Lady Macbeth's labors are doomed to failure. She cannot easily escape her essential nature. While her husband is murdering Duncan, the pretense is exposed when she nervously admits that "had [Duncan] not resembled my father as he slept, I had

275

done't." Nor, initially, can Macbeth easily escape his innate sense of right and wrong either, for his moral sensitivity is still able to activate a deep sense of guilt. When he returns from Duncan's room where he has murdered the king, Macbeth becomes fixated on the blood he has spilled. Looking at his hand in horror, he asks, "Will all great Neptune's ocean wash this blood clean from my hands?" The answer he provides suggests the enormity of his guilt: "No; this my hand will rather the multitudinous seas incarnadine." Blood, life-giving and precious, has now dyed the entire world with the unnatural color of sin. Because guilt this enormous is impossible to hide, Lady Macbeth's attempts to assuage it are pitifully inadequate. "Consider it not so deeply," she implores, but the words betray her inability to face the horror of what they've done, for thinking deeply on it can only aggravate that relentlessly nagging conscience.

Because she was so focused on obtaining the crown that she failed to appreciate her husband's deeply moral nature, she never anticipates the depth of his moral guilt and can do very little after the murder to mitigate it. She tries to manage those feelings by focusing very narrowly on the incriminating details of the murder scene, but, in the end, the cruelty she unleashed in her husband begins to separate them. While her guilt overwhelms and drives her toward madness, the very war-hardened, masculine bravery she had taunted now battles against the inner voice of his conscience and the social consequences that had previously argued against the murder. Unlike Lady Macbeth, courage and cruelty were always a part of his nature, so warrior-like, he now dares "fate into the list" so it can "champion me to the 'utterance." Though they are now on two separate but equally dangerous spiritual paths, the first fruit of evil, division, is already at work.

By murdering Duncan, the Macbeth's placed their interests before the common good. That selfishness is the essence of their sin, and that all-consuming self-interest will come to dominate their thoughts, their actions, their lives, even their sleep until there is no more room for anything of real and lasting value. Unwittingly, Lady Macbeth has unleashed the brutal animal that once fought for a good and gracious king but now fights for their survival, and this battle gradually empties Macbeth's heart of any human kindness until no feelings are left, even for his once beloved wife. Their complete isolation from each other is the personal consequence of sin. Their isolation from the community becomes the social and political consequence. Whether they yet realize it, the Macbeths have passed through the very gates of Hell, which the irritable porter humorously acknowledges the next morning as he answers the persistent knocking of Duncan's entourage:

> Here's a knocking indeed! If a man were porter of Hell Gate, he should have old turning the key. (Knock.) Knock, knock, knock! Who's there, i' th' name of Belzebub? . . . . But this place is too cold for hell. I'll devil-porter no further. I had thought to have let in some of all professions that go the primrose way to th' everlasting bonfire. . . . (2.3.1-20)

There is no turning back anymore. The king has been murdered. Life can never be poured back into what's dead and gone. The Macbeths have stepped onto the primrose path to hell. Confession and repentance are the only options to return to nature's good graces now, but time, as subsequent events will show, is not on their side.

For the Macbeths, repentance never happens. As the necessary precursor to murder, the repudiation of human nature's moral and nurturing qualities becomes increasingly difficult to reverse. The first sin makes successive ones easier until they become habitual. The answer to Lady Macbeth's demonic prayer came instantaneously, but the remainder of the play traces this hollowing out of everything that was once good in her husband. Fittingly, that process involves his war against children, who embody the future he can still only dimly perceive.   Previously, Lady Macbeth had used the imagery of vulnerable babes to define the depraved cruelty required for murder.   Now children, who threaten to avenge the wrongs they've suffered, become the cause of his relentless anxiety and restless sleep.

Because the king's sons, Malcolm and Donalbain, feared for their own lives and fled, they are blamed for their father's murder, but they eventually become instrumental in Macbeth's defeat.   But the play's other children are also instrumental in time's retribution for murder.   Because they remained in Scotland, Banquo and his son, Fleance, are of more immediate concern.   Since the witches prophesied that Banquo's descendants, not Macbeth's, would comprise a long line of Scottish kings, Macbeth decides that they too must be eliminated.   Though the thugs he hired succeed in killing Banquo, Fleance escapes, an outcome that vexes Macbeth's concern about the future. "The worm that's fled," he observes, "hath nature that in time will venom breed, no teeth for th ' present" (3.4.29-30).   Though harmless for the moment, young Fleance represents the vengeance that the future will eventually bring to Macbeth's doorstep, and that vengeance is personified in the child who escaped.

Besides Macbeth's obsessive anxiety about the future, the consequences of sin are manifested in other ways as well. One of those is the disruption of the murderers' sleep. Normally, sleep is nature's way of healing mind and body from the ordinary cares of daily life.   But murder is anything but normal.   When Macbeth emerges from the chamber where he murdered Duncan, he tells his wife that he thought he heard a voice cry "Sleep no more! Macbeth does murther sleep. . . ." From that point on, neither he nor Lady Macbeth enjoys the kind of sleep "that knits up the ravell'd sleave of care."   Her last appearance, in fact, has her sleepwalking through the castle trying to wash away the "damn'd spot" from her hands. Though she had once counseled her husband that "a little water [will clear] us of this deed," guilt will not allow either of them to forget the blood that has permanently stained their hands. With guilt large enough to dye the green sea red, such deeply troubled minds can never enjoy the necessary balm that sleep normally provides.

The need for secrecy is another consequence of their sin. Having tried mightily to hide their guilt and shame, their effort to project a façade of normalcy causes a familiar divergence between surface appearances and a hidden truth. After the Macbeth's have settled on the murder, the wife advises her husband to "look like the innocent flower, But be the serpent under it." Later, when Macbeth explains why the attendants in the king's chamber were also killed, a suspicious and wary Malcolm remarks to his brother, Donalbain, "to show an unfelt sorrow is an office which the false man does easy." Again, as his waiting guests are seated for the dinner where Banquo's ghost appears, Lady Macbeth tries to ease her husband's troubled soul, imploring him to "sleek o'er [your] rugged looks, Be bright and jovial. . . ." Throughout *Macbeth*, starting with the equivocal statements from the witches, an appearance of innocence needs to cloak the evil underneath. But nature's inherently moral design will not allow sin to remain hidden for long.

As in *Hamlet*, the ghost of a murdered father is the first indication that Macbeth's secret, abhorrent sin must be exposed. When Banquo's ghost disrupts the assembled nobles at Macbeth's dinner, it is clear that something in nature detests Scotland's unnatural violence and wants these terrible secrets to be revealed and addressed so the wounds can be healed. The morning after Duncan's murder, in fact, the Scottish nobles arriving to escort the king to his next destination report events that imply nature's revulsion:

> The night has been unruly. Where we lay, our chimneys were blown down, and (as they say) lamentings heard i' the' air; strange screams of death, and prophesying, with accents terrible, of dire combustion and confus'd events new hatch'd to th' woeful time. The obscure bird clamor'd the livelong

night. Some say, the earth was feverous, and did shake. (2.2.54-661)

Unnatural murder disrupts nature's normal order, and that disruption cannot be allowed to persist. Divinely designed for order, peace, and abundance, nature waits to be healed. Evil must be exposed and excised before the land can return to its natural moral health. When Macbeth's confused and frightened guests leave his banquet prematurely, therefore, the banquet's false display of the camaraderie and social bonding that had once unified the Scottish community is revealed as a lie. Murder has and will continue to undermine community until the murderers are brought to justice. The appearance of Banquo's ghost is the eruption of Macbeth's bloody sin into the light of day, an event that will trigger Scotland's deliverance from the shackles of tyranny. Despite every effort the Macbeths make to hide their sin and bend fate to their liking, the truth eventually emerges like the naked, newborn babe blowing the horrid deed into every eye. Though evil currently rules the land, the young eventually bring future justice into the present.

Undaunted, Macbeth continues to struggle against the inevitable. The vision of Banquo's ghost prompts him to once again seek out the weird sisters for another glimpse into a future that he desperately wants to control. Once again, though, he is allowed to see only partial truths. The witches provide three more veiled prophecies. He is told to "beware Macduff." He is told that "no man of woman born shall harm" him. And he is told that he can never be defeated until "Great Birnam Wood to high Dunsinane hill shall come against him." As the witches indicated early in the play, their method is to provide their victim with a false sense of security, the purpose for which these latest prognostications are designed. To enhance that false promise of security, the obvious solution to the first warning is another murder, this time of Macduff. And because the remaining two prophesies seem impossible, his

280

future safety and security seem within his grasp. Like the other prophecies, though, these prove to be equivocal as well. Desperate for the security his sin has precluded, Macbeth now hears what he wants to believe. Reckless hope blinds him to the realities that have begun to envelop him.

The first of these prophecies sets Macbeth's resolve to murder not only Macduff but his entire family. Macduff, however, has left for England to encourage Duncan's sons to raise an army that would free Scotland from bloody tyranny. Unfortunately, this leaves his wife and children unprotected. When news of their murders reaches Macduff, his emotional response initiates an exchange with Duncan's son Malcolm that describes manhood much differently than Lady Macbeth's earlier perverted definition:

> Mal.   Be comforted,
> Let's make us med'cines of our great revenge
> To cure this deadly grief.
> Macd. He has no children.   All my pretty ones?
> Did you say all? O hell-kite! All?
> What, all my pretty chickens, and their dam,
> At one fell swoop?
> Mal.   Dispute it like a man.
> Macd.   I shall do so;
> But I must also feel it as a man:
> I cannot but remember such things were,
> That were most precious to me. Did heaven look
>   on,
> And would not take their part? Sinful Macduff,
> They were all strook for thee! Naught that I am,
> Not for their own demerits, but for mine.
> (4.3.213-226)

Here, the loss of a wife and her precious children is cause for deeply felt grief and remorse because he wasn't there to protect them. Where Lady Macbeth had once prayed to "stop up th 'access and passage to remorse," Macduff suffers the loss of his family with genuine and heartfelt grief.   An expression of sorrow does not make him less of a man. Moreover, his sense of moral responsibility for their safety enhances rather than detracts from his understanding of what it means to be a man, a father, a husband. Manhood does not prohibit emotions like grief or tears for the loss of loved ones. It is an indication, in fact, of a deeply felt human connection to family.

Lady Macbeth's demonic prayer to dash the brains of her nursing child contrasts the vulnerable helplessness of babes with the unnatural cruelty she hopes for. But the murder of Macduff's little boy, who bravely defies his assassins, establishes once again that children will embody future vengeance. Banquo's son Fleance, supposedly the ancestor of King James who witnessed an early performance of the play, begins that theme. But Macduff's nameless son becomes the play's most vivid example. In his illuminating essay "The Naked Babe and the Cloak of Manliness," Cleanth Brooks writes:

> The logic of Macbeth's distraught mind . . . forces him to make war on children, a war which in itself reflects his desperation and is a confession of weakness. Macbeth's ruffians, for example, break into Macduff's castle and kill his wife and children. . . . But the pathos is not adventitious; the scene ties into the inner symbolism of the play. For the child, in his helplessness, defies the murderers. Its defiance testifies to the force which threatens Macbeth and which Macbeth cannot destroy. (400)

Macbeth's expectation that a babe would somehow blow the horrid deed in every eye is fulfilled by the death of Macduff's child. Time, anthropomorphized in Banquo's Fleance and Macduff's defiant little boy, will indeed redeem the Scottish nation. As Brooks suggests, the play's defiant juveniles constitute a corporate force that, despite their temporary helplessness, becomes the power that the perverse masculinity of Macbeth cannot possibly defeat.

Moreover, the genuine grief and anger of a father for the loss of a child, the very feelings Lady Macbeth sought to expunge, become part of that universal force. As Malcolm implores his distraught countryman, "Be this the whetstone of your sword, let grief convert to anger, blunt not the heart, enrage it." And as the witches foresaw, Macduff, who comes to avenge his murdered child, will confront Macbeth in his final battle. The truth hidden in the witches 'prognostication, the truth that the bloody tyrant could not comprehend, was that a cesarean procedure had ripped Macduff "untimely" from his mother's womb. Since he is the man never born of woman, a man now full of righteous anger for his brave little boy's death, Macduff enacts justice upon a once brave and noble man whose crimes have left him isolated and completely dispirited.

This gradual devaluation of Macbeth's original stature is amplified further by images of a man who is too small for the robes in which he has been dressed, a child, ironically, wearing adult clothes. The first use of the image suggests a status that doesn't belong to him. "Why do you dress me in borrowed robes?" he asks Duncan's messengers who greet him as Thane of Cawdor, a title the witches had predicted would be his. Later, that image is enhanced as Macbeth's enemies discuss the impending confrontation with Scotland's bloody tyrant:

> Now does he feel
> His secret murthers sticking on his hands;
> Now minutely revolts upbraid his faith-breach;
> Those he commands move only in command,
> Nothing in love. Now does he feel his title
> Hang loose about him, like a giant's robe
> Upon a dwarfish thief. (5.2.17-22)

As king, Macbeth has broken all faith with his people. Despite his effort to wash away the blood, the incarnadine stains, "sticking on his hands," persist for all to see. As a result, he can no longer inspire love from those he commands, and the oversized cloak of royalty loosely covers "a dwarfish thief." This image of an overly large, ill-fitting garment on a child-like figure transforms the once manly warrior of the play's first scene into an absurd thief of royal authority. By deliberately choosing to devalue his ordained nature, this once noble person is reduced to a farcical version of the original. The true manliness of Macduff is meant to be measured against this ridiculous, dwarfish figure.

Even at this late date, however, repentance is still possible. Just as the thief crucified next to Jesus was forgiven at the moment of death, Macbeth's predecessor, the first Thane of Cawdor, regained some of his lost honor by repenting before his execution. But Macbeth has committed sins so grievous that they circumscribe his options and he believes he has little choice but to soldier grimly on. As the armies of his numerous enemies gather nearby, a desperate Macbeth senses defeat but cannot see any direction that could provide an escape from a life that has become devoid of meaning:

> For mine own good,
> All causes shall give way. I am in blood
> Stepp'd in so far that, should I wade no more,
> Returning were as tedious as go o'er. (3.5.134-137)

There is emotional exhaustion in that word "tedious," for having released this river of blood, he is unable to decide whether continuing to spill more is better than repenting and paying the consequences of his terrible misdeeds. The moral confusion initiated by witches still affects his thinking. Macbeth has reached this moment of weary nihilism because he yielded to equivocation, ambition, specious moral logic, and the repetitive murders that dulled his conscience so that even the horrid scream of his dying wife fails to affect his hardened heart. As he prepares for his final battle, he understands exactly what has been lost:

This push
Will cheer me ever, or [disseat] me now.
I have liv'd long enough: my way of life
Is fall'n into the sear, the yellow leaf,
And that which should accompany old age,
As honor, love, obedience, troops of friends,
I must not look to have; but in their stead,
Curses, not loud, but deep, mouth-honor, breath,
Which the poor heart would fain deny, and dare not.
   (5.2.20-28)

Until now, Macbeth's cruelty had cowed every heart into sullen compliance, but resentment and dissension multiplied all around him. Community was destroyed. When the Macbeths chose to murder Duncan, they forfeited the blessings that come with righteous living, with living according to nature's design. There are consequences for sin, as Macbeth knew from the beginning, but he allowed the witches 'half-truths and his wife's spurious moral logic to subvert his reason and overpower his conscience.

Entering with the tyrant's head, the victorious Macduff announces that, finally, "the time is free." Duncan's son Malcolm, now hailed as Scotland's king, thanks his loyal followers with language that promises a return to the benevolent nature of his murdered father:

We shall not spend a large expense of time
Before we reckon with your several loves,
And make us even with you. . . .What's more to do,
Which would be planted newly with the time,
As calling home our exil'd friends abroad. . .
This and what needful else
That calls upon us, by the grace of Grace,
We will perform in measure, time, and place. (5.9.27-39)

Free of Macbeth's bloody reign, Scotland can once again experience the blessings they had enjoyed from the good and generous Duncan. Under Malcolm's rule, loyalty and bravery

285

will be repaid with royal largesse, exiled friends will be brought back home, and everything necessary will be "planted newly with the time. . . by the grace of Grace." Grace, God's restorative instrument, has redeemed both time and the Scottish nation.

For the Elizabethans, the notion of tragedy was a relatively simple one, derived from a blend of Latin and native influences, among them Seneca, the morality drama, and earlier history plays like Thomas Sackville's *Gorboduc*, which combined these influences in important ways for his successors, including Shakespeare. As Normand Berlin writes,

> The exact nature of tragic responsibility in *Gorboduc* has far reaching effects on Elizabethan tragedy. We noticed that, in the *Complaint*, Buckingham's evil actions led to his downfall, with Fortune and God's justice parts of the overall scheme. In *Gorboduc*, the downfall of the king is also caused by his own behavior, but his intentions are good; that is, unlike Buckingham, Gorboduc must be considered an essentially good man who committed an error in judgment. (*Sackville*, 123)

Berlin goes on to observe that this very influential early tragedy was written as a cautionary tale for Elizabeth herself, but it inverts the more conventional stories, broadly popularized by the *Mirror for Magistrates,* that depict the fall of an evil ruler. This provides significant background for a play like *Macbeth* which is a rich amalgam of these same literary threads. While Shakespeare's play may be a celebration of the government's narrow escape from Fawkes' evil plot, it achieves this with a story about a man with a functional conscience who succumbs to the manipulations of an ambitious wife and the equivocations of the witches. The murder he commits initiates their spiral into ever-deepening depravity and despair. For the Macbeths, death is a release from a self-inflicted agony; for their countrymen, it comes as a welcome relief from tyranny.

In the broadest of terms, *Macbeth* has similarities to Marlowe's *Doctor Faustus*, a man who sells his soul to the devil in exchange for a life of pleasure and wealth. But unlike Marlowe's play, which is more melodrama than tragedy, Shakespeare's has a firm but subtle grasp on the nuances of temptation, on the consequences of sin, and on the redemptive powers that work through time. Through it all, Macbeth's sin is clear and his punishment both just and inevitable. There is emotional and spiritual power in such clarity. We may admire his grim determination, but the sheer amount of blood spilled from innocent men, women, and children renders any sympathy for Macbeth more than a little unsavory. Scotland was desperate for redemption.

Ironically, given the thematic, emotional, and spiritual prominence Shakespeare gives to many of his women characters, the evil side of the spiritual war waged against Macbeth is implemented through the weird sisters and his wife. Both exert the type of magic that deceives, coerces, and eventually damns a promising man's soul. Without much evidence of the countervailing magic of love, it is difficult to escape the sense of unrelieved doom in *Macbeth*. The next play, the tragedy of *Antony and Cleopatra,* reasserts Shakespeare's conviction about the nature of love and the role women play in teaching men its value. Though it is set in the pagan world of ancient Rome and Egypt, with no reference to Biblical verses or to God at all, the light of the divine still shines brightly through the play's magnificent female protagonist, Cleopatra. Rather than a denial of God's presence in the world, it's as if Shakespeare wanted to be very clear that, even if everything else in the world shows no evidence of God, that presence is always visible through the woman who gives herself wholeheartedly and generously to the man she loves. If God's presence can't be seen anywhere else, Shakespeare seems to be saying, it is visible there. A man just has to believe what he's seeing.

Antony and Cleopatra

Although the title suggests that *Antony and Cleopatra* has two main characters, the play is really about the effect the famed Egyptian queen has upon Antony, the Roman general who gave a pivotal speech in the earlier *Julius Caesar*. In a striking departure from the preceding tragedies with their male protagonists, Cleopatra emerges as the main character in this later play. In some respects, *Antony and Cleopatra* is closer to *Romeo and Juliet*, the only other Shakespearean tragedy named after two lovers, than it is to *Hamlet, Othello, Macbeth*, or *Lear*. Both are about couples who believe they're in love; both make distinctions between reductive and richer views of love; both end with deaths that are as much celebratory as somber.

But this play also has important differences from the exuberant, joyful love of Romeo and Juliet, so aptly captured in the courtly love poetry of the sonneteers. In that youthful tragedy, love is largely foiled by misfortune. An ongoing feud and a delayed letter outlining the plan to reunite Juliet with her husband are circumstances beyond the lovers' control. Except for those unfortunate events, love might very well have triumphed. But *Antony and Cleopatra* replaces that first, exciting blush of teenage romance with a sober awareness of the difficulties resulting from human fallibility that love must struggle to overcome. Compared to Romeo, Antony is hardly as clear-sighted about his feelings for Cleopatra, whose mercurial temperament mystifies him for most of the play. Moreover, misfortune has minimal impact on these middle-aged lovers who become ensnared in the political intrigues of men vying for power and control. The expansive scope of their language reflects a view of the world and their place in it that is based on an experience of authority. These are people who command the known world. They are rarely if ever victimized by fate or chance in any ordinary sense of that word. When Cleopatra asks the honest Enobarbus who was responsible for the disastrous naval retreat that begins Antony's decline, his answer is clear: "Antony only, that would make his will lord of his reason" (3.13.4-5).

Most probably written around 1606, a year or so after *Lear*, *Antony and Cleopatra* reflects Shakespeare's interest in Roman history, most of which he learned through Sir Thomas North's translation of Plutarch's *Lives*. Experimenting with transitions of unusually short scenes, which follow in quick succession to convey the chaos of battle, Shakespeare condenses ten years of political maneuvering into a rapid flow of events. No subplot impedes the play's relentless forward progress. Even the main plot is relatively simple. Antony dallies with Cleopatra in Egypt until his Roman wife, Fulvia, forms an alliance with Antony's brother to foment rebellion in Syria. Though the rebellion is quickly put down, Caesar assumes Antony had some part in the turmoil, and he is forced to return to Rome to explain his lack of attention to family and empire. To patch up their differences, Antony agrees to marry Caesar's sister, Octavia, even though he already longs to return to his Egyptian lover. Though Caesar explicitly warns Antony not to, he goes back to Alexandria, which gives Caesar an excuse to consolidate power by eliminating all his rivals. When the Roman army enters Egypt, Antony manages to lose two crucial naval battles by following Cleopatra's retreating forces. As Caesar's troops approach, Antony hears a false rumor that Cleopatra is dead and attempts to commit suicide. Mortally wounded and near death, he learns that Cleopatra is still alive and implores his attachés to bring him to her. Hiding high up in her pyramid, she pulls him up and tries to comfort him before he dies. Though Caesar promises to respect Cleopatra's wish to remain in Egypt after her lover's death, she correctly anticipates his plan to humiliate her by parading her through the streets of Rome. Partly to avoid this shame but mostly to fulfill her dream of becoming Antony's wife, she joins him in death by committing suicide. While

290

Shakespeare's retelling of the story incorporates many of North's details, his version not only avoids North's moral condemnation of the Egyptian queen but transforms her death into a celebration of her steadfast love for Antony.

As *Macbeth* indicates, Shakespeare could make very clear distinctions between right and wrong behaviors, showing that tragic consequences usually follow when will or desire subverts judgment and conscience. Consequently, it may seem quite reasonable to assume, as Enobarbus does, that the sins of these two aging lovers make them responsible for the dire consequences that engulf them. In a very good essay on *Macbeth*, Dolores Cunningham concludes her analysis by applying *Macbeth*'s straightforward moral perspective to *Antony and Cleopatra*:

> Unless one accepts the distorted modern view of the play as a sermon on the glories of a noble love transcending everything in this world and the next, one sees that Antony and Cleopatra are presented as being so accustomed to the worship of sensual love as an absolute that they would rather lose everything than change their ways. The tragic outcome of *Antony and Cleopatra* is as firmly shaped as that of Macbeth by the failure to alter misguided affections and destructive choices. Both plays end in tragedy because the heroes and heroine give their hearts completely to those things (worldly glory, worldly love) which, however attractive, are defined in the plays as unworthy of such ultimate allegiance. . . . (79-80)

The judgment being applied here certainly sounds morally rigorous, but it isn't Shakespeare's. Projecting the lessons of *Macbeth* onto a very different play distorts the theatrical experience derived from the contrast between Rome's pragmatic emotional coldness and Egyptian warmth. Such negative evaluations of the lovers never make clear why the world is a better choice. They never account for why this play devotes its final act to the Egyptian queen. Instead, it seems far more appropriate to point out a crucial similarity to this play's older sibling, *Romeo and Juliet,* which also

291

distinguished streets marred by violence and juvenile bawdiness and a lyrical garden where reverence and love could bloom. In the end, there is remarkable consistency in Shakespeare's judgment of love's value in a world so easily susceptible to evil.

Because *Macbeth* is a play about murder and its consequences, it lends itself quite naturally to clear-cut moral judgments. *Antony and Cleopatra,* however, is about love, a presence, to paraphrase sonnet 116, whose light provides guidance through a wicked world but whose true worth remains mysterious and therefore under-appreciated. As dramatic material, love is far more complex, morally and emotionally, than an act of murder. After *Lear*'s brilliant examination of love and forgiveness, of reason's limitations and the need to mitigate its judgments with a sensitivity to those visceral feelings connecting family and community, the application of simple moral distinctions will miss much of this play's rich complexity, in particular, the nature and value of Cleopatra's love. As always, that complexity is examined through the play's multiplicity of viewpoints, divided roughly between the citizens of Rome and Egypt.

Though Shakespeare lifts some of North's descriptive passages almost verbatim, he largely resists the generally accepted view that Cleopatra corrupted Antony's Roman nobility. That view of her, however, is voiced by Demetrius, one of Antony's Roman attendants, at the very beginning of the play. As the two lovers cavort in the background, he speaks to another Roman:

> Nay, but this dotage of our general's
> O'erflows the measure. Those his goodly eyes,
> That o'er the files and musters of the war
> Have glow'd like plated Mars, now bend, now turn
> The office and devotion of their view
> Upon a tawny front; his captain's heart. . .
> Reneges all temper,
> And is become the bellows and the fan

To cool a gipsy's lust. . . . Look where they come!
Take but good note, and you shall see in him
The triple pillar of the world transform'd
Into a strumpet's fool. (1.1.1-13)

The displeasure expressed is not so much moral as it is an acknowledgment that Cleopatra has distracted Antony from his administrative and military duties. While Demetrius condemns the influence Cleopatra's sexual behavior has on Antony, the remainder of the play explores the validity of this Roman view. His view should not be seen, therefore, as simply a statement of fact but more as an assertion to be verified. What, in fact, is Cleopatra's true nature? Having created female characters like Gertrude, Lady Macbeth, Goneril and Regan, Shakespeare clearly did not over-idealize or romanticize women. But he also created strong, positive female characters like Rosalind in *As You Like It*, Olivia and Viola in *Twelfth Night*, Desdemona in *Othello*, and Cordelia in *Lear*, all of whom know more about love than the men who profess their devotion and commitment.

Antony and Cleopatra answers this implied question about the Egyptian queen in several different ways. Besides these opening lines, the play provides additional perspectives of Cleopatra. She is viewed from the vantage of various Romans, from Antony's perspective, and from Cleopatra's own viewpoint. As a result of these different perspectives, a complex view of this legendary woman emerges, making the truth of Cleopatra's identity the play's central issue. But Shakespeare also verifies her identity and her significance by devoting the last act almost entirely to her, a dazzling theatrical finale. While Antony's decline and death are certainly pitiful, his dramatic role is really to demonstrate what effect she has on him, and so he disappears from view at the end of the fourth act. What remains after he is gone is the complex truth of the Egyptian queen's heart, and it is this that Shakespeare wants us to remember.

That is not to say that Antony is irrelevant. The play provides sufficient justification for the love and admiration Cleopatra expresses for him. When Fulvia's rebellion and death compel Antony's return to Rome to deny any part in her misadventure, he patiently explains his actions to a suspicious Caesar. Quite magnanimously during that exchange, Antony never tries to use his age or his military experience to intimidate the much younger man. In fact, Antony freely admits that his Egyptian distractions have caused him to neglect his imperial duties. In another scene where Antony is not present, Caesar himself admires his rival's courage and self-discipline in the face of military hardship. And when, after Antony's final, inglorious defeat, his honest and loyal friend, Enobarbus, leaves him to join Caesar, Antony very generously sends the deserter's treasures after him. All of this shows Antony to be able, noble, generous, and, eventually, loving toward Cleopatra. His destiny is a familiar tragic paradox: he has to lose what's important, in this case, his imperial and military identity, before he can fully appreciate Cleopatra's value. His journey from that original ignorance to understanding demonstrates her effect on him. He always feels that magic in her presence but it isn't until he's on the verge of losing it that he appreciates what being near her, being part of her, has meant to him. Since this magic cannot be explained or defined, the final act belongs to her so that what Antony came to appreciate about the Egyptian queen is clear for all to see.

Throughout Shakespeare's plays, the difficulty of seeing what is true about life has been a consistent theme. All too often, characters mistake the obvious as truth only to discover how blind they have been to deeper realities. As Heilman noted in the *Lear* chapter, such blindness has many causes, the opaqueness of the world, desire's ability to distort judgment, the inaccuracies resulting from people's assumptions among them. To all the Romans who have seen Cleopatra, her sensuality, her reputation for an almost irresistible sexuality, are the most obvious facts. While this is what they see when she is near, her sexuality also embodies a force that, in many ways, stands in opposition to much of what Rome represents. Compared to the Roman preoccupations with empire, war, and death, Cleopatra is life force incarnate. Abundance and prosperity surround her, emanate from her. Having returned to Rome with Antony, Enobarbus describes life in Cleopatra's court and Antony's first, very dramatic meeting with the queen:

> Maec. Eight wild-boars roasted whole at a breakfast, and
> but twelve persons there; is this true?
> Eno. This was but as a fly by an eagle; we had much more
> monstrous matter of feast, which worthily deserv'd
> noting.
> Maec. She's a most triumphant lady, if report be square to
> her.
> Eno. When she first met Mark Antony, she purs'd up his
> Heart upon the river of Cydnus. . . .
> The barge she sat in, like a burnish'd throne,
> Burnt on the water. The poop was beaten gold,
> Purple the sails, and so perfumed that
> The winds were love-sick with them; the oars were
> silver
> Which to the tune of flutes kept stroke, and made
> The water . . .
> As amorous of their strokes. For her own person,
> It beggar'd all description: she did lie
> In her pavilion—cloth of gold, of tissue—
> O'er picturing that Venus where we see
> The fancy outwork nature. (2.2.179-201)

The Spartan-like Romans are fascinated by the seductive sensuality of the Egyptian queen and the sumptuous excesses of her court. Subtly modifying that first impression of the gypsy strumpet, Cleopatra's magic has even managed to invade Rome. Like Venus, the goddess of love, sex, beauty, and fertility, Cleopatra's magnetic feminine nature has seduced the Roman imagination. Her extravagant banquets, her fabulous wealth, her feminine beauty, her dramatic entrances, but most of all her sensual, sexual allure confirm her ability to command male attention. The very waves of the River Cydnus fall in love with her. The soldiers and generals listening to Enobarbus's description are enraptured by this report of Cleopatra's charms, though mere words cannot possibly match her actual presence. Even from faraway Alexandria, she can fire the imagination of men hardened by war and self-discipline. Though all of them disapprove of her effect on her distracted Roman lover, Agrippa cannot help but exclaim "O, rare for Antony!" For some critics, it must be said, Cleopatra's impact on others has less to do with feminine magic than with a penchant for self-dramatization. If this were true, however, the eventual betrayal of her emotional commitment to Antony would be necessary confirmation. Such a betrayal never comes.

If this kind of magic is an Egyptian trait, no one is so moved to describe Octavia, Caesar's sister, who is used to patch up the quarrel between her brother and Antony. Quickly following this enchanting description of Cleopatra, Maecenas expresses the hope that Octavia, betrothed now to Antony, will cool his desire for his Egyptian paramour:

> If beauty, wisdom, modesty, can settle
> The heart of Antony, Octavia is
> A blessed lottery to him. (2.2.240-242)

Though there's admiration here for this woman's virtues, there is no magic, nothing that compels attention or fires the imagination. The comparison is meant to point to something unique and special about the Egyptian queen. Ever the good Roman wife, Octavia proves her virtues to her new husband, but she eventually falls victim to the rivalry between spouse and brother. When Caesar informs her that Antony has returned to Egypt to be with Cleopatra, she can only exclaim, "Ay me, most wretched, That have my heart parted betwixt two friends That do afflict each other" (3.6.77-79)! Possessing no magic, Octavia can only function as a political expediency. While Caesar seems to love her, he is not above using her for the good of the empire, even though he is fully aware of Antony's Egyptian inclinations. Used by her own brother, Octavia does her duty, and in her compliant, pleasant, completely asexual demeanor, she is Cleopatra's complete opposite. Dutiful, devoted, loyal, even loving, there is much to admire in Octavia, but she will never ignite anyone's imagination the way Cleopatra can.

The frankly sexual relationship between Antony and Cleopatra certainly distinguishes this play from the far more innocent *Romeo and Juliet,* a play about desire rather than its fulfillment. But that innocence quickly dissipates in subsequent plays where sexual conduct is most often linked to the bestial aspects of human behavior. Hamlet, obsessed by his mother's sexual union with the murderer Claudius, associates her with the disease that infects Denmark. Othello's love for the innocent Desdemona is transformed into jealous hatred by Iago's lurid whisperings. In terms brimming with disgust, the mad Lear associates female sexuality with the cruel ingratitude of his daughters, Goneril and Regan. Throughout these later plays, this sexual nausea reveals more about the characters who exhibit it than it does about the object of their disgust.

Here, though, there's something qualitatively different about the treatment Cleopatra's sexual appeal receives, for, while she is really all about commitment, it is only the Romans who talk about her sensual and sexual nature. In her "salad days," she admits, she allowed herself to be carried to Julius Caesar in a mattress, but she is older now and she has Antony in her life. The problem is no longer with her sexuality but with reductive Roman assumptions about women and love. We have seen this reductive attitude before in Mercutio, in Touchstone, even in Hamlet. As a Roman, Antony is not immune to this same emotional and moral hypocrisy. Because of that ignorance, he completely undervalues Cleopatra's true worth, he forges a doomed alliance with Caesar, he returns to Egypt for the wrong reasons, and he betrays the hard-won trust of his soldiers by expecting Cleopatra to fight alongside him in the Roman fashion, ignoring how vulnerable her love has made him to her whims and fears.

Besides the erotic allusions early in the play, Cleopatra's sexual nature figures in other ways. It is part of her past connection to Rome, for Julius Caesar, the father of this play's Octavius Caesar, had a child with her, which the Romans in this play view with flippant condescension. Listening to Enobarbus describe Cleopatra's grand first encounter with Antony, Agrippa is reminded of her affair with Julius Caesar. "Royal wench!" he begins, "She made great Caesar lay his sword to bed; He ploughed her, and she cropp'd" (2.2.227ff). Egyptian fecundity is present even in this condescending quip. Because of her colorful past, the Romans feel comfortable speaking of her in this juvenile, prurient manner. For them, she is defined by her previous sexual indiscretions, which, like Antony, limits their understanding of who she is now. Consequently, that past sexual behavior has also become part of her present. It defines her even for Antony. With typical Roman aplomb, the newly married Antony decides to return to Egypt because, as he says privately, "I 'th 'East my pleasure lies." At this point in his relationship with Cleopatra, his attraction doesn't go any deeper than the physical. What he fails to comprehend, though, is that Cleopatra understands that her sexuality is the one way she can communicate love to a man who is only capable of appreciating its physical expression.

But the agricultural allusions in the memory of great Caesar plowing Cleopatra so she would crop also suggest that Cleopatra's sexuality, her physical desire for the man she loves, aligns her with nature's purpose. This notion is not unique to *Antony and Cleopatra*. Lady Macbeth tries to violate this principle with her "unsex me" speech. Many of the comedies and the late romances, like *The Tempest*, associate love with lavish feasts and bounteous nature. Here in *Antony and Cleopatra*, the Egyptian queen's dominion, the very land she presides over, partakes of Cleopatra's fertility. After Antony manages to patch up his first quarrel with Caesar, he shares some of his observations about life in Egypt with his Roman companions:

> Thus do they, sir; they take the flow o' th' Nile,
> By certain scales i' th' pyramid; they know,
> By th' height, the lowness, or the mean, if dearth
> Or foison follow. The higher Nilus swells,
> The more it promises; as it ebbs, the seedsman,
> Upon the slime and ooze scatters his grain,
> And shortly comes the harvest. (2.7.17-23)

As we have seen before, when Duncan observes the swallow's procreant cradles near Macbeth's castle, the fertility and abundance of nature reflect the moral framework of a divinely created world that, Biblically, is under man's dominion and that reflects God's desire to provide. Egypt, a land where new life emerges out of the mud and slime of the Nile, personifies the life-giving force of its queen. The play's many allusions to nature's abundant and fertile goodness, therefore, confirm the virtue of the sexuality associated with her. Love and sex are part of nature's creative force, and the lovers' desire for union is what, metaphorically, separates Egypt from Rome.

Unlike Egypt, a land of cyclical fertility, Rome is associated with war and military discipline. The contrast between a seemingly ascetic Rome and sensual Egypt is, of course, deliberate. Virtue and moral rectitude appear to reside in Rome; weak, self-indulgent sensuality, at least from the Roman point of view, dominates Egypt. Caesar, recalling Antony's exploits, cannot help but admire his rival's incredible perseverance in the face of war's hardships. "When thou once Was beaten from Modena," he muses:

> . . . at thy heel
> Did famine follow, whom thou fought'st against
> . . . with patience more
> Than savages could suffer. Thou didst drink
> The stale of horses and the gilded puddle
> Which beasts would cough at; thy palate then did deign
> The roughest berry on the rudest hedge . . . On the Alps
> It is reported thou didst eat strange flesh
> Which some did die to look on. . . . . and all this
> Was borne so like a soldier, that thy cheek
> So much as lank'd not. (1.5.56-71)

In contrast to the abundant life of Egypt, self-denial in the face of impoverishment is what built the Roman Empire and therefore what the Romans value. Before he met Cleopatra, this was Antony's identity. This masculine determination is why the play often associates him with Hercules, the demigod of legendary strength and endurance. The contrast with the luxurious beds of Egypt, where Antony now finds his pleasure, suggests that he is at a crossroad where self-denial and desire point in different directions.

Circumstances eventually force Antony to choose between them. The choice is reminiscent of Hal's dilemma in *1Henry 4* where the young prince must choose between the frivolous and self-indulgent play of Fat Jack Falstaff, stuffed with sack and capons, and the taxing duties of the throne. For Hal, a young man looking to prove his worth, it is relatively easy to forgo the temptations that Falstaff represents. He understands that duty and self-control are what the English throne needs after his father took the crown from Richard. Circumstances are much different between Rome and Egypt, however. First, unlike Falstaff, Cleopatra will prove to be much more than the self-indulgent sensualist who exists to tempt Antony into a depraved indifference to anything besides pleasure. And unlike Hal, Antony has already proven his value to Rome. But his relationship with Cleopatra promises wholly different emotions and commitments that challenge

300

him to develop unrealized aspects of his identity. Standing at the crossroad, Antony must decide either to continue thinking, acting, speaking in the role he's always known or to embrace an entirely different mode of being.

Making that decision occupies most of Antony and Cleopatra's events, and everything depends on Antony's ability to evaluate Cleopatra accurately. For a Roman steeped in the ways of war and unfamiliar with liaisons based on love rather than political expediency, such discernment does not come easily. At first, Antony is ignorant of the emotional bond that has formed out of his physical relationship with Cleopatra. Though he believes returning to Egypt after the disastrous marriage to Octavia is only for his "pleasure," it is obvious that physical union has created far deeper though little understood emotional bonds. Revealing more truth about him than he realizes, the reference to pleasure trivializes what actually draws him back to Egypt. Though he does not yet possess the vocabulary to define it more precisely, he is drawn to whatever is so captivating, so irresistible about Cleopatra's magic. The very different characterizations of Octavia and Cleopatra are meant to emphasize the magical allure of the Egyptian, and wherever the power of that force is not recognized, as it isn't in Rome, the fullness of life is no longer available. People and events continue, but it is an existence without life as it was meant to be. Although he cannot resist the power of this life force, Antony's trivialization of sex as mere pleasure reveals his ignorance of love's magic.

Whether or not Antony understands the strength of the bond that ties him to Cleopatra, she has placed considerable hope in the resilience of their connection, for she continuously tests those bonds in an effort to make them more secure, to encourage him to choose her. Right from the start, it is clear she wants something more from her relationship with Antony than he does. Their first appearance on stage begins with some playful banter. She asks him a question that should resonate after *Lear*:

Cleo: If it be love indeed, tell me how much?
Ant: There's beggary in the love that can be reckon'd.
Cleo.   I'll set a bourn how far to be belov'd.
Ant.   Then must thou needs find out new heaven, new
       earth. (1.1.14-17)

In the afterglow, love is huge and boundless. But this good-humored playfulness is quickly undermined by a troubling insecurity hiding in Cleopatra's thoughts. Well-schooled in the ways of men who too easily exaggerate professions of love to take what they want, Cleopatra—unlike Lear—does not accept Antony's words at face value. Her playful repartee quickly turns petulant when she recalls his infidelity to Fulvia, his Roman wife. "Why should I think you can be mine, and true. . . Who have been false to Fulvia?" she asks indignantly. That betrayal threatens her desire for his loyalty to her, and the conversation becomes tense. Envious of Fulvia's status as Antony's wife, Cleopatra's jealousy acknowledges a harsh truth: Antony has loyalties elsewhere.

But when news of Fulvia's rebellion sparks Antony's determination to return to Rome, she relents with touching vulnerability. Afraid she might be losing him, her words reveal both helplessness and the depth of her emotional confusion:

Ant.   I'll leave you, lady.
Cleo.   Courteous lord, one word:
       Sir, you and I must part, but that's not it;
       Sir, you and I have lov'd, but there's not it.
       That you know well. Something it is I would---
       O, my oblivion is a very Antony,
       And I am all forgotten. (1.3.86-92)

Unable to complete her thoughts coherently, she tries several times to express her fear and sorrow at their parting.

But to Antony, the melodramatic reference to his absence as her oblivion sounds emotionally manipulative, and his Roman determination is replaced by exasperation. "But that your royalty Holds idleness your subject," he replies, "I should take you for idleness itself." Egyptian idleness, according to Antony, allows time for love, but when the more important business of empire beckons, love must be put aside. While this position is understandable, his impatience with her turns it into a harsh, unwarranted, personal rebuke. Trying to put any bruised feelings aside, she begins with a reminder of her investment in their relationship but quickly moves on to an apology that is both intimate and dignified:

> 'Tis sweating labor
> To bear such idleness so near the heart
> As Cleopatra this. But, sir, forgive me,
> Since my becomings kill me when they do not
> Eye well to you. Your honor calls you hence,
> Therefore be deaf to all my unpitied folly,
> And all the gods go with you! (1.3.93-99)

With the kind of tempered fortitude reminiscent of Viola's patience with Orsino in *Twelfth Night*, Cleopatra rejects his assertion that she is the queen of all idleness by reminding him that it is difficult work to bear the weight of an emotionally uncaring Roman so near her heart. Her sexual metaphor neatly highlights the irony of a physical union that masks the labor required to overcome his emotional distance. Very aware of his preoccupation with his own pleasure, she is anything but idle. Though it isn't on the grand scale of empires, Cleopatra's work is to bring Antony to a deeper appreciation of her love.

In her precarious emotional situation, therefore, she cares very much about his perception of her, and so she regains emotional balance and finds the strength to wish him well. She recognizes that her self-concern is secondary to the honor he values, so go he must. This is the Egyptian form of Antony's much-admired fortitude and generosity. In the face of his rebuke, she accepts his determination to leave with uncommon grace. Though her emotional turmoil is evident, it is hard to see this as anything less than the sacrificial love exhibited by other Shakespearean women in other plays. Even if Antony is at first blind to her worth, her words not only validate what is in Cleopatra's heart but also demonstrate the emotional strength that will eventually transform his as well.

Additional confirmation of her love for Antony comes in several subsequent scenes, leaving no doubt that her devotion to him is genuine. Before she hears of the marriage to Octavia, she implores her servant to bring the sleeping potion, mandragora, so she might "sleep out this great gap of time My Antony is away" (1.4.4-5). Since he's already in Rome, there is no artifice at all in her longing to be with him again. Even when she learns of the marriage, she works to recover her equanimity. At first, her ire falls upon the hapless messenger, whom she strikes. But remorse quickly sets in. Eager to size up her competition, she is now desperate to learn all she can about Octavia's appearance, which the trembling messenger describes with great tact. Encouraged by this artful information, Cleopatra concludes that "all may be well enough." She is undeterred. To weaker personalities, the second Roman marriage might seem an insurmountable challenge, but, like the earlier Juliet, the strength of her love waivers only momentarily. Though Antony has yet to exhibit any similar loyalty to their relationship, hers remains steadfast no matter the circumstances, the North Star to his wandering heart.

Cleopatra certainly has her faults. She can be melodramatic when it suits her, as her jealous outburst over Fulvia shows. Her fears sometimes get the best of her, as they do when she flees the two naval battles that turn the tide against Antony. And she is not above faking her death in an ill-conceived effort to assuage Antony's rage. Yet, at this moment, she faces this very difficult test of her fidelity in a way that proves the enduring persistence of her love. By doing so, ironically, she shows herself to be a better Roman than the Romans.

While loyalty might seem a very Roman value, much of what happens in the empire's capital reveals the hollowness of their professed reverence for honor, nobility, and virtue. There is a sense in this play that, after the assassination of Julius Caesar, Rome has changed, and not entirely for the better. Now, Antony, Lepidus, and Octavius Caesar, the son of Julius, share the empire's governmental and military responsibilities. Of these three triumvirs, Octavius is considerably younger than the other two, but he wears his authority well. During the conversation where Antony explains his dalliance in Egypt while a wife and a brother rebel against the empire, Antony is always on the defensive, protecting himself from Caesar's dogged accusations.

But Caesar's confidence is not the only quality that distinguishes him from Antony, a man who is generous, who is self-disciplined in war, and who, perhaps because of his age, shows no signs of the imperial ambition that drives Caesar. In this world, a man's character has little to do with his worldly fortunes. According to a soothsayer Antony encounters before the nuptials to Octavia, Caesar is simply favored by luck and good fortune. "If thou dost play with him at any game," the oracle says, "Thou art sure to lose." And when Antony asks him whose fortunes shall rise, the soothsayer's answer is unequivocal: "Caesar's." Acknowledging the truth of this prophecy, Antony is now motivated to return to Egypt, to escape the luckier Caesar, despite his promise to marry Caesar's sister. Defying all logic and political common sense, the decision is evidence of the powerful hold that Cleopatra's magic has on this Roman.

Despite his rational and pragmatic nature, however, Caesar is not entirely without his own virtues. He not only admires Antony's military accomplishments but also expresses what seems to be a genuine love for his sister. With considerable foresight, he carefully warns Antony before the marriage:

You take from me a great part of myself;

305

Use me well in't. Sister, prove such a wife
As my thoughts make thee. . . .Most noble Antony,
Let not the piece of virtue which is set
Betwixt us, as the cement of our love
To keep it builded, be the ram to batter
The fortress of it; for better might we
Have lov'd without this means, if on both parts
This be not cherish'd. (3.2.24-32)

Caesar is very transparent about his reasons for this marriage
and the potential danger that it represents. But his view of it,
as it has been for all the Romans, is entirely pragmatic. While
the marriage is intended to "cement" the love and respect
between the two men, trusting Antony to revere and cherish
his sister, this "piece of virtue," is a risk for all involved.

In matters politic, Caesar proves to be a much better
tactician. Far more than Antony, he understands what is at
stake in this marriage. Being a Roman, he views the purpose
of this marriage almost entirely in rational and political terms.
Unlike the emotional forces at work in Antony's relationship
with Cleopatra, love has nothing to do with this very Roman
arrangement. Octavia simply has a duty "to prove such a
wife" as Caesar needs her to be. It is possible to see this as a
cynical ploy to trap Antony in a relationship that cannot last
and that will therefore provide Caesar with the excuse he
needs to eliminate all potential challengers to his ambition.
But Antony never expresses any imperial ambitions. It seems
more thematically plausible, therefore, that Caesar's very
pragmatic view of marriage aligns with what other Romans
have said about love, which, as their comments about
Cleopatra show, is largely utilitarian. No one in Rome, Caesar
included, comprehends the kind of magic and power
embodied in a woman like Cleopatra. They may recognize it,
as their recollection of the Egyptian queen in her barge
indicates, but they don't understand or appreciate it. Of all the
Romans, Antony alone responds deeply to her love. Though
he doesn't understand why at first, his actions show that,

somehow, at this time of his life, he values it more than he values what Rome has to offer. Where Caesar cunningly uses power to realize his ambitions, that pragmatic realism limits his understanding of the heart. Antony is different, and it is his generous, magnanimous spirit that distinguishes him from all the other Romans. It is this generosity to others and his openness to the full possibility of life that allow him to respond to Cleopatra.

From the Roman perspective, however, Antony has wasted precious time in sensual idleness. With a certain smug, moral superiority, they blame Cleopatra for this dotage, this decline. Pompey, who has raised a naval force to threaten the triumvirs, hears that Antony has returned to Rome. The news surprises him and he offers a mock prayer:

> But all the charms of love,
> Salt Cleopatra, soften thy wan'd lip!
> Let witchcraft join with beauty, lust with both,
> Tie up the libertine in a field of feasts,
> Keep his brain fuming; epicurean cooks
> Sharpen with cloyless sauce his appetite. . . . (1.5.20-25)

As Pompey's food imagery suggests, Antony is in Egypt feeding his appetites while true Romans are busily working to shape the world. But underneath the rational, virtuous-seeming surface of Rome lurks considerable moral dishonesty too, as Pompey's actions against the empire suggest. Though his desire is for power rather than love, he too is feeding an appetite. In plays like *Othello* and *Lear,* evil blossoms where misunderstood or unacknowledged desires transform reason's virtues into rationalizations. If Egyptian sexuality tempts Antony toward love, the Roman temptation is clearly power.

To commemorate the truce as well as the impending marriage, the triumvirs and their friends hold a celebration where wine flows freely. Even the normally cautious Caesar partakes. Quietly at the party's fringe, though, Menas whispers to Pompey that he has an opportunity to assassinate the others and seize sole control of the empire. Having just reconciled with the triumvirs, though, Pompey resists the temptation. Rather than condemning this amoral proposition, Pompey weakly mutters that, had the assassinations occurred without informing him, he would have been able to claim plausible deniability. Because power and dominance trump moral integrity, Roman virtue is largely a sham. Frustrated by such indecision, Menas disavows any further loyalty to Pompey. "For this, I'll never follow thy pall'd fortunes more. Who seeks, and will not take when once 'tis offer'd, Shall never find it more" (2.7.81ff).

Proof of that hypocrisy comes quickly. Unlike Pompey, Caesar does not hesitate to act when a similar opportunity is presented to him. For daring to raise a navy to challenge the Triumvir, Pompey is eliminated, and, with total power within his grasp, the third triumvir, Lepidus, is clearly next. Antony remains with Octavia long enough to witness the beginning of this effort to consolidate power. Offended by Caesar's behavior, he voices his complaint to his new wife:

> Nay, nay, Octavia, not only that---
> That were excusable. . . . but he hath wag'd
> New wars 'gainst Pompey; made his will, and read it
> To public ear;
> Spoke scantly of me; when perforce he could not
> But pay me terms of honor. . . . (3.4.1-7)

Caesar's political realism offends Antony's sense of honor, though he himself provides several examples of marital and emotional disloyalty. Even virtuous-seeming Roman women are subjects of a similar moral equivocation. In contrast to the self-assurance of a woman like Cleopatra, Octavia's reply to Antony is passive and perplexed. "Husband win, win brother. . . no midway 'twixt these extremes at all." In a marriage based on duty rather than love, she is unable to stand firmly with Antony, so even though he sends her to plead his case to Caesar, he follows his heart back to Egypt where he will "raise the preparation of a war." Both men have now made their fateful choice. But the circumstances that led them to this point reveal the hypocrisy of the Roman allegiance to honor and virtue.

This Rome, then, is a pale shadow of that city's former golden age. Instead, virtuous sounding men speak of honor as they wage war against admired elders and leave dutiful and innocent wives in the name of pleasure. Temptation is rejected, not for any valid reason, but because it has the wrong optics. With a strange little scene, the play argues that Pompey and Caesar's rationalized calculation of self-interest has infected every level of Roman society. In it, an obscure Roman lieutenant refuses to take military action because it might make him look too ambitious in the eyes of his superiors. "Better to leave undone," he begins, "than by our deed Acquire too high a fame when him we serve's away." He goes on to cite the example of one of Sossius's lieutenants whose "quick accumulation of renown, which he achiev'd by th 'minute, lost his favor" (3.1.16-20). Inaction, the argument goes, will be more acceptable than any action that might offend an ambitious and easily jealous superior. The moral rot evident in the resolution of Pompey's rebellion and Caesar's ambition is prevalent throughout the empire. From top to bottom, Roman values have been corrupted by various human weaknesses, and that corruption begins to make what Egypt offers considerably more attractive.

Because a more politically cunning Pompey could have easily agreed to Menas's assassination proposal, military skill or even political cunning alone cannot explain Caesar's decision to seize power, though he certainly has both. His moment has simply arrived. As the Egyptian sorcerer had foreseen, Caesar was fortunate that Menas spoke to a man who cared more for his public reputation than for power. Nevertheless, though Pompey's temptation goes nowhere, the brush with treachery prepares us for the Machiavellian tactics that the young Caesar employs. Pompey hesitates and is lost.

Caesar isn't the kind of man to make the same mistake. As soon as he learns that Antony has betrayed his sister, Caesar begins to secure all remaining imperial power for himself. After he eliminates Pompey and Lepidus, he then prepares to move on Antony, who is now in Egypt. Despite his admiration and respect for Antony's military experience, Caesar uses the dishonor shown to his sister to rationalize what he desires most: the power to rule a vast empire without complications or interference. Their respective fates now sealed, both men have made their choice.

Antony, who has been associated with the demi-god, Hercules, throughout the play, engages Caesar in two separate naval battles, even though his soldiers warn him that his advantage is on land. Encouraged by Cleopatra, he ignores the warning, only to suffer humiliating defeat after leaving the fray prematurely to follow the queen's fleeing ships. By allowing love to influence a military decision, Antony is defeated by those very same emotions. One of Antony's soldiers tries to warn his superior of his tactically foolish choice to fight at sea, which Cleopatra prefers. "We are women's men," he laments, and so a woman must now console a defeated Antony:

> Cleo.　O my lord, my lord,
> 　　　　Forgive my fearful sails! I little thought
> 　　　　You would have followed.
> Ant.　　　　　　　　Egypt, thou knew'st too well
> 　　　　My heart was to thy rudder tied by th' strings,
> 　　　　And thou shouldst tow me after. O'er my spirit
> 　　　　Thy full supremacy thou knew'st and that
> 　　　　Thy beck might from the bidding of the gods
> 　　　　Command me.
> Cleo.　O, my pardon! (3.11.54-62)

Unfortunately, this is precisely what Cleopatra didn't know about Antony until this moment, and the realization renders her all but speechless. In a moment of joy mixed with

310

profound sorrow, she can only ask for his forgiveness. Antony's deteriorating fortunes are clear when, following this defeat, he dares great Caesar to single combat. It is an empty, pathetic challenge that eventually leads the very loyal Enobarbus to desert the general he loves too much and whose decline he cannot bear to witness. The paradox, of course, is that Antony's defeat finally reveals how deeply her love is now rooted in his heart. Out of this enormous loss of worldly power and status comes much personal gain.

As soon as he has declared his love, however, it is put to the test, for Caesar sends an emissary to entice Cleopatra to leave Antony. Pretending to be receptive to the idea, Cleopatra entertains the messenger, who is about to kiss her hand when Antony reappears and completely misinterprets her intentions. He is irate, has the messenger whipped, and then sends the man back to Caesar before turning to Cleopatra in a cold fury that gives way quickly to self-pity:

> Ant.　You were half blasted ere I knew you, ha?
> 　　　Have I my pillow left unpress'd in Rome,
> 　　　Forborne the getting of a lawful race,
> 　　　And by a gem of women, to be abus'd
> 　　　By one that looks on feeders?
> 　　　　　　　. . . .
> Cleo.　Have you done yet?
> Ant.　Alack, our terrene moon
> 　　　Is now eclips'd, and it portends alone
> 　　　The fall of Antony.
> Cleo.　　　　　　　I must stay his time.
> Ant.　To flatter Caesar, would you mingle eyes
> 　　　With one that ties his points?
> Cleo.　　　　　　　Not know me yet?
> Ant.　Cold-hearted toward me?
> Cleo.　Ah, dear, if it be so,
> 　　　From my cold heart let heaven engender hail,
> 　　　And poison it in the source, and the first stone
> 　　　Drop in my neck; as it determines, so
> 　　　Dissolve my life! (3.13.153-162)

There is no pretense, no provocative play-acting for attention here. Her denial of any indifference toward him is absolute and total. Undaunted by his fury, the constancy of Cleopatra's love is unmistakable in that simple, direct question "Not know me yet?" Finally responding to her authenticity, Antony is encouraged enough to regroup and fight his second and this time decisive battle with Caesar. But not before Cleopatra tenderly helps Antony put on his armor, a dramatization of a favorite Renaissance icon of Venus similarly helping Mars. Soon after, Enobarbus hears music underground, which he interprets as the spirit of Hercules abandoning Antony. Though the fading Herculean music signals that Antony's martial and imperial decline is well underway, the visual reference to Mars and Venus indicates that his devotion now belongs to a different Roman deity. Venus has superseded Mars. The transformation of his identity is all but complete.

The second and final battle with Caesar ends like the first. This time, though, afraid of Antony's anger, Cleopatra sends word from her pyramid that she has died, which redoubles Antony's sense of loss and provokes him to fall on his own sword. But he botches the suicide only to learn that the queen is still alive. The time for anger having passed, he asks to be brought to the pyramid where he can speak his final words to her. There, she draws him up in a symbolic act of elevation where they exchange their last thoughts. He very generously assumes all blame. Full of remorse and sorrow, she is confronted by the limitations of her love:

> Ant. Not Caesar's valor hath o'erthrown Antony,
>   But Antony's hath triump'd on itself.
> Cleo. So it should be, that none but Antony
>   Should conquer Antony, but woe 'tis so!
> Ant. I am dying, Egypt, dying; only
>   I here importune death awhile, until
>   Of many thousand kisses the poor last
>   I lay upon thy lips.

```
Cleo.    . . . But come, come, Antony---
         Help me, my women--- we must draw thee up. . . .
Ant.     O, quick, or I am gone.
Cleo.    Here's sport indeed! How heavy weighs my lord!
         Our strength is all gone into heaviness,
         That makes the weight. . . .Die when thou hast
              liv'd,
         Quicken with kissing.  Had my lips that power,
         Thus would I wear them out. (4.15.14-39)
```

As in the sepulcher with Romeo and Juliet, death begins to be associated with love. This second allusion to Antony's weight recalls that earlier sexual reference when he was about to leave for Rome, as does her use of the word "sport." But the earlier irony has now been replaced by a deep pathos, for the joy of bearing his weight is intermixed with desperation and sorrow. Any blame or anger notably absent, his thoughts turn to her welfare as he implores her to befriend Caesar after he's gone. "Of Caesar seek your honor, with your safety," he instructs, to which she replies, "My resolution and my hands I'll trust, None about Caesar." Though she is already resolute for death, his passing elicits a moving tribute to the man she has long loved with all her heart:

```
         Noblest of men, woo't die?
         Hast thou no care of me?  Shall I abide
         In this dull world, which in thy absence is
         No better than a sty?  O, see, my women;
              [Antony dies.]
         The crown o' th' earth doth melt.  My lord!
         O, wither'd is the garland of the war,
         The soldier's pole is fall'n.  Young boys and girls
         Are level now with men; the odds is gone,
         And there is nothing left remarkable
         Beneath the visiting moon [faints.]  (4.14.59-68)
```

Throughout, Cleopatra's desire for Antony's love has been constant. She has worked, to use her word, to bring him to a realization of that truth. If sex and pleasure were the only vocabulary of love he understood, she would fearlessly use that to help him see more, and she returns to that theme here because it has been their common ground. But to her, he was far more than the physical aspects of love, and she pays homage, as she should, to his incomparable nobility. A bit later, in magnificent, almost dreamy poetry, her admiration for Antony is all but overwhelming:

> His legs bestrid the ocean, his rear'd arm
> Crested the world, his voice was propertied
> As all the tuned spheres. . . .
> But when he meant to quail and shake the orb,
> He was as rattling thunder. For his bounty,
> There was no winter in't; an autumn it was
> That grew the more by reaping. . . .In his livery
> Walk'd crowns and crownets; realms and islands were
> As plates dropp'd from his pocket. (5.2.82-92)

This is clearly Cleopatra expressing what she admired about Antony, but it is easy to miss the remarkable within the obvious. She knows that Antony could very easily have been, like Caesar is now, the ruler of the known world. Despite his defeat on the water at Actium, he was a better soldier on land than his rival, but he sacrificed all that was possible for her, and he did so because he lacked the bold and cunning opportunism of this Caesar, who should remind us of another opportunist, Henry Bolingbroke of *1Henry4*. In Caesar's case, he was willing to risk his sister in a marriage to a man whose heart was obviously elsewhere. What part of that decision was sincere and what part was calculated to purposely fail for Caesar's advantage? Cunning is not an attribute Shakespeare respected, as Iago should remind us. No, what Cleopatra admires about Antony is his generosity, his carelessness about things of this world, those "realms and islands" that dropped from his pocket in exchange for something of real value. That matters to her, greatly. The awe

314

and gratitude for what Antony was willing to give up for her is unmistakable.

The play begins with two very different views of the Egyptian queen. Which of those is true has been answered and will receive further confirmation by her death. Her love, which the very limited Roman imagination mistook for something shallow and small, is anything but. As she claimed early on, she alone would set the boundaries for love, and those boundaries far exceed the ordinary, exceedingly shallow version that occupies Roman imaginations. The play's final act, almost entirely given over to her, is a tribute to the magic and the mystery of the kind of devotion that lovingly envisions a giant bestriding seas and continents, shedding the wealth of empires in careless generosity from his pockets.

After Antony's death, Cleopatra is engaged in a psychological war with Caesar over her fate. Though at first she declares her intention to follow Antony, she pretends to be convinced by Caesar's assurances of a safe and dignified future. Getting final confirmation that he really intends to parade her through the streets of Rome where, as she imagines it, "I shall see some squeaking Cleopatra boy my greatness I ' the posture of a whore" (5.2.219ff), she declares, "I am again for Cydnus to meet Mark Antony." Ready, that is, to re-enact their first, very dramatic encounter as she sailed seductively in colorful barges toward the man she would come to love. Deserving of an extensive and close reading, the death that follows is at once magnificently dramatic and weighty with tragic paradox.

Just as death awaited Duncan inside a castle adorned with procreant cradles, emblems of Egyptian fertility and abundance also frame Cleopatra's demise. In rhythm with the Nile, Egypt accepts that decay and death are inseparable from life, and as Hamlet said, the readiness is all. When the "rural fellow" enters with his basket of figs hiding the poisonous asps, she calmly observes that "he brings me liberty."

315

Because death now represents deliverance from a world without her beloved, her determination is absolute:

> . . . I have nothing
> Of woman in me; now from head to foot
> I am marble-constant; now the fleeting moon
> No planet is of mine. (5.2.238-241)

As she faces her final moments, Cleopatra steels herself by denying feminine weakness and embracing the marble determination of Rome, sentiments that echo Lady Macbeth's "unsex me" speech. But the sentiment originates from a desire for love, not cruelty. Although she has already proven that her constancy to Antony is more Roman than Egyptian, she cannot undo the essential, feminine quality that makes her Cleopatra, again reminiscent of Lady Macbeth's inability to do what she asked of her husband. Like a good wife, Cleopatra wants to look her best when she meets Antony in the hereafter. Having dressed in her "best attire," she continues her journey to meet her lover again:

> Give me my robe, put on my crown, I have
> Immortal longings in me. . . . Methinks I hear
> Antony call; I see him rouse himself
> To praise my noble act. I hear him mock
> The luck of Caesar. . . . Husband, I come!
> Now to that name my courage prove my title!
> I am fire and air; my other elements
> I give to baser life. (5.2.280-290)

Of the four elements known to Renaissance science, earth and water are the lower two, fire and air belong to the heavens. Hearing the voice of her lover, Cleopatra is now joyously determined for the latter. Whatever else has been said by other Romans, be they characters of this play or simply those who judge her by overly simple moral dichotomies, this is magnificent, emotional poetry, full of longing for union with the beloved. It is the first and only time she calls Antony

316

husband, implicitly gaining the concomitant title for herself that she earns by courageously letting go of "baser life" and giving herself over to "fire and air." When her maidservant, Iras, falls, mortally poisoned by the aspic on Cleopatra's lips, the queen cannot resist one final sexual allusion. It is an essential part of who she is with Antony. Looking at Iras, she notes:

> If thou and nature can so gently part,
> The stroke of death is as a lover's pinch,
> Which hurts and is desired. (5.2.294-296)

Worried that Iras will reach Antony first, Cleopatra is moved to take the final, fatal step into fire and air:

> This proves me base.
> If she first meet the curled Antony,
> He'll make demand of her, and spend that kiss
> Which is my heaven to have. Come, thou mortal wretch
> [to the asp, which she applies to her breast]
> With thy sharp teeth this knot intrinsicate
> Of life at once untie. Poor venomous fool. . . .
> O, couldst thou speak,
> That I might hear thee call great Caesar ass
>   Unpolicied.
> Char. O eastern star!
> Cleo.   Peace! Peace!
>   Dost thou not see my baby at my breast,
>   That sucks the nurse asleep?
> Char.   O, break! O, break!
> Cleo. As sweet as balm, as soft as air, as gentle---
>   O Antony! (5.2.300-313)

If Antony is now husband through this death, Cleopatra simultaneously becomes wife and mother both. It is difficult to witness this and not feel that she has triumphed, not only over Caesar, that "ass unpolicied," but over death itself. Yes, she probably has, as Caesar points out when he sees her lifeless body, "pursu'd conclusions infinite of easy ways to dic."   But her "immortal longings" have magically transformed any fear of death she might have had into something that mimics wedded bliss.   What was little more than rhetorical flourish in *Romeo and Juliet* is much more explicit in his last tragedy.   It's as if Shakespeare wants us to fully understand what was significant about Juliet's decision in that tomb.   Once again, we witness another remarkable woman passing fearlessly through death into a love that has been perfected from what might have been only the lust of the flesh into something truly noble, splendid, and transcendent.

Not all critics are so sanguine about the implications of these deaths.   In a very thoughtful essay, John Danby writes:

> The Roman condemnation of the lovers is obviously inadequate. The sentimental reaction in their favor is equally mistaken.   There is no so-called "love-romanticism" in the play.   The flesh has its glory and passion, its witchery.   Love in *Antony and Cleopatra* is both of these.   The love of Antony and Cleopatra, however, is not asserted as a "final value."   The whole tenor of the play, in fact, moves in an opposite direction. Egypt is the Egypt of the Biblical glosses: exile from the spirit, thralldom to the flesh-pots, diminution of human kindness.   To go further still in sentimentality and claim that there is a "redemption" motif in Antony and Cleopatra's love is an even more violent error. . . . The fourth and fifth acts of *Antony and Cleopatra* are not epiphanies.   They are the ends moved to by that process whereby things rot themselves with motion. . . . Shakespeare may have his plays in which "redemption" is a theme (and I think he has), but *Antony and Cleopatra* is not one of them. (424)

Danby is right to reject the reading of Cleopatra's death as redemptive.   By way of contrast, Cordelia's return to save Lear and her sacrificial death do appear to expiate her father's sin, freeing him from all guilt.   However we resolve the ambiguity of Lear's conviction that his precious daughter is still alive, despite the obvious, Lear's unresolvable agony ends

318

with her return. His redemption, however momentary it may be, is real.

Still, Danby's moralism is far more simplistic than Shakespeare's, for Cleopatra really has no one to redeem. Caesar, who lives to incorporate the P*ax Romana*, has no interest in redemption, and there is no one of any stature who hasn't already been corrupted by Roman hypocrisy. Caesar implements the kind of *realpolitik* so familiar in our modern era, but it's good to recognize that, like many of Shakespeare's vice figures, he breaks his vow to take what rightfully belongs to others. We have seen what judgment is passed on Bolingbroke in *1Henry 4*; on Falstaff, who robs the pilgrims at Gadshill; on Sir Toby and on Iago, who both pilfer the purses of those who suffer under the illusion that they're among friends; on Lear's eldest daughters who lie to obtain a share of his kingdom. If such self-interest is the seed that sprouts into evil, it's equally important to recall the central metaphor of plays like *The Merchant* where generosity is the monetary equivalent of the mercy and forgiveness necessary for love, and that here, in this play, Antony's generosity contrasts sharply with Caesar's lack of that virtue.

Rather than being redemptive, Cleopatra's final scene shows her irresistible, life-giving, endlessly abundant love overcoming the intractable evil of death. As horrible and permanent as death certainly is, it cannot overcome Cleopatra's feminine conviction of her right to be Antony's wife, his lover, the mother of his children. In the *Lear* chapter, the quote from Berlin's *The Secret Cause* spoke of tragedy's ability to confront life's essential mysteries. Though different from Lear's tragedy, the last scene of *Antony and Cleopatra* confronts us with the amazing and profound mystery of that kind of love: What is its origin? Why do some people feel it so deeply and others not? And, ultimately, what is its meaning for those who do respond to its magic? As the great 116th sonnet has it, love somehow guides life down certain paths, but ultimately its full emotional, moral, and spiritual value can never really be comprehended by the very limited capacity of the human mind. As the Romans do, the mystery of love can certainly be reduced to sex, but the merely physical can never adequately explain the selfless devotion of an Edgar, a Cordelia, or the magnificent constancy of a Cleopatra.

Resolving the mystery of Cleopatra isn't as simple as saying that Rome is evil and Egypt is good. To achieve what Caesar does requires the cunning and sometimes ruthless application of power. While good men like Antony pay a price for that, the many years of peace that followed Caesar's actions are not without value. But such ruthless exercise of power raises the question whether what Caesar achieves is capable of enriching his life in the same way that Antony and Cleopatra enrich theirs. Similar to Hal in *1Henry 4*, Caesar sacrifices something quite precious at the personal level to achieve something grand but entirely worldly. In contrast, Antony and Cleopatra are forced by political circumstances to sacrifice something worldly but end up gaining something personal and immensely valuable. It is possible to argue that neither choice is better than the other, but *Antony and Cleopatra* demonstrates that only one choice can save and ennoble the heart. Caesar triumphs but his political skills leave little room for genuine love. Somehow, Caesar's choice diminishes the person. Because the choice, unfortunately, is stark, no one, not even the all-conquering Caesar, can have them both.

The foundations of all this drama are basic Christian concepts about love and human nature, which must eventually confront the choice between things of this world and those of the spirit. This was not the original design of creation, which began in a fertile garden that freely provided the first Adam with nature's full, indivisible bounty, including complete union, body and soul, with a loving mate and with his fully visible creator. This was the intention until sin destroyed that Eden, and the Creator sent man out into the world to work by the sweat of his brow. Ever since, the necessity of work distracts men from the women who love them. For women like Cleopatra who were born with a deeply embedded need for love, such devotion becomes part of their identity. Though men often fail to understand this, something within their nature cannot help but respond. This miracle, this magic, is what Shakespeare celebrates with his Egyptian queen. Embodied though that love is in fallible human beings, it has the power to transform lives. Its steadfast and patient persistence, its conviction that human weakness and misunderstandings must be forgiven, are dim but significant reflections of the perfect love that designed the world. Such love is the spark of divine fire that women like Cleopatra possess, and because of it, they are able to hold their men close to their hearts, even through and beyond death itself. This is the mystery that Antony and Cleopatra's tragic story demonstrates. What the two of them have is far different from what Caesar achieves, but Shakespeare makes it very clear why the final act of this play does not belong to him.

Shakespeare's final group of plays, collectively known as romances, take a step back from tragedy. Though they address similar themes and issues, they reflect changing theatrical tastes, deliberately creating a context that is less realistic and much closer to folklore or fairy tale. Ever the adapter and experimenter, Shakespeare meets audience expectations without sacrificing any of his hard-won convictions about love and human life. Perhaps the best of his final plays, *The Tempest* is an example of this great author's life-long effort to use art to educate and enlighten his audience about the value and meaning of human being.

The Tempest

Perhaps more than any other of his plays, an autobiographical element is detectable in Shakespeare's last great drama, *The Tempest*. Since a source for the play has yet to be identified, several personal and historical events may account for the unique quality of the play, which is most evident in the main character, Prospero, an elder who employs magic to redeem three men of sin. The sense that this play is more autobiographical than others is largely the result of the obvious parallel between Prospero's art and Shakespeare's. That *The Tempest* was his last major work adds some credence to this.

While few reliable records have been found to document Shakespeare's final years, it is clear that *The Tempest* was written when he was approaching retirement. Though he had purchased one of the finest Stratford homes, New Place, in 1597, evidence suggests he retired there sometime between 1610 and 1613, the year his theater, The Globe, burned to the ground. Since *The Tempest* was probably written sometime between 1610 and 1611, his retirement from the theater was likely on his mind as he composed these lines. Already wealthy and respected by his peers, he would have been about forty-six years old when he wrote the last of his great plays, including *The Tempest,* which had been preceded by two other similar romances, *Cymbeline* and *The Winter's Tale*.

Unlike anything he had done before, all three of these dramas take place in an unspecified, fairytale-like setting where the miraculous is an accepted element of experience. Even though these romances make no pretense to the realism of either history or tragedy, they still manage to examine many of the same themes that pervade his earlier plays but with a carefully calibrated balance between artistic control and artistic freedom. At the center of this exquisite jewel of a tale is Prospero, the magician who uses his art to reform whatever is redeemable in human nature, making the parallels to Shakespeare himself difficult to avoid. Quite naturally, the approaching end of his productive years might very well have initiated a period of self-reflection, an assessment of what his time in the theater had accomplished.

This personal appraisal may also have been motivated by the rapidly changing political and religious environment in the first decades of the seventeenth century. Though Shakespeare was at the height of his powers, these last productive years must have been bittersweet. His chosen profession was under serious attack. Like Elizabeth, James enjoyed and gladly supported the theater, sponsoring Shakespeare's company with notable royal largesse. But James had to contend with the growing cultural and political influence of the Puritans. Inspired by Reformation zeal, they promoted the primacy of both scripture and individual conscience over the power of Anglican bishops, who, they felt, owed their fealty more to the English throne than to God. As Puritan influence steadily transformed the House of Commons during that decade, they were able to wield considerable power over James. Though their initial aim was to remove the last remnants of Catholicism from the Anglican Church, their efforts to purify all aspects of English society eventually jeopardized the political stability that Elizabeth's religious compromises had afforded. With uncompromising zeal, the Puritans viewed any religious accommodation as a subordination of principles to convenience, and they used the pulpit, the pamphlet, and the politician to attack any religious, political, or cultural activity that violated their beliefs. London's theaters, viewed as dens of rowdy, sometimes licentious behavior, were a favorite target. To the Puritans, entertainment was an idolatrous activity that diverted attention away from productive work and spiritual devotions. Such opinions fueled their intense dislike of the theaters, and they longed for the day when all of them would finally be closed.

Such passionate opposition eventually had a chilling effect on theater attendance, the driving force behind the intense creative effort that made Elizabethan theaters so successful. Anticipating what now seemed inevitable, James Burbage, one of the co-owners of Shakespeare's Globe, bought and refurbished the Blackfriar's Theater in London for smaller, indoor productions. At first used primarily during the winter, it attracted a wealthier, better-educated clientele who brought with them different theatrical expectations. Influenced by the classically trained Ben Jonson, who authored the First Folio's dedication, this audience preferred his witty, satirical comedy or his elaborate masques, which featured light-hearted, frivolous spectacles in an idealized pastoral location. Heavy with song and dance, these plays featured easily digestible fare that was intended more for delight than for instruction. With Puritan opposition to the theaters strengthening and changing audience expectations, Shakespeare, that keen, intelligent observer of human nature, must have had some sense that the end of his theatrical career was approaching.

Collaborating with the famed architect, Inigo Jones, who designed his elaborate stage sets, Jonson established the artistic standards for the masque. For the far more accomplished Shakespeare, Jonson had become the competition. Endlessly inventive, however, Shakespeare produced a play that not only satisfied these new expectations but transformed the frothy, Jonsonian masque into a profound statement about the capabilities as well as the limitations of art. In what amounts to an implicit critique of Jonson's extravagant spectacles, *The Tempest* compares those who idealize creation with those who believe the world exists to satisfy their desires, and it argues that the purpose of art is not just to entertain but to reform whatever there is in either type still susceptible to redemption.

Further evidence that Shakespeare was responding to the challenge Jonson's plays represented is suggested by *The*

Tempest's observation of the classical unities, one of the few plays in the Folio that does so. Jonson readily acknowledged Shakespeare's natural talent and popularity but thought his rival's works ignored the standards set by the Latin and Greek models taught at university. As if to prove his adaptability, Shakespeare carefully constructs *The Tempest* to follow the unities of action, time, and place, artificial criteria that mattered so much to Jonson. Even at his age, with his achievements, it's as if Shakespeare were trying to show he could still be relevant in a theatrical world that was moving in an entirely new direction. Four hundred years later, the irony is that *The Tempest* remains one of his most popular plays while Jonson's masques, for all their flashy spectacle, have long been forgotten.

Along with an impending retirement, the Puritans, and Jonson's masques, *The Tempest* shows the influence of the many books and pamphlets about the Americas that had begun circulating throughout London. These electrified the English imagination with visions of a pristine, unblemished society, untouched by the sins of a supposedly civilized culture. Among the most notable were William Strachey's *A True Reportory of the Wreck and Redemption of Sir Thomas Gates*, Silvester Jourdain's *A Discovery in the Bermudas*, and Montaigne's *The Cannibals,* all of which, in some ways and for a variety of purposes, idealized the land and the peoples of the new world. Montaigne's essay, in fact, which romanticized the inhabitants of these far-off lands to satirize the moral hypocrisy of European society, is the source for Gonzalo's naïve utopian vision as the corrupt Italian nobles, shipwrecked by the play's storm, survey their new home.

Like Montaigne, Shakespeare was very aware that man's capacity for virtue had been adulterated with an incurably sinful nature. Man, he knew, had been gifted with not only a conscience to help him differentiate between good and evil but also with reason to help him choose wisely between the two. These tools lifted him above the animals

325

that acted purely on those instinctual desires for safety, food, and sex. From his very Christian perspective, man had indeed been created in God's image, but, because of the fall, reason, responsible for perceiving and interpreting the world, was easily corrupted by the same selfish desires that motivated the animals. So unless the fall described in *Genesis* was false, the primal innocence of the new world's inhabitants was an impossibility that *The Tempest* is careful to qualify. Whatever the intentions of the pamphlet writers, they were advancing the unbiblical notion that pristine human nature, untouched by civil and spiritual nurturing, is inherently good. While that may have been God's original design, *The Tempest* seems to argue, sin had changed all that. Theoretically, man might be perfectible, but he could never be perfect or, therefore, create a perfect social construct. That reality defines art's purpose, which was not only to delight but also to provide instruction for moral and spiritual improvement.

As a play, *The Tempest* is deceptively simple. There are no larger-than-life characters like Falstaff or Lear, both endowed with much rich vitality. It contains no intellectually and emotionally passionate speeches like the soliloquies of *Hamlet*. Where Lear's mad ravings untangle complex thematic threads of blindness, justice, and human nature, similar ideas are handled here with a deliberately delicate touch. As for the plot, nothing remarkably dramatic happens. There is no regicide, no ambiguous ghost, no agony over postponed revenge, no murder of an innocent wife, no lost battles or empires. Influenced by Jonson's masques, the plot is based on a relatively benign story taking place in a pastoral setting with plenty of entertaining songs. Realism is eschewed and magic is an accepted norm. While this light-hearted fare manages to conform to the standards of the Jonsonian masque, however, it is a tribute to Shakespeare's artistry that *The Tempest* can be viewed as both simple entertainment and as drama with a serious purpose. In Shakespeare's masterful hands, the one doesn't in any way preclude the other.

The play opens with a storm ravaging a ship carrying several members of the Italian court who are returning home from the wedding of the King of Naples's daughter. Unbeknownst to them, the storm is controlled by Prospero, formerly Duke of Milan, who has initiated a plan to punish these noblemen, particularly his brother, Antonio, for usurping his throne and exiling him and his daughter, Miranda, to this remote island. The exiled duke and his daughter reside on this unnamed island with Caliban, a savage, and Ariel, a spirit who implements Prospero's magic. Though Prospero's art keeps everyone aboard the foundering ship safe, they all come to believe they've been shipwrecked. Alonso, king of Naples, believes his son, Ferdinand, has drowned. The king's brother, Sebastian, blames him for bringing them so far from home. Very quickly, these shipwrecked noblemen divide into two morally distinguishable camps. Though there is no discernible advantage to be gained, one group plans to murder Alonso, the king of Naples, whose love for his lost son eventually leads to his redemption.

A subplot, which comically mimics this murderous plan, involves two drunken passengers from the ship who collaborate with the savage, Caliban, to murder Prospero. As a result of the similarities between the two murder conspiracies, the subplot comically mocks the moral vacuity of the wayward brothers in the main story. But there is never any doubt that Prospero knows all and controls what can happen on the island. What little dramatic tension exists is eventually resolved by the love that develops between the innocent young adults, Ferdinand and Miranda. Because of their love, the divide between Prospero and Alonso, who expresses regret for his part in Prospero's overthrow and exile, is eventually bridged. After freeing Ariel from any further obligation and giving up his magical book and staff, Prospero returns to Italy as Duke of Milan where he intends to rule with far more wisdom than he exhibited previously.

Though no audience can accept Prospero's magic as real, *The Tempest* still manages to elude the frivolous by developing several familiar Shakespearean themes. Typically, this is accomplished by the contrasting assumptions and motives of various characters. Among the most prominent of these themes is the way desire shapes perceptions of the world. Hamlet's desire for revenge, for example, shades his perception of Denmark so that everyone, good or bad, seems morally diseased. Macbeth's ambition, awakened by the witches, blurs the moral clarity that his conscience was meant to provide. *The Tempest*, however, suggests that even benign assumptions about human nature have the potential to taint perceptions of the world.

When the Italian noblemen find their way ashore after Prospero's storm, the good-natured Gonzalo, who is described in the play's list of characters as "an honest old councilor," envisions the society he would create if he were the island's ruler. His idealized vision is cynically mocked by Sebastian and Antonio, the amoral brothers of Alonso and Prospero respectively:

<pre>
Gon.   Had I plantation of this isle, my lord—
Ant.   He'd sow't with nettle-seed.
Seb.   Or docks, or mallows.
Gon.   And were the king on't, what would I do?
Seb.   'Scape being drunk, for want of wine.
Gon.   I' th' commonwealth, I would, by contraries,
        Execute all things; for no kind of traffic
        Would I admit; no name of magistrate;
        Letters should not be known; riches, poverty,
        And use of service, none; contract, succession,
        Bourn, bound of land, tilth, vineyard, none;
        No use of metal, corn, or wine, or oil;
        No occupation, all men idle, all;
        And women too but innocent and pure;
        No sovereignty—
Seb.   Yet he would be king on't.
Ant.   The latter end of his commonwealth forgets the
</pre>

Gon. All things in common nature should produce
   Without sweat or endeavor; treason, felony,
   Sword, pike, knife, gun, or need of any engine,
   Would I not have; but nature should bring forth,
   Of its own kind, all foison, all abundance,
   To feed my innocent people.
Seb. No marrying 'mong his subjects?
Ant. None, man, all idle—whores and knaves.
Gon. I would with such perfection govern, sir,
   T' excel the golden age. (2.1.144-168)

Gonzalo's idyllic society would "excel the golden age" of Hesiod, which, very much like the Biblical Eden, described a time of innocence and plenty. If Gonzalo ruled, culture, labor, laws, military preparedness—in short, everything that constitutes civilization would be unnecessary on this island because the nature that Gonzalo perceives is prodigiously abundant and good. Honest and well-meaning, Gonzalo's vision of what might be reflects his assumptions about the world and man's essential, perfectible nature. That naiveté makes him look foolishly vulnerable to the two cynical brothers, who see the world quite differently. Because Sebastian and Antonio are themselves so easily swayed by the dark desires of their hearts, they find the old man's dream unrealistic and foolish. "How lush and lusty the grass looks!" Gonzalo observes. "The ground indeed is tawny," responds Antonio. Two very different men, two very different views of the world. Where Gonzalo's world is green with promise, theirs is tawny, dry, and arid, good only for nettles, whores, and knaves. As sympathetic as Gonzalo is, the two mockers establish an alternative view that proves dangerous to ignore. Though both views contain some truth, neither naivete nor cynicism is adequate.

   What's true about the cynical notion of human nature is quickly validated after Ariel puts everyone except these two amoral brothers to sleep. Tempted by the prospect of getting the throne of Naples and forging an alliance for their mutual benefit, Prospero's sibling, Antonio, tempts Sebastian to kill his brother, the king of Naples along with his faithful counselor, Gonzalo, before they reawaken. The state of their hearts is revealed not only by the heinous plot but also by the feeble pangs of their consciences. Even though Antonio had ousted Prospero and cast the former duke and his daughter adrift at sea, Sebastian worries that his companion might be too troubled by his conscience to help kill the king. "But, for your conscience?" he asks cautiously. "I feel not this deity in my bosom," replies Antonio, a sure sign that his unrepentant heart has become inured to evil. Like Macbeth, repetitive sin has rendered conscience an ineffective deterrent to selfish desire. Although Gonzalo's virtue allows him to believe that innately good men exist within a benevolent nature, that vision is naïve, unfortunately, because such men as Sebastian and Antonio do exist and must be taken into account.

The comic subplot reinforces this view of a stubbornly selfish human nature that has fallen far from its original, innocent design. In this plotline, Caliban, the aboriginal savage of the island, encounters two of the ship's occupants, Stephano and Trinculo. Overindulging in the wine Stephano managed to save from the ship, the three hatch a plan to kill Prospero, win Caliban's freedom, and rule the island according to their whims.

Though a savage, Caliban believes he has a legitimate claim to the island. The offspring of the witch, Sycorax, Caliban had once roamed the island unhindered, surviving off the fruit of the land, much like the natives described in those idealized accounts of the new world. When the deposed Duke and his daughter arrive, he willingly shares his knowledge of the island, something that Prospero repays by trying to teach him the basics of civilization. But that initial trust is broken when Caliban attempts to rape Miranda and people "[t]his isle with Calibans" (1.2.351). Mentioned only in passing, this attempted rape exposes the human proclivity to inherently

330

amoral desires, contradicting Gonzalo's assumption that unschooled, natural man is innocent. Ignoring any of the possible consequences, Caliban is ruled by his needs rather than the other way around. Constantly rebelling against Prospero's authority, he lacks the necessary self-discipline to harness desire, listen to his conscience, and reason out the proper course of action.

Like Sebastian and Antonio, Caliban craves the freedom to do as he pleases, to take what he wants when he wants it. A version of Falstaff without the endearing wit, he behaves as if the island is there for his pleasure. In his first appearance, he is cursing Prospero for making him work. He remembers a time before Prospero's arrival when he was free to do as he pleased. Then he was a king unto himself. But with Prospero's arrival and dominion over the island, his state has changed dramatically. Despising the discipline imposed by Prospero, he laments the loss of his freedom. Now, he begins:

> I must eat my dinner.
> This island's mine by Sycorax my mother,
> Which thou tak'st from me. When thou cam'st first,
> Thou. . . made much of me. . . , wouldst give me
> Water with berries in't. . . .and then I lov'd thee. . . .
> Curs'd be I that did so! . . . .
> For I am all the subjects that you have,
> Which first was mine own king . . . . (1.2.330-342)

Like Prospero, Caliban has also been deposed, but he lost authority over the island and its bounty because his base desire threatened Miranda's innocent virtue, which civilized society is duty-bound to protect and encourage. When that duty to authority is forsaken, Shakespeare's histories remind us, chaos is the inevitable result. The issue, *The Tempest* argues, really isn't between freedom and enslavement but between license and an orderly society built on respect, duty, and love.

But Caliban is not the only character who imagines himself king of the island. Many of the play's characters imagine being the one exercising authority: Gonzalo, Sebastian, Caliban, even Prospero himself. Gonzalo, the honest one, accepts the dream for what it is. The others, though, employ various stratagems to make their dream a reality. The evil ones are willing to violate moral norms to take what they want. Prospero, though, uses his authority to educate and redeem. In either case, the play makes clear that the effort to take matters in hand, to be "mine own king," does little more than create an illusion of freedom. *The Tempest* begins, in fact, with the ship's crew struggling to control the storm-ravaged vessel while the terrified noblemen foolishly try to assert their wills upon the sailors. "What cares these roarers," the boatswain chastises, "for the name of king? To cabin! Silence! Trouble us not." Sometimes staged with Prospero rocking a model ship above this scene of terror and desperation, it is clear that what Nietzsche called the individual will to power is, in Shakespeare's view, subject to an authority that, while dimly perceived, is far more potent.

The absurdity of thinking otherwise is again lightly mocked by events in the subplot. Because of the attempted rape, Caliban had been forced to serve Prospero by doing menial tasks. After the storm, the wild native of the island encounters the drunken butler, Stephano, and the jester, Trinculo, with a cask of wine they share with the credulous islander. Because the effects of the liquor strike him as magical, he foolishly assumes those who bring it must be gods:

Cal.   [Aside] These be fine things, and if they be not sprites. That's a brave god, and bears a celestial liquor. I will kneel to him.

Ste.   Swear by this bottle how thou cam'st hither—I escap'd upon a butt of sack which the sailors heav'd o'erboard—by this bottle, which I made of the bark of a tree with mine own hands since I

	was cast ashore.
Cal.	I'll swear upon that bottle to be thy true subject,
	for the liquor is not earthly. . . .
Trin.	O Stephano, hast any more of this?
Ste.	The whole butt, man. My cellar is in a rock by the
	sea-side. . . .How now, moon-calf? How does thine ague?
Cal.	Hast thou not dropp'd from heaven?
Ste.	Out o' th' moon, I do assure thee. . . .
Cal.	I have seen thee in her, and I do adore thee. . . .
	I'll show thee every fertile inch o' th' island;
	And I will kiss thy foot. I prithee, be my god.
	(2.2.116-149)

Though he happily exchanges servitude to Prospero for the opportunity to become the "true subject" of a drunken butler and a fool, Caliban seizes this opportunity to escape from his normal drudgery, enlisting his newfound friends in a plot to murder his erstwhile master. When the three of them concur, he joyously exits the stage, singing:

'Ban, 'Ban, Ca-Caliban
Has a new master, get a new man,
Freedom, high-day!
High-day, freedom! Freedom, high-day, freedom!
    (2.2.184-186)

Caliban forsakes the well-meaning but strict Prospero and his chores only to make two drunken fools his gods. As recalcitrant, natural man, Caliban is entirely ignorant of the spiritual and moral truth that everyone is a servant of some master. For some, like Sebastian and Antonio, it is the lust for power. For others, like Ferdinand and Miranda, it is romantic love. For Caliban, it is mistaken for a butt of wine. And, for Prospero, it is the magical authority found in book, robe, and staff. For each of these characters, the choice is not between freedom and servitude but between worthy and unworthy masters. As the play's initial storm shows, the conviction that man controls his own fate, that, being his "own king," he can do whatever he chooses, is a dangerous illusion created by self-pride and a wrongfully conceived notion of freedom.

Conceptually, the problem of freedom is a problem of commitment: who or what a person decides to commit himself to. Like Caliban, Prospero's other, far better servant, Ariel, also wants his freedom. As such, he provides an alternative definition of freedom to Caliban's, who sees it as license to do as he pleases. Though he possesses a capacity for love, co-operation, and service, qualities he exhibits when Prospero and Miranda first arrive on the island, Caliban cannot subsume his basic instinct for self-satisfaction to self-control. As the curses he hurls at Prospero show, he rebels at any external authority that hinders his self-indulgence. Any effort at self-control is overpowered by desire, the divine liquor poured from the bottle. The freedom he craves would allow him to drink deeply of his own desires. As natural man, therefore, he needs constant oversight, a wearying responsibility assumed by Prospero. Without that governance, as the attempted rape indicates, whatever civilized order the island has would be quickly overthrown and each person would live according to his own desires. This is the dangerous potential inherent in man's natural state. Fallen man is a being driven by selfish and self-serving desires that sometimes bring momentary satisfaction but at the cost of moral profligacy and social chaos. Self-indulgence never brings lasting freedom or the peace that nurtures it. As Goneril and Regan from *King Lear* demonstrate, self-indulgence eventually devolves into the kind of ravenous appetite that ends up feeding on itself.

Thematically, therefore, Ariel's purpose in the play is to present a different view of freedom. When he first appears on stage, he too is Prospero's servant, assisting the old magician with the storm, the ship, and all the onboard passengers. Having accounted for all of these, he reminds Prospero of a promise:

> Ariel: Let me remember thee what thou hast promis'd
> Which is not yet perform'd me.

```
Pros:                              How now? Moody?
           What is't thou canst demand?
Ariel:              My liberty.  (1.2.243-245)
```

Ariel's history is somewhat different from Caliban's. Both
arrived on the island with the witch, Sycorax, but where the
amoral Caliban roamed free, the witch imprisoned Ariel in a
pine tree for failing to carry out some of her distasteful
commands. Unlike Caliban, who remains in foolish bondage
to his ridiculous gods, Ariel makes a moral judgment about
his master and his duties. Though he begins in a pine tree
prison, he is now moving toward freedom under Prospero's
tutelage. He isn't quite there yet but will be once he assists
the exiled duke with his effort to reform any of the ship's
passengers open to repentance. The master and the purpose
Ariel serves are morally and spiritually worthy of his loyalty.
As their relationship shows, obedient service to the proper
master is the only path to real freedom, which is the freedom
to move toward nature's original and perfect design. It is a
paradox firmly rooted in Christian thinking that self-control
and obedience to what's worthy free the servant from
ignorance, sin, and its consequent guilt.

   This paradox is elaborated further through the
romance of Ferdinand and Miranda. Separated from the other
shipwrecked passengers, Ferdinand stumbles upon the lovely
but wholly innocent Miranda and, in keeping with the spirit of
comedy, immediately falls in love. As does she. Though
there's a sense that this is part of Prospero's larger plan, the
girl's father decides to intervene. But he does so for a purpose.
He addresses Ferdinand, the bewitched young lover:

```
Pros:                          Soft, sir, one word more.
   [Aside] They are both in either's pow'rs; but this swift
                      business
           I must uneasy make, lest too light winning
           Make the prize light. (1.2.450-453)
```

To verify the quality of Ferdinand's devotion to his daughter, Prospero gives Ferdinand the menial task of hauling logs to their shelter, the same task previously assigned to Caliban. Prospero's island, clearly, is far different from Gonzalo's idealized society where "nature should produce without sweat or endeavor." In Prospero's world, work is a form of service, an exercise that reflects a willingness to give something from the self for the greater good of spouse, family, and society.

Both Ferdinand and Caliban are required to work, but each accepts their tasks with completely different attitudes that measure their readiness for a place within a family and civil society. Caliban resists the drudgery, curses his master, and seizes upon the first opportunity to escape from his burdens. Ferdinand, on the other hand, understands that his labor has a purpose and will be rewarded with the promised abundance that benevolent nature has embodied in Miranda. Unlike Caliban and the two amoral nobles, Sebastian and Antonio, Ferdinand is comfortable with the notion that selfless service is a part of nature's design. He is not distracted by an illusion of unrestrained freedom, which is nothing more than slavery to desire. He has chosen the worthy master. Where Gonzalo's idealized vision of society requires nothing of its inhabitants, Ferdinand's mature acceptance of Prospero's work requirement prepares him for the duties owed to a loving wife and a peaceful, orderly society.

How these two young lovers respond to Prospero's demand is indicative of a virtue that differentiates them from Caliban and the amoral nobles, Sebastian and Antonio, all of whom mistake unlicensed desire for the mirage of freedom. The lovers 'innocent virtue is evident in the scene where Ferdinand and Miranda exchange vows of love to each other. He is carrying logs hither and yon; she feels compelled to provide relief:

> Fer: The very instant that I saw you, did
>   My heart fly to your service, there resides,

> To make me slave to it, and for your sake
> Am I this patient log-man.
>
> Mir: Do you love me?
>
> Fer: O heaven, O earth, bear witness to this sound. . . .
> Beyond all limit of what else i' th' world,
> Do love, prize, honor you. . . .
> Wherefore weep you?
>
> Mir: At my own unworthiness, that dare not offer
> What I desire to give; and much less take
> What I shall die to want. . . .
> I am your wife, if you will marry me;
> If not, I'll die your maid. To be your fellow
> You may deny me, but I'll be your servant,
> Whether you will or no. (3.1.64-86)

Miranda's humble joy at the prospect of such love echoes the very same sentiments that Portia expressed when Bassanio chooses the lead casket in *The Merchant*. The same language of generosity and service is evident here: Ferdinand is her willing slave; Miranda is his unconditional servant, ready to help, with or without marriage. And though Prospero is watching this scene from afar, they are making these pledges freely. Love, that wondrous, mysterious conviction of the heart, gives itself over to the other willingly, freely, joyously. True love is impossible, Shakespeare argues over the course of his career, without this generous surrender of self to other. Love is an open-ended, generously given commitment to service, and, from that, much goodness flows.

Interestingly, the pristine innocence of these lovers illuminates Gonzalo's utopian vision of society from a different perspective. In his musings, Gonzalo had dreamed of the women on his island as "innocent and pure," which is surely true of both Miranda and Ferdinand. Together, they represent a kind of love that is almost otherworldly, an unblemished state of pure innocence. But in a world that contains Sebastian and Antonio, that kind of innocence is terribly vulnerable. At the end of the play, when she sees the

337

men from Naples and Milan, including those unrepentant plotters, Sebastian and Antonio, she cannot help but exclaim, "O brave new world that has such people in't!" It is an ironic exclamation, for like Edgar in *King Lear*, Miranda's naïve innocence makes her vulnerable to their evil. The world, unfortunately, won't let her retain that innocence forever. Men who only listen to their selfish desires will eventually despoil that simplicity, but that youthful innocence is precious nevertheless. Like the story of Eden, it serves to remind what should be, what could be chosen. And of what has been lost to selfish willfulness. Gonzalo's utopia may be subject to worldly cynicism, but, like the story of Eden, the truth it reflects serves to condemn human sinfulness.

Caliban's story demonstrates that freedom is not to be confused with license. Suffering under the delusion he will gain freedom by murdering Prospero, Caliban is only substituting one set of masters he momentarily prefers, Stephano and Trinculo, for another, Prospero, who displeases with his enforced demands for obedience. He's simply exchanging one master for another. That master can be either God or Mammon, flesh or spirit, self or others, good or evil. Mankind may choose a master freely, but in some fashion he remains enslaved to that choice. Choosing a master is the extent of freedom available in a fallen world, but the consequences of that choice determine what kind of life follows because that master will either betray his servants, as Stephano and Trinculo do, or prove his worthiness.

Like the unregenerate, natural man of the island, Sebastian and Antonio are equally subject to the selfish desires of their hearts. They are takers, not givers; rebels, not servants. Witty, sophisticated, civilized, they misread and misunderstand the good intentions of Gonzalo, who tries to comfort Alonso as he mourns the apparent loss of his beloved son, Ferdinand. Throughout, they exhibit neither generosity nor compassion. They mock Gonzalo unmercifully. They plan to kill Alonso to seize power for themselves even though there's no obvious way for them to return home yet. Like Caliban, they simply want what they want. Motivated entirely by self-interest, they take advantage of whatever opportunity fate presents to them.

Deftly establishing the moral similarities between Caliban and the plotters, the comic subplot exposes the error of choosing the wrong master. Where the courtiers plot the murder of Alonso and Gonzalo, Caliban and his drunken masters plot to kill Prospero. Both plots serve to comment on the backstory of the original overthrow of Prospero back in Milan, where Antonio usurped his brother's control of the city. What each of these events has in common is the taking of something not theirs for personal gratification – for power, for "freedom," for greed. This is the elixir that makes men drunk, that subverts their judgment, that leads them out of paradise into the fallen world of sin, corruption, and, ultimately, chaos. That the comic subplot to kill Prospero is foiled by a clothesline of flashy garments, which catch the eyes of Stephano and Trinculo and diverts them from their mission, implies that the effort to satisfy their desires is an illusion not worth the effort. Man will be betrayed whenever he mistakes the real for the illusory, whenever he chooses the unworthy things of this world instead of whatever his conscience knows to be good.

The consequences of either choice are made clear by the two banquet scenes that take place near the middle of the play, both of which are orchestrated by Ariel. At the end of Act III, the first banquet is presented to the shipwrecked Italian nobles, who are famished by their ordeal. Being subject to physical hunger, of course, is symbolic of their enslavement to all desires of the flesh. The lavishly furnished banquet table that appears and tantalizes them quickly vanishes, leaving their hunger unsatisfied. Ariel delivers this stern message to Alonso and the two plotters; his words are reminiscent of Hal's final words to Falstaff at his royal coronation parade:

You are three men of sin, whom Destiny,
That hath to instrument this lower world
And what is in't, the never-surfeited sea
Hath caus'd to belch up you; and on this island
Where man doth not inhabit—you 'mongst men
Being most unfit to live. I have made you mad. . .
But remember
(For that's my business to you) that you three
From Milan did supplant good Prospero,
Expos'd unto the sea (which hath requit it)
Him and his innocent child; for which foul deed
The pow'rs, delaying (not forgetting) have
Incens'd the seas and shores—yea, all the
        creatures,
Against your peace. Thee of thy son, Alonso,
They have bereft; and do pronounce by me
Ling'ring perdition. . . shall step by step attend
You and your ways. . .
Which here. . . is nothing but heart's sorrow
And a clear life ensuing. (3.3.53-82)

Ariel states his purpose plainly: these "three men of sin" need
to remember what they did to Prospero and Miranda. The
vanishing banquet symbolically reenacts their callousness,
which took away everything that had at one time sustained the
exiled duke and his daughter. For supporting the coup that
abandoned a father and his innocent daughter to dire
uncertainty, the king, Alonso, must now endure a similar loss
of a child. Separation, sorrow, and perdition are the wages
earned by a heart closed to tender mercies. Before repentance
is possible, sin must be exposed and remembered.
Symbolically, the banquet vanishes before any of these men
are satisfied to indicate that none of nature's sustaining bounty
will ever be available to them unless they change. The
"Destiny that. . . instrument[s] this lower world" rejects them,
belches them up onto this remote island to present them with
the opportunity to acknowledge and repent. As it did for Lear,
a tempest has come to shake complacent and morally lazy man

out of selfishness and self-delusion.   But the chastisement also contains a message of hope.   There is a benevolent purpose, an over-arching plan within nature that works toward their redemption if they are open to it.

As both Prospero and Alonso show, the unconditional love of a parent for his child becomes the only avenue into the promised redemption.   Where evil separates and divides, love is always defined and experienced through union.   It holds spouses, families, communities, and nations together.   The necessary prerequisite for redemption, however, is a heart that remains open to feelings so basic that, as Cordelia admitted, they cannot be heaved into the mouth.   It is Alonso's love for his son that enables his repentance.   He is salvageable. Sebastian and Antonio, who never express anything like that tenderness   toward   anyone,   remain   recalcitrant   and unredeemable. Like the wicked daughters in *King Lear*, their cynicism blinds them to the possibility of goodness, of forgiveness, of redemption.   Like Caliban, Sebastian and Antonio lack any awareness of a choice that might benefit them far more than the path of self-indulgence they've chosen. Enslaved   to   self,   they   remain   ostracized,   emotionally, morally, and spiritually if not physically, from a civil society that will always regard them with suspicion.   Like Caliban, Sebastian and Antonio have made their fool their god.

But the first banquet with its bitter aftertaste is soon followed by a contrasting second. The next one for Ferdinand and Miranda is a sweet celebration of their innocent love, which they've preserved by co-operating with Prospero's hard-earned wisdom.   Because they have persisted in that obedience, they are provided with all the bounty of nature. Their banquet suggests that all manner of sustenance, physical, emotional, and spiritual, is available to them precisely because of their desire to serve the other over the self. But that kind of emotional and spiritual control is hard work, a constant struggle against any desire that threatens to subvert that selfless attitude. Instilling that spiritual vigilance is the reason for the work that Prospero obliged Ferdinand to do, and it trained both young lovers about the necessity of self-discipline. Their generous, selfless spirit makes that hard work of self-discipline a joy, however.

Though the second banquet functions as Prospero's blessing on the pair, he is fully aware that desire can always overpower whatever restrains man's behavior, so he insists that Ferdinand must continue to exercise self-control by abstaining from physical intimacy until the lovers are officially married. Ferdinand's willing consent to this stands in sharp contrast to Caliban's attempted rape of Miranda. Self-control, which is the obedient submission to a higher good, is a choice that leads somewhere far different from the destination that awaits those who only serve themselves. After the fall, Eden is no longer available. The Sebastians and Antonios of the world will always be present in the post-Edenic garden, but the utopian dream, the Edenic memory, reminds man of what he might eventually become if he chooses to follow the worthy master.

For most of the play, it isn't entirely clear what Prospero's intent is for the three men of sin, whether he intends to punish or reform them. But, from a Christian perspective, the persistence of sin in a fallen world makes further demands on the victims of that sin. Instead of revenge, it demands forgiveness, the turning of the other cheek. In *Hamlet* and other plays, Shakespeare examined the personal and social consequences of revenge. Those consequences were unacceptable to both providence and mankind. The only alternative available in a world where everyone is imperfect and fallible is forgiveness, a foundational principle of the New Testament as well as the Lord's Prayer. Grievously hurt by a brother's betrayal, by a forced removal from power, by the callous exile to the sea and an uncertain fate, Prospero possesses the power to crush his enemies completely but chooses otherwise. Moved by Ariel's pity for the suffering aristocrats of Naples and Milan, Prospero makes a decision:

> Though with their high wrongs I am strook to the quick,
> Yet, with my nobler reason, 'gainst my fury
> Do I take part. The rarer action is
> In virtue than in vengeance. They being penitent,
> The sole drift of my purpose doth extend
> Not a frown further. (5.1.25-30)

Completely different from power, which can enforce someone's will on another, forgiveness makes a demand on the injured party. Similar to the self-discipline that Prospero asked of Caliban and Ferdinand, forgiveness demands that the aggrieved relinquish any desire to personally punish the wrongdoer. Faced with a choice between revenge or mercy, Prospero must now enact the same truth that he has been trying to teach to others: that the self-discipline holding selfish desires in check promotes God's design for the fallen world and that only obedience can provide the freedom that makes all of nature's abundant provisions available.

Prospero himself has to undergo his own tempest before he understood this lesson fully, and even now, at this crucial moment, it takes an act of will. Instead of indulging selfish desires, conformity to the design of nature demands rigorous self-discipline, but the rewards for doing so are great. The bountiful promises of love are enough to motivate the sacrificial service of Ferdinand and Miranda, but that emotional self-discipline must also be matched with the moral self-discipline that makes forgiveness possible. When Prospero puts aside any inclination for revenge, therefore, he demonstrates that he has acquired the self-discipline that was missing from his tenure as Duke of Milan, for, as Prospero explains to Miranda, his brother, Antonio, was able to seize his title and authority because of his obsession with magic:

> My brother and thy uncle, call'd Antonio. . .
> He whom next thyself
> Of all the world I lov'd, and to him put
> The manage of my state. . . being so reputed

In dignity, and for the liberal arts
Without parallel; those being my study,
The government I cast upon my brother,
And to my state grew stranger, being transported
And rapt in secret studies. (1.2.66-77)

Just as Caliban chooses the wrong master when he follows his
two foolish gods, Prospero had at one time allowed his
fascination with magic to distract him from his duties. Magic
had become his master. As he admits to Miranda, by
"neglecting worldly ends," he "awak'd an evil nature" in
Antonio that blossomed into mutiny and their forced removal
from Milan. Based on the association of Prospero's art with
Shakespeare's, those "secret studies" weren't in themselves
problematic, for the secret arts he learned during those hours
now enable Prospero to reform Alonso and regain his civil
authority in Milan. What made his obsession with magic
problematic is that he allowed it to become his false idol. In
effect, Prospero lost his dukedom, suffered exile to a remote
and desolate island, and endangered his daughter because he
made the same mistake that Caliban does. It is for this reason
that Prospero now refers to his magical powers as this "vile
art." Like anything of this world, it has the power to tempt
man away from his real purpose. Vigilance and discipline are
necessary to avoid any such distraction.

In the final scene, all of the unresolved issues are
settled. For his faithful service, Ariel is given his freedom.
Even Caliban recognizes that he needs to be "wise hereafter,"
that he needs to "seek for grace," that he has been "a thrice-
double ass . . . to take this drunkard for a god, and worship this
dull fool." Most importantly, however, Prospero and Alonso
are reconciled through the love of Ferdinand and Miranda,
who greets these "three men of sin" with the naiveté of the
innocent. "O wonder!" she exclaims with joyful excitement.
"How beauteous mankind is! O brave new world, that has
such people in't!" And since much has indeed changed for the
better, forgiveness has indeed created a brave new world.

344

Touched by the miracle that he has experienced, Alonso returns the stolen dukedom to Prospero and asks him to "pardon me my wrongs" (5.1.119). Because Prospero chose forgiveness over revenge, much good has been generated.

But perfection remains elusive. Those devious brothers, Sebastian and Antonio, remain silent throughout the reconciliations except to observe that "the devil speaks in" Prospero when, in an aside to them, he threatens to reveal their attempt to murder Alonso. Their incipient evil has not changed, and its presence will always threaten people like Miranda whose precious innocence makes them vulnerable. It is precisely because of such resilient evil that Gonzalo's utopia remains an impossibility. Prospero's acceptance of mercy's necessity ends up being more realistic, and that lesson has prepared him well for his return as Duke to Milan.

The final mystery of *The Tempest* is why Prospero disposes of his magic, which was instrumental in bringing about not only young love but repentance and reconciliation as well. Perhaps because it has served a very useful purpose, his renunciation of that power contains a hint of melancholy. As he releases the noblemen from his charms and brings them to that final scene of reconciliation, he pledges to leave his magic behind:

> Graves at my command
> Have wak'd their sleepers, op'd, and let 'em forth
> By my so potent art. But this rough magic
> I here abjure; and when I have requir'd
> Some heavenly music (which even now I do)
> To work mine end upon their senses that
> This airy charm is for, I'll break my staff,
> Bury it certain fathoms in the earth,
> And deeper than did ever plummet sound
> I'll drown my book. (5.1.48-57)

The idyllic island where Prospero's "potent art" worked to transform the hearts of his sinful countrymen will soon fade into the past. What's left is the real world, the world where real sins await real forgiveness. *The Tempest* identifies the origin of sin in selfish desire. It demonstrates how even those with good intentions are distracted by false idols and, therefore, why everyone needs and benefits from forgiveness. It reminds us that what is sinful in human nature threatens innocence and eliminates the possibility of both individual and social perfection. And it suggests that art's role is to remind us of these heartbreaking truths about what is possible, what is lost, and why mankind is afflicted with suffering and death but also blessed with the incalculable joy of love.

Though Shakespeare went on to collaborate with others in the writing of three or four additional plays, some see this as his good-bye to the theater. It is indeed difficult not to see Prospero as a type for Shakespeare. Both of them, after all, are dramatists. Prospero, through his servant Ariel, orchestrates the tempest and its consequences, including the two banquet scenes. The purpose of this benign magic is to educate and enlighten, never to harm. Prospero can be strict and demanding, but, with the benevolent authority of a caring father, it is always to instill the spirit of self-sacrifice and discipline that will enable his willing students to maintain their allegiance to good rather than to evil. As Ms. Colie writes in *Shakespeare's Living Art*:

> This, then, is Prospero's "art": to heighten nature's
> effects so that the miraculous achievement of human
> kindness, human solidarity, and human gentleness
> may be seen for the rarity it is: the patient, gifted
> work of self-civilizing men and women, who, on the
> one hand, pull themselves out of a bestial life and, on
> the other, resist the moral temptations omnipresent
> in the complexity of any society and civilization. (291)

But that art is by no means omnipotent, for it cannot change the evil plotters of the court, all of whom remain firmly focused on the unworthy. The similarities between Prospero's magic and Shakespeare's art, which was also benevolent,

346

morally instructive, and limited make it entirely appropriate to recall Shakespeare's cultural and personal circumstance: an aging man about to retire from a theater under attack by sometimes legalistic and judgmental moralists. The possible termination of what he loved, of everything he had accomplished, might well have raised questions about the purpose of his professional life. Sir Phillip Sydney's *Defense of Poesie* may have come to mind, for Sydney countered the moralists by arguing that art's purpose was to instruct, to clarify the distinction between moral right and wrong with something that also pleased the imagination, making the lesson that much more durable. While it has no real power, art, Sydney argued, has a significant purpose. That seems to be the conclusion of *The Tempest* as well.

Rather than a farewell to art, Prospero's rejection of his magic seems to be an acknowledgment of both its strengths and its limitations, a mature assessment of what Shakespeare had devoted his life to. Art can teach. It can both delight and instruct, as Sydney had argued. But it cannot act. It can only play. It wields no power in the real world. Instead, it works in the realm of the mind, the heart, and the spirit. It helps to reshape man's crudest natural instincts into something better. Instead of revenge, the wronged can learn to choose forgiveness. Instead of selfishness, man can choose sacrificial love. Instead of evil and the chaos that follows from it, man can choose good, which results in harmony and a delightful harvest of nature's bounty. Even from a state of obstinate sinfulness, mankind can imagine the possibility of innocence. He can experience the bounty available from providential nature if he subsumes his selfish desires to a master worthy of obedient and loving service. There, Shakespeare seems to be saying, is where man can find true freedom: freedom from chaos, freedom from want, freedom from sin.

The island where *The Tempest* takes place is a magical setting where the difference between good and evil can easily be discerned, where true and innocent love prevails, where

347

lives can be transformed for the better, where forgiveness engenders reconciliation. It is a pastoral, idyllic setting whose unreality we willingly but only momentarily accept as real. Like Prospero, we know it cannot last beyond the two hours or so that actors practice their art, their magic, onstage. Like Prospero, we must leave the magic behind and return to our real lives, drab and ordinary as those might be. But it is precisely there that our choices matter most. As he draws the action to its proper conclusion, Prospero is completely transparent about this:

> Our revels now are ended. These our actors
> (As I foretold you) were all spirits, and
> Are melted into air, thin air. . . . the gorgeous palaces,
> The solemn temples, the great globe itself,
> Yea, all which it inherit, shall dissolve,
> And like the insubstantial pageant faded,
> Leave not a rack behind. We are such stuff
> As dreams are made on; and our little life
> Is rounded with a sleep. (4.1.148-158)

The passage refers to all three levels of our experience of *The Tempest*: the magical island, capable of transforming Alonso; the play that the audience has just witnessed; and, of course, our lives in this world, with its "insubstantial pageants." All are "rounded with a sleep." All must come to an end. The question is, what have we learned? How will that change our lives? While it still matters, will we move away from what makes us susceptible to evil and toward what's good?

Instead of retiring in triumph, as Shakespeare was about to do, Prospero returns to the "real" world of Milan. That is proof that he too has been transformed by the island. He lost his dukedom because he chose to study his books rather than rule his people. On the island, he used his magical authority to transform hearts and minds, and Prospero will take that same authority, without the magic, back to Milan. But there, in Milan, "every third thought shall be [his] grave" because the inevitability of that final sleep will serve to keep him focused on what matters, what's real. What uncivil natural man values, those flashy garments hanging on a line, isn't real and won't matter in the end. The ability to distinguish between good and evil, however, matters greatly, and in this realm, art, like Shakespeare's art, has a real and valid purpose.

The Wonder of Shakespeare

After looking closely at these eleven plays, most readers will likely come away with two impressions: how artfully this man could present those deeply felt moral truths shared with his fellow countrymen and, through that art, a strong inkling of what the man himself might have been like. As mentioned in the introduction, Jonson, the man who penned the dedicatory poem for the First Folio, claimed that the plays bore the image of the artist who wrote them. They reflect, that is, what the man believed and probably how he bore himself in the world. That his fellow actors saw fit to undertake the arduous and financially risky proposition to publish his works is a strong indication of the affection they held for him.

Perhaps the basis for that regard is too obvious to be stated, but a recent biography by Stephen Greenblatt, the Harvard professor who articulated New Historicism's foundational principles mentioned briefly in the first chapter, draws a very different conclusion. Unlike Thomas Campion, a Catholic who refused to denounce his religious convictions and who paid for that with his life, Greenblatt's Shakespeare is a morally timid individual unable to live out any of his core values. Citing evidence that Shakespeare's father might have had Catholic leanings, he suggests that William likely absorbed that sentiment but suppressed it while working with a theater company financially supported by an aggressively Anglican aristocracy. Moreover, from Shakespeare's migration to London soon after marrying Anne Hathaway, Greenblatt extrapolates an estrangement resulting from his homosexual inclinations. Because of this engrained hypocrisy, he suggests, Shakespeare's retirement in Stratford had to have been devoid of any recognizable faith and love. He concludes:

Shakespeare began his life with questions about his faith, his love, and his social role. He had never found anything equivalent to the faith on which some of his contemporaries had staked their lives. If he had once been drawn toward such a commitment, he had turned away from it many years before. To be sure, he had infused his theatrical vision with the vital remnants of that faith, but he never lost sight of the unreality of the stage and never pretended that his literary visions could simply substitute for the beliefs that led Campion to his death. And though he may have had brief glimpses of bliss, he had never found or could never realize the love of which he wrote and dreamed so powerfully. (*Will in the World* 388)

For Greenblatt, Shakespeare's clandestine Catholicism, his suppressed homosexuality, his exodus to London to escape a marriage he didn't want, concludes with an emotionally and sexually unhappy life. Since the few records specifically about Shakespeare's life have to do with baptisms, weddings, land contracts, and legal proceedings, it is virtually impossible to know anything about his private life, let alone whether he knew anything about bliss. If this speculative historical view is legitimate criticism, then the equally plausible assertion that those marvelous female creations, his Rosalind, Cordelia, or Cleopatra, were only possible because he had enjoyed the company of such steadfastly loving women.

This kind of speculation is contradicted by Jonson's claim that these moving, sometimes glorious plays accurately reflect who the author was and what he was like. This from a man who worked with and knew Shakespeare personally. When Jonson wrote his poem, Shakespeare had been dead for almost seven years, so he had little reason to resort to flattery. In fact, anecdotal evidence indicates that Shakespeare was not only loving and forgiving but the cause of those virtues in others, to paraphrase that great wit, Falstaff. His professional relationship with his fellow actors and with Jonson makes the point.

Despite his education and a comic predisposition, Jonson had a reputation for a choleric temper. Early in his career, he quarreled with a man by the name of Gabriel Spenser, one of the actors in Shakespeare's theater company. Their disagreement ended sordidly when Jonson killed his antagonist in a duel. Though a legal loophole allowed Jonson to avoid execution, he could not escape other consequences altogether. Phillip Henslowe, one of the founding members of Shakespeare's company, was greatly dismayed by Spenser's death. In a letter to a friend, he complained that he had "lost one of my company, which hurteth me greatly; that is Gabriel, for he is slain in Hogsdon Fields by the hands of Benjamin Jonson, bricklayer" (Wells 134). The reference to Jonson as a lowly bricklayer reflects Henslowe's displeasure with the rival playwright's actions. As a result of that unfortunate death, the managers of the Globe Theater refused to perform Jonson's next comedy, *Every Man In His Humour*. But Shakespeare, also one of the founding members of the company, read the manuscript and intervened on Jonson's behalf. Not only was the play performed at the Globe, but Shakespeare apparently acted one of the significant parts. This gesture resurrected Jonson's stage reputation, and he and Shakespeare became relatively good friends as a result. They disagreed on many aspects of the theater, but from that time on Jonson never forgot the kindness Shakespeare had shown him.

In the fall of 1623, however, almost thirty years after this incident, Jonson had an opportunity to repay Shakespeare's compassion. A remarkable literary event was about to occur, the publication of Shakespeare's collected plays. Two men who had partnered with him at the Globe Theater, John Hemmings and Henry Condell, had been working since their colleague's passing to preserve his plays. All three men had been business partners, good friends as well as fellow actors. Their friendship was so solid, in fact, that John and Henry helped care for William's fatherless children after his death. Though it isn't known for sure if Condell had been with Shakespeare from the start of their theatrical careers, Hemmings not only had been but had also witnessed the writing and production of each play. Because of his intimate knowledge of the plays and of their author, he was the perfect choice, therefore, to oversee such an important and arduous task as a collected edition. Without their familiarity with the plays and the author himself, confidence in the canon would be much weaker.

The First Folio project was something of a financial gamble, however, because the physically larger folio editions were generally more expensive than the average Elizabethan would be willing to pay. Moreover, it was unusual, almost presumptuous, to package theatrical works as literature. But Hemmings and Condell clearly understood the cultural value of what they were dealing with. To lend the Folio the proper caché, therefore, they dedicated it to William Herbert, Earl of Pembroke, who had long been a major sponsor of Shakespeare's theater company. This too was somewhat presumptuous, for, normally, only poets dedicated their volumes to an important aristocrat. Unlike petty dramatists, poets considered their works to be literary art and used such dedications to win the patronage of wealthy nobles willing to pay to see their names in print. But Hemmings and Condell took one additional step to ensure the success of their effort: they asked Jonson to write a commemorative verse for the Folio's cover pages. Because of Shakespeare's earlier kindness, Jonson's poem of some eighty lines was warm and full of genuine admiration. Shakespeare's work, he wrote, is far superior to that of those renowned English poets, Chaucer and Spenser. He even equates Shakespeare with the great Greek playwrights, Aeschylus, Euripides, Sophocles for tragedy, and Aristophanes, Terence, and Plautus for comedy.

From a man well-educated in both Greek and Latin literature, this was high praise indeed.

The First Folio, then, represents the remarkable devotion of three men to a friend's life and art, and western culture owes them a debt of gratitude for that vision and persistence. What is worth speculating about is why Jonson, Hemmings, and Condell would participate in such a financially risky and culturally presumptuous undertaking if not for the love and respect they felt for both the plays and the man who wrote them.

Furthermore, when Shakespeare accommodates Jonson after the fateful duel with Spenser, it exemplifies the generous encouragement and forgiveness that is required of believing Christians. Much of the available public record about Shakespeare's life deals with commonplace events like baptisms, school enrollment, contracts on material for his family, and his theatrical enterprise. None of this evidence reveals very much about the man's emotional state, his motives, or his spiritual convictions. Reading between the lines of all this material to draw out inferences may be fun, but it should not be mistaken for anything other than the speculation that it is.

Because we have no documents that are clearly in his own hand other than the plays, Shakespeare the man will always remain something of an enigma, and the only reliable documentation we have of him is what Hemmings and Condell edited into the First Folio. What we see in these plays is what we can reasonably determine about the man: extraordinary talent, a marvelous facility with language, an ability to view people objectively and with minimal personal prejudice, a consistent sense of fairness and balance, an awareness of the universality of sin and suffering, a keen understanding of what genuine love demands and what it promises, and a deeply felt conviction of God's presence, His love and mercy, in human endeavors. In light of such enduring truths, whether he was gay or Catholic seems either improbable, irrelevant, or both.

In the end, Shakespeare's enduring appeal rests upon his relationship with his audience, which contrasts sharply with his friend and rival, Jonson, who could be quite prickly about the public reception his plays received. Somewhat peeved by Shakespeare's success despite his ignorance of classical standards, Jonson tried to educate his audience about the necessary rules of dramatic structure. In his short but illuminating book on Shakespearean comedy, *A Natural Perspective*, Northrop Frye describes with sly irony Jonson's introductory comments to the very convoluted and long-forgotten comedy, *The New Inn*:

> There is something very disarming in the way that Jonson, both here and in the entr'actes to his next play, *The Magnetic Lady*, attempts to instruct us in the art of liking Jonson. He would call our attention particularly to the extraordinary skill with which the play has been constructed. Is not his protasis logically and clearly laid out in the first act, his epitasis developed from it with equal clarity and logic, his fourth act a catastasis or cleverly disguised recognition scene, where the recognitions are false clues, and his fifth act a brilliantly resolved catastrophe, where all is made clear? (15)

Though it was most likely counter-productive, Jonson, it seems, was not above haranguing his audience about their ignorance of rhetorical and dramatic standards. Not surprisingly, Jonson's haughty marketing strategy never burnished his reputation as brightly as Shakespeare's selfless attention to theatrical success. Never one to slavishly follow any rule except what worked on stage, Shakespeare's only concern was pleasing his audience. As much businessman as playwright and actor, he understood that his job was not to insult his audience but to motivate them to return to his theater for more. In the end, his lack of a university education actually helped him avoid any obsessive adherence to rules, academic or otherwise. After *Titus*, his short experiment with Senecan tragedy, what he did possess and what he learned to trust was an uncanny ability to please his audience, to give them plays they not only enjoyed but plays that also enlightened.

Above all, Shakespeare was a master storyteller. As the very dramatic opening scene of *Hamlet* indicates, he knew how to capture an audience's attention. He absorbed and experimented with both comic and tragic conventions, using only those that made theatrical sense, discarding those, like Seneca's grotesquely bloody spectacles, that didn't. He intuitively understood dramatic rhythm and pacing; he understood that tension could be built in successive waves only to be relieved in the final scenes. That awareness of rhythm and pacing made him fearlessly unrestrained about mingling genres, much to the dismay of his less imaginative rivals and critics. *Lear*, for example, intermixes the comic fool with the deeply tragic experience his royal master was undergoing. And there is a shade of tragic pathos in Malvolio's comic imprisonment in a symbolically darkened cell. Comfortably foregoing any pretense of realism in his late romances, he blithely incorporates supernatural spirits and magic into a story that functions quite well as fairytale, as serious drama, or as an elegant combination of both. Throughout his career, Shakespeare's attention to the art of storytelling is what immediately captivates an audience and brings it willingly and happily into the plot.

Based on existing attendance records, Londoners were quite willing to spend a penny or two to set aside their daily cares and watch two hours of make-believe transpire on stage. Shakespeare was very aware of the inherent power in this ability to create imaginary worlds, some realistic, as in the histories, some not, as in the romances. He was also fully aware that his audiences were, in some sense, participants in the plays because of their imaginative involvement in those stories. And he was grateful for their attention, often thanking them at the end of his plays. Alone on stage, the magician Prospero provides a representative epilogue for his play, *The Tempest:*

> Let me not,
> Since I have my dukedom got,
> And pardon'd the deceiver, dwell
> In this bare island by your spell,
> But release me from my bands
> With the help of your good hands.
> Gentle breath of yours my sails
> Must fill, or else my project fails,
> Which was to please.   Now I want
> Spirits to enforce, art to enchant,
> And my ending is despair,
> Unless I be reliev'd by prayer,
> Which pierces so, that it assaults
> Mercy itself, and frees all faults,
> As you from crimes would pardon'd be,
> Let your indulgence set me free. (Epilogue 5-20)

With faint echoes of the Lord's Prayer, this charming appeal for a minute or two of enthusiastic applause to indicate their willingness to forgive the play's faults and dispel the illusion also deftly manages to allude to the play's themes of mercy and freedom.   Unlike Jonson's grumpy antagonism, Shakespeare cultivated this symbiotic relationship with his audience, a posture that reflects a gentle and humble spirit appreciative of their patronage and their attention.   It is undoubtedly that spirit that endeared him not only to his audience but also to his co-workers who were instrumental in bringing that First Folio to publication.

Clearly, though, there was much more to Shakespeare's popularity than good public relations and intriguing stories.   It is fair to say that Shakespeare's popularity among his fellow Londoners rested in large part on a bedrock of shared ideas, values, and assumptions presented with deliberate attention to dramatic and artistic detail. As the

357

close readings in the previous chapters have indicated, this consummate artist usually constructed parallel dramatic structures to encourage comparisons between characters. Such comparisons develop a variety of themes that acquire further nuance through an intricate web of imagery. How much of Shakespeare's structural and thematic complexity could his Elizabethan audience actually appreciate, though? Does such close analysis read more into the plays than the average Elizabethan would ever find? To assume they could not distinguish between good and bad drama is not borne out by historical evidence. As Alfred Harbage notes in *Shakespeare's Audience:*

> There is no need to magnify the individual [Elizabethan] spectator. All that Shakespeare had to offer was immediately apparent to him no more than it is to us. He was willing to accept on the average much less than Shakespeare offered. But he preferred Shakespeare. . . . He found in these plays room for his soul at its widest dimension. He preferred too much to too little. He could grasp some things, touch others, and sense the presence of more. (160)

The Elizabethans experienced Shakespearean drama, then, exactly as audiences do today, which is to say with a pleasure that is not diminished by an awareness that these plays contain a richness sensed in performance but only understood through a careful reading of the text.

The pleasure derived from these plays has manifold causes and strikes different people in different ways, but what shines through most clearly to nearly everyone, even today, are those shared values. Precisely because Shakespeare lacked a university education, he shared an affinity with his audience that eluded Jonson. As Harbage mentions elsewhere, the greater portion of his audience was composed of the working classes of London, people who had acquired an education similar to Shakespeare's own (82). As a result, author and audience worked with a set of common assumptions and beliefs. As Frye astutely observes:

> It is consistent with Shakespeare's perfect objectivity that he should show no signs of wanting to improve his audience's tastes, or to address the more instructed members of it with a particular intimacy. His chief motive in writing, apparently, was to make money, which is the best motive for writing yet discovered, as it creates exactly the right blend of detachment and concern. He seems to start out with an almost empathic relation to his audience: their assumptions about patriotism and sovereignty, their clichés about Frenchmen and Jews, their notions of what constitutes a joke, seem to be acceptable to him as dramatic postulates. (*A Natural* 38)

This set of shared opinions and values, including religious values, it should be noted, removes any incentive to preach or educate, to insert authorial statements where they aren't needed. With no incentive to preach, characters are free to speak for themselves. Withholding any judgment and allowing characters to exhibit unique personalities through their language is what Frye means by Shakespeare's "perfect objectivity." Where Jonson craved attention and accolades, the egoless Shakespeare disappears behind his story, allowing his characters to come alive for themselves. As a dramatic tool, this verisimilitude takes advantage of the normal desire to understand what people are really like behind their public faces. It is why, even today, readers delve into the motives of these characters and seek to understand why they do what they do.

To some extent, then, Bloom is right to extol Shakespeare's ability to create uniquely vital characters. While each is given a voice suitable to their thematic purpose, their individuality evokes genuine emotional responses, just as real people do. Falstaff's playfulness, Hamlet's inquisitive intelligence, and Lear's justifiable outrage at being grievously wronged inspire genuine feelings of delight, awe, and

359

sympathy. They speak in ways and about topics that seem significant, yet also absolutely true to life. But, as we have seen, acknowledging that is not sufficient. It may very well be reasonable to prefer Falstaff to Hotspur, Hamlet to Polonius, Lear to Gloucester, but the implicit invitation to contrast characters includes an invitation to recognize their similarities as well: to see how both Falstaff and Hotspur dilute the real meaning of honor; to recognize how both Hamlet and Polonius misread what they observe; to recognize that the mad Lear and the blind Gloucester have both been victimized by opportunistic and selfish children. Though uniquely individual within their dramatic context, each of these main characters is meant to be evaluated and judged by their similarities to and differences from other characters. While vitality of characterization is certainly noteworthy, it was one tool among many Shakespeare used to enhance his story, to draw his audience into the play's action, and to validate what they knew was right and good.

But life-like characterizations were not the only means by which he acquired the involvement of his audience. Another means by which Shakespeare deliberately met the assumptions and expectations of his audience was his reliance on dramatic convention. This was particularly true of his comedies and late romances, both of which lend themselves to plot patterns and character types. Comic confusions of identity are initiated by disguised twins or the displacement of court aristocrats onto a remote island where what once seemed normal suddenly appears to be completely abnormal. Regardless of their origins in classical comedy, these conventions were recognizable artistic patterns to his audience. The development of Shakespearean tragedy, however, was a bit different.

Perhaps fortunately, there were no widely accepted conventions for tragedy. The only well-known pattern for tragic action was Seneca, and while Shakespeare tried that formula once, he quickly saw its limitations and moved on.

Beginning with Thomas Sackville's, *Gorboduc*, first performed in 1561, three years before Shakespeare was born, the Elizabethan fascination with their own history eventually generated an alternative pattern for Shakespeare's tragedies. As Normand Berlin writes, Sackville's play about the Duke of Buckingham:

> . . .confronts the important question of tragic responsibility in a way that directly anticipates later Elizabethan tragedy. . . . Sackville fuses the ideas of Fortune, individual responsibility, and God's justice; he makes [the protagonist] responsible for his own actions which cause him to become a slave of Fortune and which lead to his fall and death. At the same time, Sackville surrounds this fusion with an air of mystery (the constant use of the question), emphasizes the idea of mutability, and propels the narrative by means of the revenge theme. . . . In this tragical narrative, therefore, Sackville brought to Elizabethan tragedy one approach to the complexity of tragic responsibility – a tragic character who errs but is sympathetic. . . . (*Thomas Sackville* 121)

Because this tragic pattern of great men who err and fall from fortune's favor was played out many times throughout English history, it evolved quite naturally from Shakespeare's experiments in the history genre. The story of the self-involved royal protagonist of *Richard II* proved to be a very workable tragic pattern, one that provided depth and richness to human suffering. After the delightful experiment of *Romeo and Juliet*, which effortlessly turns a comic pattern into a courtly love tragedy, the capacity for ruthlessly honest self-examination became the gateway to the great tragedies of *Hamlet*, *Macbeth*, *Lear*, and, yes, Cleopatra, a woman who knew what she wanted and was willing to wait patiently, like the Viola of *Twelfth Night*, for her man to understand who she really was.

One final and very significant difference between Jonson and Shakespeare, one that may very well explain the difference between their reputations four hundred years later, is Shakespeare's willingness to experiment with different genres. For all his immense talent, Jonson was primarily a comic or satiric dramatist only. Unlike Shakespeare, he never had the inclination or the natural talent to produce anything vastly different in kind. But Shakespeare's forays into different genres like history, comedy, tragedy, and romance forced him to confront commonly experienced human problems from different perspectives, in different moods, with different types of language. By doing so, these different perspectives cross-pollinated each other, and the result is often a more fully-rounded understanding of character and issues. Even common comic types like Shylock or Malvolio are given some very human qualities that soften their hard edges. It is this comprehensiveness, as some critics term it, that separates Shakespeare from his contemporaries. By way of contrast, Jonson adhered to a theory of comedy that was based on the four humours, roughly equivalent to accepted Elizabethan psychological categories. Funny as these comic types could be, they were two-dimensional characterizations and could never be confused with the very human vitality of Juliet's nurse or the Falstaff of *1Henry 4*.

Along with his sensitivity to the common assumptions of his audience, then, Shakespeare's very thoughtful and intelligent experimentation with different genres served to enrich all his plays. Not only do his characters gain unique and very human qualities as a result, but the themes explored in each play, whether comedy or tragedy, have an intellectual depth that continues to attract critical attention four centuries later. This is not to say that his ideas are in any way *avante garde* for his time or ours. Far from it, in fact. Instead, they are commonplace, a worldview shared with a solidly Christian audience. Rather than Bloom's anachronistic nihilism, the ideas promulgated in Shakespeare's plays reflect the ancient and enduring truths of the Bible that were familiar to every church-going Elizabethan. If Richard II's failure to fulfill his royal duties led to the loss of his crown, his self-indulgent nature was easily recognized by the audience who shared the same sin in less significant ways. All are punished for their complicity, declares the prince at the end of *Romeo and Juliet*. The ancient wisdom of the Bible requires the moral humility that can recognize the essential commonalities of human existence, including the pervasiveness of sin, the need for forgiveness, the hunger for union with another that reflects the very nature of the divine.

All of these factors differentiate Shakespeare from the other playwrights of his era, including the best of his rivals, Marlowe and Jonson. Marlowe, possibly an atheist, died young and wrote only one or two plays that maintain any interest today. Except for an occasional academic production of his *Doctor Faustus*, his works are rarely performed on stage anymore. Because Jonson's comedies and satires reveal the kind of wit and invention that still resonates with modern audiences, his works have enjoyed a somewhat better fate. But neither of these authors exhibit the depth, richness, or wisdom that is so evident in Shakespeare, almost from the beginning of his career. There are many explanations for this, as this chapter has argued, but central to all of them is a humility that is completely aware of our necessary dependence on divine grace. On this, Northrop Frye deserves the last word:

> What Shakespeare has that Jonson neither has nor wants is the sense of nature as comprising not merely an order but a power, at once supernatural and connatural, expressed most eloquently in the dance and controlled either by benevolent human magic or by divine will. Prospero in particular may appropriately be said to make nature afraid, as he treats nature, including the spirits of the elements, much as Petruchio [in *The Taming of the Shrew*] treats Katharina. . . .[In] the myth of nature in Shakespeare. . .the emphasis is thrown, not on the visible rational order that obeys, but on the mysterious personal force that commands. As a somewhat bewildered

Theseus remarks [in *A Midsummer Night's Dream*], after the world represented by his authority is turned upside down by the fairies in the forest:

> Such tricks hath strong imagination,
> That, if it would but apprehend some joy,
> It comprehends some bringer of that joy.
> (*A Natural* 71)

Shakespeare's view of nature, including human nature, is not theological in any ordinary or obvious sense. For him, the attributes of the "bringer of joy" seem to remain largely mysterious, what Hamlet, paraphrasing the gospel of Matthew, refers to as that "special providence in the fall of a sparrow." Anything more than that eludes the fallible human eye, and there is not much sense in peering through the gray fog of this world to try to catch a better glimpse of the eternal. That will come in due time.

What can be known, what can be valued and cherished, is the evidence of the divine working within the world of human experience. This is the very premise of the Bible itself, which teaches that such evidence is all around. And that conviction is the source of Shakespeare's contagious admiration for all the miracles, both small and large, evident in our world. We need only think of Cordelia, without whom Lear would never be more than an angry old man raging at the ingratitude of his wicked daughters. Or of Juliet, without whom Romeo would indeed be little more than "fortune's fool." Or of the innocent and ever-faithful Desdemona, murdered by an uncomprehending husband who has been duped by the devil incarnate. Or, finally, of the magnificent Cleopatra, whose love for Antony transforms her last moments on earth into divine fire and air. None of this has anything to do with feminism, either, for, given Goneril and Regan, given Lady Macbeth or Gertrude, it is not really about the social, political, or financial stature of women. It is, however, about the spark of the divine visible through the loving relationship some men have with some women, both of whom must first be blessed with a heart habitually vulnerable to the world and therefore to each other. This, to use Frye's terminology, is the force in nature that, despite evil and human folly, brings two lovers together. It is the force that reconciles parents to children. It excises the evil of Macbeth and restores social order and peace. This is the evidence that can be seen and acknowledged for what it reveals as well as what it cannot. In God's design for the world, human love is meant to reflect divine love. It is the divinely provided instrument we can use to glimpse His nature. While none of this provides an escape from suffering or death, human imagination can, as Theseus attests, apprehend through such things both the joy and the cause of joy.

If Shakespeare's assumption about women in love could never be mistaken for modern feminism, neither should it be mistaken as strictly religious either. It seems especially noteworthy that his final tribute to this kind of love, *Antony and Cleopatra*, is set in the pagan environs of ancient Rome and Egypt, decades before that historic birth in Bethlehem. Shakespeare certainly had been exposed to the sectarian struggles between Catholics and Protestants and the horrors perpetrated in the name of "the one true" religion. The distinction he establishes in that play between the worldly and pragmatic Romans, who see love as sexual attraction employed in the service of political expediency, and the feminine luxury of Egypt suggests that the particular manifestation of the divine within the human knows no bounds, pays no attention whatsoever to the preconceived and limited notions of the religious. As the Bible stipulates, that force mentioned by Frye has been at work in human affairs from the very first moment of creation. Though it is an integral part of experience, it ultimately defies human comprehension. Other than a recognition that this is our experiential connection to the divine, the origin and manifestations of that love remain a mystery. What, we may rightly ask, can fully explain Juliet's feud-and-grave-defying connection to Romeo? Or Cordelia's sacrificial bond to the father who had so cruelly rejected her? Or Cleopatra's immortal longing to be Antony's wife, a mother to his children? These things defy the simplistic reductions of an Iago or even the well-meaning Enobarbus, friend to Antony. By its unshakeable constancy, genuine love defines how we must act in the world, yet its miraculous presence will forever remain essentially mysterious.

The various influences that coalesced to make love the primary concern of Shakespeare's art is part of that mystery. Ideas from Ovid, courtly love conventions, and his Christian faith made that possible at the very time that theaters were flourishing in London and a young man from Stratford looked for work. All of this very well might not have happened, and we would have been the poorer for that cultural void. Each of these three influences played a part in the way he presented the experience of love on stage, but it was his Christian faith that gave his presentations the kind of moral depth and richness that made his greatest plays possible. At the very heart of those plays, Shakespeare demonstrates his conviction that our human nature involves us in intractable sin and, as a consequence, necessitates forgiveness. Only through such acts of loving generosity do we confirm our connection to the divine.

Coda: Sonnet 116

So, the attentive reader might ask, what exactly is the significance of the cover art, which seems to have nothing whatsoever to do with Shakespeare? And why this title? The answers lie within Shakespeare's 116th sonnet, which is a succinct but somewhat puzzling definition of love. Though the focus of this book has been his dramatic art, this particular sonnet complements the insights and themes already discussed in those previous chapters, and, as such, it deserves some attention of its own. Though poetry can be almost as intimidating as a Shakespearean play, we will proceed, briefly, with three specific goals: first, to show how this sonnet summarizes Shakespeare's view of love; second, to reinforce the notion that reading Shakespeare has relevance even today; and third, to explain the reason for the cover art and the title.

The title, of course, is a reference to one line from this sonnet where the speaker declares that love "is an ever-fixed mark that looks on tempests and is never shaken." In the speaker's opinion, love's primary attribute is that it is fearlessly constant in its devotion to the beloved, never wavering regardless of circumstances. As the discussion of individual plays has shown, many of the most attractive characters are women who live out this notion. But the sonnet is a very intriguing definition of love because in fourteen compact lines it reiterates this notion of constancy as well as many additional key ideas from the plays.

To make sense of this sonnet, we will analyze each of its four-line sections individually. To begin properly, we must imagine a narrative voice speaking to a friend who is about to marry his betrothed. The speaker wants to offer some heartfelt advice about marriage and relationships. The first four lines of the sonnet indicate what love is by negation, by addressing what it is not. Since the opening two lines allude to the portion of the wedding ceremony where the minister asks the congregation if there are any objections to the marriage, there's a suggestion that the speaker is concerned about the friend's reasons for marrying, a concern that, if left unaddressed, might force the speaker to voice his objection during the ceremony. Because the poem attempts to clarify what love is, it would be reasonable to assume that this concern is for a friend who might have misunderstood that concept. This is the background to the first four lines of the sonnet.

> Let me not to the marriage of true minds
> Admit impediments; love is not love
> Which alters when it alteration finds,
> Or bends with the remover to remove.

The prevailing idea here is that love is a mutually shared idea of constancy and commitment that will never waver, regardless of circumstances. Love, the poet declares, is constant and durable. It does not alter or change. It does not retreat or give up, even if the other person involved wants to. Any human connection that fails to meet that criterion cannot be called love. Love, then, should not be confused with fickle emotions that wax and wane with circumstances. Love is constant.

The next four lines include the phrase referenced by our title, *The Ever-Fixed Mark*. They drive home this notion of constancy with a highly suggestive image that invites our imagination to explore additional implications of true love. Having alluded to what love is not, the speaker now tells us what love is. For this portion of the sonnet, the scene changes, and we find ourselves aboard a small ship at sea. Beginning with Homer's *Odyssey*, a journey is traditionally a metaphor for some sort of life experience that induces a significant change. In this portion of the sonnet, rootless wandering is transformed into a journey toward a chosen destination. Using two additional images, a recognizable landmark and a star, we learn that love is not only constant but that it provides guidance and direction to a person's life. After concluding that love will never alter, the speaker continues:

> O no, it is an ever-fixed mark
> That looks on tempests and is never shaken;
> It is the star to every wand'ring bark,
> Whose worth's unknown, although his highth be
>   taken.

The wandering bark is a small sailing vessel alone on a vast, featureless ocean. Though it is on a journey, it is currently wandering, aimless and without direction, but desperate for a way to orient itself so that it can reach some desired destination. This second quatrain alludes to two ways the anxious sailors can regain some sense of direction. The first way to orient this wandering ship is by sighting a fixed landmark, the "ever-fixed mark." It could be a lighthouse, say, or a familiar bay, that will show them the way to a place of safety and refuge. Even during the worst storms, that landmark remains visible, a reliable indicator that the ship is on the right course. That reliability, especially during a threatening storm, is a source of immense comfort. Instead of being lost, the ship and its crew gain certainty about both direction and destination.

So the first significant point of the landmark image is that love provides the kind of guidance that changes a person from a lost, wandering traveler to one with a known destination. Love's guiding power is transformative. But the image includes a second, more subtle implication. It suggests that the difference between wandering aimlessly or finding a direction involves a choice, that the choice is in fact an existential one. We are either blown about by the winds of random circumstance, letting those determine where we end up, or we are in fact captains of our ship, responsible for setting a direction and reaching a destination. The control gained by using the landmark is never absolute because storms are an inevitable part of the world in which we travel, but the landmark allows us to find our way. Since these points of reference are a metaphor for love, the speaker suggests, choosing love provides the control that allows us to find both meaning and direction or purpose in life. Random circumstances no longer take us wherever the sometimes ill winds blow. We can choose to trust these guiding landmarks or not, but that choice determines not only where we end up but also whether the eventual destination is the one we envisioned for ourselves. The second significant point of the image, then, is that choosing love as a guiding principle of life has important consequences for a person's identity and purpose in life.

The second image of this quatrain, the star, takes us even further out to sea, away from land altogether, where there is nothing to differentiate one direction from any other. The only way the captain can orient his ship that far from land is by the North Star, a different kind of landmark, but one that is also always there like a steadfast friend, like the speaker himself. What's a bit different here is that the star is remote, high above us, a brilliant light in an otherwise dark sky. While calculating the height of that star with a sextant can determine latitude or longitude, there are qualities of the star we'll never understand. Though we have its guiding light, what the star is made of, what its intrinsic value is, can never be fully known. There are limits to what man can understand about the star, and because of that limitation, words can never adequately describe what it actually is. This, the poet declares, is also the nature of love. The guidance, the sense of direction, the comfort provided, all of which constitute its value or worth to the traveler, can only be experienced, but the star's essential qualities, its worth, defy verbal quantification or analysis. In some fundamental way, the essential nature and value of love will always remain mysterious. Our efforts to describe or explain love are only vague approximations of the actuality, of the actual experience. While we desperately need this light to find our way home, it ultimately remains beyond our comprehension. Not because its value is insignificant, but because our skills, our language, our reason and our imagination, are inadequate to assess its full value.

Love, then, is a necessary, guiding presence in our lives that endures all but that defies our best efforts to explain not only what it is but also why it is. It is simply there, a fact of life, a choice made available to us, an option we can choose to trust or not. In our journey through life, we are all faced with the choice to participate in the experience of love or not to participate in it. We can choose to let the star guide our journey or to continue wandering aimlessly. Either choice entails some risk. By continuing to wander aimlessly through life, we may never experience genuine love. We let circumstances control what happens. But to be guided by something we can only dimly comprehend risks reaching the wrong destination or getting to the right destination for the wrong reasons. It is crucial, therefore, that we correctly evaluate the star's intended purpose, its capacity to guide our journey, trusting in its goodness even though we will never fully understand it. Though words can do very little to elucidate the essential mystery of this guiding principle, we will know it by its constant endurance, and if we are comfortable with that mystery and let it guide our way, it will bring us to the very destination we long for. A successful journey, therefore, takes discernment (is my sextant evaluating the star's height correctly?), a willingness to trust and to risk all (the decision risks the safety of crew, cargo, and ship), faith that the star will always be there, even through the worst storms, and persistent effort to keep checking the star for guidance.

Choosing love as the guide for life must be intentional, a choice or decision that has consequences. Genuine love isn't random, emotional, or fickle, something that comes upon us by chance and leaves when the weather turns ugly. Love,

Shakespeare is reminding us, isn't something that is done to and for us by the other person. To experience love, we must be prepared to be and do what it requires. As captains of our ship, we must decide to trust the guidance it provides. Since the sonnet puts us on the ship gazing at the star through our sextant, choosing to use it to get us to our destination, we are the ones who must possess the necessary qualities to participate in the experience of true love. The nature of the image and the way it is presented indicate that genuine and enduring love requires these qualities from us. Loving well is our responsibility. It is a choice we make to endure life's tempests without forsaking love's steady, guiding influence. In these enormously suggestive images, this is what the speaker is trying to tell his friend before he walks down the aisle to take his vows.

The sonnet concludes by acknowledging the consequences of a decision to let love guide our lives and to provide our identity and purpose. By making that commitment, love stays faithfully with us forever. Not even relentless time and all the physical changes that come with age can diminish genuine love. It shines its bright, consistent light even out to the very edge of death's dark night.

> Love's not Time's fool, though rosy lips and cheeks
> Within his bending sickle's compass come,
> Love alters not with his brief hours and weeks,
> But bears it out even to the edge of doom.
>   If this be error and upon me proved,
>   I never writ, nor no man ever loved.

Once genuine love becomes our identifying and guiding principle, we arrive at a place that remains secure and safe forever. Time may change the appearances of people and things, but the security and safety genuine love provides are permanent. We may never be able to adequately describe or explain it, but it is present and visible and enduring.

Shakespeare was certainly aware of other aspects of love, of course. In his comedies, especially, irrational love often overpowers couples with complete randomness. *A Midsummer Night's Dream*, for example, features a forest spirit who, for the amusement of the king and queen of fairyland, sprinkles magic dust on the eyelids of sleeping mortals so that they fall in love with the first person they see upon waking. Not surprisingly, amusing chaos results as young and fervent lovers are bewildered by the surprised reactions of those they choose to pursue. But while his comedies often deal with the amusing aspects of love, Shakespeare also recognized that the outcome and experience of love depend upon attitudes and values that people hold, that love may begin randomly but requires much more of us to endure. How a person loves reflects the secret assumptions about life and people within his heart. Opportunities for love may occur with some randomness, but what a person does with the opportunity depends entirely upon the assumptions about love and human nature that a person holds dear. And the assumptions that people hold dear vary. Some are true and some are only apparently so, but whatever their motivating beliefs about human nature are, it will show not only in their words and actions but in the eventual consequences of their choices. Following what's actually true, the North Star, brings a person to a place that generates good consequences, like comfort, security, and emotional nourishment. Following what only seems true ends in a far different place. Recall the two very different banquet scenes in *The Tempest*. There's a certain, inevitable justice to all this, which is part of the star's mystery.

Even at this juncture, Shakespeare's relevance should already be apparent, for his 116th sonnet challenges prevailing notions about love, which, if we're honest about it, is viewed from two somewhat contradictory perspectives that coexist in an uneasy partnership. From one perspective, love is all about emotions, feelings, and irrational sexual chemistry. Without these, the experience many believe should be emotionally thrilling seems lifeless and contrived. But as the brief mention of *A Midsummer Night's Dream* suggests, Shakespeare is not only aware of these aspects of love but makes gentle fun of such powerful and seemingly random emotions in all of his romantic comedies. He acknowledges these as a stubborn fact of life. The powerful emotions that come with love can lead people into absurd and sometimes humorous consequences. That is an inevitable part of being in love. But even though love includes an irrational, emotional component, those fickle emotions that come and go are not the most essential quality of love. The alternative basis for love is what the 116th sonnet addresses with its suggestive image of the ever-fixed mark.

But a definition of love that is largely based on the legitimacy of feelings is only one faulty assumption that Shakespeare confronts. Besides implicitly rejecting the significance of love's irrational aspects, the 116th sonnet promotes values like constancy that dispute the other, somewhat contradictory assumption that love can be both conditional and transactional. This assumption, so prevalent in our time, holds that a relationship deserves to continue only as long as one person's effort to make the other person happy is reciprocated in both degree and kind. This requires some understanding of what makes each person happy and then a concerted effort to meet those needs. If the effort to understand isn't forthcoming or if no understanding can be reached, then there's no reason for the relationship to continue. Even within relationships, this seems acceptable because primacy is given to personal happiness and self-fulfillment. Fundamentally, the parties enter the relationship as a means to have personal needs fulfilled. Since the reciprocity involved in fulfilling each other's needs is conditional, the quality of the relationship is subject to analysis and evaluation of whether those needs are being met. Though much lip service is paid to romance, there is very little of that underlying the very pragmatic assumptions prevalent in secular notions of love. We may agree that we have an obligation to the happiness of the other person in the relationship, but the primary reason each individual enters that relationship is to satisfy his or her own so-far unmet needs, to decrease loneliness and sadness and to increase happiness.

It is precisely this focus on love as the means to self-fulfillment that the 116th sonnet warns against. While love isn't just emotions, Shakespeare seems to be saying, it also isn't genuine if it is seen as something that another person must do to enhance our well-being. The sonnet puts the responsibility squarely on the one who is on the journey. As captain of the ship, we must choose to trust and follow the star. We decide to let it take us to a particular destination. In other words, the first responsibility we have is to do what must be done, to accept the right guidance, to get our values right. Only when the right attitudes and values inform our motivations will love take us toward a worthy beloved. Bassanio from *The Merchant of Venice* wins Portia's heart because he chooses the right casket.

As the previous chapters have shown, the plays go into considerable detail about what those values are and what obstacles people encounter to understand and act upon those values. We could stop teasing out any additional inferences of the sonnet's metaphor right now and still have very satisfying discussions about the plays based on those alone. But one additional element of the sonnet's metaphor deserves scrutiny and reflection because it adds further depth and richness to what has already been said about Shakespeare's definition of love in this sonnet. Currently, love is often considered to be something we feel or know, something internal to our being. Tradition has it that love originates somewhere within the human heart. But in the sonnet, the guiding star of love is something external, high above the ship and its captain, who uses its distant light to find his way. Paradoxically, the light of the star is both transcendent and external to us while, at the same time, its guiding light makes it also imminent and personal. The star's light connects that mysterious heavenly body to the ship, almost as if there's no separation at all. By using the star as a metaphor for love, Shakespeare very deliberately seems to imply a connection between some external, heavenly source of love and genuine love here on earth. The star metaphor conveys a suggestion that divine love offers direction and guidance for human relationships.

For the Elizabethans, this implication of the star would have been neither obscure nor forced. Having recently emerged from the church-centric Middle Ages every aspect of their lives was influenced by Christian beliefs. Intimately familiar with the Bible, Shakespeare's audience would understand that this is precisely how God's love supposedly works in his people. This dimension of the star metaphor provides additional clarity and meaning to the earlier implications. As 1John 4:19 declares, "we love because He first loved us." There is a referential connection between God's love and our own, and the love that connects the divine to the human will be both transcendent and immanent at the same time. When the Biblical God's sacrificial, merciful and unwavering love for his people becomes the model that guides our attitudes and behaviors, life ceases to be aimless because that orientation gives us identity and purpose. And it is the only reliable way, the metaphor suggests, to reach our destination.

This facet of the metaphor also clarifies the implication made earlier that our understanding of the star is necessarily limited. After the fall, mankind no longer has the perceptual capacity to understand love's transcendent aspects. Where *Genesis* describes a God that once walked with Adam, that familiarity is no longer possible after the fall. The height, the distant remoteness, is knowable, but the full nature and worthiness of the love that is available to us is not. It is divine; we are not. Despite the guidance it can still provide, therefore, there is something inherently mysterious about its constant

376

involvement with an inescapably flawed people. What man can know, however, is the portion of that love that is imminent, divine love's manifestations within human relationships. Though our ability to distinguish true from false is limited even at this level, constancy is evidence of the divine nature of genuine love.   That is a miracle that should inspire reverent awe for a God who has provided all of love's abundant wealth when it is embraced as the guiding principle for life within created nature.

While this may seem a lot to glean from a fourteen line sonnet, there is much in the plays that confirm the relevance of these observations to an understanding of Shakespeare's plays. For a variety of reasons, Shakespeare never overtly advocates for Christian beliefs in his art, but, given the pervasive influence of the church in every aspect of Elizabethan life, it would be equally surprising if his plays showed no Christian influence at all. Christianity exerted as significant an influence on Shakespeare's life, his thinking, and therefore his art as Ovid, Plautus, or Seneca, other literary influences readily acknowledged by scholars and academics. Though the times made it too dangerous to venture into the politics of religion, the plays do exhibit the influence of basic Christian ideas about human weakness and the necessity of forgiveness. For Shakespeare, those basic Christian concepts become a defining quality of the durable love that originates with God but which is imperfectly reflected in human love. That very Biblical perspective is evident in one of the most touching scenes in all of literature: the tender moment when Lear's youngest daughter, Cordelia, gently forgives the father who grievously misjudged her. Shakespeare's plays are so effective, touch us so deeply, precisely because he demonstrates the consequences of human nature's best inclinations without denying, at the same time, that humans also possess a great capacity for evil. The decision to follow the star makes all the difference. It is no exaggeration to recognize that the lives of individuals and the stability of nations depend on that choice.

There are many understandable reasons why interest in Shakespeare's plays has endured for nearly half a millennium. Some do so to understand the intricacies of his plays' construction, how plot, imagery, characterization are used to demonstrate his insights about the lives people endure and enjoy. That is a perfectly valid reason for looking at these works, for the construction of the plays is truly remarkable. But there is additional poignancy and beauty to be found in his grasp of meaning and joy right alongside the humorously absurd. With endearing grace for our follies, his comedies revel in the simple joys of love and family and friendship. In his tragic mode, there is an appreciation of the miraculous at the very center of immense suffering, for he is able to detect the fragile sweetness of life at the very moment that we are asked to drink from the cup of bitterness. It is this uncanny balancing act, this ability to see and accept the contradictions of human existence not only without condemnation but with such graceful understanding of our potential and our failures that continues to amaze his devotees. That ability to balance contradiction without judgment is a clear indication of how deeply Shakespeare grasped the essential truths of his Christian faith. Rather than acting as a constraint upon his art, those truths serve to deepen and enrich his depiction of life and the essential nature of man.

The various influences that coalesced to make love the primary concern of Shakespeare's art is part of that mystery. Boyhood ideas from Ovid, courtly love conventions popularized by the Elizabethan sonneteers, and his Christian faith encouraged that fascination with love at the very time that theaters were flourishing in London and a young man from Stratford looked for work. All of this very well might not have happened, and we would have been the poorer for that cultural void. Each of these three influences played a part in the way he presented the experience of love on stage, but it was his Christian faith that gave his presentations the kind of emotional and moral depth as well as the spiritual richness that made his greatest plays possible. At the very heart of those plays, Shakespeare demonstrates his conviction that the prevalence of intractable sin necessitates forgiveness which is an act of loving generosity confirming our connection to the divine. Sonnet 116 takes as its premise that holding firmly to the belief that our love for each other should be modeled on God's faithful, unwavering, selfless love for us, is the only way to experience love's full and abundant grace. Following our willful desires, however, as Falstaff does, threatens to turn this demi-Eden we inhabit into the Boar's Head tavern. It is precisely this choice that separates Cordelia from her sisters. Even today, the choice for every breathing, sentient person is exactly the same.

Works Cited

Berlin, Normand. *The Secret Cause: A Discussion of Tragedy*. U of Massachusetts P, 1981.

---,*Thomas Sackville*. Twayne Publishers, Inc.,1974.

Bindoff, S.T. *Tudor England*. Penguin Books, 1950.

Bloom, Harold. *Shakespeare: The Invention of the Human*. Riverhead Books, 1998.

Brooks, Cleanth. "The Naked Babe and the Cloak of Manliness." *Modern Shakespearean Criticism: Essays on Style, Dramaturgy, and the Major Plays,* edited by Alvin B. Kernan, Harcourt Brace Jovanovich, Inc., 1970, pp.385-403.

Brown, John Russell. *Shakespeare and His Comedies*. Methuen & Co. LTD, 1957.

Chute, Marchette. *Shakespeare of London*. E.P. Dutton Co., Inc, 1949.

Colie, Rosalie L. *Shakespeare's Living Art*. Princeton UP, 1974.

Cunningham, Dolora G. "Macbeth: The Tragedy of the Hardened Heart." *Approaches to Macbeth*, edited by Jay L. Halio, Wadsworth Publishing Company, Inc., 1966, pp. 70-80.

Danby, John. "Antony and Cleopatra: A Shakespearean Adjustment." *Modern Shakespearean Criticism: Essays on Style, Dramaturgy, and the Major Plays,* edited by Alvin B. Kernan, Harcourt Brace Jovanovich, Inc., 1970, pp.407-426.

Ellis, Havelock, ed. *Christopher Marlow: Five Plays*. Hill and Wang, 1956.

Frye, Northrop. *Anatomy of Criticism: Four Essays*. Princeton UP, 1968.

---,*A Natural Perspective: The Development of Shakespearean Comedy and Romance*. Harcourt, Brace, And World, Inc.,1965.

Greenblatt, Stephen. Will in the World: How Shakespeare Became Shakespeare. W.W. Norton & Company,2004.

Harbage, Alfred. *As They Liked It: A Study of Shakespeare's Moral Artistry*. U of Pennsylvania P, 1947.

---,*Shakespeare's Audience*. Columbia UP, 1941.

Heilman, Robert Bechtold. *This Great Stage: Image and Structure in King Lear*. U of Washington P, 1967.

---, *Magic in the Web*. U of Kentucky P, 1956.

Highet, Gilbert. *The Classical Tradition: Greek and Roman Influences on Western Literature*. Oxford UP,
        1949.

Hubler, Edward. "The Economy of the Closed Heart." *Shakespeare: Modern Essays in Criticism*, edited by Leonard F. Dean, Oxford UP, 1967, pp. 467-476.

Kernan, Alvin B. "The Henriad: Shakespeare's Major History Play." *Modern Shakespearean Criticism: Essays on Style, Dramaturgy, and the Major Plays,* edited by Alvin B. Kernan, Harcourt Brace Jovanovich, Inc., 1970, pp.245-275.

Levin, Harry. *The Question of Hamlet*. Oxford UP, 1959.

Lewis, C.S. *The Allegory of Love: A Study in Medieval Tradition*. Oxford UP, 1967.

Loomba, Ania. *Shakespeare, Race, and Colonialism*. Oxford UP, 2002.

Rabkin, Norman. *Shakespeare and the Common Understanding*. The Free Press, 1967.

Rose, Mark. *Shakespearean Design*. Belknap Press of Harvard University, 1972.

Spencer, Theodore. *Shakespeare and the Nature of Man*. Collier Books, 1966.

Tillyard, E.M.W. *The Elizabethan World Picture*. Random House, 1941.

Wells, Stanley. *Shakespeare and Co*. Pantheon Books, 2006.

The New Jerusalem Bible. General editor, Henry Wansbrough, Doubleday, 1985.

The Riverside Shakespeare. General editor, G. Blakemore Evans, et. al., Houghton Mifflin Company, 1997.

Made in United States
North Haven, CT
23 February 2022

16411284R00212